D1599258

THE UNITED LIBRARY
2121 Sheridan Road
Evanston, Illinois 60201

Community Identity in Judean Historiography

Community Identity
in Judean Historiography

Biblical and Comparative Perspectives

DS
115.5
.C647

Edited by

GARY N. KNOPPERS and KENNETH A. RISTAU

Winona Lake, Indiana
EISENBRAUNS
2009

© Copyright 2009 by Eisenbrauns.
All rights reserved.
Printed in the United States of America.

www.eisenbrauns.com

Library of Congress Cataloging-in-Publication Data

Community identity in Judean historiography : biblical and comparative
perspectives / edited by Gary N. Knoppers and Kenneth A. Ristau
      p.   cm.
"This volume is largely the outcome of presentations made in the
Ancient Historiography Seminar of the Canadian Society of Biblical
Studies/Société canadienne des études bibliques at its 2007 annual
meeting in Saskatoon, Saskatchewan"—Introduction.
    Includes bibliographical references and indexes.
    ISBN 978-1-57506-165-8 (hardback : alk. paper)
    1. Jews—History—To A.D. 70.—Historiography—Congresses.
2. Jews—Identity—History—Congresses.   3. Jews—Identity—
Historiography—Congresses.   4. Ethnicity in the Bible—Congresses.
5. Bible. O.T.—Historiography—Congresses.   6. Bible. O.T.—Criticism,
interpretation, etc.—Congresses.   I. Knoppers, Gary N., 1956–
II. Ristau, Kenneth A.
    DS115.5.C655   2009
    933.0072—dc22

                                                              2009010552

The paper used in this publication meets the minimum requirements of the
American National Standard for Information Sciences—Permanence of Paper for
Printed Library Materials, ANSI Z39.48-1984.⊚™

For our mothers,

Barthie Maria Boon Knoppers and Brigitte Karin Ristau,

whose stories, sacrifices, and devotion
contributed so much
to the development of our identities

Contents

Contributors to
Community Identity
in Judean Historiography

Ehud Ben Zvi is a Professor in the Department of History and Classics and the interdisciplinary Program of Religious Studies at the University of Alberta (Edmonton) and a former president of the Canadian Society of Biblical Studies / Société canadienne des études bibliques.

Mark J. Boda is Professor of Old Testament at McMaster Divinity College and Professor in the Faculty of Theology at McMaster University (Hamilton, Ontario).

James Bowick is a graduate student at McMaster Divinity College (Hamilton, Ontario).

Louis C. Jonker is Associate Professor of Old Testament in the Faculty of Theology at the University of Stellenbosch (South Africa).

John Kessler is Professor of Old Testament at Tyndale Seminary (Toronto).

Gary N. Knoppers is the Edwin Erle Sparks Professor of Classics and Ancient Mediterranean Studies, Religious Studies, and Jewish Studies at The Pennsylvania State University and a former president of the Canadian Society of Biblical Studies / Société canadienne des études bibliques.

Mark Leuchter is Director of Jewish Studies at Temple University (Philadelphia).

Kenneth A. Ristau is a doctoral student at The Pennsylvania State University and the original coordinator and chairman of the Ancient Historiography Seminar of the Canadian Society of Biblical Studies / Société canadienne des études bibliques.

Kenton L. Sparks is a Professor of Biblical Studies in the Department of Christian Studies at Eastern University (St. Davids, Pennsylvania).

Katherine M. Stott received her Ph.D. in 2005 from the University of Queensland (Australia) and held the Izaak Walton Killam Memorial

Postdoctoral Fellowship at the University of Alberta (Edmonton, 2005–7). She is Acquisitions and Production Editor at Gorgias Press and currently resides in Orange, Australia.

John Van Seters is Professor Emeritus in the Department of Religious Studies at the University of North Carolina (Chapel Hill). He resides in Waterloo, Ontario.

Introduction

This volume is largely the outcome of presentations made in the Ancient Historiography Seminar of the Canadian Society of Biblical Studies/Société canadienne des études bibliques at its 2007 annual meeting in Saskatoon, Saskatchewan. The Ancient Historiography Seminar aims to bring together a diverse group of methodologically distinct junior and senior scholars to discuss their research, foster understanding, and publish on topics related to historiography in the ancient Mediterranean world.[1] Participants are encouraged to approach the proposed topics from their own methodological perspective(s), whether literary, historical, archaeological, epigraphic, or otherwise. For 2006, the Seminar explored the different functions of historiography in the Hebrew Bible, Apocrypha (or Deutero-Canon), New Testament, and early Patristic writings.[2] For 2007, the steering committee decided to pursue the theme "Identity Formation and Ethnicity in Biblical Historiography," which resulted in the present publication.[3]

In debating the complicated issues of collective identity, social location, and ethnicity, modern ethnologists follow a variety of different, albeit sometimes overlapping paths. It will be useful to look at a few of these issues and/or paths before proceeding to a discussion of the chapters included in this volume.[4] Some ethnographers stress the factors of ancestral origins, blood relations, shared values, geographical location, and common social, familial, and religious institutions in attempting to pinpoint group identity. Assumed cultural, national, or somatic traits bind the society together. Founding myths, ancestral claims to a shared territory, and related lineage structures function as corporate markers to authenticate collective membership and to lend internal

---

1. The Ancient Historiography Seminar was given a renewable three-year term by the Canadian Society of Biblical Studies/Société canadienne des études bibliques, beginning in 2006.

2. Culminating in the volume *The Function of Ancient Historiography in Biblical and Cognate Studies* (ed. Patricia G. Kirkpatrick and Timothy D. Goltz; Library of Hebrew Bible/Old Testament Studies 489; New York: T. & T. Clark, 2008).

3. In 2008, the Seminar explored the theme "Economy and Society in Ancient Israelite Historiography," and in 2009, the Seminar is exploring the theme "Prophets and Prophecy in Ancient Israelite Historiography."

4. Readers interested in the vast secondary literature on these matters should consult the footnotes to the contributors' essays in this volume.

cohesiveness to the group in question. Other scholars view ethnicity and group identity as being much more situational, relative, and transitory in character. Factors of lineage, social customs, and religious structures are not denied, at least not altogether. Nevertheless, the boundaries that separate different *ethnē* are viewed as malleable and continually shifting. In this view, claims of common descent, ties to land, social customs, and cultic practices function as indices of ethnic identity but do not function as necessary criteria of ethnic identity. Group identity is not regarded as an abiding or absolute norm. The social behaviors of group members at a certain moment in time should not be assumed to be incontrovertible indicators of permanent identity. Ethnic boundaries are culturally permeable and historically relational. If a shift in group identity occurs, the boundaries of affected groups will also change.

To complicate matters further, collective identities need not be entirely exclusionary or hierarchical in classification. Corporate classifications may be multiple and overlapping. One might be a resident of a particular city, a member of a special guild, a practitioner of a certain profession, a participant in a given religion, and a citizen of a larger people. Seen from this perspective, both the definition of the group and the definition of the other are inextricably related, changing, and ongoing processes that are always subject to revision. In this respect, one may speak of identity formation and reformation rather than presuppose any kind of ongoing static identity.

It is not possible to address all of the aforementioned issues, much less do so in the introduction to a volume of specialized studies. Nevertheless, the questions raised by ethnographers are important and quite relevant to the study of ancient Judah in the Neo-Babylonian and Persian periods. Indeed, it is fascinating to observe how many of these modern questions are also questions that were debated in some shape or form already in antiquity. Is *Judean*, for instance, an ethnic, territorial, religious, national, or international designation? What is the relationship between Israel and its land? What is Israel? Might Israel be the patriarch Jacob, the ancestor of a people, a composite of twelve or more tribes, the northern tribes, a united kingdom, a northern state, Judah (a southern state), the children of the exile, a transnational and transtemporal entity, or a group of laity (as opposed to priests, Levites, gatekeepers, and musicians)? What are the markers of Judean identity —a tie to the land (even if one does not necessarily live there), an ancestral link to the patriarch Judah, a prior link to the ancestor Israel/ Jacob, centralization of worship in Jerusalem, political administration by the Davidic family, allegiance to the Torah, shared social memory, the experience of exile, common religious practices, or some combination of the above?

Increasingly, biblical scholarship has recognized the significant value of biblical historiography as a vehicle to (re)shape collective identity. One has only to look at some of the debates within the biblical writings themselves to appreciate how important the issues of identity and ethnicity are for understanding the history of ancient Israel and Judah. Inasmuch as many of the historical books, the Prophets, and the Writings address a larger collective, however they understand or define that collective and set that collective over against other collectives, these literary writings are incredibly rich sources for inquiries into ancient representations of identity and ethnicity.

The essays in the present volume deal with issues of self-identification, community identity, and ethnicity in Judean and ancient Near Eastern historiography. The scholars address a range of issues, such as homeland-Diaspora relations, the representation and ongoing relevance (if any) of the Davidic Dynasty to Israelite identity, the relationship between the people of Judah and the land, the function of exile in Judean collective memory, the various notions about the future of the Israelite people in postmonarchic writings, the relationship between the preexilic and postexilic priesthoods, the relationship between royal ideology in Yehud and royal ideology in the center of the Persian Empire, the opposition between political autonomy and political subservience as alternative strategies for Judean group survival, the relative importance of Torah and Jerusalem to Israelite identity, and the relationship between identity formation in Yehud and the Judean (re)definition of neighboring peoples. The contributors approach these matters from a variety of theoretical and disciplinary vantage points. For example, some pursue an innerbiblical perspective (pentateuchal sources/writings, Former Prophets, Latter Prophets, Chronicles, Ezra, Nehemiah), while others pursue a cross-cultural comparative perspective (ancient Near Eastern inscriptions, classical historiography, Western and non-Western historiographic traditions). The methods employed include comparative analysis, historical criticism, epigraphy, source criticism, rhetorical criticism, (new and old) literary criticism, redaction criticism, ethnographic analysis, and even social psychology. The result is, hopefully, a wealth of new insights on the role of biblical texts in the construction and promotion of community identity and ethnicity.

The exploratory essay of Kenton Sparks, "Israel and the Nomads of Ancient Palestine," mines various biblical texts for the characterization of Palestinian nomads, or seminomads, as a means to clarify aspects of early Israelite origins.[5] Sparks avers that the biblical texts from the monarchic period onward tend to reflect primarily negative views of nomads, especially the Ishmaelites, Amalekites, Qenites, and Rechabites. He argues that this representation inveighs against the wholesale invention of a nomadic origin tradition in that period, although he also acknowledges that some affiliation may be reflected in the occasional positive representation of the Midianites in the earliest, probably premonarchic biblical strata. The Midianites are the one group with whom the early Israelites are most often linked in important ways. Sparks suggests that this representation, although not conclusive in itself, is consistent with the hypothesis that Israel, or at least Yahwistic Israel, emerged from the south and east.

Naturally, no investigation into Israelite or Judean community identity could neglect to look at attitudes toward the monarchy and the central role of David. John Van Seters takes up this cause in his thought-provoking essay, "David: Messianic King or Mercenary Ruler?"[6] Van Seters argues that there are essentially two representations of David preserved in Samuel–Kings: an earlier, promonarchical account by the original Deuteronomist, dating to the Neo-Babylonian period, and a second, antimonarchical account, or *David Saga*, dating to the Persian period. The latter work is the focus of Van Seters's analysis, specifically its presentation of David's repeated recourse to the use of foreign mercenaries. Comparisons are drawn between the presentation of hired professional soldiers in the book of Samuel and the presentation of hired professional soldiers in classical writings. Van Seters contends that the very portrayal of David's mercenaries, consisting principally of two groups—Philistines on the one hand and Cherethites and Pelethites on the other hand—provides one indication that the *David Saga* is a late work, because the Cherethites and Pelethites may be identified as belonging to special categories of light-armed troops, namely, Greek peltasts and Cretan archers. In this reading, the very unflattering portrayal of David as a ruthless, egotistical, and devious ruler by the writer of the *David Saga* counters the Deuteronomistic presentation of David as a divinely chosen and blessed king. A related

---

5. For background to his understanding of the links between ancient ethnicity and collective identity, see his *Ethnicity and Identity in Ancient Israel: Prolegomena to the Study of Ethnic Sentiments and Their Expression in the Hebrew Bible* (Winona Lake, IN: Eisenbrauns, 1998).

6. This study is programmatic for a forthcoming monograph on the history of the David story.

function of this Persian-period work is to subvert the "messianic utopianism" present in older royal traditions (e.g., Ps 132).

The insightful treatment of Katie Stott, "A Comparative Study of
the Exilic Gap in Ancient Israelite, Messenian, and Zionist Collective
Memory," considers the curious absence of detailed historical information in major biblical texts about the so-called exilic period. Stott notes
similar gaps in ancient Messenian and Zionist collective memory. As
the author points out, *lacunae* of this sort can be telling. In all three
cases, a period of exile marks a distinct phase in the social memory of
the community, but comparatively little is actually said about the par-
ticulars of community life during this time. In making these historical
comparisons, Stott rejects the explanation that the gaps result from
either a lack of available evidence or a dearth of basic knowledge.
Rather, she argues that the treatment of the period in question as a gap
has to do with the (re)formation of group identity. The gaps are ideologically driven, a means to create continuity between the community's present and its idealized past. An additional function of such an
approach to group dislocation is to strengthen the people's claims to
the land from which they had been exiled.

The focus of Ehud Ben Zvi's far-ranging study is also comparative
in orientation, but he concentrates on the shared features of two of the
Hebrew Bible's major historical writings, "Are There Any Bridges Out
There? How Wide Was the Conceptual Gap between the Deuteronomistic History and Chronicles?" Many treatments of the relationship
between the Deuteronomistic work and the Chronistic work focus on
variations, gaps, and differences. By examining how the two literary
works diverge in coverage, style, structure, themes, and historical contexts, scholars attempt to identify the most important or distinctive
traits of each particular writing. Ben Zvi's analysis pursues the conver-
gences between the two works, demonstrating that the conceptual gap
between the Deuteronomistic History and Chronicles is not as wide as
is generally thought. The literati responsible for each literary work
employed similar historiographical techniques and shared similar
ideas about deferred and nondeferred judgment, prophets and prophecy, David and the Davidides, the exclusive legitimacy of the Davidic
Dynasty in the monarchic period, the importance of national history,
and pan-Israelite identity. With respect to constructions of "the other,"
the two works present similar notions about non-Israelite peoples and
non-Israelite political dynasties. Hence, Ben Zvi argues that the intellectual horizons of the respective literati are close in several important
ways, despite real differences between the two groups. The writers

responsible for the Deuteronomistic History and Chronicles shared many traits, regardless of the ways in which the latter attempted to re-shape the intellectual traditions of the former.

The interests of James Bowick in his programmatic paper are rhe-torical, cross-cultural, and ideological. His essay entitled "Characters in Stone: Royal Ideology and Yehudite Identity in the Behistun Inscrip-tion and the Book of Haggai" consists of two main parts. The first in-volves a careful literary analysis of the Old Persian panel of the Behistun Inscription, while the second explores the theme of kingship in Haggai. After analyzing the intricate organization of the Behistun Inscription, Bowick compares the ideology of kingship presented in this famous text with notions of human kingship in the prophetic book of Haggai. Bowick shows that Behistun and Haggai both present the authority of kingship as divinely derived in a number of striking ways. Nevertheless, in the Behistun text, Darius is an active agent, favored by the divine, whereas in Haggai Zerubbabel is a passive recipient of divine favor and a beneficiary of divine action.

The subject of John Kessler's contribution to this volume also in-volves one of the prophetic books. His carefully nuanced study, "The Diaspora in Zechariah 1–8 and Ezra–Nehemiah: The Role of History, Social Location, and Tradition in the Formulation of Identity," com-pares an important theme in Zechariah (1–8) with a related theme in one of the Writings, arguing that the former views the Diaspora as an aberration and envisions a full return, while the latter (Ezra–Nehe-miah) accepts the reality of the Diaspora and recognizes its members as authentic Yahwists who can support and even lead the community in Yehud. Kessler argues that this difference in perspective illustrates how historical circumstance, changing history, and socioreligious lo-cation can (re)shape tradition and contribute to the (re)formation of community identity.

Like Kessler's essay, the essay by Gary Knoppers ("Ethnicity, Gene-alogy, Geography, and Change: The Judean Communities of Babylon and Jerusalem in the Story of Ezra") deals with important issues in the history of homeland-Diaspora relations. Knoppers examines the pre-sentation of the Diaspora community in the Ezra story and shows that it plays an important, central, and defining role, despite the apparent focus of the larger book on the Yehud community. In fact, the Ezra story presents the exile as the defining characteristic of its community and is fundamentally about that exilic community bringing its prac-tices and traditions to bear on the life of the community in Yehud. The writers not only recognize the phenomenon of the ongoing Diaspora in the history of the Judean people but they also endorse the continuing contributions that the Diaspora makes to the homeland. Rather than the homeland community regularly coming to the aid of the derivative Diaspora community, the opposite is true. Consequently, the Ezra story is not simply a story of restoration but also of transformation and a new international definition for the Israelite people.

The wide-ranging study of Mark Leuchter also deals with the Ezra story, but his focus is on the history of the Israelite priesthood. His paper, "Ezra's Mission and the Levites of Casiphia," is a carefully plotted analysis of the tensions within the account of Ezra's mission. He argues that these tensions reflect attempts to reconcile the Zadokite, or mythosacral, and Levitical, or sociosacral, Priestly traditions. In the end, Leuchter sees the character of Ezra as embodying this reconciliation, mediating between the Zadokite and Levitical traditions and the role of the temple and the Torah in the community, because of his Zadokite heritage, on the one hand, and his identity as a teaching scribe and recruitment of the Levites at Casiphia, on the other hand. Significantly, this mediation of the two traditions presages the greater reconciliation of textual traditions in the final redaction of the Torah.

Louis Jonker's stimulating essay focuses on the portrayal of one of the most troubled monarchs in the Chronicler's work, "Textual Identities in the Books of Chronicles: The Case of Jehoram's History." In his methodologically nuanced essay, Jonker draws on ethnicity studies and the discipline of social psychology to investigate the way in which the Chronicler's changes to the Jehoram narrative (over against the Deuteronomistic History) reflect identity issues. Jonker emphasizes the extent to which historical writings that address the collective nature of community history have the capacity to redefine the ongoing process of identity formation in the community to which this historical writing is directed. The sociopsychological notion of "textual identities" provides the theoretical basis for this reading. In his analysis, historical traditions are repeated not for the sake of reconstructing the past but for the sake of self-categorization in a new present. He argues that the Chronicler's narrative reflects changes in the sociopolitical dynamic of the relations between Yehud and its neighbors in the context of the Achaemenid kingdom. During this time, Judeans were coming to terms with their provincial existence within a much larger, Persian imperial dominion—"amidst other similar provinces to the north and to the south"—and defined their uniqueness by the "Yahwism practiced in Jerusalem in continuation of the Davidic covenant."

Ken Ristau's essay draws attention to the importance of the same historiographic work examined by Jonker for confronting the possible relationships among political independence, provincial dependence, royal ideology, national lament, and collective conscience. His finely detailed treatment, "Reading and Re-reading Josiah: The Chronicler's Representation of Josiah for the Postexilic Community," contends that the story of Josiah in Chronicles conditions its audience toward accepting both the dependent status of Yehud in the Persian period and the absence of a Davidic monarchy. Of particular interest to Ristau is the manner in which the depiction of Josiah's death reshapes the Josianic legacy for the postmonarchic community. When Josiah appears as "the king of Torah and of tears," the narrative validates national lament and encourages its readers to engage such topics as the nature of God's judgment, the existence of tragedy in the divine and human economy, and the larger role of imperial authority.

The perceptive treatment of Mark Boda explores a related but different dimension of the Chronicler's work, "Identity and Empire, Reality and Hope in the Chronicler's Perspective." Boda recognizes that the final chapters of Chronicles introduce readers to Judah's future as a dependent community and direct them toward accepting a time of colonial status in the Persian period. Nevertheless, the Chronicler also provides important alternative views of political organization within his work. Boda finds these striking presentations of a strong indigenous polity to be especially prominent in the representations of Hezekiah and Manasseh. He avers that the portrait of Hezekiah models faith, legitimate resistance against empire, and hope for independence, while the portrait of Manasseh models a penitent king and the road to the renewal of the kingdom and its monarchy. In this way, the introduction to the colonial status of Judah in the Persian period, as reflected in the last chapters of Chronicles, is mitigated by alternative portraits that provide a basis for future hope in the restoration of the Davidic monarchy and resistance against imperial domination.

GARY N. KNOPPERS
The Pennsylvania State University
KENNETH A. RISTAU
The Pennsylvania State University

Note to reader

The abbreviations in this book follow the *Society of Biblical Literature Handbook of Style for Ancient Near Eastern, Biblical, and Early Christian Studies* (ed. P. H. Alexander et al.; Peabody, MA: Hendrickson, 1999).

Israel and the Nomads
of Ancient Palestine

KENTON L. SPARKS

Eastern University

Two basic models of early Israel's origins predominate in our guild. One theory holds that the earliest Israelites were essentially Canaanites who migrated from the lowland city-states into the highlands; the other believes that the Israelites came from nomadic stock, from groups of nomadic or seminomadic pastoralists who abandoned their tents for settled life. For a long time I was of the former opinion, but in the last few years my research has steered me in a different direction. Though my position on this question remains in the hypothetical stages, at present my working hypothesis is indeed that many or most of the earliest Israelites were nomadic in origin. In this paper, I will consider the matter in light of Israel's attitudes toward the nomadic groups that lived on its social and spatial periphery. I will begin with general comments before giving attention to some of the important nomadic peoples mentioned in the Bible. Before beginning my discussion in earnest, I should point out that purely nomadic cultures are exceedingly unusual. Whether we are speaking of pastoralists such as the Shasu and Amalekites or of camel nomads such as the Midianites, Ishmaelites, and Arabs, the evidence on hand suggests that all of these so-called nomadic cultures had significant sedentary populations.[1] In many cases, even the nomadic elements of the population are better described as seminomadic. The nomadic profile of these peoples was accentuated in the Bible because, for obvious reasons, the Israelites normally had contact with the more mobile elements of the population.

---

1. Regarding the sedentary elements of the Shasu and Amalekites, see 1 Sam 15:5 (the Amalekites) and R. Giveon, *Les Bédouins Shosou des Documents Égyptiens* (Leiden: Brill, 1971) 71–77, 112–15 (the Shasu). As for Midianites, Ishmaelites, and Arabs, these three groups were closely associated with settlements in northwest Arabia, as is well documented. For the relevant sources, see my discussion of these groups below.

Israel and the Nomads

Let us begin with Israelite attitudes about nomadic life. If the earliest Israelites did not hail from nomadic origins but rather from Canaanite society proper, as some scholars believe, then how did it come about that the Israelites embraced a nomadic portrait of their origins? One answer avers that pastoral nomads were for the Israelites a kind of "noble savage," whose simple lifestyle and freedom of movement appealed to people living in Israel's more complex, sedentary society. It is thought that Jeremiah's admiration for the nomadic Rechabites provides a prominent example of this Hebrew sentiment, as Karl Budde first suggested over a century ago.[2] But in fact, at this point, there are real questions about the nature of Rechabite society. It is supposed now that theirs was a not a clan of pastoralists so much as of itinerant craftsmen, such as appear in the simple societies of modern times. Moreover, if we may judge from the anthropological observations of living cultures, it is by far the rule that settled populations regard nomads with suspicion and animosity. A primary reason for this is that, in most nomadic cultures, the society's economic viability requires the periodic and even systematic raiding of settled populations living nearby.[3] So the comparative evidence is largely stacked against the theory that Israel embraced a "nomadic ideal."

Respecting Near Eastern texts, the only explication of the nomadic ideal that I know of appears in a Mari letter, but there the ideal is expressed by a fellow who actually had a nomadic background.[4] As for the Hebrew Bible itself, it is perhaps the prophet Hosea who brings us closest to a nomadic ideal.[5] He appears to construe the history of Israel

---

2. K. Budde, "The Nomadic Ideal in the Old Testament," *New World* 4 (1895) 725–45. See also J. W. Flight, "The Nomadic Idea and Ideal in the Old Testament," *JBL* 42 (1923) 158–226; W. G. Dever, "Israelite Origins and the 'Nomadic Ideal': Can Archaeology Separate Fact from Fiction?" in *Mediterranean Peoples in Transition: Thirteenth to Early Tenth Centuries BCE* (ed. S. Gitin, A. Mazar, and E. Stern; Jerusalem: Israel Exploration Society, 1998) 220–37.

3. W. Goldschmidt, "Career Reorientation and Institutional Adaptation in the Process of Natural Sedentarization," in *When Nomads Settle: Processes of Sedentarization as Adaptation and Response* (ed. P. C. Salzman; New York: Praeger, 1980) 52 (48–61); P. C. Salzman, "Processes of Sedentarization among the Nomads of Baluchistan," in ibid., 99 (95–110); L. E. Sweet, "Camel Raiding of North Arabian Bedouin: A Mechanism of Ecological Adaptation," *American Anthropologist* 67 (1965) 1132–49; D. C. Wright, "Nomadic Power, Sedentary Security, and the Crossbow," *Acta orientalia Academiae Scientiarum Hungaricae* 58 (2005) 15–31.

4. P. Marello, "Vie nomade," *Florilegium Marianum* 1 (1992) 115–25.

5. P. Humbert, "La logique de la perpective nomade chez Osée," in *Vom Alten Testament: Karl Marti zum siebzigsten geburtstage* (ed. K. Budde; BZAW 41; Giessen: Alfred

in terms of a story that began with monotheistic nomads who worshiped Yahweh and ended with polytheistic *sendentaires* who worshiped Baal. Hosea's solution for Israel's idolatry and infidelity was a return to that "golden age" when nomadic Israelites faithfully worshiped Yahweh in the wilderness (see Hos 2:16–17);[6] Israel would once again "dwell in tents" (Hos 12:10). Certainly, this is a nomadic ideal of some sort, but I do not believe that it qualifies as the nascent ideology from which Israel's nomadic origins sprung. Hosea's viewpoint simply presupposes the nomadic origins of Israel and does so with rhetoric that construes a return to tent living not as reward but as punishment. So the prophet was not enamored with nomadic life per se; he was enamored with the God who found the Israelites wandering in the wilderness.

A similar perception of nomadic life appears in the comparative evidence from Mesopotamia. Though the Assyrians viewed nomads as a perennial threat to social stability and carried out regular campaigns against them,[7] they nevertheless remembered that their own Semitic ancestors "lived in tents."[8] We cannot be certain, but I suspect that in Assyria as in Israel sedentary populations embraced a quasi-evolutionary view of human society that understood sedentary living as a development from more-primitive nomadic lifestyles. This is almost certainly why the author of Num 24:20 could describe the nomadic Amalekites as ראשית גוים, that is, 'first among the nations'.[9] In

---

Töpelmann, 1925) 158–66; idem, "Osée le prophète bedouin," *Revue d'Histoire et de Philosophie Religieuses* 1 (1921) 97–118.

6. For discussion, see my *Ethnicity and Identity in Ancient Israel: Prolegomena to the Study of Ethnic Sentiments and Their Expression in the Hebrew Bible* (Winona Lake, IN: Eisenbrauns, 1998) 164–66.

7. See I. Eph'al, *The Ancient Arabs: Nomads on the Borders of the Fertile Crescent, 9th–5th Centuries B.C.* (Jerusalem: Magnes, 1984) 20–59.

8. See Assyrian King List "A," in *The Context of Scripture* (ed. W. W. Hallo; 3 vols.; Leiden: Brill, 1997–2003) 1.463–65; *ANET* 564–66.

9. Scholars have long wrestled with this phrase, which has been variously interpreted to mean "the oldest of nations," "the strongest of nations," and "the nation that first met Israel as it came out of Egypt." In my opinion, it is the first option that best suits the poem in Numbers, since ראשית contrasts poetically with the אחרית ('end') of Amalek. Some scholars are troubled by the apparent conflict between this reading of Numbers and Gen 36:12, which makes Amalek a grandson of Esau. I do not view the tension between Num 24:20 and Gen 36:12 as being significant for our interpretation of the Numbers passage. In the first place, we are dealing with a poetic text in Numbers that is prone to exaggeration and accentuates impressions rather than providing raw facts. In the second place, conflicting ideas often appear in the Hebrew traditions, so there is no reason to demand so much coherence in the traditions. And in the third place, a similar perception of Amalek's antiquity appears in 1 Sam 27:8. Noth and Budd essentially agree with

the end, I would say that, for ancient Israelites, the tradition of nomadic ancestors was one thing; to live the nomadic life was another.
And the anthropological evidence bears this out. As a rule, nomads
prefer to settle down and remain settled. They only move about because security and economic necessity demand it.[10]

So in the anthropological evidence, and in the Hebrew and Assyrian
sources, one finds that settled peoples tend to have fairly negative
views of nomads. Indeed, this pejorative posture toward nomads and
nomadic life is much closer to what we find when we examine the
Hebrew Bible in more detail. Israelite perspectives on the Midianites,
Ishmaelites, and Amalekites provide good examples.

The Midianites

Midianites were caravaning nomads. They appear mainly in the Pentateuch and in the book of Judges, where we sometimes find them
closely associated with—or even identified with—the group known in
the Bible as the Ishmaelites. In historical terms, however, the Midianite
profile differs from that of the Ishmaelites, inasmuch as the Midianites
appear to be the older group. Gideon's victory over the Midianites in
Judg 6–8, for example, was already a piece of war nostalgia in the
eighth century B.C.E., when Isaiah of Jerusalem recalled it as the "day
of Midian" (Isa 9:4). That the tradition must be still older, as is true of
many traditions in the book of Judges, goes without saying. The Midianites are enemies of Israel in the book of Numbers as well, where God
prescribes their extermination on account of their role in the apostasy
at Peor (Num 31). But this is by all accounts a very late text that has
little to do with Midian and much to do with legitimizing priestly pro-
tocols.[11] De Vaulx has suggested that Midian appears in this priestly
lore because the narrative in Numbers was modeled after the battle ac-

---

my assessment; Gray and Davies lay out the options but do not stake out a position. See
M. Noth, *Numbers: A Commentary* (OTL; Philadelphia: Westminster, 1968) 193; P. J. Budd,
Numbers (WBC; Waco, TX: Word, 1984) 270; G. B. Gray, *A Critical and Exegetical Commen-
tary on Numbers* (ICC; Edinburgh: T. & T. Clark, 1912) 374–75; E. W. Davies, *Numbers*
(NCB; Grand Rapids: Eerdmans, 1995) 276–77.

10. C. Frantz, "The Open Niche, Pastoralism, and Sedentarization in the Mambila
Grasslands of Nigeria," in *When Nomads Settle: Processes of Sedentarization as Adaptation
and Response* (ed. P. C. Salzman; New York: Praeger, 1980) 62–63 (62–79); E. Marx, "The
Tribe as a Unit of Subsistence: Nomadic Pastoralism in the Middle East," *American An-
thropologist* 79 (1977) 345 (343–63); N. Swidler, "Sedentarization and Modes of Economic
Integration in the Middle East," in *When Nomads Settle*, 23 (21–33).

11. See Noth, *Numbers*, 226–33; Budd, *Numbers*, 325–34; Gray, *A Critical and Exegetical
Commentary on Numbers*, 417–25; Davies, *Numbers*, 319–21.

count in Judg 6–8, which strikes me as plausible but hardly certain.[12] What is certain is that, when it comes to Israelite perspectives on Midian, the Midianites come off poorly in traditions that are relatively early and also in late traditions. So there is no evidence that a so-called "nomadic ideal" has shaped the biblical perspectives on Midian.

Now it seems to me that the negative view of Midian that predominates in the Israelite tradition paradoxically suggests the antiquity of the only positive tradition about Midian, namely, the tradition that associates Moses and Yahweh with the Midianites and their priest, variously known as Jethro, Reuel, and Hobab. I submit that this is a tradition no late Israelite novelist would simply invent. To be sure, as Van Seters has pointed out, the presentation as we have it in Exodus is not ancient, for in certain ways it appears to mimic other biblical traditions that are themselves not so early.[13] Still, in the end, the core tradition that directly associates Yahweh with peoples and locales outside Israel proper is old, as we could surmise from the handful of texts, often ancient, that associate Yahweh with regions in the south—with Sinai, Edom, Mount Seir, Teman, and Paran.[14] These areas were (and still are) frequented by nomadic groups. For this reason, I believe the memory of Yahweh's homeland is ancient by biblical standards, dating to the early Iron era or perhaps even earlier. As a result, when it comes to Israelite perspectives on Midian, the biblical portrait provides an odd juxtaposition of affection and antipathy: affection in the very earliest period (because of a shared cultural and religious heritage) and antipathy in all later periods (because the Midianites were Israel's nomadic opponents). Notably, these conflicting portraits of Midian do not reflect mere ambivalence; they reflect contrary feelings from different historical junctures. Affections with a positive valence toward Midian are associated with Israel's earliest history, and those with a negative valence appear in all subsequent periods. What would explain the development of this affective pattern? I will return to this problem below, but first, a digression.

Some scholars have questioned the assumption that the Midianites were nomadic. Knauf and Mendenhall, in particular, have argued that the Midianites are better understood as a settled population.[15] Their

---

12. J. de Vaulx, *Les Nombres* (SB; Paris: Gabalda, 1972) 355.

13. J. Van Seters, *The Life of Moses: The Yahwist as Historian in Exodus–Numbers* (Louisville: Westminster/John Knox, 1994) 29–34.

14. See Deut 33:2; Judg 5:4–5; Hab 3:3; Isa 63:5; Ps 68:8, 17.

15. E. A. Knauf, *Midian: Untersuchungen zur Geschichte Palästinas und Nordarabiens am Ende des 2. Jahrtausends v. Chr.* (Abhandlungen des deutschen Palästinavereins; Wiesbaden:

conclusion is based on a presumed connection between the biblical Midianites and a type of Late Bronze/Iron Age pottery found in north-west Arabia, Sinai, the Negeb, and in Transjordan.[16] This pottery assemblage is generally poor in terms of its repertoire and quality, reflecting as it does the unevenness of either hand forming or a very slow pottery wheel. The pottery's saving grace, as it were, is its bichrome and polychrome decoration, which features geometric, zoomorphic, and occasionally anthropomorphic figures in various shades of red, black, and brown. The conclusion that this pottery belonged to the biblical Midianites is problematic but, if the Midianite traditions in the books of Exodus and Judges go back to the early Iron period—and I believe that they probably do—then those who made this pottery are in the right places at the right time. Knauf's and Mendenhall's assertions that these Midianites were settled peoples rather than nomads is based on the observation that this Midianite ware is very prominent at Qurayyah, a major archaeological site in northwest Arabia.[17] Here we find a city wall, a strongly fortified citadel, and irrigation works that are indicative of extensive agricultural activity. Numerous settlements with this pottery have also been discovered in the coastal mountains west of Qurayyah. For Knauf and Mendenhall, this is sufficient evidence to prove that the Midianites were not nomadic, but they are only partly right about this.

Petrographic analysis has confirmed that nearly all of the Midianite ware—in Arabia, in the Sinai, in the Negeb, in Transjordan, and in the Arabah—was manufactured in Qurayyah itself.[18] This is indicative not of a wholly settled society but of a dimorphic society, which included both people living a nomadic, caravan lifestyle and settled peoples, who resided in ecological niches within the Hejaz and Arabah and at strategic locations along the trade routes. Thus, a large number of so-called Midianite settlements—even if these include large settle-

---

Harrassowitz, 1988) 1–42; G. F. Mendenhall, "Midian," *ABD* 4.815–18.

16. B. Rothenberg and J. Glass, "The Midianite Pottery," in *Midian, Moab and Edom: The History and Archaeology of Late Bronze and Iron Age Jordan and North-West Arabia* (ed. J. F. A. Sawyer and D. J. A. Clines; JSOTSup 24; Sheffield: JSOT Press, 1984) 65–124; G. Bawden, "Painted Pottery of Tayma and Problems of Cultural Chronology in North-west Arabia," in ibid., 37–52.

17. Knauf, *Midian*; Mendenhall, "Midian."

18. Rothenberg and Glass, "The Midianite Pottery"; P. J. Parr, "Archaeological Sources for the Early History of North-West Arabia," in *Sources for the History of Arabia, Part 1* (2 vols.; Riyadh: Riyadh University Press, 1979) 37–44.

ments such as Qurayyah—cannot be taken as evidence of a fully settled society. Whether the Midianite-ware society should be equated with biblical Midian is a question still worth asking.[19] More certain, I think, is that it was a dimorphic society, which included both settled and nomadic populations, as was the case with the Arab societies that followed it. Moreover, in these later proto-Arab and Arab societies we find various kinds of nomadism, including not only camel nomadism—practiced by groups who traveled into the deep desert—but also bovine and ovine pastoralism.[20] From this we may safely assume that some nomadic Midianites were pastoralists of this sort. The reasonableness of this conclusion is reinforced by the fact that, in the Late Bronze and early Iron periods, the development of camel nomadism was still in its nascent stages; and of course, the Egyptians tell us that the nomadic Shasu were pastoralists with flocks and herds.[21]

Continuing with this digression, even if the Midianite ware did not really belong to the biblical Midianites, the material evidence left behind by its caravaning society has a direct bearing on our understanding of biblical Midian. It is sometimes maintained that the domestication of the camel and camel nomadism did not really develop until the first millennium.[22] While it is true that exploitation of the camel came into its own during the first millennium, there is ample evidence that the camel was domesticated earlier and that camel nomadism was practiced during the latter parts of the second millennium. Our evidence for dromedary domestication includes ancient representations of camel riders (with saddles behind the camel's hump!) that date to the third and second millennia B.C.E.[23] To this we can add our oldest picture of a rider on the camel's hump, which dates to the ninth century (Tell Halaf).[24] Given that camel nomadism requires only that

---

19. See P. Bienkowski, "Midian, Midianites," in *Dictionary of the Ancient Near East* (ed. P. Bienkowski and A. Millard; Philadelphia: University of Pennsylvania, 2000) 198.

20. As we may deduce from certain booty lists, in which the Assyrians claim to have seized sheep, goats, and cattle from Arabs in the regions to the immediate south of Palestine. See Eph'al, *The Ancient Arabs*, 83–86.

21. P. Anastasi IV; translation in *ANET* 259.

22. See, e.g., N. P. Lemche, *Prelude to Israel's Past: Background and Beginnings of Israelite History and Identity* (Peabody, MA: Hendrickson, 1998) 62.

23. W. Dostal, "The Evolution of Bedouin Life," in *L'Antica Società Beduina* (ed. F. Gabrieli; Rome: Centro de Studi Semitici, Istituto di Studi Orientali—Università, 1958) 11–33.

24. Ibid.; R. D. Barnett, "Lachish, Ashkelon and the Camel: A Discussion of Its Use in Southern Palestine," in *Palestine in the Bronze and Iron Ages: Papers in Honour of Olga Tufnell* (ed. J. N. Tubb; London: Institute of Archaeology, 1985) 15–30.

camels are domesticated for burden-bearing, not for riding, we can safely conclude that camel domestication was accomplished before the first millennium. As for camel nomadism itself, the evidence of the Midianite ware is conclusive: it was distributed via camel caravans during the latter part of the second millennium. Hence, the biblical portrait of the Midianites as camel nomads need not be viewed as anachronistic; in fact, insofar as we date the traditions about the biblical Midianites to the Iron I period (which seems quite reasonable), an association of the biblical Midianites with the Midianite ware is implicit and probably right.

But returning to the main theme, I promised to take up the matter of Israel's conflicting portraits of Midian, which paint the Midianites in both good and evil hues. To repeat, these portraits do not reflect mere ambivalence; they reflect contrary feelings from different historical situations. Affections with a positive valence toward Midian are associated with Israel's earliest history, and those with a negative valence appear in all subsequent periods. What would explain the development of this affective pattern?

If we suppose for the sake of discussion that a significant core of early Israelite society was nomadic, then the anthropological evidence helps us understand this dynamic among settling nomads, in which early affections for their nomadic brethren are replaced by antipathies. In many cases, settling nomads begin to develop an identity apart from members who remain nomadic.[25] This is especially true when the settlers develop an economy that no longer needs the nomadic element; the nomads become threats rather than assets. As a result, if the highlands of Late Bronze/Iron I Palestine were settled by pastoral nomads who also took up agriculture, as some scholars suggest, then we should anticipate the following pattern. First, the early settlers valued

---

25. For relevant discussions, see V. Azarya, "The Nomadic Factor in Africa: Dominance or Marginality," in *Nomads in the Sedentary World* (ed. A. M. Khazanov and A. Wink; Richmond, UK: Curzon, 2001) 252 (250–84); R. Bulliet, "Sedentarization of Nomads in the Seventh Century: The Arabs in Basra and Kufa," in *When Nomads Settle: Processes of Sedentarization as Adaptation and Response* (ed. P. C. Salzman; New York: Praeger, 1980) 45–46 (35–47); W. Irons, "Nomadism as a Political Adaptation: The Case of Yomut Turkmen," *American Ethnologist* 4 (1974) 638–39 (635–58); E. Marx, "The Tribe as a Unit of Subsistence: Nomadic Pastoralism in the Middle East," *American Anthropologist* 79 (1977) 354 (343–63). For closely related discussions concerning changes in social structure among sedentarizing nomads, see W. Goldschmidt, "Career Reorientation and Institutional Adaptation in the Process of Natural Sedentarization," in *When Nomads Settle: Processes of Sedentarization as Adaptation and Response*, 48–61; P. C. Salzman, "Processes of Sedentarization among the Nomads of Baluchistan," in ibid., 95–110.

and appreciated their nomadic origins. Second, because the highland settlers were both pastoralists and agriculturalists, these settlers soon developed some measure of economic independence. Third, as a result of this independence, the settlers came to view the nomads as threats to the security of settled life. One consequence of this development would have been that early affections for nomadic brethren were finally replaced by animosity toward them.

This scenario more or less dovetails with the biblical portrait of Midian. Here there is a distant memory of Israel's nomadic origins and of its early affections for the nomads, as well as evidence of its eventual turn against the nomadic threat. Now this evidence by no means proves that early Israelites had recently lived as pastoral nomads, but it is commensurate with this explanation of Israel's origins.

The Ishmaelites

Our discussion of Midian proceeds organically into a discussion of the people that the Israelites called Ishmaelites. This is in part because the Bible closely associates the Midianites with the Ishmaelites and in part because the archaeological and textual evidence associates the two peoples with the same geographical and ecological niches.

Israelite sentiments about the Ishmaelites are ensconced in Yahweh's pronouncement to Hagar that Ishmael would be "a wild ass of a man, with his hand against everyone, and everyone's hand against him; and he shall live at odds with all his kin" (Gen 16:12). Who the Ishmaelites were in Israelite eyes is suggested on the one hand by explicit descriptions of their nomadic lifestyle, which involved caravans, tents, and camels; and on the other hand by the tradition about Ishmael's twelve sons, who turn out to be the eponyms of nomadic Arab tribes that are also mentioned in the Neo-Assyrian texts.[26] The earliest Assyrian textual references date to the mid-ninth century, and at this point the Arabs were already a formidable military opponent—one

---

26. While acknowledging a connection between Ishmael and the Arabs, Eph'al wishes to preserve a distinction between them, so that *Ishmaelite* is an early term, relating to an Iron I tribal confederation, and *Arab* is a later term, designating the nomadic lifestyle in general. In my opinion, this distinction is based on his dubious conclusion that the biblical texts about Ishmael date to the Iron I period. Because these texts probably date to the first millennium, I see no point in preserving this distinction. For the relevant discussions, see I. Eph'al, *The Ancient Arabs*, 231–40; idem, "'Ishmael' and 'Arab': A Transformation of Ethnological Terms," *JNES* 35 (1976) 225–35; E. A. Knauf, *Ismael: Untersuchungen zur Geschichte Palästinas und Nordarabiens im 1. Jahrtausends v. Chr.* (Abhandlungen des deutschen Palästinavereins; Wiesbaden: Harrassowitz, 1989).

part of the coalition that successfully resisted the Assyrian army at Qarqar in 853 B.C.E.[27] The texts imply that the Arabs employed about 1,000 battle camels in the confrontation so that, already by the ninth century, the camel was more than the pack animal that it was for the so-called Midianite society. The Arabs do not figure in our Assyrian sources again until the reign of Tiglath-pileser III, when the Assyrians moved to annex western areas of the Fertile Crescent to their empire. Here there are eighth-century references to Arabs promising their loyalties and paying tribute to Assyria, and, notably, the Arabs were frequenting the same areas and travel routes as the earlier Midianite society—in Arabia, along the King's Highway in Transjordan, in the Arabah, the Negeb, and in northern Sinai, heading toward Egypt.

Chronologically speaking, the Bible associates the Ishmaelites with the era before the settlement, in connection with the Abraham and Joseph stories, but these biblical traditions cannot be so ancient. The Joseph story is probably the older source here, inasmuch as it provides political commentary on conditions in the northern kingdom;[28] as for the Abraham traditions, these are to my mind exilic or postexilic in their formulation.[29] So it appears that the Israelites employed the term *Ishmaelite* in both halves of the first millennium, in a manner akin to, and in the same time frame as Mesopotamian uses of the term *Arab*. This may suggest that the Israelites at first referred to the caravan cultures from Arabia as *Midianites* and then later called them *Ishmaelites* and *Arabs*.

In spite of the obvious similarities between the Midianite and Ishmaelite cultures, Israelite feelings about Midian are in every way more extreme. Israel does not express the strong affections for Ishmael that it once had for Midian, nor does it develop the intense animosity for Ishmael that it eventually developed toward Midian. *Ambivalent* is the word that best describes Israelite attitudes about Ishmael. This am-

---

27. See Shalmeneser III's Kurkh Monolith Inscription in RIMA 3, 11–24. Translation in *ANET* 278–79.

28. W. Dietrich, *Die Josephserzählung als Novelle und Geschichtsschreibung: zugleich ein Beitrag zur Pentateuchfrage* (Biblisch-theologische Studien 14; Neukirchen-Vluyn: Neukirchener Verlag, 1989); D. M. Carr, *Reading the Fractures of Genesis: Historical and Literary Approaches* (Louisville: Westminster, 1996) 277–83.

29. The traditions about Abraham are now widely regarded as late compositions. For the relevant discussions by Van Seters, Blum, Carr, Rose, Schmid, Thompson, and others, see my *Pentateuch: An Annotated Bibliography* (Institute for Biblical Research Bibliography 1; Grand Rapids: Baker, 2002) 22–33.

bivalence not only contrasts with Israelite attitudes about Midian; it contrasts as well with Israel's more extreme animus against Ammon, Moab, Edom, and Amalek. These differences need to be sorted out.

Let us begin with the contrast between Israel's attitudes about Ishmael and Midian. Israel had no early memory of affection for Ishmael because the Ishmaelites first emerged as a discrete identity after the Israelite settlement. This being so, what is found in the Bible is found in the anthropological evidence; settled peoples are usually suspicious of their nomadic neighbors, because the nomads represent a threat to social and political stability. So why was Israelite hostility so much more pronounced in the case of the Midianites, who were culturally similar to the Ishmaelites? The difference probably stems from political and economic considerations. Israel's tribal societies were poorly integrated before the monarchy; they could only have sporadically policed the activities of local nomads. As long as this was the case, the nomadic peoples were a serious threat to the security of the Israelite tribes. This would have been particularly true of people who lived along the trade routes in Transjordan, as reflected in the conflict between Israel and Midian in Judg 6–8.[30] It was only with the rise of the monarchies that the Hebrews could better secure their borders and take advantage of nomadic trade, which they eventually managed to do.[31]

This explains why Israel's sentiments for Ishmael contrasted so starkly with its hostility toward Ammon, Moab, Edom, and Amalek. These four entities represented economic and political threats to Israel. The first three were territorial states that vied for control of nearby regions, and the last group—the Amalekites—were nomadic pastoralists who constantly threatened peace in peripheral regions to the south. By way of contrast, the Ishmaelite caravans served a vital role in promoting trade in the region. As Eph'al has noted, this economic link was undoubtedly one of the things that prompted these early Arabs to join Israel in the ninth-century coalition against Shalmaneser of Assyria.[32] So it was by no means a romantic notion of nomadic life that motivated Israel to link itself closely with Ishmael in the genealogical tradition. It was instead a matter of economic calculus.

---

30. Notice as well the fame of Hadad of Moab, which accrued to him after his defeat of the Midianites in Transjordan (see Gen 36:35).

31. See Eph'al, *The Ancient Arabs*, 86–87.

32. Ibid.

The Amalekites

The correctness of this assessment of Ishmael is reinforced by a closer look at Israelite attitudes toward Amalek. For in the case of the Amalekites, though Israel admitted an ethnic association with them, one looks in vain for some word of acceptance or affirmation (with one possible and very obscure exception). From the beginning of the biblical story onward, the Amalekites are marked for extermination, ostensibly because of their early conflicts with Israel in the desert wilderness. The last chapter in this story appears in the fictional tale of Esther, where Mordecai, from the family of Kish, gets the best of Haman, the Agagite.[33]

The contrast between Israelite sentiments for Ishmael and Amalek may depend upon the different kinds of nomadism the two groups practiced. Whereas the Ishmaelites were mainly proto-Bedouin traders who specialized in camels, the Amalekites were primarily bovine and ovine pastoralists, whose movements were limited to areas of pasturage closer to Israel.[34] The Bible suggests that they sometimes moved into the valleys and hill country of Palestine as well, as does the earlier Egyptian evidence regarding nomadic Shasu pastoralists.[35] This kind of nomadism brought the Amalekites into direct competition with Israelite pastoralists and agriculturalists dwelling in these areas[36] and was one cause of the perpetual conflict between Israel and Amalek. The conflict was further exacerbated by the tendency for Amalekites to raid Israelite villages, flocks, and herds. This assumption follows from the general anthropological evidence, which shows that nearly all nomadic groups practice raiding,[37] and it follows as well from specific anthropological observations in the region. These observations suggest that nomadic groups living in the marginal areas south of Israel could not easily survive apart from the business of caravaning or the raiding of nearby populations.[38]

---

33. The relevant text is 1 Sam 15, which pits Saul, the son of Kish, against the Amalekites and their king, Agag.

34. G. L. Mattingly, "Amalek," *ABD* 1.169–71; cf. 1 Sam 15:15, which lists "sheep and oxen" as the livestock of Amalek.

35. See Num 14:25, 45; Judg 6:33; 12:15. For the relevant texts from the reigns of Seti I and Ramses II, see *ANET* 254 and P.Anastasi I in E. F. Wente, *Letters from Ancient Egypt* (SBLWAW 1; Atlanta: Scholars Press, 1990) 106–7. See also texts and discussion in Giveon, *Les Bédouins Shosou des Documents Égyptiens*, 39–131.

36. Mattingly, "Amalek."

37. See n. 3 (p. 10).

38. M. Haiman, "Agriculture and Nomad: State Relations in the Negev Desert in the Byzantine and Early Islamic Periods," *BASOR* 297 (1995) 29–53; Sweet, "Camel Raiding

At any rate, my basic observation about the Amalekites is this: though they represent the nomadic group whose *Lebensart* comes closest to the pastoral nomadism that Israel envisioned for its own origins, Amalek is at the same time the nomadic group that Israel most despised. Thus the biblical evidence regarding Amalek does not lend any support to the idea that the Israelites embraced romantic notions of pastoral nomadism.

As mentioned, however, there may be one case in which the Hebrew traditions look positively upon the Amalekites, and this singular exception—if it is one—fits very nicely with all that I have said so far. I have in mind an obscure reference in the Song of Deborah (Judg 5:14), which claims that some of Israel's troops came 'from Ephraim, whose roots are in Amalek' (מני אפרים שרשם בעמלק).[39] Text critics have speculated that this text is corrupt. Some of the versions do not reflect שרשם but instead suggest a verb; BHS proposes אשרו (from אשר, meaning 'to advance, to tread'). The Greek translators tried to make sense of שרשם itself, resulting in 'Ephraim *uprooted them* [εξερριζωσεν] in Amalek'. Another possible corruption involves עמלק itself. Some Greek witnesses read εν τη κοιλαδι ('in the valley') instead of 'in Amalek', thus reflecting בעמק instead of עמלק. Similar confusion regarding עמלק appears in a comparison of MT Judg 12:15 with the versions. The Hebrew has "Abdon . . . was buried in Pirathon, in the land of Ephraim, in the hill country of the Amalekites [עמלקי]," but the Lucianic Greek has Σελλημ instead of Αμαληκ, and the Old Latin has *Aellen*. The editors of BHS therefore proposed to emend the Hebrew to בהר אפרים בארץ שעלים ('in the highlands of Ephraim, in the land of Shaalim'), but the textual evidence for this emendation does not appear to be very strong.

The tendency for the BHS editors to edit out Amalek in these two texts (Judg 5:14; 12:15) seems to mirror an earlier tendency in the versions. Possibly, the translators of the versions could not really believe what they were reading in the Hebrew, which (as Mark Smith has pointed out) seems to imply "not simply a neutral mention of Amalek but a positive indication of kinship between the tribe of Ephraim and Amalek."[40] For the ancient translators, as well as for the BHS editors, this view of Amalek seemed so at odds with the strong animus against

---

of North Arabian Bedouin." A vivid description of nomadic robbers at work appears in P.Anastasi I (see Wente, *Letters from Ancient Egypt*, 107).

39. The discussion of Judg 5:14 and 12:15 in this paragraph depends upon the textual apparatus of BHS.

40. M. S. Smith, *The Origins of Biblical Monotheism: Israel's Polytheistic Background and the Ugaritic Texts* (Oxford: Oxford University Press, 201) 145.

Amalek in the rest of the Hebrew Bible that it must be wrong. The ancients therefore emended and changed the texts, and the BHS editors
followed suit. As it turns out, the versions are actually further evidence
for this fact: some early texts in the Hebrew Bible reflect a period when
the distinctions between nomadic Amalekites and Israelites were not
so clear. Perhaps the earliest Ephraimites were essentially settling
Amalekites. If this is right, then in the case of Amalek we have the same
pattern as we did regarding Midian: Israelites had affection for the nomads in the earliest period, and then antipathy for them after the
settlement. So these texts from Judges are precisely what we would expect if early Israel hailed from nomadic (even Amalekite!) roots.

The Qenites and Rechabites

Our survey of Israelite perspectives on the nomad is incomplete without consideration of two other nomadic groups, the Qenites and Rechabites. It is precisely with respect to these groups that some scholars
find the best evidence for Israel's romantic view of nomads. Each of
them deserves individual attention, but a few general comments about
the Qenites and Rechabites are in order. First, in both cases Israelite
sentiments toward them were sufficiently positive to allow these nomads to live in proximity to, or among, the Israelites. This was not true
of the Midianites and Amalekites, or of the Ishmaelites, who traveled
and camped in proximity to Israel but did not really live among them.
In this respect, the Qenites and Rechabites are unique among Israel's
nomadic neighbors. Another point of uniqueness regards ethnicity.
Neither the Qenites nor the Rechabites appear to have been Israelites,
at least not in any straightforward way. The Qenites were generally
understood as the children of Cain, and their immunity from Israelite
aggression in 1 Sam 15 was granted, not on the basis of ethnicity, but
on the ostensible basis of their kindness toward Israel at the time of the
Exodus. It is true that an alternative tradition feebly connects the Qenites to Israel through their association with Midian, who was in turn a
son of Abraham by Keturah. But on the whole, the Qenites seem to be
regarded not as Israelites but as friendly neighbors of Israel.

As for the Rechabites, little is said in the Bible about their origins.
Our only hint is the late genealogy in 1 Chr 2:55, which connects them
with the Qenites. So, insofar as the Qenites are regarded as non-Israelites, the same may be cautiously inferred about the Rechabites. The
main point is that neither group was fully incorporated into Israelite
society. Why, then, were the Qenite and Rechabite nomads at the

same time both spatially intimate with and ethnically distant from the Israelites?

In the case of the Qenites, at least, the answer to this question may be provided by attending to their occupation. It has long been suspected, and in many quarters is essentially accepted, that the Qenites were itinerant metalsmiths. One part of the evidence for this is their name, which can mean 'to forge' or 'a metalworker', as it does in Arabic and Syriac. Another part of the evidence is that the eponymous ancestor of the Qenites, Cain, had a son who was the patron saint of metallurgy (Tubal-cain).[41] Then there is the traditional homeland of the Qenites to consider. This land lay in regions to the south of Palestine proper, where copper deposits were mined and processed as early as the third millennium B.C.E. When this circumstantial evidence is considered together with their nomadic lifestyle, one can see why it is so tempting to conclude that the Qenites were metalsmiths. There is also other evidence for this identification that is less well-known.

It is common in simple societies for metalsmiths to live itinerate lives.[42] This is in part because they must travel to gather raw materials and then bring them back to customers and in part because they are among the very few who possess the requisite metallurgical skills. These skills are naturally valued by the individuals whom the smiths serve, with one result being that the smiths often enjoy a degree of acceptance and protection within the societies that benefit from their work. Nevertheless, it is usually the case that the smiths remain a separate ethnic group. Some scholars attribute this relative marginality to suspicions that arise in response to the magical appearance of metalwork,[43] while other scholars believe it is intentionally pursued by the smiths themselves, as one strategy for protecting their exclusive access to the technology.[44] Perhaps there is some truth in both explanations. At any rate, because of their marginality and relative independence, one finds that in times of war the smiths are wholly neutral. During attacks on Bedouin camps in Arabia, for example, one can find the smiths practicing their craft with a spirit of impunity, defending neither

---

41. B. Halpern, "Qenites," *ABD* 4.17–22; P. M. McNutt, "In the Shadow of Cain," *Semeia* 87 (1999) 45–64.

42. Idem, "The African Ironsmith as Marginal Mediator: A Symbolic Analysis," *Journal of Ritual Studies* 5 (1991) 75–98; idem, "The Kenites, the Midianites, and the Rechabites as Marginal Mediators in Ancient Israelite Tradition," *Semeia* 67 (1994) 109–32.

43. Ibid.

44. F. S. Frick, "The Rechabites Reconsidered," *JBL* 90 (1971) 279–87; D. C. Benjamin, "A Response to McNutt: 'The Kenites, the Midianites, and the Rechabites as Marginal Mediators in Ancient Israelite Tradition,'" *Semeia* 67 (1994) 133–44.

themselves nor their neighbors.[45] They do so with confidence because all of the Bedouin protect them and because any loss of property will soon be set right. Fellow members of the blacksmith clan who live among the attacking Bedouin tribe will ensure this.

Understood in this anthropological context, the sociological niche of the Qenites comes into clearer focus. Consider their forefather, Cain, for instance. It was his family that first worked in metals and that was sentenced to an itinerant life. At the same time, his was a protected family that bore a mark of immunity from violence. This mark was not necessarily a visible mark, as is sometimes supposed. Perhaps it was, like the beast's mark in the Apocalypse, an ideological marker ever visible to those "in the know." In the world of ancient Israel, everyone knew to live at peace with the smiths and to offer them protection. Vivid illustrations of this phenomenon appear in the books of Judges and Samuel. In the Battle at Kishon Brook, we find that the Qenites are at peace with both of the warring factions (Israel and Hazor). Similarly, in Saul's slaughter of the Amalekites, Saul directs the Qenites out of harm's way.[46] This is probably not a reflection of Israel's nomadic ideal; it is more likely a reflection of the high regard that Israel had for Qenite technology. For with respect to the Qenite's nomadic lifestyle, Israel's sentiments are summed up in the words of Cain: "My punishment it too great to bear" (Gen 4:13).

As for the Rechabites, who are supposedly related to the Qenites, the Bible gives us very little to go on. They lived in tents and they practiced neither agriculture nor viticulture (Jer 35:6–7). It is possible that they were pastoralists of a sort, but if they were, it is very odd that they sought refuge from Babylon in the urban confines of sixth-century Jerusalem (Jer 35:11). A more natural course of action would have been to take their flocks into marginal areas, farther away from Babylon's strategic interests.[47] From this I conclude that Rechabites were probably itinerant craftsmen, perhaps metalworkers, whose social status vis-à-vis Israel was similar to that of the Qenites. This conclusion is further reinforced by their abstinence from alcoholic beverages, which was—according to Frank Frick—a shrewd protocol for protecting their trade secrets.[48]

---

45. A. Musil, *The Manners and Customs of the Rwala Bedouins* (Oriental Explorations and Studies 6; New York: American Geographical Society, 1978) 281.

46. See Judg 4–5; 1 Sam 15:6. Whether 1 Sam 15 is mainly history or fiction is really beside the point, I think.

47. Frick, "The Rechabites Reconsidered," 285.

48. Ibid.

Conclusions

My survey of Israelite perspectives on nomads and the nomadic life is complete. What conclusions can be drawn from it? Foremost, I do not see any evidence that the Israelites embraced a romantic view of nomadic life that could have served as the catalyst for inventing a tradition about their nomadic origins. On the contrary, the Israelites did not much care for the nomads, and the nomads they tolerated were mainly those who provided economic or technological services to the Israelites. The singular exception to this rule appears in Israel's earliest memories of Midian, which preserve a tradition that connects Israel's origins, and its god, with foreign peoples and regions in the south. By no means does this prove that the Israelites were largely the descendants of pastoral nomads. But this evidence is certainly commensurate with this explanation for Israel's origins.

Another important point is this: it is clear from the biblical data that the Israelite traditions tended to conflate one nomadic group with others. One reason for this is that there were probably genuine associations between the nomads. Some Qenites apparently lived among the Midianites and Amalekites, for example.[49] There were also occasions where common cause brought different nomadic groups together, as we see when the Midianites and Amalekites fought side by side (Judg 6–8). Another reason for the conflation of one nomadic group with another is the lexical elasticity of the terms used in Israel to describe the nomads. Once a term entered the Hebrew vocabulary to describe a particular nomadic group—such as "Midian"—it was natural to employ it in a generic sense, so that it referred to the nomadic lifestyle in general or to particular kinds of nomadic life, such as caravan nomadism as opposed to pastoral nomadism.[50] Of course, the ancients were not always fastidious in their formulation and use of ethnic categories. When the Israelites made Amalek the son of Timna, for instance, the link between them was probably their common nomadic lifestyle;[51] however, it remains the case that the two groups generally lived out different modes of nomadism, because the town of Timna should be associated with caravaning routes, but the Amalekites were (primarily) nomadic pastoralists.

---

49. Cf. Judg 1:16; Exod 3:1; 1 Sam 15.

50. The reference to Midianites in the story of Joseph is likely such an instance, because this story probably dates well after the Iron I period (see Gen 37:28–36).

51. Gen 36:12; 1 Chr 1:36.

An obvious implication of these observations is that it is probably unwise to trace the early Israelite settlers back to a particular nomadic group, such as the Midianites or Qenites. As Israel's historical memory suggests, nomads and migrants from different places—especially from the south and east, as well as from within Canaan proper—would have contributed to the settlement. The religious evidence bears this out. Yahweh appears to have been a local god from somewhere in the south. It is possible that many nomadic groups knew of and respected this deity, but it seems unlikely that Yahweh was originally prominent for so many different settlers. We could surmise as much from the name of the early tribal confederation, which, as Mark Smith has pointed out, was not *yiśrā-yāh* but *yiśrā-ʾēl*.[52] But this is, of course, another chapter in Israel's fascinating story.

---

52. Smith, *The Origins of Biblical Monotheism*, 143.

David:
Messianic King or Mercenary Ruler?

JOHN VAN SETERS
Waterlook, Ontario

Introduction

The problem of David's role in the formation of identity for the entity known in the biblical literature as "Israel" and for the people of Judah from the time of the Judean monarchy onward is bound up with the increasing recognition in recent years that the two states of Israel and Judah did not share a common origin, as the biblical tradition suggests. The notion that there was originally a sacred twelve-tribe league that changed over time into a single united monarchy has been largely discredited, and what we must accept in its place is the more likely view that each of the two kingdoms evolved gradually as two distinct entities.[1] Even though they shared a common deity, Yahweh, and perhaps some religious traditions and social customs, it is remarkable how much the Bible still preserves the impression that Judah and Israel maintained through much of the monarchy period quite separate traditions of origin and "archaic" history. A case in point is the obvious fact that all of the stories of the judges belong to the northern region of

---

1. See T. L. Thompson, *The Mythic Past* (London: Basic Books, 1999) 164–68; D. Edelman, "Saul ben Kish in History and Tradition," in *The Origins of the Ancient Israelite States* (ed. V. Fritz and P. R. Davies; JSOTSup 228; Sheffield: Sheffield Academic Press, 1996) 142–59; idem, "Did Saulide-Davidic Rivalry Resurface in Early Persian Yehud?" in *The Land That I Will Show You: Essays on the History and Archaeology of the Ancient Near East in Honor of J. Maxwell Miller* (ed. J. A. Dearman and M. P. Graham; JSOTSup 343; Sheffield: Sheffield Academic Press, 2001) 69–95; P. R. Davies, "The Origin of Biblical Israel," in *Essays on Ancient Israel in Its Near Eastern Context: A Tribute to Nadav Naʾaman* (ed. Y. Amit et al.; Winona Lake, IN: Eisenbrauns, 2006) 141–48; I. Finkelstein, "The Last Labayu King: King Saul and the Expansion of the First North Israelite Territorial Entity," in ibid., 171–87; idem, *David and Solomon: In Search of the Bible's Sacred Kings and the Roots of Western Tradition* (New York: Free Press, 2006); J. Blenkinsopp, "Benjamin Traditions Read in the Early Persian Period," in *Judah and the Judeans in the Persian Period* (ed. O. Lipschits and M. Oeming; Winona Lake, IN: Eisenbrauns, 2006) 629–45.

Israel,[2] and Saul's rise to the status of king in Benjamin seems to be in complete continuity with this tradition. Within the Saul story it has long been recognized that there is an early source in 1 Sam 9:1–10:16; and that chaps. 11, 13, and 14 are entirely Benjaminite and originally had no connection with either Samuel or David.[3] Saul's career is summed up in 1 Sam 14:47–48 as the conclusion of this account.[4] Consequently, it seems entirely reasonable to assume that until the late monarchy period various regions in Israel, and Benjamin in particular, had their own traditions about heroes from an archaic past.

Furthermore, it appears increasingly likely that it was only after the demise of the northern kingdom of Israel and the movement of many northern refugees into the south in the late eighth and seventh centuries B.C.E. that the identity of the people of Judah began to merge with that of the people of Israel. This also entailed the merging of origin traditions and archaic histories, including the origin of the monarchy, in such a way as to articulate a common identity.[5] A major factor in this development was undoubtedly the shift in the administrative center from Jerusalem to Mizpah in Benjamin during the Neo-Babylonian and early Persian periods for the combined regions of Judah and Benjamin under the control of one governing authority.[6] This strengthened the perception that Israel and Judah were one people, with Israel being the more dominant of the two. However, if Judah and Israel were to be understood as one nation under Yahweh, then nowhere was it more important to find a way to express this unity than in a common origin of the two monarchies, because it was the institution of the monarchies with their distinctive royal ideologies that had defined the nature of the two peoples for centuries as two distinct entities. Only by means of the myth of a common united monarchy in which the traditions of the

---

2. The exception is the story of Othniel in Judg 3:7–11, but this tale is clearly an artificial creation. Hence, the exception merely proves the rule.

3. See J. Van Seters, *In Search of History* (New Haven: Yale University Press, 1983) 250–64 for details.

4. I do not think it is possible, however, to date Saul's reign or to reconstruct his achievements by the use of archaeology or the analogy of the Amarna age Labayu of Shechem, as Finkelstein does (see n. 1 above). He uses too many details from the Persian period of the David story for his reconstruction. Even the story of Saul's war against the Ammonites in 1 Sam 11 is a completely idealized hero tale, in my view, that has little historical value.

5. Davies places this process in the Neo-Babylonian and Persian periods, whereas Finkelstein locates the literary development in the eighth century. My view is that there are two major levels in the Saul-David story; one is Neo-Babylonian and one late Persian.

6. See O. Lipschits, *The Fall and Rise of Jerusalem: Judah under Babylonian Rule* (Winona Lake, IN: Eisenbrauns, 2005) 88–126, et passim.

first kings, Saul and David, played a part could this division be over-come.[7] The historian who first attempted to produce a continuous inte-grated history of the two peoples of Israel and Judah was the Deuter-onomist (Dtr). It is to this historian of the Neo-Babylonian period, probably writing from Mizpah, that we must attribute the story of Da-vid's rise to power as successor to the first Israelite king, Saul.[8]

The form of identity for the people of Judah from the tenth to the sixth century was that of a monarchy known as the "House of David" because presumably David was the founder of a dynasty whose kings ruled over Judah for this entire period. When a history of the nation was compiled by Dtr at the end of the state, it is not surprising that the succession of kings from the time of David to the last of his line should constitute the backbone of this work and that David as the founder of the dynasty should hold a special place in it. In keeping with this, Da-vid is presented by Dtr as a model ruler, just in all his deeds, obedient to all Yahweh's laws, and a king to be emulated by all subsequent rul-ers. This history of the monarchy was complicated by the fact that, after the demise of the Kingdom of Israel to the north, a large influx of Israelites into northern Judah produced a particularly close association between Judah and the neighboring region of Benjamin, and this in-spired the need for a common history of the two regions. Thus, the his-tories of the two monarchies were combined into one with a synchro-nism developed to link them together. However, this combined history complicated the story of the origin and founding of Israelite kingship, because Benjamin had its own tradition of a founding monarch, that of the pious and valiant Saul. He could not be denied his place as the first king of Israel, who won independence from the Philistines as David had for the Judeans. Consequently, as a link between the two tradi-tions, the story of David's rise to power within the court of Saul and the one ultimately to succeed him was formulated by Dtr to bring the Ben-jaminite and Judean traditions together to create the myth of the united monarchy.[9] Within Dtr's account of David's rise, it is David who

---

7. Albrecht Alt, in his *Staatenbildung der Israeliten in Palestina* (1930) had attempted to account for the apparent duality of the united monarchy in historical terms; see A. Alt, "The Formation of the Israelite State in Palestine," *Essays on Old Testament History and Re-ligion* (Oxford: Blackwell, 1966) 171–237. In this he was followed by many other scholars, most notably M. Noth, *The History of Israel* (New York: Harper, 1960) 164–224.

8. The role of Mizpah was already suggested by M. Noth, *The Deuteronomistic History* (JSOTSup 15; Sheffield: JSOT Press, 1981) 145 n. 1.

9. Consequently, I do not view it as appropriate to use any of the textual material from either the story of David and Saul or the so-called court history to reconstruct the history of Saul, as Finkelstein and Edelman do (see n. 1 above). The older Saul tradition

fights against the Philistines as commander under Saul with apparent
great success, although not a single detail is given of these frequent encounters in 1 Sam 18–19.[10]

This reconstruction is admittedly speculative, but it seems to me to
be the only way to explain the elaborate attempt to account for the fact
that two separate founders of their respective kingdoms became the
first king of the same "people of Israel" through the actions of the same
deity. In my view, it was Dtr who developed this complex "historiographic" solution to the problem of identity for the combined entity. I
will not attempt here to defend this thesis in detail but focus only upon
the figure of David in the Deuteronomistic History (DtrH) as the just
king for the whole people. David is chosen by Yahweh, the god of Israel
and he is anointed as king over all the tribes of Israel. The role of Judah
is played down as only a part of that larger whole. The divine promise
to David of an enduring succession speaks only of kingship over Israel
and never mentions Judah. The state of Judah becomes a kind of con-
solation award given to Solomon's son "for David's sake" after Israel
proper is lost to Solomon (1 Kgs 11:36–39). David is still the model king
for Jeroboam to emulate, and the latter could have secured the same
"sure house" for Israel that David's offspring had for Judah if he had
not broken the divine law.

To be sure, Dtr also combined his ideal David with the notion of
obedience to the law of God—that is, Deuteronomy—so that the king
is responsible for maintaining the state as living in accordance with
this law, and deviation from it inevitably brings disaster. But beyond
the destruction of the two kingdoms, Israel by the Assyrians and Judah by the Babylonians, there is still some hope in a restoration of the
House of David and a return to the ideal of the founding era. To this

---

is restricted to texts within 1 Sam 9–11, 13–14. Edelman also works on the assumption
that there was a historic rivalry between David and Saul that "resurfaced" in the early
Persian period. The view adopted here is that a rivalry of this sort is a myth. The sociological method used in support of the united monarchy and the great state of David by
C. Schäfer-Lichtenburger ("Sociological and Biblical Views of the Early State," in *The Origins of the Ancient Israelite States* [ed. V. Fritz and P. R. Davies; JSOTSup 228; Sheffield:
Sheffield Academic Press, 1996] 78–105) is seriously flawed by the early date that she
attributes to so much of the David story, most of which is of Persian date. More on this
below.

10. The independent story of David and Goliath in 1 Sam 17 is a rather careless attempt at combining the destinies of Saul and David. Saul recruits conscripts from the
sons of Jesse in Judah, and he is even presented as the king of Jerusalem (17:54). This presumably explains why the battle is fought in the strategic region west of Jerusalem and
not in his own territory of Benjamin.

extent, the election of David and the founding of the temple by his son
Solomon still forms a powerful focus for popular identity beyond the
destruction of the state. This can be seen ultimately in the work of the
Chronicler, who feels at liberty to dispense entirely with the history of
the Israelite state and focus entirely upon David as the founder of the
Jerusalem temple community. And it is reflected in the history of messianic ideology in later Judaism and the longing for the restoration of
the golden age of David.

However, the portrayal of David within the biblical corpus in 1 Sam
16–1 Kgs 2 is hardly uniform in its presentation of a model king. The
fact that David, the Judean, replaces Saul, the Benjaminite, as king and
the open conflict between the House of Saul and David's men have, in
the past, suggested an apologetic and propagandistic motive in the account of David's rise to power (HDR), on the model of various Near
Eastern royal apologies. This work has long been regarded as a contemporary product of the tenth century that was used as a source by
Dtr for his history. But if the combination of the Saul tradition with the
story of David's rise could only have come about in the late Judean
monarchy, at the earliest, then there is nothing that prevents it from
being the product of Dtr himself. Likewise, the so-called Succession
Narrative (SN), which also presupposes the struggle between the
House of David and the House of Saul throughout, must be viewed as
a late work and not as an apology for either David or Solomon.

Consequently, because there is much in both the story of David's
rise to power and the history of David's court that is quite incompatible
with Dtr's idealization of David, and even openly antagonistic to Dtr's
ideology of kingship, it becomes important to find a way of controlling
the historical and social parameters within which such a work (or
works) was composed.[11] One of the rather pervasive features that one
encounters in the texts that contain a negative portrayal of David is the
dominant role of mercenaries. In the account of David's rise, David is

---

11. I refer specifically to the corpus of texts in 1 Sam 17:55–18:4; 19:18–21:10; 22:6–23;
23:6–14, 19–24; 25:1–28:2; 29:1–30:31; 2 Sam 1:1*, 5–10, 13–16; 2:4–4:12; 5:3*, 4–5; 6:1*, 3b,
6–12, 14, 16b, 20–23; 9:1–10:14, 19b; chaps. 11–20; 1 Kgs 1:1–53; 2:5–9, 13–46. In my book
(*The Biblical Saga of King David* [Winona Lake, IN: Eisenbrauns, 2009], I try to justify this
source division and the unified character of this work, which I designate the *David Saga*
(DS). This includes but goes beyond what I identified in my earlier work as the Court History of David. Cf. my *In Search of History*, 277–91; idem, "The Court History and DtrH," in
Die sogenannte Thronfolgegeschichte Davids: Neue Einsichten und Anfragen (ed. A. de Pury
and T. Römer; OBO 176; Freiburg, Switzerland: Universitätsverlag / Göttingen: Vandenhoeck & Ruprecht, 2000) 70–93.

portrayed as a mercenary leader in the employment of the Philistines, and after David becomes king he himself makes frequent use of foreign mercenaries within his own army. Because the development of the use of mercenaries in the first millennium is well documented, in particular the use of Greek mercenaries by Near Eastern monarchs, this military history should give us a good control over the dating and social context of an extensive part of the David story.[12]

Use of Mercenaries in the Near East

In a recent paper, I have given an extensive survey of the rise of the professional army and the use of foreign mercenaries during the period from the time of the Assyrian Empire in the mid-eighth century down to the late Persian period, and there is no need to repeat it here.[13] From my survey, the following conclusions may be drawn:[14]

1. The organization of the professional military elite in the time of the Assyrian Empire by Tiglath-pileser III and the frequent devastation of the land by Sargon and Sennacherib led to the bankruptcy of many small farmers and the rise of brigand bands that raided small towns and villages for booty. Soldiers taken as prisoners by the Assyrians, especially men with special skills, often became professional soldiers used by the Assyrians as garrison troops in foreign lands.
2. The earliest use of *Greek* mercenaries in the Near East was the employment of soldiers from the region of Ionia and Caria by the Saite rulers of Egypt. This was the result of an alliance between the Lydian kings, who controlled the region of Ionia, and the Saite rulers of Egypt. They were particularly important from the sixth century down to the time of the Persian conquest of Lydia and Egypt, when the use of mercenaries from Ionia and Caria, which was now under Persian control, came to an end.

---

12. The significance of this phenomenon is completely misunderstood by Schäfer-Lichtenburger in her "Sociological and Biblical Views of the Early State." Consequently, she misdates the texts in which these occur.

13. J. Van Seters, "David the Mercenary," in *Israel in Transition: From Late Bronze II to Iron IIA (c. 1250–850 BCE)*, vol. 2: *The Texts* (ed. L. L. Grabbe; European Seminar in Historiography 8; London: T. & T. Clark, forthcoming).

14. The following is a list of useful publications that may be consulted on this subject: H. W. Parke, *Greek Mercenary Soldiers: From the Earliest Times to the Battle of Ipsus* (Oxford: Clarendon, 1933); G. T. Griffith, *The Mercenaries of the Hellenistic World* (Cambridge: Cambridge University Press, 1935); F. E. Adcock, *The Greek and Macedonian Art of War* (Berkeley: University of California Press, 1957) 19–25; Yvon Garlan, *War in the Ancient World: A Social History* (New York: Norton, 1975) 93–103; D. B. Redford. *Egypt, Canaan, and Israel in Ancient Times* (Princeton: Princeton University Press, 1992); Serge Yalichev, *Mercenaries of the Ancient World* (London: Constable, 1997); R. Waterfield, *Xenophon's Retreat: Greece, Persia and the End of the Golden Age* (Cambridge: Harvard University Press, 2006).

3. The next phase began at the end of the Peloponnesian wars (late fifth century) when there was a surplus in Greece of soldiers with no other means of livelihood, including officers and generals, who hired themselves out to Persian satraps and rulers (e.g., Xenophon and his portrayal of mercenaries in the *Anabasis*). Important here is the rise in the use of special light-armed troops, such as the peltasts and the Cretan archers, because these are mentioned several times in the David story!

4. This development of the extensive use of professional soldiers and foreign mercenaries by the state in the late Persian period redefined the nature of the monarchy. Instead of the king's being the leader of an army of the people (the citizen conscripts, whom he led into battle against a common enemy), the king became the one who financed and employed a body of professional soldiers to fight for profit and the aggrandizement of the court. The army had little in common with the people of the land who now paid these soldiers for their protection or suffered the consequences.

This military history of the use of foreign mercenaries, especially Greeks, allows us to fit the David story into a rather clearly defined social context.

David and the Army

Once we understand the nature of mercenary armies, we are able to make some interesting comparisons between David's role as leader of the armed forces in Dtr's presentation of David and this role as portrayed in the later supplementary source. In Dtr's account, from the time that David enters into the service of Saul (1 Sam 16:14–23), he quickly establishes himself as the leader of the citizen army and replaces Saul in this role in the frequent battles against the Philistines (1 Sam 18). It is David's success in this capacity, because "Yahweh is with him," that works to the detriment of Saul and that leads to Saul's jealousy and the falling out between them. When David is forced to flee from Saul, who seeks his life, he collects a band of distressed peasants, but the only military activity in which they engage, according to Dtr, is to defend the small towns of Judah against Philistine marauders (1 Sam 22:1–2; 23:1–5).

After Saul's death, when David is made king by all the tribes of Israel, they do so because they recognize him as the one who led them into battle under Saul, and thus David becomes their divinely appointed leader (*nāgîd*) to fight the wars of Yahweh (2 Sam 5:1–3*). And once David becomes king, he continues to lead the citizen army against the Philistines and all the other nations around the land of Israel (2 Sam 5:17–25; 8:1–14; 10:15–19a). The victories of David are the victories of

Yahweh, to whom he dedicates the spoils. There is complete solidarity between king and people in the conduct of these wars. In fact, David's whole career in the DtrH is defined by his participation in fighting the wars of Yahweh, and only at the end of his life, when Yahweh has given him rest from his enemies that surrounded him does he receive the divine promise of a perpetual dynasty, a "sure house."[15] Yahweh's anointed one is, above all, the one who carries out the mission of liberation from oppression and the bringer of peace to God's people.

Against this background of Dtr's royal ideology, something radically different is presented in an extended revision of the DtrH by a masterful literary work that I will designate the *David Saga* (DS).[16] According to this version of the David story, once David has left Saul's service and gathered together a band of men, some of whom were foreigners (note Ahimelek the Hittite in 1 Sam 26:6),[17] he forms them into an elite military force that he can offer for hire to the Philistine king of Gath to fight the king's battles for him (1 Sam 27:1–28:2). In this capacity David conducts continuous raids on the villages of the aboriginal population and massacres the population, entirely for his own personal gain, paying part of the booty to his overlord. In return for his service, he receives the town of Ziklag as his private domain. It is true that he avoids raiding the Judean cities, the enemies of the Philistines, and in doing so he proves disloyal to his overlord, whom he has sworn to serve. Yet this deception is only to serve his own political ambition and not for any higher purpose. When the Philistines gather for the decisive battle against Saul and the Israelites, David expresses his eagerness to participate and is only deterred from doing so by the other Philistine commanders who do not trust him (1 Sam 29). When David carries out a reprisal expedition against the Amalekites, who have raided Ziklag in his absence (1 Sam 30), his booty is piously declared to be the "booty that Yahweh has given us." But none of it is dedicated to Yahweh, as in the DtrH. Instead, much of it is distributed as political gifts to the elders of Judah in the various cities of the region, who will later make him king.

The clear indication that David is primarily concerned about his own welfare and ambitions and is quite prepared to massacre Judeans

---

15. 2 Samuel 7 originally stood immediately before 1 Kgs 2:1–4. The whole of 2 Sam 9–24 (except 10:15–19a) + 1 Kgs 1–2 (except 2:1–4,10–12) are later additions. The wars of 2 Sam 8:1–15; 10:15–19a originally stood after 5:25. 2 Samuel 8:16–18 is also a late addition.

16. See my book *The Biblical Saga of King David*.

17. The "Hittites" were, of course, condemned to eradication by Deuteronomy. See also Uriah the Hittite in 2 Sam 11.

if his demands are not met comes in the episode regarding the estate owner Nabal (1 Sam 25). In this instance he imposes his "protection" on the men tending the flocks of sheep and goats of this rich landowner, with the expectation that he will be richly "rewarded" for his service. There is no prior agreement about this service, so it is something of a protection racket. When David's men ask for their payment, they are rebuffed, and David prepares to massacre the whole population of this large estate and take what he wants. It is only the intervention of Abigail, Nabal's wife, who saves the day by flattering David with a much greater prize, his ambition to be king, which would be in jeopardy if he sheds innocent blood among the Judeans. She reminds David of his career as one who fights the "wars of Yahweh," which was the case during his service under Saul but hardly reflects his current activity as a mercenary. It also makes a mockery of what he will do under Achish, his Philistine overlord, when innocent blood is shed with impunity, and later during his struggle against the House of Saul.

After Saul's death, David takes his band of mercenaries and all of their wives and dependents to Hebron and sets up his base of operation there (2 Sam 2:3). The Judeans anoint him king, with little obvious choice (v. 4). David is very much like the Greek tyrants of the fourth century, who ruled their cities with large mercenary bodyguards. He now no longer does any fighting himself but allows his professional elite to do it for him, and they continue the same kind of marauding for booty as payment that is typical of mercenary soldiers (3:22). David's men under Joab now engage in warfare against the Israelite forces and the House of Saul under the command of Abner, with the first encounter in Benjamin (2:12–32). The battle is indecisive, but events in the struggle create a personal animosity between the two generals of the opposing forces. When there is a falling-out between Abner and the Israelite king, Ishbosheth, Abner attempts to make a deal with David to transfer the allegiance of the Israelite tribes to David in exchange for the total command of the army (3:12–39). This plan, however, is thwarted by Joab's murder of Abner in revenge for the killing of his younger brother, but also to safeguard his own place as leader of the army. The destinies of the two kingdoms are entirely in the hands of generals, and the kings, the anointed ones, are mere puppets.

After David becomes king of Israel, he has a good treaty relationship with Nahash, the king of the Ammonites. This is the same king against whom Saul had conducted a holy war to rescue Jabesh-gilead (1 Sam 11), and therefore it completely contradicts Dtr's view of David as one who fights against the enemies of Yahweh (see above). Nahash's

son, however, on taking the throne to succeed his father, unwisely
snubs David's messengers and humiliates them, and this becomes the
casus belli against the Ammonites (2 Sam 10:1–14). The Ammonites hire
33,000 Syrian mercenaries to aid them in the protection of the capital.
The elite forces under Joab take on the Syrian mercenaries, while
Abishai and the regulars take on the Ammonites, and both of the Israelite commanders are successful in the open field. This results in the
Ammonites' retreating into their city and the end of the campaign.
When military activity is resumed in the next fighting season, David's
special professional forces, which include foreigners such as Uriah the
Hittite and the general conscripts from Israel and Judah, take to the
field against the Ammonites (chap. 11). This time they are accompanied by the ark in a holy war with all the strictures of abstinence from
feasting and sex that this entails. David, however, remains in Jerusalem; he does not lead them in the fight and is certainly not bound by
any of the limitations of such a campaign but violates the wife of one
of his foreign soldiers, a Hittite, who by contrast is scrupulous about
keeping the restrictions. This makes a complete mockery of the principles of holy war as laid out in Deuteronomy. The Hittite, Uriah, obeys
the strictures of the Deuteronomic law and loses his life as a consequence, while Yahweh's anointed breaks all of the laws of God with
impunity. When David finally captures the capital city of the Ammonites, he merely treats it as his own personal property, assuming the
crown of their king (or god?) and all of the booty, with none of it dedicated to the deity (2 Sam 12:30–31; cf. 8:11). The idealism of Dtr's presentation of David as Yahweh's *nāgîd* and his anointed is made to
confront the hard "reality" of political power and the conduct of war as
the author of the *David Saga* understands it.

The Absalom revolt is another instance that points up David's use of
foreign mercenaries and professional soldiers against his own people
in a civil war. The whole account is heavily loaded with irony. First,
Absalom begins his coup in Hebron, the heartland of Judah, where he
is anointed and declared king (2 Sam 15:10–11; cf. 19:10) and begins his
move against his father. This career path, of course, parallels David's,
except that Absalom has the strong support of the representatives of
both Judah and Israel. David has only the support of his personal en-
tourage in Jerusalem. Second, David is heavily dependent upon two
groups of foreign mercenaries, Philistines and Greeks, which make up
two of the three divisions of his army. The Philistine mercenaries are
from Gath, a band of 600 men under Ittai the Gittite. This Philistine

leader swears his loyalty to David, invoking the Hebrew deity, Yahweh, and will not be dissuaded from serving under David in the present crisis. His loyalty and trustworthiness is in marked contrast to the loyalty and trustworthiness of David and his men in service to the king of Gath.

The other group of mercenaries consists of the Cherethites and the Pelethites, who, as we have seen above, are the Greek peltasts and Cretan archers. These, together with the "servants of David" (that is, his elite professionals), are set in opposition to Absalom's forces, which consist primarily of a large conscript army of Judeans and Israelites. It is David's professional army with its largely foreign contingent of mercenaries that defeats the army of Israel, with the slaughter of 20,000. David himself plays no role in the decisive battle itself; the command of the army is completely in the hands of the generals, who conduct the war as they see fit. Absalom, who makes the mistake of taking to the field himself, against the advice of his wisest counselor, loses his life and the war.

No sooner is the civil war with Absalom over than another rebellion breaks out over a dispute between the Israelites and the Judeans, led by Sheba, a Benjaminite (2 Sam 20). David intends to replace Joab, commander of the army, with Amasa, Absalom's former commander of the citizen army, but Amasa cannot muster the conscripts in time to fight the rebellion. David must resort to using his professional army, including the Greek mercenaries under Abishai. When Amasa does appear on the scene, belatedly, he is murdered by Joab, just as Joab murdered Abner, so that his control of the army remains unchallenged. It is Joab who, without any prior approval from David, makes all of the decisions about the prosecution of the war and negotiates the terms of peace to end it. Throughout this source document (DS), the generals are in complete command of all the military affairs, to which the king merely acquiesces. Furthermore, this prolonged internal strife, which leads to such great loss of life, completely undermines the statement by Dtr in 2 Sam 7:1 that Yahweh had given David "rest from all his enemies surrounding him." According to DS, throughout David's reign there is constant turmoil and bloodshed, both within his own family and in the nation as a whole.

During the final struggle for the throne between the two sons of David, Adonijah and Solomon, the military commanders play a prominent role. Adonijah looks like he has a very strong position with the support of Joab and the army. Solomon's party, however, has Benaiah, son of Jehoiada, commander of the Greek mercenaries (Cherethites and Pelethites), who also functioned as the palace guard along with the elite corps of "mighty men." Once the senile David is manipulated into giving Solomon his assent, the coup can be carried out very quickly, with Zadok the priest and Nathan the prophet anointing Solomon as king, accompanied by the foreign mercenaries.[18] As a general without an army at his immediate disposal, Joab is powerless in these circumstances. It is this same commander of the mercenaries, Benaiah, who after David's death carries out the execution of Adonijah, the rightful heir, and Joab, his rival. This makes completely ludicrous the royal ideology of Yahweh's anointed that is articulated through Dtr's presentation of the reign of David.

Conclusion

Throughout this essay I have focused on two different and contrasting portraits of David as a military leader, both before he came to power and after he became king. These portrayals reflect two quite contradictory conceptions of the monarchic state and its anointed king. In the earlier version (the DtrH), David is identified as Yahweh's chosen one through his success in leading the armies of Israel, because "Yahweh is with him" during his service under Saul. He has the love and support of all the people and no enemies within the state, except the rejected Saul. After Saul's death he is recognized as the chosen one and anointed by all the people, and as such he leads them to complete victory over all their enemies. This sets the stage for the golden age of Solomon, the building of the temple, and the period of tranquility. As such, the messianic age of David in the past is the model and hope for the messianic age in the future (2 Sam 7:9–10).

By contrast, the later document, the *David Saga*, presents the origin of David's kingship in his role as the leader of a ruthless mercenary band, who is quite willing to work for the Philistine king of Gath with pretended loyalty, while looking out entirely for his own interests. It is this same mercenary band that becomes the core of David's military support after he is made king of Judah and wins the protracted war against the House of Saul to gain control of the whole nation. David, as king, retires from fighting any more "wars of Yahweh" and leaves all

---

18. See also the parallel situation in 2 Kgs 11, in which the priest Jehoiada, supported by a palace guard of Carian mercenaries, carries out a coup against the queen, Athaliah, and anoints the young prince, Jehoash, as king. The reference to Carians as mercenaries places this text in the Saite (i.e., Neo-Babylonian) period.

military activity in the hands of his old elite corps, supplemented by a large number of foreign mercenaries. The victories of David's generals do not bring "rest" to the nation or to David's household, which is constantly torn apart by violence and civil strife to the very end. Indeed, the prediction of Nathan that the sword would not depart from David's "house" has an ironic reference not merely to David's immediate household but to the whole of the "House of David"—that is, his dynasty. Thus David, in the DS, is the man ultimately responsible for the destruction of Judah, just as, in the DtrH, Rehoboam is responsible for the fall of the kingdom of Israel. This portrayal of David reflects the social reality of rulers in the late Persian period, and with its revision of the earlier Dtr presentation it attempts to subvert the messianic utopianism that the older tradition fosters (cf. Ps 132). The Chronicler excised from his own account of David and Solomon almost all traces of this revisionist presentation in order to preserve and enhance this utopian age. Consequently, any construction of Jewish identity in the late Persian period must take this antimonarchic and antimessianic revisionist perspective into account.

A Comparative Study of the Exilic Gap in Ancient Israelite, Messenian, and Zionist Collective Memory

KATHERINE M. STOTT
Gorgias Press

An often-noted feature of biblical historiography is the noticeable gap
between the fall of Judah (described in 2 Kgs 23:31–25:30; 2 Chr 36; Jer
32:43) and the return(s) from Babylon depicted in the books of Ezra
and Nehemiah. As L. L. Grabbe observes, "there is no narrative of exile, only of going into and returning from it."[1] To be sure, certain passages have been understood by some as compositions that reflect an
exilic perspective (see, for example, Ezekiel; Isa 40–55) or that construct the exilic experience from a later vantage point (Ps 137). Furthermore, the large bulk of biblical literature has been regarded in
certain circles as the product of the "exilic period."[2] However, the fact
remains that we learn very little from the literature of the Hebrew
Bible about the state of people in exile.[3]

Author's note: The research for this essay was undertaken during the period that I held
the Izaak Walton Killam Memorial Postdoctoral Fellowship. I would like to acknowledge
the Killam Trust for the financial support provided.

1. L. L. Grabbe, "Introduction," in *Leading Captivity Captive: "The Exile" as History and
Ideology* (JSOTSup 278; Sheffield: Sheffield Academic Press, 1998) 17.

2. See, e.g., R. Albertz, *Israel in Exile: The History and Literature of the Sixth Century
B.C.E.* (trans. David Green; Studies in Biblical Literature 3; Atlanta: Society of Biblical Lit-
erature, 2003); J. Van Seters, *In Search of History: Historiography in the Ancient World and
the Origins of Biblical History* (New Haven, CT: Yale University Press, 1983; repr. Winona
Lake, IN: Eisenbrauns, 1997). Note that I use the term *exilic period* to refer to the period
between the fall of Judah in 587/586 B.C.E. and the return under Cyrus in 538, although
I do so in the recognition that its usefulness has been strongly questioned; see, e.g., R. P.
Carroll, "Exile! What Exile? Deportation and the Discourses of Diaspora," in *Leading
Captivity Captive: 'The Exile' as History and Ideology* (ed. L. L. Grabbe; JSOTSup 278; Shef-
field: Sheffield Academic Press, 1998) 62–79; Grabbe, "Introduction"; C. C. Torrey, *Ezra
Studies* (Chicago: University of Chicago Press, 1910) 289.

3. It should be acknowledged that some brief glimpses of life in exile are provided in
the historical books. See, for example, the account of Jehoiakin at the end of Kings and
Jeremiah (2 Kgs 25:27–30; Jer 52:31–34).

The absence of historical narrative in the Hebrew Bible pertaining to the exilic period is especially curious, given the central importance that the notion of exile plays in the conceptual world of this literature.[4] In this essay, I will attempt to gain some clarity on this tension by analyzing the biblical construction of Israel's past from a comparative perspective. It is the contention of this essay that this approach can shed light on the reasons for the "exilic gap" in biblical literature.[5] Additionally, it helps to illuminate other features surrounding the representation of the exilic period in the Hebrew Bible both in terms of the way the concept of *exile* is depicted/understood and how this period is situated and constructed in relation to the broader periodization of Israel's past.

Exile in Messenian and Zionist Memory

As the title of this paper suggests, parallels to the biblical treatment of exile can be found in ancient Messenian and Zionist conceptions of the past in which exile plays an equally pivotal yet similarly marginalized role.[6] While the experience of exile is formative to the identity of both communities, the period of exile is telescoped in the collective memories of each group. Despite the considerable length of the exilic period for these communities, it is remembered as little more than a brief interruption in a much longer historical time-frame. The period of exile is understood in the collective memory of both communities as a temporary gap between a glorious ancient past and the celebrated reestablishment of the nation in the homeland.

Writing in the second century C.E., the Greek traveler and geographer Pausanias provides the most complete and detailed surviving account of the Messenian past (see *Descr.* 4). Though not a Messenian himself, Pausanias relies extensively on two local sources from the Hellenistic period, and thus it is presumed in modern scholarship that

---

4. The trope of the loss and return to the land is repeated throughout the biblical literature. See, e.g., S. Talmon, "'Exile' and 'Restoration' in the Conceptual World of Ancient Judaism," in *Restoration: Old Testament, Jewish and Christian Perspectives* (ed. J. M. Scott; Leiden: Brill, 2001) 113–19. See also Carroll, "Deportation and Diasporic Discourses."

5. See the comments in ibid., on the potential insights that might be gained from a comparative approach.

6. By *Zionist*, I am referring to the movement founded at the end of the nineteenth century as a response to growing anti-Semitism across Europe, which sought the establishment of an independent Jewish state in Palestine. For a more extensive discussion of the history of the movement and its goals, see Y. Zerubavel, *Recovered Roots: Collective Memory and the Making of Israeli National Tradition* (Chicago: University of Chicago Press, 1995) 13–15.

his account reflects Messenian perceptions of their past as conceived in the postexilic period.[7] Pausanias's account begins with the first settlement and earliest rulers of the region up until the Trojan War and then describes how the Messenians were eventually conquered by the Spartans in two major wars. Despite their valiant efforts to maintain their independence, the Messenians were successively defeated, some being reduced to the status of helot and others forced into exile. Two centuries later, people who had toiled as helots under the Spartans rebelled in an attempt to regain their freedom. They were unable to regain control of their homeland at that time but eventually settled in Naupactas. A century or so later, however, the fate of the exiled Messenians took a significant turn for the better. In 369 B.C.E., the Thebans, under their general Epaminondas, defeated the Spartans at Leuctra, after which he resolved to reestablish Messenian independence. In so doing, he gathered together the Messenians from the various lands in which they were dispersed and founded the city of Messene at the base of Mount Ithome as the new capital of Messenia. Never again would the Messenians—who, as Pausanias points out, had wandered for almost 300 years outside their land and maintained their local customs and Doric dialect—be subdued by the Spartans.

Like the Hebrew Bible, it could be said that the Messenian past is periodized in Pausanias's account into three main phases: antiquity, the exile, and the postliberation period. Moreover, in much the same way as scholars of the Hebrew Bible speak of a gap in biblical literature during the exilic period, similar observations have been made about Pausanias's Messenian history:

> In Book 4 of Pausanias, his lengthy discussion of the history of the Messenians, a gap in the story can be easily discerned. Essentially his narrative runs through the Second Messenian War, the exploits of the great hero Aristomenes, and the final conquest of the Spartans, then "fast-forwards" to the period immediately prior to liberation—with very little mentioned between. Apart from a brief reference to the fifth-century helot rebellion and some description of Messenians in exile, Pausanias jumps over a time-span of fully some fifty Olympiads [287 years]. The end result, of course, is a version of the Messenian past that elides the period of Spartan domination.[8]

---

7. While scholars appear to agree on this point, there is much less consensus about the historicity of this material. S. E. Alcock ("The Pseudo-History of Messenia Unplugged," *TAPA* 129 [1999] 333–41) provides a review of the debate that also serves as a useful introduction to modern scholarship on Messenian historiography.

8. Alcock, "The Pseudo-History of Messenia," 338. See also E. L. Bowie, "Past and Present in Pausanias," in *Pausanias historien: Huit exposés suivis de discussions* (ed. J. Bingen

Thus, just as the Hebrew Bible provides very little detail about what happened to the Israelites in exile, and just as there is no historiography of the exile in the Hebrew Bible, Pausanias provides few details about the Messenians in exile.

Keeping in mind this common feature in Israelite and Messenian social memory, as preserved in the Hebrew Bible and Pausanias, respectively, the Zionist case can also be introduced into the discussion. In a study that explores the emergence and development of Zionist constructions of Jewish history as manifested in a wide range of sources,[9] Zerubavel sees a similar pattern in the conception and periodization of the past to the pattern that is observable in the Hebrew Bible and Pausanias. According to Zerubavel, Zionists also constructed the past in terms of three main periods: antiquity, exile, and national revival. Moreover, the period of exile represented a "hole" or "gap" between the two national periods. The memory of this period was significantly repressed, despite spanning some 18 centuries.[10]

Explaining the Gaps

The terms *telescoping* and *structural amnesia* are used in wider literature to describe the shortening or neglect of a given period in social memory/historiography, and there are various reasons why this may occur. One possible explanation for gaps, as Momigliano points out in his essay on time in ancient historiography, is the limited amount of available and/or reliable evidence for a given event/period.[11] However, while this consideration might explain some instances where lacunae are detected in historiographical texts, the shortage of available evidence did not necessarily prevent ancient historians from writing

---

and O. Reverdin; Vandoeuvres-Genève: Hardt, 1996) 213–16; and H. Sidebottom, "Pausanias: Past, Present, and Closure," *Classical Quarterly* 52 (2002) 494–99, for their comments on Pausanias's tendency to juxtapose events from different times.

9. Sources include "public school textbooks, educational brochures produced by youth movements ... affiliated with Zionist parties, publications of the Israel Defense Forces' education headquarters, newspaper articles, television and radio programs, popular songs, jokes, plays, poems, children's stories, novels," and interviews (Zerubavel, *Recovered Roots*, xvii).

10. The considerable difference in the length of the exile between Zionist and biblical thought is recognized, though not considered to undermine the heuristic value of the comparison.

11. A. Momigliano, "Time in Ancient Historiography," in *Essays in Ancient and Modern Historiography* (ed. Arnaldo Momigliano; Middletown, CT: Wesleyan University Press, 1977) 191.

about a given era.[12] Two cases in point are, in fact, Israelite and Messenian narratives pertaining to their preexilic past. Although these histories may mention actual events or historical figures, suggesting that they are based at least to some extent on reliable tradition (and even older written sources in certain instances), particular claims that they convey about the past stand in questionable relation to historical realities that they purport to portray.[13] A good example in the case of Messenian history is argued by Luraghi, who holds that the Messenians as a national entity did not exist in the "preexilic" period but was an identity forged later and projected back into earlier times.[14] As for the Israelites, the modern discussions about the historicity and evidentiary basis for many elements of the biblical portrayal of the preexilic past are well known, a notable example in this instance being the debate surrounding the historicity of the united monarchy.[15] These studies suggest that historically reliable material was, in these cases, not available, not sought out, or only selectively taken into account for the purpose of fashioning these histories, and imply that there was a certain level of "creative" thinking involved, either by the writers who produced these accounts and/or by the societies within which they emerged.[16] If this scholarship is to be given credence, the question must be asked why similar creative effort was not devoted to the exilic period. As for the Zionists, it is hardly reasonable to suggest that 2,000 years of history is overlooked due to a lack of available information. In all of these cases, the gap has little to do with available material and appears to be more ideologically driven. In this regard, it is useful to distinguish between what might be termed temporal blanks and temporal gaps—the former left vacant due to lack of information and the

---

12. A good example concerns traditions about the early history of Rome in the histories of Livy and Dionysius of Halicarnassus. The lack of contemporary sources from this early period did not prevent these writers from covering it in their accounts.

13. For an examination of source citations and the use of sources in the Hebrew Bible, see my *Why Did They Write This Way? Reflections on References to Written Documents in the Hebrew Bible and Ancient Literature* (London: T. & T. Clark, 2008).

14. N. Luraghi, "Becoming Messenian," *Journal of Hellenic Studies* 122 (2002) 45–69. A similar argument was made much earlier by L. Pearson, "The Pseudo-History of Messenia and Its Authors," *Historia* 11 (1962) 397–426.

15. See, among others, T. L. Thompson, *Early History of the Israelite People: From the Written and Archaeological Sources* (Leiden: Brill, 1992) 301–51.

16. By *creative*, I do not necessarily mean the whole-scale fabrication of tradition but simply the recognition that these records cannot be read as a straightforward and innocent recollection of the past. Instead, the needs and agendas of the communities that produced them along with the complicated dynamics of how societies remember and forget need to be taken into consideration.

latter created (either knowingly or unknowingly) for a particular purpose.[17]

In seeking to explain temporal gaps in social memory, as opposed to temporal blanks, scholars commonly explain that the past has lost relevance for the present. This is a well-known feature of oral societies, which adapt and modify their genealogies to suit the current social and political circumstances. As D. Henige points out,

> It has long been recognized that, in most societies where kinship is the primary means of social and political control, genealogies are likely to be foreshortened. In these segmentary genealogies only the first few founding generations and the most recent four to six legitimizing generations are remembered. Since the purpose of these genealogies is both to reflect and to justify current social patterns based on kinship considerations it serves no purpose to preserve the memory of useless ancestors. Such genealogies tend to remain approximately the same length over time, but their components change constantly; relevance and utility are guiding principles.[18]

Although the interim period of exile represents a gap in Israelite, Messenian, and Zionist social memory, there is a considerable difference between the nature of this gap and the gap that often appears in the social memory of oral societies. In the oral societies mentioned above, segments of the past are forgotten because of a lack of relevance for contemporary circumstances. However, in the case of Israelite, Messenian, and Zionist memory, the period of the exile, although significantly deemphasized, if not deliberately suppressed, is certainly not forgotten. It would have been possible for these groups at the time of their (re)establishment to advocate a total rupture with the exilic past and yet each refrained from doing so.[19] Possibly this is because a rejection of this sort would have undermined the claim for historical continuity with the ancient past but also, and perhaps more importantly, because this experience serves a critical role in the self-understanding of these communities.

---

17. I derive these terms from M. Sternberg, "Time and Space in Biblical (Hi)Story Telling: The Grand Chronology" (in *The Book and the Text: The Bible and Literary Theory* [ed. R. Schwartz; Oxford: Blackwell, 1990] 96), though I define them differently.

18. D. P. Henige, *The Chronology of Oral Tradition: Quest for a Chimera* (Oxford: Clarendon, 1974) 27.

19. In the Zionist case, as Zerubavel (*Recovered Roots*, 21) points out, "a movement of the Young Hebrews (also known as the Canaanites) advocated a full rupture between members of the new Hebrew nation and the Jews of Exile"; their stance, however, "provoked a highly critical response" and was "largely rejected" by the majority.

A comparison of Israelite, Messenian, and Zionist attitudes towards exile illustrates that these communities held somewhat different conceptions of exile from one another, and yet, for all three, the experience played a vital and defining role. In biblical literature, exile is characterized by a mixture of both negative and positive understandings.[20] While the downfall of the monarchy and the expulsion from the land are seen as a form of punishment from the LORD for the community's past iniquities, the exile is also understood as a formative and necessary learning process that is vital for Israel's development.[21] As Ben Zvi observes, the notion that "Israel = exiled Israel" (I = EI) pervades the literature of the Hebrew Bible.[22] Indeed, regardless of whether all members of this community actually experienced exile or not,[23] the idea is that I = EI is central to the community's self-definition, reflecting "the inner discourse(s) of Yehudite Israel concerning issues such as who [. . .] Israel [is]."[24]

In contrast to the combination of both positive and negative connotations that are associated with the concept of exile in the Hebrew Bible, attitudes toward exile and Diaspora in Zionist thought are manifestly more negative. These attitudes are discussed in some detail by Zerubavel, who observes that "Zionist collective memory construct[ed] Exile as a long, dark period of suffering and persecution."[25] According to Zionist thinking, "life in exile turned the Jews into oppressed, submissive, weak, and fearful people, who passively accept their fate."[26] Essentially, exile was viewed as "pollution" or "disease."[27] Unlike the community of the Second Temple period who found a constructive explanation for the exile and managed to see some positives in this devastating experience, Zionists maintained a strongly condemnatory stance toward exile even after the foundation of the Israeli

---

20. These positive and negative evaluations are apparent both across the spectrum of books of the Hebrew Bible and also within individual books.

21. For the concept of *exile as learning process*, see Carroll ("Deportation and Diasporic Discourses") on Hosea.

22. E. Ben Zvi, "Inclusion and Exclusion from Israel as Conveyed by the Use of the Term 'Israel' in Post-Monarchic Biblical Texts," in *The Pitcher Is Broken: Memorial Essays for Gösta W. Ahlström* (JSOTSup 190; Sheffield: Sheffield Academic Press, 1995) 100.

23. As Ben Zvi (ibid., 112) points out, there is "evidence for the integration of those who remained in the land into Yehudite Israel"; see further his discussion of this evidence on pp. 111–12.

24. Ibid., 148–49.

25. Zerubavel, *Recovered Roots*, 18.

26. Ibid., 19.

27. Ibid., 20.

state.[28] By no means, however, was the concept of exile any less central to the self-definition of Zionists than it was for the community in Yehud, although the function that exile played in the development of this identity operated in different ways. While for the community of the Second Temple, the notion that I = EI became a central aspect of their self-understanding, for Zionists their identity was defined in reaction and contrast to the exilic experience.[29] Indeed, as Zerubavel points out, "the darker the imagery associated with the Exile, the greater was the promise that Zionism offered."[30]

Messenian attitudes toward exile represent yet another variation on exilic understandings, which can be contrasted with both ancient Israelite and Zionist perceptions. In Pausanias's account, the experience of exile, though understood at least partly in terms of divine retribution (as in biblical thought),[31] is given a much more positive spin than it receives in either Israelite or Zionist memory. Although Messenians are dispersed across many lands, they are depicted as maintaining their local customs and Doric dialect over a period of almost three centuries in exile; hence their experience is conceived as far less devastating or disruptive to social cohesion than it is in either Israelite or Zionist thought. Furthermore, while the fall of Messene is lamented, and the exile is depicted as an unsatisfactory state that the ill-fortuned Messenians were compelled to endure before being restored to the land that was rightfully theirs, neither of these experiences is remembered in an especially negative way. In fact, the defeat suffered by the Messenians at the hands of the Spartans is narrated in order to present them in the best possible light; as Luraghi points out, "no occasion is missed to emphasize their gallantry in the face of the ruthless Spartans."[32] Furthermore, the few descriptions that Pausanias provides of life in exile tend to be fairly positive. In chap. 25 of Pausanias's account, for example, he describes the exploits of exiled Messenians living in Naupactus who set out to conquer the Acarnanians of Oeniadae. Ac-

---

28. Ibid., 22. It is worth noting here that Zionists are only a subset of modern Jewry and not the only group with a concept of exile. Some modern Orthodox Jews also have a concept of exile but maintain that it persists—that the State of Israel is illegimate—and moreover, they do not interpret this exile in the same negative way but more closely mirror the biblical vision of the "first" exile.

29. Zerubavel, *Recovered Roots*, 18.

30. Ibid., 22.

31. See N. Luraghi, "Aristomenes and Miloš Obilić: Of Memory, Defeat, and Nation Building," paper read at the Fifth Meeting of the European Network for the History of Ancient Greece, Brown University, Providence, RI, April 15–17, 2005.

32. Ibid., 5.

cording to Luraghi, Pausanias portrays these Messenians as being "filled with a desire to show that they had won something notable with their own hands."[33] Though they were only temporarily successful in this endeavor, the image presented here of the highly active character of Messenians in exile[34] is to be contrasted with the more passive picture that emerges in Zionist and biblical constructions.[35]

Just as the concept of exile plays a central role in Israelite and Zionist self-perception, the same can be said for the Messenians. However, while exile was for Israelites and Zionists a period of foreign domination and control, for the Messenians it is construed as an escape from subjugation under the Spartans. By defining themselves as a once-exiled community (regardless of the historicity of the claim), the Messenians constructed their past so as to avoid being perceived (and understanding themselves) as victims. Implicit in Pausanias's insistence that all Messenians, even individuals who toiled for some time as helots, had left the region after the revolt in the fifth century, at the latest, is the message that the community established by Epaminondas consisted of freemen not slaves. While there is evidence to suggest that Spartans in the postliberation years denied the Messenians' right to sovereignty and territory based on the argument that these people were former helots, the concept of exile offered the Messenians an avenue to resist the identification and maintain a sense of integrity and independence.[36]

In a discussion of the gap in Messenian social memory, Alcock suggests that this "occlusion of history" may represent "a deliberate, willed forgetfulness."[37] This hypothesis is supported by external evidence which, though scanty and of debatable reliability, paints a rather grim picture of the ways in which helots were treated. Thucydides, for example, attests that as many as 2,000 helots were tricked and slaughtered by the Lacedaemonian authorities (4.80.3–4).[38] Likewise, Plutarch, who

---

33. Ibid., 7.

34. Also worth noting in this regard is the way exile is constructed in terms of a colonial enterprise over which the Messenians had some level of control, as opposed to a state of enforced banishment that the expelled community was powerless to fight.

35. One exception to the passive portrayal in the biblical literature appears in Micah, which envisages the deported remnant as a lion among the nations (5:7–9). For a discussion, see Carroll, "Deportation and Diasporic Discourses."

36. See Isocrates, *Archid.* 28. For a discussion, see N. Luraghi, "Becoming Messenian," 63.

37. Alcock, "The Pseudo-History of Messenia," 339.

38. Scholars are divided with regard to the historical reliability of this particular story, though few question that the helots were cruelly exploited. For a variety of perspectives

also describes this incident, details various other cruelties to which the helots were subjected (*Lyc.* 28). According to Plutarch, who cites Aristotle as his authority, members of the Spartan secret police force, the *Krypteia*, were from time to time dispatched to kill helots.[39] Additionally, he claims that the *ephors* (Spartan magistrates) annually declared war on the helots so as to justify mass murder of them.[40] In these sources perhaps we find an explanation for Pausanias's silence about the fate of the subjugated Messenians.

This idea that the period of Spartan domination in Messenian social memory is willfully forgotten because it is too painful and humiliating to be remembered provides another possible reason why a given period may be telescoped in the collective memory of a community and may be of some import for understanding not only the Messenian but also both the Israelite and Zionist cases. As Henige discusses, the desire to conceal periods of foreign domination or natural/political cataclysm is a common motivation for the telescoping of tradition.[41]

---

on this story, see, for example, P. Cartledge, "Raising Hell? The Helot Mirage—A Personal Re-view," in *Helots and Their Masters in Laconia and Messenia: Histories, Ideologies, Structures* (Cambridge: Center for Hellenic Studies and Harvard University Press, 2003) 20–22; S. Hornblower, *A Commentary on Thucydides Vol. II, Books IV–V.24* (Oxford: Clarendon, 1991) 266–67; R. Talbert, "The Role of the Helots in the Class Struggle of Sparta," *Historia* 38 (1989) 22–40; M. Whitby, "Two Shadows: Images of Spartans and Helots," in *The Shadow of Sparta* (ed. A. Powell and S. Hodkinson; London: Routledge, 1994) 87–126.

39. Plato also mentions this institution, though he says nothing about this practice (see *Leg.* 1.633b–c). The nature of the *krypteia* has long intrigued scholars. One well-known early study is that of H. Jeanmaire, "La Cryptie Lacédémonienne," *Revue des études grecques* 26 (1913) 121–50. For a more recent discussion, see J. Ducat, "Crypties," *Cahiers de Centre Gustav Glotz* 8 (1997) 9–38; idem, "La Cryptie en question," in *Esclavage, guerre, économie en Grèce ancienne: Hommages à Yvon Garlan* (ed. P. Brulé and J. Oulhen; Rennes: Presses universitaires de Rennes, 1997) 43–74.

40. For a discussion of this passage about the *ephors*, see G. E. M. De Ste. Croix, *The Class Struggle in the Ancient Greek World: From the Archaic Age to the Arab Conquests* (London: Duckworth, 1981) 48, 149; N. Richer, *Les éphores: Études sur l'histoire et sur l'image de Sparte (VIIIe–IIIe Siècles avant Jésus-Christ)* (Paris: Sorbonne, 1998) 249–51. Other classical writers that mention the helots, such as Herodotus (e.g., *Hist.* 6.58.3; 6.75.2; 7.229.1; 9.28.2) and Xenophon (e.g., *Lac.* 1.4; 6.3; 7.5; 12.2–4) paint a milder perspective than the examples mentioned above, giving rise to conflicting views in modern scholarship regarding the Spartan treatment of helots. On one side of the debate are scholars who view the stories of brutality as representative of historical reality; see, e.g., Cartledge, "Raising Hell?" 20–22. On the other side are scholars who question the historical reliability of these stories and downplay their significance; see, e.g., J. Ducat, *Les Hilotes* (Bulletin de correspondance hellénique Supplement 20; Athens: École Française d'Athènes, 1990); Talbert, "The Role of the Helots." The position that scholars adopt on this matter tends to be deeply intertwined with their attitudes concerning the extent to which fear of the helots affected politics and society in Sparta.

41. Henige, *The Chronology of Oral Tradition*, 5.

Furthermore, because individuals who have suffered some trauma may experience amnesia as a means of coping,[42] we might ask whether structural amnesia in social memory and historiography may also, in some cases, be explained on similar grounds.

Within the wider literature on the dynamics of remembering and forgetting in the formation of social memory, the suggestion arises that traumatic events can result in collective repression, especially in the immediate aftermath of an event.[43] However, there are some questions about the extent to which this phenomenon provides an adequate explanation for the exilic gap in either the Zionist or Israelite cases. Although Israelis showed a clear tendency to repress/deny the Holocaust in the decade or so immediately following the war and were obviously

---

42. See, for example, Freud's ideas on trauma as outlined in "Remembering, Repeating, and Working Through" (1914; *SE* 12.147), "Mourning and Melancholia" (1917; *SE* 14.239), *Beyond the Pleasure Principle* (1920; *SE* 18.3), and *Moses and Monotheism* (1939; *SE* 23.3). *SE* refers to *The Standard Edition of the Complete Psychological Works of Sigmund Freud* (trans. ed. J. Strachey and A. Freud; London: Hogarth and the Institute of Psychoanalysis, 1953–74).

43. A much discussed example is the silence that ensued in the aftermath of the Holocaust, although the reasons for this are complex and must be considered from the various perspectives of the individuals involved. F. R. Ankersmit ("The Sublime Dissociation of the Past: Or How to Be[Come] What One Is No Longer," *History and Theory* 40 [2001] 300) points out that this event was for a "long time withheld from conscious memory" because it was "so threatening and so painful." However, while this may provide an explanation for the silence of German perpetrators and Jewish victims, it is not the only reason that the genocide of the Jews was marginalized in postwar collective memory. Another significant reason that very little was said about the Holocaust in the initial aftermath is that the true extent of the catastrophe had not yet become known; see R. Hilberg, "Opening Remarks: The Discovery of the Holocaust," in *Lessons and Legacies*, vol. 1: *The Meaning of the Holocaust in a Changing World* (Evanston, IL: Northwestern University Press, 1991) 11–17. It is also important to recognize that various communities had their own motivations for sidelining this disaster that were not directly or necessarily related to the trauma of the Holocaust experience. P. Lagrou ("Victims of Genocide and National Memory: Belgium, France, and the Netherlands 1945–1965," *Past and Present* 154 [1997] 181–222) discusses how various European countries failed to perceive the genocide of their own Jewish populations due partly to anti-Semitism and partly to their own preoccupied efforts at coping with the trauma of the war. Furthermore, trauma is not the only factor to consider in explaining the marginalization of the Holocaust in Zionist social memory in the first decade or so after the war (see below). Further discussion on trauma and collective repression, with particular reference to the Holocaust, can be found in J. C. Alexander, "Toward a Theory of Cultural Trauma," in *Cultural Trauma and Collective Identity* (ed. J. C. Alexander et al.; Berkeley: University of California Press, 2004) 7; S. Friedlander, "Trauma, Transference, and 'Working through' in Writing the History of the Shoah," *History and Memory* 4 (1992) 39–57; B. Giesen, "The Trauma of Perpetrators: The Holocaust as the Traumatic Reference of German National Identity," in *Cultural Trauma and Collective Identity*, 112–54; N. J. Smelser, "Psychological Trauma and Cultural Trauma," in ibid., 50–51.

haunted by the memory of this disaster, trauma may not be the only reason for the amnesia.[44] Zerubavel suggests that the silence was not so much a response to the trauma, which most Zionists/Israelis did not directly experience for themselves, but rather a desire to dissociate themselves from the Holocaust because it was seen as the very epitome of all that was despised about life in exile.[45] Zerubavel also observes that Holocaust victims were construed in this period as submissive, passive, and, in essence, as going "like sheep to the slaughter."[46] It was not until much later, in the 1960s, that Palestinian Jews realized the extent of the terror to which European Jews had been subjected, and the experience of the Holocaust was recast as a formative element of Jewish and Israeli national identity.[47]

Just as there are problems in the Zionist case, there are also shortcomings to the hypothesis that the exilic gap in the historical books represents a deliberate attempt to repress the exile due to the traumatic nature of this experience. The most significant counterargument to this suggestion is the fact that the historical books are very much concerned with coming to terms with the exile. While they do not narrate the period of the exile, the memory of this experience shapes the content and message of biblical historiography set in both the preexilic and the postexilic periods. If the gap in biblical narrative pertaining to the exile reflects the repression of this experience, one wonders why the memory of this experience was not completely expunged.

There is another shortcoming to the hypothesis that trauma explains the narrative gap surrounding the exile in the Hebrew Bible. This concerns the relationship between traumatic events and the construction of history. The direct impact of trauma on historical narrative

---

44. See Zerubavel, *Recovered Roots*, 75. As Friedlander notes, however, "the silence was breached . . . by the debates from 1951 on concerning the reparations agreement with Germany, the Kastner trial and finally the Eichmann capture and trial" ("Trauma, Transference, and 'Working through,'" 48). See also A. Oz, *A Tale of Love and Darkness* (Orlando: Harcourt, 2004).

45. As Zerubavel (*Recovered Roots*, 72) points out, a distinction may be drawn between the Yishuv leaders from Europe who "vacillated between their deep anxiety about the fate of the Diaspora Jews and their ideological commitment to dissociate from what it represented" and the Hebrew youth "who had no personal recollection of life in Europe."

46. Ibid.

47. A similar perspective is advanced by T. Segev, *The Seventh Million: The Israelis and the Holocaust* (trans. H. Watzman; New York: Holt, 1993), who discusses how changing perceptions of the Holocaust have shaped Israeli national identity. According to Segev, the leadership of the Yishuv did very little to help European Jews during the war (pp. 73–81).

is mitigated by the fact that historiography is written retrospectively and involves a delay in time between the events it addresses and its own production. A good example is the situation that arose after the Holocaust, which was marked at first by silence and then followed by a later proliferation of historical accounts. Although the reasons for this silence are complex and varied, as noted above, it is partly attributable to the fact that a certain amount of time is required to reflect upon events if they are to be understood and contextualized.[48] Turning to the historical books in the Hebrew Bible, we can see that, while the memory of exile plays a central role in the thinking of biblical writers, they were sufficiently removed from the period to reflect upon its impact and try to explain the catastrophe within a broader historical context. This distance between biblical historiography and the events it records is another observation that weakens the suggestion that the absence of narrative about the exile in the Hebrew Bible is primarily attributable to a posttraumatic response.

If the exilic gap was not created by the individuals who produced the literature of the Hebrew Bible in an attempt to repress the memory of this experience, one might suppose instead that the gap preexisted in the collective historical memory that biblical writers drew upon to tell their story of Israel's past. In other words, the discontinuity in the construction of Israel's past that is evident in the historical books may replicate a gap in the Israelite social memory brought about by the trauma of exile. However, there are problems with this hypothesis as well. One major difficulty with the notion that the exilic experience was repressed in Israelite social memory because of its traumatic impact is the fact that other, arguably more-devastating events in Israel's past, notably the fall of Israel and Judah and the destruction of Jerusalem, remained in the community's memory and are narrated in some detail in the biblical literature. Another difficulty is posed by the literary sources outside the historical books that show Jews flourishing in the Diaspora, providing an alternative and far less negative perspective on life outside the land.[49]

In addition to these considerations, there is a problem of a far more fundamental order. Even if the trauma of exile caused collective amnesia and subsequently limited what biblical historians were able to say

48. This period of "latency" between traumatic events and their subsequent elaboration is discussed by C. Caruth, *Unclaimed Experience: Trauma, Narrative, and History* (Baltimore: Johns Hopkins University Press, 1996).
49. See, for example, the books of Daniel, Esther, and Tobit.

about life outside the land, the question still remains why, being removed somewhat from the experience themselves, they allowed this gap to shape their account completely. As noted earlier in this essay, a lack of direct knowledge about a given event/period rarely prevented historians of antiquity from covering it in their account if it was appropriate to their purposes. The corollary of this is that events/periods not expedient to an historian's objectives can be omitted or sidelined, and it is to this possibility as an explanation for the exilic gap that attention is now turned.[50]

An important key to unlocking the reason for the exilic gap in the three case studies examined in this essay lies in their common purpose as national commemorative narratives that define and construct the identity of the community within which they are formulated by reference to the past. As such, these narratives, including the way in which they periodize the past, inevitably reflect the ideological interests of the community responsible for their production. These interests determine how the past is periodized, as well as which periods are to be emphasised in recounting a nation's history and which are to be sidelined/repressed. It is within such a context that the exilic gap in Israelite, Messenian, and Zionist memory is best understood.

The exilic gap in these traditions represents the marginalization of this period because it is not useful to the construction of the past that these communities wish to project. Although it plays a significant role in defining who these communities are, how they see themselves, and why they construct the past in such a way, it is not a period of the past that they want to emphasize in the creation of their (new) identity. On the contrary, each of these communities sidelines/elides the exilic period in order to establish a connection/continuity with the more ancient past, which is perceived as a time during which each of these nations flourished and enjoyed political autonomy in their homeland. Antiquity is represented as a golden age to which the present commu-

---

50. If the trauma of the exile has shaped the literary character of any texts in the Hebrew Bible, this is perhaps most evident in the prophetic books. In a study of the impact of trauma on narrative, R. Winslow ("Troping Trauma: Conceiving /of/ Experiences of Speechless Terror," *Journal of Advanced Composition* 24 [2004] 607–33) identifies various typical characteristics of crisis literature, which the prophetic literature can be seen as sharing, including the dependence "on tropes to indicate the profound psychological and moral depths of traumatic experience," and the "creation of arational, atemporal, and nonlinear constructs." For a study that explores biblical prophecy as a response to trauma in the book of Jeremiah, see, for example, K. M. O'Connor, "Jeremiah's Two Visions of the Future," in *Utopia and Dystopia in Prophetic Literature* (ed. E. Ben Zvi; Göttingen: Vandenhoeck & Ruprecht, 2006) 86–104.

nity aspires and in relation to which it imagines its future.[51] The construction of the past provides a model for the future that is to some extent (though not entirely) represented as a revival/restoration of the ancient period.[52]

The identity of the communities examined in this essay is very much based on a connection to the homeland. As a result, periods of the past in which this bond is broken are deemphasized/shortened. In biblical literature, a gap of this sort not only marks the exilic period but also the period prior to the exodus, when the Israelites lived in Egypt.[53] While Genesis and Exodus provide detailed stories surrounding the two leaders, Joseph and Moses, who mark Israel's entry into and departure from Egypt, very little is said about the experience of the Israelites during this period. All that we learn from the historical books about this time is that the Israelites multiplied and came to be oppressed by the Egyptian authorities, working for them as slaves. Although the period of oppression is said to last for 400 years (see Gen 15:13), the experience is allocated virtually no narrative description.

Interestingly, in an attempt to establish an indisputable link between the community and its land, each of these narratives similarly sidelines competing/alternative perspectives and/or aspects of the past that might compromise this goal. For instance, each narrative creates the impression that the homeland was empty during the period of exile, despite the speciousness of such claims. Biblical scholars are familiar with the discussion surrounding what is termed the "myth of the empty land" that is promulgated in certain biblical texts such as 2 Chr 36:20–21, even though a construction of this sort is undermined by archaeological evidence[54] and other passages within biblical literature.[55]

51. E. Ben Zvi, "What's New in Yehud? Some Considerations," in *Yahwism after the Exile: Perspectives on Israelite Religion in the Persian Era—Papers Read at the First Meeting of the European Association for Biblical Studies, Utrecht, 6–9 August, 2000* (ed. R. Albertz and B. Becking; Studies in Theology and Religion 5; Assen: Van Gorcum, 2003) 39–40.

52. For instance, although Israel was ruled by kings in its golden age, monarchy is not perceived as the ideal form of government in the literature of the Hebrew Bible.

53. So also S. Japhet, "Periodization between History and Ideology II: Chronology and Ideology in Ezra–Nehemiah," in *Judah and the Judeans in the Persian Period* (ed. O. Lipschits and M. Oeming; Winona Lake, IN: Eisenbrauns, 2006) 491–508.

54. Other passages that convey the impression of total exile and empty land include 2 Kgs 24–25, esp., 24:14, 25:11(–12), 25:26, and Jer 36:29. For archaeological evidence, see H. Barstad, *The Myth of the Empty Land: A Study of the History and Archaeology of Judah during the "Exilic" Period* (Oslo: Scandinavian University Press, 1996); C. Carter, *The Emergence of Yehud in the Persian Period: A Social and Demographic Study* (JSOTSup 294; Sheffield: Sheffield Academic Press, 1999) 119–35; idem, "Ideology and Archaeology in the Neo-Babylonian Period: Excavating Text and Tell," in *Judah and the Judeans in the Neo-Babylonian*

This sort of strategy is also a feature of Zionist social memory that overlooks centuries of inhabitation of the land of Palestine. As Peteet points out, "strikingly missing" in the Zionist construction of the past "are the 3000 years in which this space was populated by a complex variety of peoples and passed through multiple and complex historical eras, the Roman, Byzantine, and Islamic, among others. Spatio-historical telescoping was intended to visually support and reproduce a geographic construction of Palestine as nearly unpopulated until the advent of twentieth-century Jewish settlement."[56]

In his account of the Messenians, Pausanias also intimates, as noted above, that there were no descendents of the old Messenians left in the

---

Period (ed. O. Lipschits and J. Blenkinsopp; Winona Lake, IN: Eisenbrauns, 2003) 301–22. Similar conclusions about the population of Neo-Babylonian Judah are reached by O. Lipschits, "Demographic Changes in Judah between the Seventh and the Fifth Centuries B.C.E.," in ibid., 323–376. But compare with E. Stern (*Archaeology of the Land of the Bible, Volume II: The Assyrian, Babylonian, and Persian Periods 732–332 BCE* [ABRL; New York: Doubleday, 2001] 303–11, 321–26, esp. p. 324), who speaks of a "gap" in the archaeological record of the former territory of Judah for this period. While Stern allows for some continuity of settlement into the Neo-Babylonian period (especially in the region of Benjamin), he believes that destruction elsewhere was nearly total.

55. For example, Jer 52:28–30, on which see R. P. Carroll, *Jeremiah: A Commentary* (London: SCM, 1986) 868–70; Jer 39:10; 52:16 (note that nothing is said in these chapters about the eventual departure of the people who were left to be vinedressers and tillers of soil [see 2 Kgs 25:12], although perhaps the departure of these people is implied in Jer 43:6–7); Ezek 33:24–29, which seemingly refers to a non-exiled remnant living in the land of Israel after its destruction, though it is envisaged that this remnant will also be destroyed; Hag 2:2–4; Zech 3:6–13; 6:9–15; 8:2–8, on which see B. Oded, "Where Is the 'Myth of the Empty Land' to Be Found?" in *Judah and the Judeans in the Neo-Babylonian Period* (ed. O. Lipschits and J. Blenkinsopp; Winona Lake, IN: Eisenbrauns, 2003) 62. Of relevance in this regard are also the books of Ezra and Nehemiah, which speak of opposition faced by the returnees from צרי יהודה 'adversaries of Judah' (Ezra 4:1; צרינו 'our adversaries' in Neh 4:5[11]), עם־הארץ 'the people of the land' (Ezra 4:4; "peoples of the lands" in Ezra 9:2, 11), and אויבינו 'those against us' (e.g., Neh 4:9[15]; 6:1). To whom exactly these designations may refer is a much debated issue in biblical scholarship. In Ezra 4:2, the "adversaries" identify themselves as foreigners who were brought to the land under King Esarhaddon of Assyria, though some scholars are skeptical of this claim; see, e.g., L. L. Grabbe, "'The Exile' under the Theodolite: Historiography as Triangulation," in *Leading Captivity Captive: 'The Exile' as History and Ideology* (ed. L. L. Grabbe; JSOTSup 278; Sheffield: Sheffield Academic Press, 1998) 94; Oded, "Where Is the 'Myth of the Empty Land'?" 62. Various modern scholars suspect that the "adversaries" were descendents of the people who were not deported to Babylon; see, e.g., Barstad, *The Myth of the Empty Land*; R. P. Carroll, "The Myth of the Empty Land," *Semeia* 59 (1992) 79–93. In any case, the references are commonly taken as evidence against the notion that the land was uninhabited when the people of Israel returned.

56. J. Peteet, *Landscape of Hope and Despair: Palestinian Refugee Camps* (Philadelphia: University of Pennsylvania Press, 2005) 39. See also Zerubavel, *Recovered Roots*, 22, 34.

region at the time of Epaminondas's campaign.[57] This claim, however, may not have been driven so much by a need to justify rights to the land as to counter Spartan allegations that the citizen body of the community formed by Epaminondas consisted of freemen returning from exile and not Spartan slaves.

Another aspect of the past that is given little acknowledgment in the biblical, Zionist, and Messenian narratives concerns individuals who continued to live in exile/Diaspora and who did not return to the homeland. While the books of Ezra and Nehemiah cultivate the perception of a mass return from exile, sources external to the historical books indicate, as noted above, that Jewish life continued for many people outside the land, in Babylonia, Egypt, and elsewhere.[58] Likewise, Zionist social memory downplays the experience of the Jews who remained outside the land of Palestine during and after the Zionist immigrations.[59]

Although Pausanias gives the impression that all exiled Messenians returned under Epaminondas, external evidence paints a somewhat different picture in this case as well. Diodorus Siculus describes some of the activities of exiled Messenians but makes no mention of a return to the Peloponnese (14.34.3–6; 14.78.5; 14.111.1). Furthermore, there is reason to doubt the notion of the *grande rentrée* of Messenians depicted in Pausanias's account. Pausanias gives the impression that the citizen body of the new polity established by Epaminondas consisted entirely of returning Messenians. However, this particular understanding of the founding of Messene was not the only perspective that circulated in ancient times. A different point of view is expressed by the Athenian orator Lycurgus, who "mentions Troy and Messene as two examples of cities that had been deserted by their inhabitants at some point in the

57. Luraghi, "Becoming Messenian," 63; idem, "Messenian Ethnicity and the Free Messenians," in *The Politics of Ethnicity and the Crisis of the Peloponnesian League* (ed. P. Funke and N. Luraghi; Cambridge: Cambridge University Press, forthcoming) 8.

58. B. Becking, "'We All Returned as One!': Critical Notes on the Myth of the Mass Return," in *Judah and the Judeans in the Persian Period* (ed. O. Lipschits and M. Oeming; Winona Lake, IN: Eisenbrauns, 2006) 3–18, on the perception of a mass return from exile. See, e.g., R. Zadok, *The Jews in Babylonia during the Chaldean and Achaemenian Periods: An Onomastic Study* (Haifa: Haifa University, 1979); and L. Pearce, "New Evidence for Judeans in Babylonia," in *Judah and the Judeans in the Persian Period* (ed. O. Lipschits and M. Oeming; Winona Lake, IN: Eisenbrauns, 2006) 399–412, on the Jews in Babylonia; B. Porten, *Archives from Elephantine: The Life of an Ancient Jewish Military Colony* (Berkeley: University of California Press, 1968), on the Jews in Elephantine.

59. Zerubavel, *Recovered Roots*, 34.

past and never recovered."[60] According to Lycurgus, Messene was established again as a city 500 years after its destruction by men of "indiscriminate origins" (*Ag. Leo.* 62). As Luraghi points out, "Lycurgus took for granted that the citizens of the state were not descendents of the Messenians of the past, and he expected his audience to concur."[61] Another perspective on the matter is presented by Diodorus, who describes the citizen body of the new state founded by Epaminondas as consisting of both the remnants of the Messenians and any others who wished to join (15.66.1).[62]

Summary

The foregoing analysis of the various aspects of the past that ancient Israelite, Messenian, and Zionist narratives exclude discloses their highly selective representation and functions as a tool to elucidate the principles and ideologies that guided and underlay their production. This analysis supports the hypothesis that the exilic gaps in the collective memory of the three groups under examination represent temporal gaps rather than blanks that both construct and reflect cultural identity. To bring this discussion to a conclusion, I offer some comments with regard to the contribution of this analysis. First, this study illustrates the usefulness of a comparative approach that goes beyond traditional boundaries of location and time for understanding biblical historiography. Second, it demonstrates the value of studying not just what is said in historiographical texts but also what is left out. Although there may be some temptation in examining silences and narrative gaps in historiography to uncover what actually happened in these periods, there is also much to be gained from accepting discontinuities and silences and considering why they exist. There is great potential for this approach to be applied on a broader scale to biblical historiography and for a much more detailed study to be conducted on this topic.

---

60. Luraghi, "Messenian Ethnicity," 9.
61. Idem, "Becoming Messenian," 64.
62. Another ancient perspective about the founding of Messene is that which seems to have been advocated by the Spartans, namely, that the citizen body comprised former helots.

Are There Any Bridges Out There?
How Wide Was the Conceptual Gap between the Deuteronomistic History and Chronicles?

EHUD BEN ZVI
University of Alberta

Introduction

There is no doubt that there is a substantial difference between the (hi)stories (hereafter, "history" or "histories") constructed and narrated in the book of Chronicles and those in the Deuteronomistic Historical Collection, that is, the collection of books usually referred to as the Deuteronomistic History (DtrH).[1] For instance, the two histories begin and reach their explicit narrative conclusion at different places.[2] Many episodes, even central episodes, in one do not appear in the other, and vice versa.[3] Even when they include reports about the same period, they often construe it in substantially different ways.[4] Moreover, the

---

Author's note: A note about the background that led to the choice of the question that opens this contribution: this work originated in an oral presentation at the 2007 meeting of the Canadian Society of Biblical Studies that took place at the University of Saskatchewan, Saskatoon. Near the university campus, where the talk was delivered, stands a very prominent bridge that marks the city landscape and that most participants in the meeting had to cross daily to arrive at or leave the campus area.

1. In referring to the Deuteronomistic History as a collection of books, I wish to stress that I view this corpus as a multivocal and complex corpus rather than as a tightly written, univocal, coherent unity.

2. The same holds true for the Primary History or, as it might also be called, the Primary Historical Collection. In speaking of the Primary History as a collection, I mean to say that this work is not a tightly-knit and well-integrated unity but, rather, a collection of books or writings. The Primary History is a work to which Chronicles is more comparable than the DtrH, from the viewpoint of the general temporal span with which it deals and which it construes for the intended and primary readerships.

3. So, for example, the period of the "Judges," as construed in the book of Judges, has no parallel in the temporal account of Chronicles.

4. See, for instance, the characterization of the reigns of Abijah and Manasseh.

characterization of shared central personages in these histories is at times clearly dissimilar.[5]

None of this is the result of chance. One of the most fundamental social and ideological roles of Chronicles, as most likely understood by its intended and primary readers was to shape, communicate, and encourage its readers to visit and vicariously relive through their reading a somewhat different past than the one shaped, communicated by, and relived through the reading of the Deuteronomistic History, and for that matter, the Primary History.[6] A related social and ideological role of Chronicles was to create a set of complementary histories in such a way that the readers of each would approach their relevant text in a way informed by the other. Certainly, ancient (re)readers (hereafter, readers) who internalized Chronicles would have approached the Deuteronomistic History and the Primary History in ways different from readers without knowledge of Chronicles.[7] In other words, Chronicles was meant to influence the reading and interpretation of already existing authoritative works,[8] while at the same time being influenced by

5. Perhaps the most obvious case is David—that is, the David of Samuel compared with the David of Chronicles. There are also substantial differences in the characterizations of Solomon, Abijah, Asa, and Manasseh, to mention just a few kings in Kings and Chronicles.

6. In referring to the readers of Chronicles, the Primary History, and the Deuteronomistic History, I want to stress that I am referring to the intended and primary readerships of these different literary works.

7. The Deuteronomistic History served as a source for Chronicles. See, among many others, S. L. McKenzie, "The Chronicler as a Redactor," in *The Chronicler as Author: Studies in Text and Texture* (ed. M. P. Graham and S. L. McKenzie; JSOTSup 263; Sheffield: Sheffield Academic Press, 1999) 70–90; I. Kalimi, *The Reshaping of Ancient Israelite History in Chronicles* (Winona Lake, IN: Eisenbrauns, 2005); J. Van Seters, "Creative Imitation in the Hebrew Bible," *Studies in Religion* 29 (2000) 395–409. For a different position, see A. G. Auld, "What If the Chronicler Did Use the Deuteronomistic History?" in *Virtual History and the Bible* (ed. J. C. Exum; Leiden: Brill, 2000) 137–50; idem, "What Was the Main Source of the Books of Chronicles?" in *The Chronicler as Author*, 91–99; idem, *Kings without Privilege: David and Moses in the Story of the Bible's Kings* (Edinburgh: T. & T. Clark, 1994). Notice also his recent clarification that he does not (and did not) claim that the individuals responsible for the present form of the book of Chronicles did not know the book of Samuel.

8. Simply, for the sake of illustration, Chronicles identifies Mt. Moriah as the site of the Jerusalemite temple (2 Chr 3:1). Ancient readers who accepted this identification would have their own readings of the patriarchal narratives in Genesis strongly colored by such an understanding. On Mt. Moriah in Chronicles, see I. Kalimi, *An Ancient Israelite Historian: Studies in the Chronicler, His Time, Place and Writing* (Studia semitica neerlandica 46; Assen: Van Gorcum, 2005) 129–31. It is worth noting that, even if Chronicles is not an innovator here but reflects a position common to Jerusalemite-centered discourses of the Persian period, it still presents itself as literature meant to convey the "actual" meaning

them. Thus multiple constructions of (and virtual visitations of) the past became interwoven in a web of meanings that not only represented better as a whole the horizon of thought of Persian-period Jerusalem but also, because of its relative openness, allowed its literati to use and reuse the past in manifold ways, according to different circumstances. Thus, Chronicles was both a self-standing work, as any other authoritative book in the repertoire of Yehud, and was asking its readers to approach it as such. At the very same time and at a different interpretive level, Chronicles was a work whose (hi)story clearly evoked, interacted with, and was written, read, and reread in ancient Israel in ways strongly informed by the "classical" version in the social memory, a memory shaped by books such as Genesis, Samuel, and Kings that were considered authoritative also from the perspective of the readers of Chronicles.[9]

This being so, Chronicles, by logical and social necessity, consistently presented itself to its readers as both similar and dissimilar, continuous and discontinuous with existing memories of the past and with their accepted renderings in narratives that were included in the

---

of older pentateuchal texts. See my "Revisiting 'Boiling in Fire' in 2 Chron. 35.13 and Related Passover Questions: Text, Exegetical Needs, Concerns, and General Implications," in *Biblical Interpretation in Judaism and Christianity* (ed. Isaac Kalimi and Peter J. Haas; Library of Hebrew Bible/Old Testament Studies 439; London: T. & T. Clark, 2006) 238–50. On the general issue, see Gary N. Knoppers, who writes, "[a]fter reading the Chronicler's composition and its selective incorporation of earlier writings, ancient readers may have understood those earlier writings differently" (*1 Chronicles 1–9* [AB 12; New York: Doubleday, 2004] 133).

9. Concerning the claim that Samuel and Kings were treated as "classical" texts from the perspective of the readers of Chronicles, see Van Seters, "Creative Imitation in the Hebrew Bible." Of course, texts can bear authority within a particular community of readers even if their literal story is not taken as the only possible representation of a social memory (compare the Gospels). The case is particularly clear in ancient Israelite historiography in which rhetorical and didactic needs trumped what today we may consider "the reconstruction of the most likely historical event." For this reason, even within the same book there exist reports that would be construed as logical contradictions within a literal, full, and only mimetic mode of reading (e.g., Josh 11:23 and 13:1; 1 Sam 14:47–48, 52; 17:54; and 2 Sam 5:6–9; 2 Chr 17:6, and 20:33).

Because of their common use, I referred above to "literal" and "literally." It should be noted, however, that the terms are a bit of a misnomer for the phenomenon I described. A more precise term would be "letteral." The letteral meaning of a text—that is, the "literal-as-written" meaning of the text, is only one of the possible "literal" meanings that communities of readers may associate with a text. See G. Loughling, "Using Scripture: Community and Letterality," in *Words Remembered, Texts Renewed: Essays in Honor of John F. A. Sawyer* (ed. J. Davies et al.; JSOTSup 195; Sheffield: Sheffield Academic Press, 1995) 321–39 (esp. pp. 324–25).

repertoire of authoritative texts held by the literati, among whom one
is to find both the authorship and primary readership of Chronicles.
This characterization of Chronicles as both continuous and discontinuous with other literati's memories and, above all, with their written,
authoritative texts shaped much of Chronicles and was communicated
to the latter's readers, again, through multiple ways. Among them, one
may mention the choice of a language that is both saliently and unmistakably evocative of Samuel and Kings—after all, Chronicles repeats
much of these texts. However, Chronicles is also written in Late Biblical Hebrew (LBH) and is therefore clearly unlike Samuel and Kings.
One may mention also the manner in which Chronicles conforms, as
expected, to a shared basic outline of Israel's past, while simultaneously reshaping substantially many of the narratives and their main
characters, and all within the limits of the allowable (hi)storical malleability of the community of literati for which the work was written.

Because some of these matters have been discussed elsewhere,[10] I
focus here on another component of the crucial and careful interplay
in Chronicles between continuity and discontinuity, between resemblance to historical traditions and the kind of creative discontinuity
that enabled its readers to (vicariously) experience slightly different
pasts and, therefore, allowed them to shape additional "sites of memory" and images of the past. As is well-known, the general tendency in
contemporary research has been to highlight the differences between
Chronicles and the Deuteronomistic History in terms of basic world
view.[11] The position advanced here serves to bring some balance into

10. See Van Seters, "Creative Imitation in the Hebrew Bible"; and my *History, Literature and Theology in the Book of Chronicles* (London: Equinox, 2006).
11. The tendency to emphasize differences between Chronicles and the Deuteronomistic History so as to widen as much as possible the gap between them has a very long
history of interpretation, which in part is entangled with that of the dating of the pentateuchal sources and particularly the Priestly work (P). Thus, for instance, a postexilic
date of P was associated with an evaluation of the picture of the monarchic period that
Chronicles portrays as carrying essentially no historical value for the historical reconstruction of the period. A Josianic date for the Deuteronomic work (D), however, tended
to be associated with a positive evaluation of the historicity of Kings in particular (and
not only with respect to its account of Josiah's reign). Thus a strong tendency to stress the
difference between the two historical narratives developed. Other factors contributed to
this trend. For instance, in the case of Julius Wellhausen—who was a child of his own
times—his negative evaluation of what he construed to be Judaism and which he associated with Chronicles played a major a role. The more negative his appreciation of Chronicles, the more he tended to show that Kings, Samuel, and Judges were different at least
in the main. (To be sure, according to him, these books were at a late ["Judaic"] stage
"tampered" with.) Had Wellhausen not stressed the difference between these books and

this question by taking into serious account the multivocality of both the Deuteronomistic History and Chronicles. This study points to a number of observations that converge to show strong continuity (and at times even overlap) between at least some "voices" within the Deuteronomistic History and voices that are either usually associated with or considered "distinctive" of Chronicles. Moreover, most of these observations directly relate to ideologically central issues in Chronicles. In most of these instances, Chronicles highlighted or further developed some viewpoints already existing in the Deuteronomistic History, implicitly or explicitly. Needless to say, because the approach in Chronicles to these matters points to strong elements of continuity, it cannot but also point at an accompanying sense of discontinuity. This is the case because Chronicles, by necessity, echoes particular voices of the Deuteronomistic History in a very different literary and ideological setting and, therefore, makes these voices interact and inform a different set of voices from those with which their "partners" in the Deuteronomistic History informed and interacted. After all, meanings in these books are always both contextual and cotextual.[12]

Observations: Converging Lines

Deferred and Non-deferred Judgment and Related Issues of Agency

As is well known, according to 2 Kgs 24:3 the destruction of monarchic Judah was due to Manasseh's sin (see also 2 Kgs 21:11–14; 23:26–27; Jer 15:4). But, to be sure, this is not the only "voice" in the Deuteronomistic

---

Chronicles, he would have remained without any "worthy" biblical historiographical narrative, historically or theologically. Likewise, the (later) widespread perception of Chronicles as a very problematic source for the reconstruction of the history of monarchic Judah led in some circles to a tendency to stress that Kings is different, for the alternative would have left historians of the monarchic period with very few reliable sources with which to write a detailed history of the period. A study of these matters demands a separate discussion and, in any event, stands well beyond the scope of the present paper. For Wellhausen's position on Chronicles, which in various ways continues to exert a strong influence in Chronicles research, see J. Wellhausen, *Prolegomena to the History of Ancient Israel* (Cleveland: Meridian, 1957; orig. publication, 1883) 171–227. For research on Chronicles in the 19th century, see M. P. Graham, *The Utilization of 1 and 2 Chronicles in the Reconstruction of Israelite History in the Nineteenth Century* (SBLDS 116; Atlanta: Scholars Press, 1990).

12. Of course, a similar argument may be advanced about Josephus and biblical traditions (see below). This interaction between discontinuity and continuity is a systemic feature of successful attempts at renarrating and reshaping a past that is in the main agreed upon within a community.

History or in Kings for that matter. The far more common voice relating the fall of monarchic Judah, Jerusalem, and the temple to a long history of cumulative sin that goes back to the very beginnings of the nation appears also in the very same report on Manasseh's reign in Kings (see 2 Kgs 21:15; cf. Lev 26:14–43; Deut 31:15–22; Hosea, passim). This voice echoes in Huldah's prophecy (2 Kgs 22:14–20) and is embedded in the inner logic of the ubiquitous construction of the fall of northern Israel (both in the Deuteronomistic History and in the prophetic literature). It is the latter's sins—certainly not Manasseh's—that resulted eventually in its fall.[13] Yet, the fall of northern Israel is ubiquitously presented as an interpretive key through which the readers of Kings were supposed to understand the fall of monarchic Judah. There is also a less salient, third voice in Kings. This voice creates an association between the Babylonian Exile and Hezekiah (see 2 Kgs 20:14–19). Despite their differences, all of these voices share a world view in which (a) the usual complementary dyad of king-people plays an important role, and (b) punishment might be deferred and sin may accumulate.[14]

There has been a common misperception that Chronicles is all about immediate and individual retribution and that there is neither "accumulated sin (n)or merit as in the book of Kings."[15] Similarly, Chronicles supposedly contains no reference to deferred or even to transgenerational punishment. In fact, Chronicles contains numerous examples

---

13. The idea that the sin that leads to the destruction of the monarchic polities is conceived as *only* monarchic in the Deuteronomistic History and is later "democratized" *only* in Chronicles is incorrect. There are clear voices in Kings that point to a "democratized" sin (see 2 Kgs 17:7–17; 21:8, 14; at times characterized as a DTR-N voice), and Chronicles is not immune to the idea that the king may lead the people astray. Note, for instance, the immediate reversal of the people as soon as Ahaz dies. See my *History, Literature and Theology*, 167–68, 220–22.

14. The two obvious cases are Hezekiah and Josiah. It may be noticed also that both the Deuteronomistic History and Chronicles assume that the divine decision to divide the Davidic/Solomonic kingdom was made during Solomon's life but implemented only after his death. In the case of the Deuteronomistic History, the divine decision is explicitly construed as punishment for wrongdoing (1 Kgs 11:33). Chronicles construes the decision differently. For its take on the matter, see my *History, Literature and Theology*, 117–43.

15. Citation from R. W. Klein, *1 Chronicles* (Hermeneia; Minneapolis: Fortress, 2006) 46. Of course, he is not the only scholar who advanced this position. See, for instance, the highly influential words of S. Japhet, "the deeds of one generation are not 'visited on' another: any ideology of 'the sins of the fathers' or ancestral merit . . . has no place in the book," *The Ideology of the Book of Chronicles and Its Place in Biblical Thought* (Beiträge zur Erforschung des Alten Testaments und des antiken Judentum 9; rev. ed.; Frankfurt: Peter Lang, 1997) 162.

that belie this claim.[16] For the present purposes, it is worth stressing that not only does Chronicles contain the crucial prophecy of Huldah (2 Chr 34:22–28; cf. 2 Kgs 22:14–20),[17] which implies deferred punishment and cumulative sin (see also 2 Chr 36:21 and cf. 2 Kgs 22:13), but its Huldah prophecy is more salient in Chronicles than in Kings, because there is no voice in Chronicles ascribing the destruction to Manasseh, and there is only a vague allusion to Hezekiah's (mis)deed (2 Chr 32:25–26). Thus, the concept of deferred judgment is communicated to the ancient readers of both the Deuteronomistic History and Chronicles.

To be sure, unlike Kings, Chronicles does not refer to the tradition about Manasseh's responsibility for the fall of Judah; but, interestingly enough, it may reflect one of the major inconsistencies between the main literary and ideological *topos* of deferred judgment and the way in which it was textualized and brought to bear into the memory of the literati in the case of the Manasseh of Kings. When judgment or the materialization of any divinely appointed catastrophe is deferred, the deferral is often conceived as a divine reward for the good deeds of an individual who is spared the experience of such a tragedy. Ancient readers of Kings who were aware of this *topos* would probably have wondered about the picture of Manasseh in Kings. Why would punishment have been deferred until after his death? Did he do something to deserve it?[18] Significantly, Chronicles constructs his image as a king who also did much good, and in fact, it shifts the crucial moment of the declaration of YHWH's irrevocable punishment that seals the fate of Judah completely to the account of Josiah, a very pious king, for rhetorical and ideological purposes.[19] In any case, this section of Chronicles

---

16. See my *History, Literature and Theology*, passim.

17. There are no substantial differences between the two pericopes.

18. Of course, Chronicles did not *have* to answer these questions. After all, Chronicles conveys also to its intended and primary (re)readers that at times YHWH's actions are impossible to explain (e.g., YHWH's decision to divide the Solomonic kingdom in two, which significantly took place during Solomon's days but was divinely implemented later—because of the piety of Solomon?).

19. I discussed the rhetorical and ideological purposes in "Observations on Josiah's Account in Chronicles and Implications for Reconstructing the Worldview of the Chronicler," in *Essays on Ancient Israel in Its Near Eastern Context: A Tribute to Nadav Naʾaman* (ed. Y. Amit et al.; Winona Lake, IN: Eisenbrauns, 2006) 89–106. The usual explanation for the positive characterization of Manasseh in Chronicles relates it to his longevity. Long life is a blessing; his (later) actions were the reason for such a blessing. This explanation does not contradict but complements the suggestion that another impetus for the positive characterization of the king may have come from considerations related to the topos of deferred judgment/catastrophe. The argument that, because Chronicles avoids the references in

rather than rejecting the use of the motif of deferred punishment in Kings manifests it in a way that is more consistent with the topos.[20]

To be sure, although Chronicles knows of deferred punishment/catastrophe, there is no doubt that it communicates numerous examples in which there is no deferral. By doing so, Chronicles presents itself as a whole to its readers as a work in which seemingly contradictory positions are advanced, so as to balance and inform each other. Significantly, the same holds true for the Deuteronomistic History. For instance, David is punished with the death of his first son born to Bathsheba, Jezebel is killed and the dogs eat her flesh, the punishment of the people of Gibeah (and Benjamin) is certainly not deferred to later generations, and the system of apostasy and punishment that characterizes much of the book of Judges is predicated on non-deferred punishment.[21] At the same time, the reference to Manasseh points to an obvious case of deferred punishment. In other words, both Chronicles

---

Kings to Manasseh's sins as being responsible for YHWH's decision to destroy Judah, the topos of deferred judgment could not have served as an impetus for the characterization of Manasseh does not hold water. The communities within which and for which Chronicles was written were well aware of this claim (after all, they knew the Deuteronomistic History). Moreover, on other occasions Chronicles develops its story in a way that interacts with, responds to, and balances sections of the Deuteronomistic History that were not included in Chronicles. See, for instance, the story of Rehoboam's building activities (only) in Chronicles and the activities of Jeroboam (only) in Kings.

20. The relevant section of Kings uses Manasseh as the main person responsible for the destruction so as to develop its lionized image of Josiah. This is part of a pattern: Ahaz-Hezekiah; Manasseh-Josiah. The tendency toward the occurrence of the topos of deferred punishment in a way that is more consistent with its usual attributes in narrowly construed pericopes in Chronicles is congruent with its general (though certainly not absolute) tendency toward higher consistency between ideological expectations and narrative within narrowly construed pericopes (as opposed to the book as a whole). This holds true for "Deuteronomistic" expectations as well as many others. See G. N. Knoppers, "Rethinking the Relationship between Deuteronomy and the Deuteronomistic History: The Case of Kings," CBQ 63 (2001) 393–415 (esp. pp. 395–96) and my History, Literature and Theology, 210–42. For typical examples of the topos of deferred judgment for the righteous in biblical literature, see the example associated with Hezekiah in 2 Kgs 20:17–18 // Isa 39:6–8; with Josiah, 2 Kgs 22:14–20 // 2 Chr 34:22–28. An interesting twist in this motif is the case of an individual subjected to a premature, divinely caused death so that he will not undergo a punishment that cannot be deferred much more. See the case of Abijah, son of Jeroboam, in 1 Kgs 14:13. The text there reinforces the principle while at the same time conveying that the best a pious Jeroboamite can expect is to die before an impending disaster, not to become king and defer it for awhile, something that only Davidides may do. On this matter, see below. For another twist in the deferred-judgment motif, see 1 Kgs 11:34, in which the merit of the father saves the son from experiencing a deserved punishment.

21. I have deliberately chosen examples for which there is no parallel in Chronicles.

and the Deuteronomistic History maintain that both deferred and non-deferred divine judgment/calamity were at work in Israel's past (and likely future) and shape a balanced ideological approach on the matter in the readers. Their position on this issue is to a large extent anticipated and consistent with the position of the discourse of the Persian-period literati in general, and appears in pentateuchal traditions and in prophetic literature as well as other places.[22] It is also worth noting that the same holds true in historical works such as Herodotus, Xenophon, and of course Josephus.[23] In other words, there is nothing unexpected about the coexistence of the two approaches in the Deuteronomistic History and Chronicles.[24]

Non-deferred judgment inevitably raises the matter of the relationship between divinely caused disaster and agency. Both the Deuteronomistic History and Chronicles assume that, at times, later generations may pay for the sins of preceding generations.[25] Although at times there is not much that the people populating the world portrayed in either one of these ancient Israelite histories can do about these matters,[26] both histories communicate that the fulfillment of a deferred

---

22. For examples of non-deferred judgment/calamity, see instances such as Onan in Gen 38:9–10, Miriam in Numbers 12, and Zimri son of Salu and the Midianite woman in Numbers 25. Deferred punishment is implied in the case of Moses and, above all, in the references to Israel's future exile. Note that the omen-nomen traditions in prophetic literature suggest an idea of a predetermined punishment that is deferred to the time of the deity's choice.

23. On Herodotus, see the defeat of Persia during the days of Xerxes, which is explained in terms of both the long-term imperial hubris of the empire and the individual hubris of Xerxes. On Xenophon, see J. Dillery, *Xenophon and the History of His Times* (New York: Routledge, 1995); F. Pownall, "Condemnation of the Impious in Xenophon's Hellenica," *HTR* 91 (1998) 251–77. For a clear instance of deferred judgment, see Josephus's account of the episode about Hezekiah's dealings with the messengers of the king of Babylon (*Ant.* 10.33–34), and for non-deferred judgment, the death of the combatants at Massada. It is worth noting that the absence of a note explaining the fall of monarchic Judah in terms of Manasseh's deeds here (just as in Chronicles) does not point to a rejection of the idea of deferred punishment. On the interesting characterization of Manasseh in Josephus, which in turn was influenced by that in Chronicles, see L. H. Feldman, "Josephus' Portrayal of Manasseh," *JSP* 9 (1991) 3–20.

24. Neither in ancient Israel nor in Greece did historiographical writers and their readers think that such a combination was logically impossible.

25. No one doubts that this is the case in Kings. As for Chronicles, see not only the case of Josiah's generation but also of people who had to live in exile because the land had to make up for its Sabbaths, a total of 70 years (2 Chr 36:21). See also 2 Chr 29:9.

26. David's people fall because of the census in both Chronicles and Samuel. For further examples in Chronicles, see, for instance, the case of people living in forced exile (2 Chr 36:21). Moreover, one cannot assume full agency for Judahites under the spell, as it were, of bad kings, or kings under a "divine spell," as was the case with Rehoboam

calamity does not necessarily imply that those who will experience its full impact *must* be deprived of agency. For instance, Zedekiah remains a bad king in Chronicles, even if the destruction of monarchic Judah was unavoidable already by Josiah's time. Similarly, the calamity that fell upon the House of David following his actions toward Bathsheba and Uriah the Hittite did not remove any agency (or culpability) from Amnon and later from Absalom for their deeds. The Chronicler and the Deuteronomist do not stand on opposite ideological sides; in both Chronicles and the Deuteronomistic History, the idea of (a) an already sealed and absolutely irrevocable future known to YHWH and at times to particular individuals[27] is not construed as necessarily inconsistent with the notion of (b) personal free choice and agency.[28]

Prophets and Prophecy

Prophets in Chronicles are often and correctly portrayed as serving a number of roles. Among other roles, they serve to warn addressees before divine punishment (and thus fulfill the relatively common motif of giving a warning before divine punishment),[29] to explain to individuals the significance of their actions and the future consequences, to communicate godly world views, and to write history.

All of these features find clear counterparts in the Deuteronomistic History. To begin with, one of the roles of the generic prophets in Kings, a role that is essential to the construction of the image of "the prophets of old" in the DtrH, is to warn people of the calamity to which their actions may lead.[30] The idea that YHWH sent warnings to the people about the impending destruction and that these were ignored is present in Kings (e.g., 2 Kgs 17:13–15, 22–23), Jeremiah (see Jer 7:25; 25:4; 26:9; 35:15; 44:4), Zech 1:3–5, and, particularly relevant to this es-

---

during the secession of the north. I have discussed these matters elsewhere (*History, Literature and Theology*, passim).

27. See Moses in Deut 30:1–6, Joshua in Josh 24:19, "YHWH's servants, the prophets" in 2 Kgs 21:10–15, Josiah (and Huldah) in both Kings and Chronicles, or David in 1 Chr 16:35. On the latter, see my "Who Knew What? The Construction of the Monarchic Past in Chronicles and Implications for the Intellectual Setting of Chronicles," in *Judah and the Judeans in the Fourth Century* B.C.E. (ed. O. Lipschits, G. N. Knoppers, and R. Albertz; Winona Lake, IN: Eisenbrauns, 2007) 349–60.

28. Compare the general spirit of *m. 'Abot* 3:15.

29. See esp. Japhet, *Ideology*, 184–90.

30. I discussed the main roles of these figures elsewhere, "'The Prophets': Generic Prophets and Their Role in the Construction of the Image of the 'Prophets of Old' within the Postmonarchic Readership of the Book of Kings," *ZAW* 16 (2004) 555–67.

say, 2 Chr 36:15–16.[31] Prophets in the world of Chronicles explained to kings the significance of their actions for the future (e.g., 2 Chr 12:5; 25:15), and so did, for instance, Nathan in 2 Samuel 12. Prophets are aware of Yʜwʜ's will in both the Deuteronomistic History and Chronicles (e.g., 2 Kgs 22:16–17; 24:2; 2 Chr 25:16; 34:22–25, and cf. Amos 3:7). Prophetic speeches are aimed at teaching the divine world view in Chronicles and in Kings, "all the (divine) teaching that I have commanded your ancestors and that I have sent you through my servants, the prophets" (2 Kgs 17:13). Because within the world of Chronicles, divine teaching is conceived as saliently textualized, it is only a logical (and perhaps even a necessary) step for the book to imagine prophets as interpreters of Scripture, [32] whether the Scripture they are interpreting was associated in the repertoire of the literati with periods earlier or later than those in which the prophet was set in Chronicles.[33]

The same tendency toward full textualization may explain why the Chronicler (i.e., the implied author of the book of Chronicles) refers to written works of prophets among his sources for regnal accounts (e.g., 1 Chr 29:29; 2 Chr 13:22; 20:34; 26:22; 32:32) and therefore implies that prophets were also "historians" who left records of their own times. If prophets understood the significance of past events (a point shared by both the Deuteronomistic History and Chronicles), then Chronicles

---

31. In 2 Kgs 17, the text deals with the fall of Samaria but from the perspective of the readers of the book clearly points to the fall of Judah and Jerusalem (and see explicit reference to Judah in v. 13). From the perspective of the present text, the "they" in vv. 13–14 can only refer to both Judah and Israel. See P. A. Viviano, "2 Kings 17: A Rhetorical and From-Critical Analysis," *CBQ* 49 (1987) 548–59 (esp. p. 551). The saliency of these verses is indicated by the shift toward Yʜwʜ as the subject (in comparison with previous verses) in v. 13 and then to the position of the speaker. See also R. D. Nelson, *The Double Redaction of the Deuteronomistic History* (JSOTSup 18; Sheffield: Department of Biblical Studies, University of Sheffield, 1981) 58.

32. See, for instance, W. M. Schniedewind, *The Word of God in Transition: From Prophet to Exegete in the Second Temple Period* (JSOTSup 197; Sheffield: Sheffield Academic Press, 1995); idem, "The Chronicler as Interpreter of Scripture," in *The Chronicler as Author: Studies in Text and Texture* (ed. M. P. Graham and S. L. McKenzie; JSOTSup 263; Sheffield: Sheffield Academic Press, 1999) 158–80; Y. Amit, "The Role of Prophecy and Prophets in the Chronicler's World," in *Prophets, Prophecy and Prophetic Texts in Second Temple Judaism* (ed. M. H. Floyd and R. L. Haak; Library of Hebrew Bible/Old Testament Studies 427; London: T. & T. Clark, 2006) 80–101; P. Beentjes, "Prophets in the Book of Chronicles," in *The Elusive Prophet: The Prophet as a Historical Person, Literary Character and Anonymous Artist* (ed. J. C. de Moor; OtSt 45; Leiden: Brill, 2001) 45–53 and see the extensive bibliography in p. 46 n. 11.

33. I elaborated this point in my "Who Knew What?"

would have assumed that at least some of them would have written their explanations (see 2 Chr 26:22; cf. 2 Chr 20:34).[34]

The point in this section, and in any other section of this paper for that matter, is *not* to show that there are no differences between the Deuteronomistic History and Chronicles. The point is to show that there are substantial lines of conceptual convergence between the two. Certainly, the Deuteronomistic History and Chronicles did not construct the very same institution of prophets and prophecy. For instance, in Chronicles characters who are not prophets may temporarily fulfill the role of prophet.[35] In Chronicles, even a foreign king (Necho) may fulfill such a role. This is not the case in the Deuteronomistic History, even if it also "Israelitizes" good foreigners such as Hiram (compare with the figure of Jethro in the Primary History). Here, as on the matter of the prophet as an interpreter of Scripture or history, Chronicles develops existing notions further as it understands (and "translates") them in a way that relates to its own world of knowledge and ideological prism.

Finally, it is worth noting that there are substantial and perhaps even larger differences in the conceptualization of the role of the prophet within the Deuteronomistic History itself than between the main voices in Kings and Chronicles. For instance, prophets play no role as such in Judges and Joshua (cf. Deut 17:18–20), and there was a substantial voice in the Deuteronomistic History according to which prophets—and by implication, prophecy—were of only secondary political and, perhaps, theological importance (see the basic structure of the regnal reports; and a text such as 2 Kgs 14:26).[36] This voice sharply differs with the other voices mentioned above, whether they appear in in Kings or Chronicles.

David and the Davidides

The differences between the Davids of Chronicles and Samuel are all too obvious and do not require further elaboration.[37] But what

---

34. Cf. Klein, *1 Chronicles*, 42; T. Willi, *Die Chronik als Auslegung: Untersuchungen zur literarischen Gestaltung der historischen Überlieferung Israels* (FRLANT 106; Göttingen: Vandenhoeck & Ruprecht, 1972) 231–41. Chronicles is also influenced by the prophetic books and their superscriptions (Schniedewind, *Word of God*, 218).

35. Cf. Amit, "The Role of Prophecy."

36. See my "Prophets and Prophecy in the Compositional and Redactional Notes in I–II Kings," *ZAW* 105 (1993) 331–51.

37. However, there are also important points of convergence besides the obvious sharing of narrative elements that reflects (a) the dependence of Chronicles on the Deuteronomistic History and above all (b) its dependence on the corpus of "core facts" about

about the memory of David represented by 2 Kgs 14:3; 16:2; 18:3; 22:2 (see also 1 Kgs 15:11)? Even the one reservation about "Uriah, the Hittite," advanced in 1 Kgs 15:3–5 does not reappear in any of these verses. Are not the readers of these texts invited to imagine him as a paragon of virtue, who did not turn aside from YHWH's path to the right or to the left? A David imagined within these parameters is likely to look much more like the David of Chronicles than the David of Samuel. Moreover, even the close association of the temple in Chronicles with both David and Solomon finds an earlier echo in 2 Kgs 21:7.[38]

The Deuteronomistic History as a whole is clearly multivocal about hope (or lack thereof) for a future David. Some texts in the Deuteronomistic History allowed or even nurtured among the ancient readers of this collection of books a sense of hope for the coming of a future Davidide (e.g., 2 Sam 7:16), but others balanced such an approach and raised the possibility that the Davidides might not return to power (e.g., 1 Sam 2:30).[39]

David that were agreed upon by the literati. Among these less obvious elements is the characterization of David as a speaker of psalms (cf. 2 Sam 22 with Ps 18 and 1 Chr 16:18–36 with Ps 105:1–15; 96:1–13; 106:1 (?) and 106:47–48).

38. It may be mentioned that the Solomon of Chronicles is consistent with a voice in 1 Kings that lionizes Solomon (and with the construction of Solomon in Proverbs, Pss 72:1, and 127:1, as well as with the references to Solomon in 2 Kings), while it rejects the strong critique of Solomon that is also present in 1 Kings. On the latter, see M. A. Sweeney, "The Critique of Solomon in the Josianic Edition of the Deuteronomistic History," *JBL* 114 (1995) 607–22; D. A. Glatt-Gilad, "The Deuteronomistic Critique of Solomon: A Response to Marvin A. Sweeney," *JBL* 116 (1997) 700–703; cf. M. Z. Brettler, "The Structure of 1 Kings 1–11," *JSOT* 49 (1991) 87–97.

39. Note the presence of the crucial temporal term עַד־עוֹלָם in both 1 Sam 2:30 and 2 Sam 7:16. 1 Samuel 2:30 may have served as *an* introduction and interpretive key to the book of Samuel as a whole. A full debate on these matters—which in any case must involve the issue of whether postmonarchic readers saw a reflection of themselves in the suffering David who was aware of having grievously sinned (a motif that characterizes the latter part of Samuel), and therefore the latter stood typologically for Israel—cannot be carried out here. It suffices to note that the Deuteronomistic History as a whole and as read within a postmonarchic setting is multivocal on these matters. The books in the Deuteronomistic History, Chronicles, and prophetic literature all exhibit some degree of multivocality on this issue, though not always the same cluster of balancing meanings. The same holds true for texts belonging to other genres that existed within Persian, Jerusalem-centered Yehud (e.g., Ps 132:11–12). In other words, it is clear that the discourse of the period as a whole did not prefer unequivocal, categorical answers. These matters deserve, of course, a separate discussion that goes beyond the scope of this paper. (On the reading of the David of Samuel that develops, among others, a portrayal in which David's "consciousness of having sinned" plays an important role, see F. H. Polak, "David's Kingship: A Precarious Equilibrium," in *Politics and Theopolitics in the Bible and Postbiblical Literature* [ed. H. G. Reventlow, Y. Hoffman, and B. Uffenheimer; JSOTSup 171; Sheffield: Sheffield Academic Press, 1994] 119–47.)

To be sure, the readers of Judges are led to believe that there is a need for a monarchy, and readers of Samuel that it should be Davidic. But from the perspective of both the Deuteronomistic History and the Primary History, the failure of the divinely chosen Davidic Dynasty to shape a long-term stable society, guided by YHWH, is not only obvious but just the last—although the most catastrophic—of an extensive series of failures of leadership models for Israel's polity,[40] none of which succeeds in the long run and none of which is portrayed as being successfully (or even unsuccessfully) retried. The point of bringing back this series of failures for continuous remembrance was, of course, not to convey a sense of necessary and inevitable doom, but to highlight the message that the long-term welfare and stability of Israel, including its hold on the land, did not depend on any particular type of leadership or the actions of any individual but on "following" YHWH's teaching / "listening" to YHWH's word.[41] Of course, the centrality of

---

40. Moses, Joshua, and the elders of his time, charismatic leaders such as the judges, a prophet-priest such as Samuel, and dynastic lines of kings such as Saul's and David's are all presented in this collection of works, one after the other. Each of them obtains a promising beginning for Israel. Yet the narratives are unequivocal: each of these beginnings eventually ends up with lack of success. The readers of the Primary History and the Deuteronomistic History are informed that Moses has already been told that, after his death, Israel will act in a corrupt manner (see Deut 4:25–28; 31:16), i.e., his leadership provided an excellent "beginning" but not a stable, sociopolitical foundation for the establishment of the Israel that should be. Joshua does not appoint a successor, nor does he create a stable community in which the people follow YHWH's teachings (see Judg 2:6–13; see also Josh 23:12–26; 24:15–20 in which the future actions of Israel are prefigured). The book of Judges does not express in equivocal language that the judges who followed Joshua did not provide the previously mentioned foundation (e.g., Judg 2:18–19; 3:12; 4:1; 6:1). The leadership of the house of Eli is presented as a dead end and so is that of the house of Samuel (e.g., 1 Sam 2:22–34; 4:10–18; 8:1–3). Significantly, the report about the sinful behavior of Samuel's sons immediately precedes and explains the people's request for a king. The text then deals with the Saulide "experiment" and its disastrous end, which sets the stage for the Davidic Dynasty, but the latter has an even more disastrous end. On these matters and on the Primary History and the Deuteronomistic History as a truncated creation story of the divinely-guided and divinely-rewarded Israel that will and should exist in the future, see my "Looking at the Primary (Hi)story and the Prophetic Books as Literary/Theological Units within the Frame of the Early Second Temple Period: Some Considerations," *SJOT* 12 (1998) 26–43.

41. There is, of course, a multiplicity of voices about the monarchy in the Deuteronomistic History. Although diachronic in perspective, see McKenzie, *The Trouble with Kingship*, and the contributions in *Israel Constructs Its History* (ed. A. de Pury, T. Römer, and J.-D. Macchi; JSOTSup 306; Sheffield: Sheffield Academic Press, 2000) 286–314 with bibliography. Needless to say, whatever the process by which the Deuteronomistic History arrived at its present form, its ancient (Persian period) readers would not have understood the text in terms of multiple univocal redactions but as a multivocal text. For the claim that the promise to David is never compromised in the Deuteronomistic History, see J. Harvey, "The Structure of the Deuteronomistic History," *SJOT* 20 (2006) 237–58.

the concept of following Yhwh's teaching or "listening" to Yhwh's word is a ubiquitous Deuteronomistic theme, but it is also a Chronistic theme, and in fact, stands at the ideological core of much of the Hebrew Bible, cutting across literary genres and linguistic choices.[42]

Finally, the Deuteronomistic History and the Primary History do not conclude with any explicit statement about a future Davidic restoration. The reference to Jehoiachin's release and his new status as one who is maintained by and becomes a life-long courtier to "the king" is consonant with the hope for a future return of the Davidides to (limited) power—after all, it tells its readers that the Davidides have survived the turmoil of history—but also connotes a strong sense of Jehoiachin's and the Davidides' (and Judah's?) acceptance of *"the* king" (i.e., the king of Babylon) as such and provides an unmistakably positive characterization of a foreign human king who is *"the* king" of the Davidides.

Despite all its differences with the Deuteronomistic History (and the Primary History), the basic approach of Chronicles regarding these matters is quite similar. For instance, on the one hand, the readers are told that Yhwh confirmed a Davidide in Yhwh's house and in Yhwh's kingdom forever, and his throne will be established forever (1 Chr 17:14; compare the careful choice of words in 2 Chr 9:8); but, on the other hand, they are told that the kingdom and the house were destroyed and that eventually Yhwh will give all the kingdoms of the earth (including, of course, Judah) to Cyrus (certainly not a Davidide) and has commanded him to build the temple for Yhwh in Jerusalem (2 Chr 36:23). Just as the Deuteronomistic History (and the Primary History), Chronicles concludes with a note that advances a positive characterization of the foreign king and implicitly calls for Israel's acceptance of his royal status over Judah, which is explicitly presented as reflecting Yhwh's will.[43]

The highly and uniquely developed genealogy of the Davidides in 1 Chr 3 draws the attention of the readers of the book not only to its past importance but also to the fact that this lineage survived "the ravages of history."[44] The report of the lineage in Chronicles may be consonant with dormant messianic or quasi-messianic aspirations such as those expressed in some prophetic books, which are focused on hopes for a distant, utopian future that will be brought about by Yhwh at the

---

42. See further below.

43. This feature can be easily explained in terms of the Persian-period background within which all these works reached their present compositional form.

44. See Knoppers, *1 Chronicles 1–9*, 332–36 (citation from p. 335).

time of the deity's choosing. But, even if this is the case, the genealogy likely conveyed a number of additional messages. For instance, it was an unmistakably emphatic statement about the vast decline in the status of the Davidides, from David to the later members of the lineage. This statement of decline is consonant with and reflects a status quo in which Davidides need not play their "traditional" role in the present for the community to be pious and lead its life in accordance with YHWH's will.[45] Moreover, a community centered around a temple already built is a community for which "David" (and "Solomon") are alive and well, as it were, through the ordinances for the cult and the temple.[46] All in all, the genealogy in 1 Chr 3 allowed itself to be understood by its intended and primary (re)readers in different ways, depending on the ideological and pragmatic context/s in which it was read. All these seemingly separate meanings informed and balanced each other. Similar things may be said of the take of the Deuteronomistic History and the Primary History and of prophetic literature for that matter on David and his dynasty.

The Exclusive Legitimacy of the Davidic Dynasty in the Monarchic Period

Both the Deuteronomistic History and Chronicles emphasize the legitimacy of the Davidic Dynasty. In Chronicles, northern dynasties are by definition illegitimate, but the (re)readers of 1 Kgs 11:29–38 are told that Jeroboam would have initiated an enduring dynasty that was legitimate in the sight of YHWH. Chronicles rejects a voice of this sort in the Deuteronomistic History, but its position seems to be not so far from the one reflected in 2 Kgs 17:21a, according to which the crowning of Jeroboam and Israel's rejection of the House of David are sins in themselves. Moreover, the LXX version of the division of the kingdom, which is itself as "Deuteronomistic" as the MT (and which may or may not precede the MT version) portrays Jeroboam as one who wanted to

---

45. This perspective may be compared with the issues raised in the previous discussion about the failure of all models of leadership to achieve these goals, by themselves, according to the Deuteronomistic History and the Primary History.

46. For a discussion on these matters as they pertain to Chronicles, see Knoppers, *1 Chronicles 1–9*, 332–36; and my contribution to "In Conversation and Appreciation of the Recent Commentaries by S. L. McKenzie and G. N. Knoppers," in Melody D. Knowles, ed., "New Studies in Chronicles: A Discussion of Two Recently-Published Commentaries," *Journal of Hebrew Scriptures* 5/20 (2004–5) 39–43, and Knoppers's response in the same (pp. 88–93). Also see the excursus in my "Gateway to the Chronicler's Teaching: The Account of the Reign of Ahaz in 2 Chr 28,1–27," *SJOT* 7 (1993) 216–49 (republished in *History, Literature and Theology in the Book of Chronicles* [London: Equinox, 2006] 230–31).

make a ruling dynasty by and for himself and, as such, in opposition to YHWH and doomed from the beginning.[47] Again, Chronicles is not so far from voices within the Deuteronomistic tradition.

Divine Teaching (Torah)

The Deuteronomistic History and Chronicles share a general world view according to which YHWH's teaching is central to Israel and to its identity. As mentioned above (pp. 72–73), both histories communicate to their readers that the fate of Israel depends, not on any model of leadership, but on whether Israel follows YHWH's teaching or rejects it.[48] Time and time again, both the Deuteronomistic History and Chronicles associated and asked their readers to associate this teaching/Torah with a written record (of teachings) to be read (e.g., Deut 17:18–19; Josh 1:8; 8:31–32; 23:6; 24:26; 2 Kgs 14:6; 22:8; 1 Chr 16:40; 2 Chr 17:9; 23:18; 25:4; 31:3; 34:14–15).[49] For the present purposes, there is no need to dwell on the social and ideological significance of the emphasis on the written character of divine teaching or on the implications of a so-called nomistic viewpoint. It suffices to notice that these positions are central to the Deuteronomistic History (at least in its present form) and Chronicles and that they were imprinted in the minds of their respective readerships. It is significant that the same general considerations about writtenness apply to the prophetic books, which present themselves to their readers as YHWH's word, and that the "nomistic" viewpoint is so prevalent in the larger discourse of postmonarchic Yehud that it is even retrojected into their constructed memories of the patriarchs (see Gen 26:5; cf. Deut 11:1).

It is worth stressing that both the Deuteronomistic History and Chronicles include the crucial episode of the finding of the book of the divine teaching during Josiah's period, and both emplot it such a way that it communicates to the readers the symbolic priority of the written authoritative text over the temple,[50] even if the temple is central in

---

47. See A. Schenker, "The Division of the Kingdom in the Ancient Septuagint: LXX 3 Kingdoms 12.24 a–z, MT 2 Kings 11–12; 14 and the Deuteronomistic History," in *Israel Constructs Its History* (ed. A. de Pury, T. Römer, and J.-D. Macchi; JSOTSup 306; Sheffield: Sheffield Academic Press, 2000) 214–57.

48. The same holds true for the Primary History. The view of the constructed patriarchal period in Gen 26:5 is particularly worth noting.

49. Following YHWH's teaching/word requires knowledge of it. Once YHWH's teaching is construed as being present in written texts, the literati, at least in their own eyes, become absolutely necessary, because they serve as brokers of YHWH's knowledge and word to the general population.

50. See, for instance, T. Römer, "Du Temple au Livre: L'idéologie de la centralization dans l'historiographie deutéronomiste," in *Rethinking the Foundations: Historiography in the*

both works. In either case, the text they carry is fully congruent with the text-centered nature of the Persian period in Israel and with the social and ideological processes that led to the production of prophetic, historical, and pentateuchal books at this time and in these communities. In either case, two crucial ideological points are conveyed: (a) the written teaching of YHWH legitimizes the temple, not the other way around; and (b) Israel may live without a temple, but Israel may not exist without YHWH's teaching.

To be sure, readings of the Deuteronomistic History as a stand-alone textual record suggested to its readers that the written teachings, and in particular Josiah's book resembled but did not equate with the book of Deuteronomy.[51] In contrast, the readers of Chronicles, for whom the concept of Scripture was central, were asked to imagine an integrative Scripture that includes Deuteronomy as well as other pentateuchal texts. Yet one must keep in mind that the ancient readers of Chronicles likely read the Deuteronomistic History, not only as a stand-alone textual record, but also in a way that was informed by pentateuchal texts. In this respect, they would have read the Deuteronomistic History as part and parcel of the Primary History. This sort of reading would have provided them with an additional understanding of the identity of Josiah's book, this time in terms consonant with the world view of Chronicles.

"National" History and "All Israel":
Transtemporal, Ideologically Conceived Israel

Both the Deuteronomistic History and Chronicles belong to the genre of "national" history. Both tell the story of an ethnotheological, transtemporal entity, "Israel."[52] The very existence of these histories points not only to a sense of group self-awareness among the composers and readers of the histories but also to (a) the readers' self-identification as Israel and (b) the centrality of people's corporate, transtemporal identity in their ideological discourses. In fact, the only other permanent and central character in the histories, besides Israel,

---

Ancient World and in the Bible: Essays in Honour of John Van Seters (ed. T. Römer and S. L. McKenzie; BZAW 294; Berlin: de Gruyter, 2000) 207–25. I discussed these matters as they relate to the account in Kings in my "Imagining Josiah's Book and the Implications of Imagining It in Early Persian Yehud" (*Studien zur Sozial- und Religionsgeschichte Israels und seiner Umwelt: Festschrift für Rainer Albertz zu seinem 65. Geburtstag* [AOAT 250; Münster: Ugarit Verlag, 2008] 193–212) and as they relate to Chronicles, in "Observations on Josiah's Account in Chronicles."

51. See my "Imagining Josiah's Book."
52. This is, of course, the case of the Primary History, as well.

is YHWH, the God of Israel. Whereas "national" histories are rare in the ancient Near East prior to the Hellenistic era (they may represent a response of cultural "peripheries" in interaction with the Achaemenid or later Hellenistic empires),[53] "national histories" are the norm in ancient Israelite historiography. This historiography is strongly shaped by the powerful sense of "ethnocultural" centrality that characterized the postmonarchic and most likely Persian-period works that eventually became included in the HB. It is particularly significant that the ethnocultural group at the center of these works is never political Judah or Yehud but a religious ethnocultural and transtemporal group, a theologically conceived Israel at whose center stood Jerusalem and Judah since David's times, by divine decision.

To be sure, there are differences. The Deuteronomistic History conveys the centrality of "all Israel" by means of books such as Deuteronomy, Joshua, Judges, Samuel, and by the "synchronistic" retelling of northern and southern histories that constructs a world in which the life of the two kingdoms is understood as deeply intertwined. This is not the main way in which the concept of "all Israel" is shaped and reflected in Chronicles, but a very similar basic concept may be found there.[54] Moreover, the relation and ideological subordination of the northern kingdom and its past to Judah is reflected and shaped in different forms. Thus, for one thing, the Jerusalem-centeredness of "all Israel" along with the ideological marginality of northern Israel are communicated in the Deuteronomistic History by the rhetorical use of the fall of the northern polity and the characterization of its sin in terms of a warning message to Judah/Jerusalem in the world portrayed in the book. The demise of the northern realm is also used as an interpretive key for the description of the events in Judah from the perspective of the ancient readers of the book of Kings (especially with respect to 2 Kgs 17:7–17).[55] Chronicles, instead, explicitly refers to the northern polity only in terms of its interaction with Judah, presents the latter as the real stage on which the fate of Israel is decided and as the

---

53. Cf. A. Momigliano, "Eastern Elements in Post-exilic, Jewish, and Greek Historiography," *Essays in Ancient and Modern Historiography* (Middletown, CT: Wesleyan University Press, 1977) 25–35. Compare and contrast A. Kuhrt, "Israelite and Near Eastern Historiography," in *Congress Volume: Oslo 1998* (ed. A. Lemaire and M. Sæbø; VTSup 80; Leiden: Brill, 2000) 257–79 (esp. pp. 268–76). For examples of historiographical works by and about "peripheries" in Hellenistic times, see the works of Berossus and Manetho.

54. See in the latter, for instance, the role of genealogies, and texts such as 2 Chr 28:9–15; 30:1–11; 31:1.

55. It is worth noting that many of the sins explicitly mentioned in 2 Kgs 17:7–17 reflect the Deuteronomistic portrayal of cultic (mis)behavior in Judah specifically.

main manifestation of Israel. In other words, Chronicles communicates a similar sense of Jerusalem-centeredness and of northern marginality but through other rhetorical means.[56]

In sum, despite all their differences, the Deuteronomistic History and Chronicles shared an understanding that "all Israel" was at the center and, for both, "all Israel" was Jerusalem-centered. Both shared an understanding of northern Israel as part and parcel of "Israel" while at the same time peripheral to an "Israel" whose center was in Jerusalem and Judah. Needless to say, the same holds true for the rest of the works that ended up in the Hebrew Bible with the exception of the pentateuchal books, which were co-opted into this view in Yehud as they were read in a way informed by the Deuteronomistic History or by Chronicles.[57]

Constructions of "The Other": The "Israelitization" of the
"Pious" Other and Exclusionary Boundaries

Both the Deuteronomistic History and Chronicles construe similar boundaries around "all Israel." As they do so, they construe "the other." It is worth noting that both contain reports that serve to partially "Israelitize" the "pious other"—that is, to construe the "pious other" in terms of ideal Israelite norms of behavior, while at the same time maintaining its foreign character. The speech of the queen of Sheba in 2 Chr 9:5–8, which constitutes an excellent illustration of this tendency, has a very clear parallel that constructs the same meaning, insofar as it is relevant to the point discussed here, in 1 Kgs 10:6–9. Huram's letter in 2 Chr 2:10–15, which is another excellent illustration, is consonant with and perhaps may be seen as an expansion and development of a characterization already implied in 1 Kgs 5:21. To be sure, Chronicles and the Deuteronomistic History are not the only texts that show converging lines in this regard. For instance, the Primary History and Jonah are similar to them in exhibiting this motif.[58] In other

---

56. I discussed the way in which northern Israel is presented as marginal in my *History, Literature and Theology*, 195–209.

57. Thus, for instance, the story of the golden calf becomes a diatribe against northern sanctuaries, and the tabernacle becomes a direct precursor of the temple in Jerusalem and the like. On Exod 32 and 1 Kgs 12:25–33, see M. Aberbach and L. Smolar, "Aaron, Jeroboam, and the Golden Calves," *JBL* 86 (1967) 129–40. See also the excellent discussion of the interplay between pentateuchal traditions and Jerusalem-centered texts by A. G. Auld, "Leviticus: After Exodus and before Numbers," in *The Book of Leviticus: Composition and Reception* (ed. R. Rendtorff and R. A. Kugler; VTSup 93; Leiden: Brill, 2003) 41–54 (esp. pp. 43–48) and the examples provided there.

58. Concerning the Primary History, see, for instance, Gen 14:18–20; Exod 18:10–11. The sailors and the repentant Ninevites in Jonah provide another example.

words, both the Deuteronomistic History and Chronicles show elements of a larger discursive attitude.

As for patterns of explicit exclusion and oppression of the other, one
clear example will suffice. It is well known that in the world of Chronicles non-Israelites were conscripted for forced labor by Solomon but
not Israelites (see 2 Chr 2:16–17; 8:7–9). This is usually contrasted with
the picture emerging from 1 Kgs 5:27–32 (cf. also 1 Kgs 11:28). But
again, this was not really an innovation of Chronicles, because it actually reflects the approach and image of the past explicitly stated in
1 Kgs 9:20–22. The real difference between the Deuteronomistic History and Chronicles here is that the Deuteronomistic History is multivocal, while Chronicles takes up only one of the voices that existed in
Deuteronomistic tradition.

Constructing Other Dynasties: The House of Ahab

How does Chronicles construe Israelite royal dynasties other than
David's that existed within the world of knowledge of the ancient
readers of Chronicles? Of course, they are illegitimate and sinful (see
above), but is there something else in their characterization that plays
an important role in Chronicles' construction of the past and to which
the readers of Chronicles are asked to pay attention by clear markers in
the text? Certainly, there is not much reference to any of them in
Chronicles, but given the lack of narrative about the northern kingdom, it is worth noting that Chronicles does refer to Ahabites. Moreover, the House of Ahab plays a particularly important ideological role
that is saliently marked in Chronicles: Ahabites are implicitly, but saliently, construed as possessing a quasi-mythical power to entice Davidic kings, including some of the best of them. These kings approach
the House of Ahab again and again, not only for no apparent reason,
but also contrary to any reasonable expectation. For instance, in
Chronicles Jehoshaphat is at the height of his power when he initiates
an alliance with Ahab, for which he has no rational need within the
world portrayed in the book (see 2 Chr 17:1–18:1). He is then induced
by Ahab to wage war against Aram (וַיְסִיתֵהוּ; see 2 Chr 18:2) and almost
loses his life as a result. The often noted difference between 2 Chr
20:35–37 and 1 Kgs 22:49–50 is also consistent with the tendency in
Chronicles to stress the power of the Ahabites to lead Davidic kings
astray.[59] Jehoshaphat's successor, Jehoram, is the addressee of a letter

---

59. On the account of Jehoshaphat in Chronicles, see G. N. Knoppers, "Reform and
Regression: The Chronicler's Presentation of Jehoshaphat," *Bib* 72 (1991) 500–524. The
difference between 2 Chr 20:35–37 and 1 Kgs 22:49–50 reflects a number of matters. For

that draws the attention of the readers of Chronicles to his irrational
aping of the ways of the House of Ahab (2 Chr 21:12–15; cf. 2 Chr 21:6).
Not only is no comparable letter sent to any other Davidic king in
Chronicles, but the sender is identified as Elijah, a central figure in the
discourse/s of postmonarchic Israel. Even more remarkable is that the
readers of Chronicles were explicitly informed that Ahaziah, Jehoram's successor, was 42 years old when he became king (2 Chr 22:2).
This is one of the cases in Chronicles in which its ancient readers were
explicitly required to approach the text with a non-mimetic strategy of
reading. After all, they were informed *twice*, including once in the immediate literary context of 2 Chr 22:2 that his father could not have
been older than 40 when he died and was succeeded by Ahaziah (2 Chr
21:5, 20) and *twice* that Ahaziah/Jehoahaz was his youngest son (2 Chr
21:17; 22:1).[60] Surely, ancient readers knew that Jehoram could not
have begotten his youngest son, never mind the older brothers, before
he himself was born. As in similar cases in which a narrowly referen-
tial reading of Chronicles makes no sense, seeming incongruity serves
to draw the attention of readers to the "true" message of the text.[61] In
this case, the point is to highlight an unequivocal image of Ahaziah as
a mature person at the time of his ascension to the throne king. He was
not a boy[62] simply influenced by his Ahabite mother and members of
her house (see 2 Chr 22:2–5) but an adult, 42 years of age, a mature Davidic king who should have been able to make his own decisions but in
fact simply did what the Ahabites told him to do. The Davidic king,
due to Ahabite influence, became like a boy—a simple Ahabite pawn
with no will of his own. Significantly, the inability of the Davidic kings
to stand up to the Ahabites in general and, in particular, the timidity of

---

the present purposes, it suffices that this difference is consistent with the tendency in
Chronicles to stress the power of the Ahabites to lead Davidic kings astray.

60. It is worth stressing that Chronicles diverges from (MT) Kings on the reported
age of Judahite kings at the point when they came to the throne. The only other case concerns Jehoiachin (2 Chr 36:9; cf. 2 Chr 24:8).

61. For a general discussion of the rhetorical value of this construction from the perspective of the readers of Chronicles, along with its implications for understanding the
ancient modes of reading Chronicles and numerous other examples, see my *History, Literature, and Theology*, 44–77.

62. Numerous markers in the text might have suggested that he was young when his
father died. See the double reference to his being the youngest of his brothers, the con-
notation of 21:17, the sense of temporal proximity conveyed by the literary proximity of
2 Chr 21:16–17 and 18–19, and the statements that he followed the advice of his mother
and 2 Chr 22:3b. On the use of literary proximity to convey temporal proximity, see Kalimi, *Reshaping*, 18–34.

Ahaziah led directly to a Judah in which no Davidic king reigned for about a sabbath of years and caused the dynasty itself to totter at the brink of extinction. From the perspectives of the readers of Chronicles, all these considerations evoked and reinforced a mental association between the House of Ahab and the eventual destruction of monarchic Judah and the fall of the Davidic line.[63]

Any reader of Chronicles and the Deuteronomistic History would easily notice vast and obvious differences between the narratives about the Ahabites in Kings and the references to them in Chronicles (see, for instance, the presence of extensive Elijah and Elisha narratives in Kings). This said, some common conceptual elements do appear. First, it is really the House of Ahab, not of Omri. Second, it is not a "regular" Israelite dynasty in Kings either. The narrative space given to the Ahabite period in northern Israel far surpasses the narrative space given to any other northern dynasty. Moreover, the coverage given to the reign of Ahab surpasses the space allocated to most kings of either Judah or Israel. Thirdly, although on the whole very negative, the image of the Ahabites (and particularly Ahab) is multifaceted also in both Kings and Chronicles. Fourthly, and even more important, Ahabites are construed in Kings as influencing and even partially shaping the conduct and future of Davidic kings.[64] In fact, there is a clear voice in Kings that construes the fall of the Davidic House as a result of the actions of kings of Judah who followed the model of the Ahabites, even centuries after their death. The account of Manasseh is partially evocative of the image of Ahab both directly (cf. 1 Kgs 16:33 with 2 Kgs 21:3) and indirectly, since the readers of Kings were supposed to construe Ahab (and the Ahabites, by extension) as a paradigmatic embodiment

---

63. It is worth noting that, despite all these central ideological features, the portrayal of the House of Ahab in Chronicles is not flat at all or one sided, but multifaceted. I discussed some of these matters mentioned above, the general portrayal of the House of Ahab in Chronicles, and its value for any historical reconstruction of the historical Omrides in my "The House of Omri/Ahab in Chronicles," in *Ahab Agonistes: The Rise and Fall of the Omri Dynasty* (ed. L. L. Grabbe; Library of the Hebrew Bible/Old Testament Studies 421 / European Seminar on Methodology in Israel's History 6; London: T. & T. Clark, 2007) 41–53.

It is likely that the association of the House of Ahab with the fall of the House of David has to do with the image of Athaliah (an Ahabite) as the only non-Davidic ruler of Judah and the associated image of the near fall of the Davidic Dynasty at the time. In Chronicles, however, the House of David could not be replaced by an Ahabite or, for that matter, by any other Israelite.

64. Aside from well-known narratives, such as 1 Kgs 22 and 2 Kgs 3, see the statements in 2 Kgs 8:18, 27, and esp. 21:3.

of the sinful behavior of the kings of (northern) Israel and their people (see 2 Kgs 17:11*, 16–17* and 23:8*, 4a*; see also 21:3).[65] In other words, the Deuteronomistic History led its readers to create a mental association between the House of Ahab and the eventual destruction of monarchic Judah and the fall of the Davidic line. To be sure, Chronicles develops further some aspects of the construction of the Ahabites, but in some central matters the Deuteronomistic History showed Chronicles the way. Despite all the differences between them, when it comes to the main ideological attributes associated with the House of Ahab among postmonarchic literati (cf. Mic 6:16), Chronicles develops in a particular way what already existed at least in an incipient way in the Deuteronomistic History.

Historiographical Commonalities

A large number of additional observations or sets of observations in the category of converging lines of historiography may be advanced. A few examples suffice. There are numerous cases in which Chronicles implicitly interacted with claims advanced in the Deuteronomistic History—even if the latter are omitted in Chronicles—as it advanced a different, counter or complementary image of the past evoked in the Deuteronomistic History. For instance, one of the reasons for the presence of the list of fortified cities in Chronicles' account of Rehoboam's reign is the reference in 1 Kgs 12:25 to Jeroboam's building projects.[66] Whereas the Deuteronomistic History and Chronicles differ a great deal in the details, the two can interact, because they both share a "set of rules for the rhetorical game."

This observation, in turn, leads us to the numerous converging lines between the Deuteronomistic History and Chronicles (and the Primary History, for that matter) that are related to matters of historical writing. For instance, it was neither expected nor demanded of the readerships of Chronicles, the Deuteronomistic History, or the Primary History that one must approach these works only from the perspective of

---

65. Much has been written on the account of Manasseh in Kings. Among recent monographs, see Percy S. F. van Keulen, *Manasseh through the Eyes of the Deuteronomists: The Manasseh Account (2 Kings 21:1–18) and the Final Chapters of the Deuteronomistic History* (OtSt 38; Leiden: Brill, 1996); Francesca Stavrakopoulou, *King Manasseh and Child Sacrifice: Biblical Distortions of Historical Realities* (BZAW 338; Berlin: de Gruyter, 2004). For my own contribution, see "The Account of the Reign of Manasseh in 2 Kgs 21:1–18 and the Redactional History of the Book of Kings," *ZAW* 103 (1991) 355–74 and the bibliography there.

66. See my *History, Literature, and Theology*, 103–6.

full and complete mimesis between past events and historical narrative.[67] From the perspective of the (implied) authorship and readership of these three histories, the point was not what exactly happened but what can be learned from or taught by a story about what happened.[68]

One may note also that both the Deuteronomistic History and Chronicles understood successful royal building activities and multiplication of progeny as blessings,[69] and both used the rhetorical tool of referring to existing written sources to convey authority, while at the same time claiming implicitly to supersede and supplant them as the main sources of knowledge for the community. This is because they purported to convey to the community all the information that was really important for it, while the remainder is construed as "the rest [i.e., the least important] of the deeds of. . . ."[70]

It is worth noting that, at times, the implied narrator of Chronicles seems to be filling gaps and fleshing out matters that were hinted at but not developed in the memory of the past that the readers of the Deuteronomistic History were supposed to create. As the latter virtually visited and revisited these sites of memory through their reading of the books in the Deuteronomistic History, the presence of "gaps" called for acts of imagination to fill them. For instance, the Deuteronomistic History hints at reform by Jehoshaphat (1 Kgs 22:47) and reports a few details of reforms carried out by Asa and Hezekiah (1 Kgs 15:12–13; 2 Kgs 18:4). Chronicles develops these matters. As it does so, it places itself as independent from but complementary to and in continuity with the Deuteronomistic History and the Primary History, which were considered "authoritative" (Pentateuch) or at least "classical" (Joshua–2 Kings) by the literati who actually wrote, read, and reread Chronicles. To some extent, one may compare this process that bridged and separated Chronicles and the Deuteronomistic History with the process

---

67. I discussed the matter at length in ibid., 44–77. See also p. 80 above.

68. The same holds true for Josephus; see S. Mason, "Contradiction or Counterpoint? Josephus and Historical Method," *Review of Rabbinic Judaism* 6 (2003) 145–88.

69. See, for instance, Judg 10:3–4; 1 Kgs 4:20. Pentateuchal texts (and therefore, the Primary History) emphasized time and again the blessing of progeny. Of course, this is also true for other ancient historiographical traditions. Building activities play an important role in Mesopotamian texts that are meant to create an image of the past, among other things.

70. On general rhetorical matters associated with explicit references to written sources in ancient historiographic works, see K. Stott, *Why Did They Write This Way? Reflections on References to Written Documents in the Hebrew Bible and Ancient Literature* (Library of Hebrew Bible / Old Testament Studies 492; London: T. & T. Clark, 2008).

that bridged biblical texts and their "retelling" in the *Antiquities* of Josephus, even though the gap between Chronicles and the Deuteronomistic History as understood by their primary readerships was certainly much narrower than the gap between the readerships of the Primary History and Josephus's *Antiquities*.

Some Conclusions

The point of this study is certainly not to "harmonize" the Deuteronomistic History and Chronicles. Harmonization only blunts their messages and is detrimental to the study of the ideological world of the literati who produced and first read these histories, as well as detrimental to any understanding of these works in their primary, historical setting. Similarly, any attempt to gloss over the differences between Chronicles and the Deuteronomistic History would be, at best, counterproductive. There are clear differences in style and structure between the two, which, of course, reflect and communicate a substantive divergence with regard to meaning. Above all, each work creates its own story of the past, presents its own characterization of the main figures of the past, and shapes its sites of memory to be imagined, visited, and revisited by its ancient readers.

This said, intellectual historians of ancient Israel and particularly of the Jerusalem-centered Yehud in which I locate the production of the Deuteronomistic History and Chronicles in their present forms (the former in the earlier Persian period; the latter in the late Persian period) cannot but notice that neither work is univocal. Multiple voices appear in both of them. This is, by itself, an important point of similarity. Moreover, some of the voices heard in one overlap, to some extent, with the voices heard in the other. From the perspective of the study of the social setting of the creation of knowledge (and literature) in Jerusalem-centered Yehud, there is nothing "strange" about these observations. In fact, they should have been anticipated, given that there was a substantial level of continuity between the literati of the early and the late Persian period and their worlds of images, ideas, and memories.[71]

---

71. Scholars who work with diachronic approaches to the Deuteronomistic History are likely to conclude that the postmonarchic literati responsible for Dtr-N or Dtr-2 or the Persian-period edition of DtrH or a post-Deuteronomistic redaction of the books of Joshua–2 Kings or any combination of the above shared some central ideological motifs with the individuals responsible for Chronicles. The bibliography on proposals for the redaction history of the DtrH is immense. For a recent diachronic study of the DtrH and its different (and hypothetical) redactional layers, see T. Römer, *The So-Called Deuteronomistic History: A Sociological, Historical and Literary Introduction* (London: T. & T. Clark, 2005).

The converging lines mentioned here draw attention to the fact that, particularly at the level of ground ideas, core ideological concepts, and basic communicative (rhetorical) grammar as well as general historiographical tendencies, the gap between Chronicles and the Deuteronomistic History (in its present form) was not as large as often claimed. The works' underlying ideological systems shared much more and at a much deeper level than usually assumed, and so did the Persian-period literati responsible for each of them, even if they lived in different sub-periods and even if, consequently, their "world of knowledge" was far from identical (that is, the individuals who were responsible for Chronicles knew the Deuteronomistic History [and the Primary History], but the reverse is not true; those responsible for Chronicles knew of integrative, authoritative Scripture, but this was probably not the case for the individuals responsible for the Deuteronomistic History). Moreover, it is not by chance that Chronicles often shares these converging lines not only with the Deuteronomistic History but also with pentateuchal and even prophetic books, because the triad of pentateuchal, prophetic, and historical books evolved together, and together reflected the authoritative repertoire and shaped the general intellectual (and ideological) horizon of the few literati of Jerusalem-centered (early) Yehud who produced, read, and reread these books.[72]

The preceding discussion leads to a clear affirmative response to the question in the title of this paper: there were bridges. Of course, even the best bridges and, particularly, the best among them cannot but draw attention to the existence of a gap that needs bridging. In this case, even the most converging lines mentioned here point at differences on the surface of the Deuteronomistic and Chronistic narratives and even more importantly to differences at the level of the multiple didactic meanings created through the literati's continuous rereading of these narratives (both the Deuteronomistic History and Chronicles) in a way informed by their different sets of co-texts, each of which led to complementary sets of meaning that are, by necessity, different.[73]

All in all, this study demonstrates that the analysis of continuity and discontinuity between the Deuteronomistic History and Chronicles can profit much from taking into account that which goes beyond

---

72. On these matters, see also my "Reconstructing the Intellectual Discourse of Ancient Yehud," forthcoming in *Studies in Religion*.

73. These sets of co-texts included passages in literary proximity to the relevant pericopes within a particular book, the particular book as a whole, the entire literary collection with which the book was associated in its primary setting, the whole repertoire of authoritative texts available to the literati, and the like.

the surface differences between the two works. The categorical claims about their differences must not be rejected but set in proportion to their similarities.

Characters in Stone:
Royal Ideology and Yehudite Identity in the Behistun Inscription and the Book of Haggai

JAMES BOWICK
Mcmaster Divinity College

Introduction

The Behistun monument, engraved into the side of a cliff in Iran, features a 3 × 5.5 meter relief of Darius and accompanying text in Babylonian, Old Persian, and Elamite.[1] Darius is shown standing with his left hand holding a bow and his right hand raised toward a winged-disk figure of Ahuramazda.[2] Before Darius are nine rebel kings, each with their hands tied behind their backs, joined by a rope around their necks, each distinctively carved in the typical ethnic dress of his people. Beneath Darius's left foot is the liar-king Gaumata. The winged

---

Author's note: This essay represents the initial part of a larger project, which will compare the literary techniques used for characterization in the Behistun Inscription, Herodotus, and Ezra. I gratefully acknowledge Mark Boda, Gary Knoppers, Cindy Nimchuk, and Ken Ristau, whose suggestions were invaluable, as well as the contributions of my colleagues at Mcmaster Divinity College, especially Andrew McGinn and Eleanor Filyer.

1. An Aramaic translation on papyrus was also found in Egypt. See A. Cowley, *Aramaic Papyri of the Fifth Century* B.C. (Oxford: Oxford University Press, 1923); N. Sims-Williams, "The Final Paragraph of the Tomb-Inscription of Darius I (DNb, 50–60): The Old Persian Test in the Light of an Aramaic Version," *Bulletin of the School of Oriental and African Studies* 44 (1981) 1–7; J. Tavernier, "An Achaemenid Royal Inscription: The Text of Paragraph 13 of the Aramaic Version of the Bisitun Inscription," *JNES* 60 (2001) 161–76.

2. The close connection between Darius and Ahuramazda in the inscription suggest strongly that the winged figure is Ahuramazda. Some scholars, however, hold that the winged figure may be the daemon of the king or one of his ancestors; they cite Zoroastrian doctrine and Herodotus. These arguments assume that Zoroastrian doctrine has remained unchanged since the Achaemenid period and also that Herodotus is right, rather than emphasizing the apparent implications of the inscriptions on the monument itself. See M. Cool Root, *King and Kingship in Achaemenid Art* (Leiden: Brill, 1979) 169–71; M. Garrison and M. Cool Root, *Seals on the Persepolis Fortification Tablets*, vol. 1: *Images of Heroic Encounter, Part I: Text* (2 vols.; OIP 117; Chicago: Oriental Institute, 2001) 69.

figure of Ahuramazda, hovering above the captives, faces Darius with his right hand raised in a way similar to Darius, handing Darius a ring with his left. Behind Darius are two Persians, one with a spear, the other with a bow. All the characters are identified with inscriptions, except for Ahuramazda and the two Persians. The Old Persian text is directly beneath the relief, while the Babylonian is to the left, and the original Elamite to the right of the relief. A second copy of the Elamite was carved beneath the Babylonian, to the left of the Old Persian. When the original Elamite inscription was almost complete to the right of the monument, the figure of Skunka, the ruler of the Scythians, was added. To make room, it was necessary to obliterate the Elamite text, which was then reinscribed beneath the Babylonian version.[3]

Although much work has been done analyzing the texts of Behistun, especially in conjunction with the Greek texts, to determine the sequence of events leading up to Darius's ascension to the throne, only in the past 15 years have scholars such as Jack Balcer and Gernot Windfuhr carefully studied the literary features of the text.[4] The texts of both the Behistun Inscription and the book of Haggai place the events they describe within the first three years of Darius's rule,[5] and both reveal something of their community's understanding of kingship and its rulers.[6] This essay will begin by examining the literary and rhetorical features of the text of the Old Persian inscription, with special attention to characterization and Persian attitudes toward kingship. Building on this analysis, the essay will compare the attitudes toward kingship found in the Behistun Inscription with the attitudes toward kingship reflected in the biblical book of Haggai.

---

3. G. Cameron, "The Elamite Version of the Bisitun Inscription," *JCS* 14 (1960) 60–61; P. Briant, *From Cyrus to Alexander: A History of the Persian Empire* (trans. P. T. Daniels; Winona Lake, IN: Eisenbrauns, 2002) 124, 127.

4. J. Balcer, "Ancient Epic Conventions in the Bisitun Text," in *Continuity and Change: Proceedings of the Last Achaemenid History Workshop* (ed. H. Sancisi-Weerdenburg, A. Kuhrt and M. Cool Root; Leiden: Nederlands Instituut voor het Nabije Oosten, 1994) 257–64; G. Windfuhr, "Saith Darius: Dialectic, Numbers, Time and Space at Behistun (DB, Old Persian Version)," in ibid., 265–81.

5. The book of Haggai dates the oracles in it to the second year of Darius (1:1, 15; 2:10), while the main text of Behistun claims to record events that occur entirely in Darius's first year (§59), with an appendix describing events that are placed in the following two years (§71).

6. The Behistun Inscription directly reveals royal ideology by representing speech of the king. The prophecies of Haggai were compiled, preserved, and valued by the community of Yehud sometime after the prophecies themselves were given. How the compiler shaped these prophecies and what this says about kingship are the subject of the second half of this paper.

This approach puts two principal areas of common inquiry in the study of Behistun beyond the scope of the study. First, no effort will be made to determine the truth value of any claims of the Behistun text. The claims of the narrative in the inscription, written in the voice of Darius, offer a glimpse into Persian thought, whether the events happened as described or not. Questions about the veracity of these claims will not be raised, nor will the Greek sources commonly used to reconstruct the history of this period be cited, because I will be analyzing the narrative world of the Behistun text to understand foremost what it is saying and what literary techniques are being used to present the truth claims.[7] Only after Behistun has been understood in its own right will I turn to the Hebrew Bible for comparison. Specifically, the book of Haggai will be read as a historiographic narrative with the intent of determining how the Yehudite community understood kingship. While it is not common to view Haggai as historiography or as narrative, because it consists of a collection of prophetic oracles, recent scholarship demonstrates that the book as a whole can be read as a prophetic narrative. Rather than reading the book as a collection of oracles to which some narrative material has been added, I will use a prophetic narrative model, which describes a sequence of events, including the oracles themselves, to form a coherent story.[8] Reading Haggai as a narrative whole will reveal something of the Yehudite community's understanding of kingship, which will then be compared to the perspective of the Behistun text and what it reveals of Persian ideas of kingship.

Behistun: Orientation

Although the Elamite section of the Behistun Inscription is more likely the original text, the Old Persian is significant.[9] The content of the Old

---

7. On the veracity of the Behistun account, see for instance A. Olmstead, "Darius and His Behistun Inscription," *AJSL* 55 (1938) 392–416; A. Poebel, "Chronology of Darius' First Year of Reign," *AJSL* 55 (1938) 142–65; and "Chronology of Darius' First Year of Reign (Concluded)," *AJSL* 55 (1938) 285–314; A. Olmstead, *History of the Persian Empire* (Chicago: University of Chicago Press, 1948) 107–18; more recently, E. Bickerman and H. Tadmor, "Darius I, Pseudo-Smerdis and the Magi," *Athenaeum* 66 (1978) 239–61; M. Lang, "Prexaspes and Usurper Smerdis," *JNES* 51 (1992) 201–7.

8. See for instance, D. Petersen, *Haggai and Zecharia 1–8: A Commentary* (OTL; Philadelphia: Westminster, 1984) 32–36; P. Redditt, *Haggai, Zechariah, Malachi* (NCB; Grand Rapids: Eerdmans, 1995) 11–12; M. Floyd, "The Nature of Narrative and the Evidence of Redaction in Haggai," *VT* 45 (2004) 470–90.

9. The text of the Old Persian is not the first text inscribed; however, the image of the monument itself, copied elsewhere, is primary, and Darius's original verbal instructions

Persian text generally follows the earlier versions, but the characters are much more skillfully and deeply incised.[10] It contains material that the other texts are missing: Behistun §70 reads, in part, "By the favor of Ahuramazdā this (is) the form of writing which I made, besides, in Aryan, and on clay tablets. Both on clay tablets and on parchment it has been placed."[11] In the same place, in Elamite, it reads, "I made a script (or inscription) of another kind in Aryan which previously had not existed."[12] Many believe it was in order to record the Old Persian version that the Old Persian language was put into writing. Darius, it is argued, had the cuneiform script for the Old Persian language developed specifically for this monument.[13] For these reasons, this study will focus on the literary features specifically of the text as found in the Old Persian version.

concerning what to write were quite probably in Old Persian; C. Tuplin, "Darius' Accession in (the) Media," in *Writing and Ancient Near Eastern Society: Papers in Honour of Alan R. Millard* (ed. P. Bienkowski et al.; Library of Hebrew Bible/Old Testament Studies 426; New York: T. & T. Clark, 2005) 217; W. J. Vogelsang, *The Rise and Organization of the Achaemenid Empire: The Eastern Iranian Evidence* (Leiden: Brill, 1992) 177.

10. Cameron, "The Elamite Version," 60–61.

11. All translations of the Behistun text are from R. Schmitt, *The Bisitun Inscription of Darius the Great: Old Persian Text* (Corpus Inscriptionum Iranicarum, Part I: Inscriptions of Ancient Iran 1—The Old Persian Inscriptions, Texts 1; London: School of Oriental and African Studies, 1991) unless otherwise noted. See also L. W. King and R. C. Thompson, *The Sculptures and Inscription of Darius the Great* (London: British Museum/Oxford University Press, 1907); S. Sukumar, *Old Persian Inscriptions of the Achaemenian Emperors* (Calcutta: University of Calcutta, 1941); R. Kent, *Old Persian: Grammar, Texts, Lexicon* (2nd ed.; New Haven, CT: American Oriental Society, 1953). On the text of Behistun, see also L. Gray, "Notes on the Old Persian Inscriptions of Behistun," *JAOS* 23 (1902) 56–64; W. Jackson,"The Great Behistun Rock and Some Results of a Re-Examination of the Old Persian Inscriptions on It," *JAOS* 24 (1903) 77–95; R. Kent, "The Textual Criticism of Inscriptions," *JAOS* 40 (1920) 289–99; idem, "Old Persian Texts," *JNES* 2 (1943) 105–14; idem, "Cameron's Old Persian Readings at Bisitun Restorations and Notes," *JCS* 5 (1951) 55–57; N. Debevoise, "The Rock Reliefs of Ancient Iran," *JNES* 1 (1942) 76–105; W. Eilers, "The End of the Behistan Inscription (Col. V:18–20 and 34–36)," *JNES* 7 (1948) 106–10; G. Cameron, "The Old Persian Text of the Behistun Inscription," *JCS* 5 (1951) 47–54; W. C. Benedict and E. von Voigtlander, "Darius' Bisitun Inscription, Babylonian Version, Lines 1–29," *JCS* 10 (1956) 1–10.

12. M. A. Dandamaev and V. G. Lukonin, *The Culture and Social Institutions of Ancient Iran* (Cambridge: Cambridge University Press, 1989) 278–79.

13. J. Balcer, *Herodotus and Bisitun: Problems in Ancient Persian Historiography* (Stuttgart: Franz Steiner, 1987); Dandamaev and Lukonin, *Culture and Social Institutions,* 281; Briant, *From Cyrus to Alexander,* 127, contra R. Hallock ("On the Old Persian Signs," *JNES* 29 [1970] 52–55), who argues based on the number of wedges in the different characters that the base text for developing OP cuneiform was CMa, which reads, "I am Cyrus the King, an Achaemenian" (Kent, *Old Persian,* 116). There is reason to believe that this text was also by Darius.

The text consists of 76 paragraphs, each one (except the first) introduced with the words "Proclaims Darius, the King." These 76 fit into
the following outline: §1–9 Introduction and Lineage, §10–14 Darius
Defeats Gaumata, §15–54 Rebellions Put Down, §55–70 Conclusion,
§71–76 Epilogue: Year 2 and 3. In the first section, §1–9, the narrator,
speaking as Darius, asserts Darius's membership in the royal family,
lists the nations that came to him, and describes his rule as just. The
second section, §10–14, narrates the events that led to Darius's rise. Cyrus had a son, Cambyses, who had a brother, named Smerdis. Before
his death, Cambyses slew Smerdis. A magus named Gaumata seized
power, claiming to be Smerdis, the brother of Cambyses. The people
followed him, fearing that anyone who denounced him would be slain.
Finally Darius and a few men rose up and slew Gaumata, the false
Smerdis, restoring the throne to the royal family and making Darius
king. However, all was not well, as the third section, §15–54, reveals. A
number of rebellions broke out throughout the land, and Darius and
his generals had to put them down. The conclusion, §55–70, records
Darius's insistence that what has been said is true and gives advice on
kingship to those who follow, including an injunction to protect the
Behistun monument itself. The epilogue, §71–76, describes rebellions
during the second and third year that Darius put down. By narrating
Darius's lineage, ascent to the throne, and his many victories in the
first year, the Behistun text seeks both to establish Darius's right to the
throne and to discourage future rebellions.

Genre
Before considering the literary features of the text, I think that it is
important to define the literary genre of the Behistun narratives. The
text, accompanied as it is by the relief and boasting of the works of the
king predominantly in the first person, is reminiscent of other royal inscriptions. A literary analysis assumes that the text is in fact a careful
literary composition, with characteristics of one or more genres. The
genre has been examined by both Balcer and Windfuhr, although they
take different approaches and arrive at different conclusions as to the
nature of the text. Their examinations prove useful in demonstrating
some of the characteristics of the text and point the way to further
study.
Balcer thinks that the Behistun narrative reflects ancient Indo-
European conventions, as described by Dumézil and others.[14] Dumézil,

---

14. Balcer (ibid., 257) cites a number of sources.

drawing on linguistic studies that describe the histories and development of languages, including languages no longer extant or even attested, developed a comparative approach to myths and the social
structures they reveal, and also proposed theories of interrelationship
and genealogy.[15] Dumézil compared ancient Indian myths with those
of Italic, Germanic, and Celtic peoples to search for common themes
and structures that shed light on the myths and social structures of
the original Indo-Europeans.[16] At Behistun, Balcer finds the Indo-
European tripartite divisions of sovereignty, force, and nourishment
manifest in the divisions of priest, warriors, and herder-cultivators.[17]
Additionally, the specific story of Darius told by Behistun has themes
from the Indo-European epics. Gaumata is a trickster but is also the seriously flawed king and the opponent of Darius, the intruding hero.[18]
As the epic intruding hero, Darius must first prove himself by conquer-
ing his enemy and then undertake some act on behalf of a small band of
supporters, whom Balcer sees as Darius's six colleagues who, along
with Darius, were the seven conspirators that overthrew Gaumata. After this, the intruding hero must act on behalf of the entire people.[19]

The Behistun narrative differs from the epic conventions, as noted
by Balcer, in that the epic hero usually meets a tragic fate, either per-
ishing or losing a great deal . Balcer, however, notes that in *The Odyssey*
and *Cid* the hero's society is revitalized, and the end of the story ushers
in a stable society.[20] Further, Balcer's assertion that "Darius' emphasis
upon his colleagues, the six fellow conspirators against Bardiya, is
strong" is overstated.[21] It is not until §68 that they are mentioned at all.
There they are named, and it is noted that "at the time [they] were
there, whilst I slew Gaumāta the magus who called himself Smerdis.

15. G. Dumézil, *L'idéologie tripartie des Indo-Européens* (Brussels: Berchem, 1958);
B. Lincoln, *Priests, Warriors, and Cattle: A Study in the Ecology of Religions* (Berkeley: Uni-
versity of California Press, 1981); S. Littleton, *The New Comparative Mythology* (rev. ed.;
Berkeley: University of California Press, 1973); M. Vereno, "On the Relations of Dume-
zillian Comparative Indo-European Mythology to History of Religions in General," in
Myth in Indo-European Antiquity (ed. G. J. Larson; Berkeley: University of California Press,
1974) 180–90; J. Oosten, *The War of the Gods: The Social Code in Indo-European Mythology*
(London: Routledge & Kegan Paul, 1985); G. James Larson, "Introduction: The Study of
Mythology and Comparative Mythology," in *Myth in Indo-European Antiquity*, 1–16.
16. See Littleton, *Comparative Mythology*, 7–19, for a helpful overview of Dumézil's
theories.
17. Balcer, "Ancient Epic Conventions," 258, 263.
18. Ibid., 261.
19. Ibid., 261–62.
20. Ibid., 262–63.
21. Ibid., 261.

At that time these men strove as my followers" (§68). While this may be significant recognition for the individuals, it is hardly a strong emphasis within the text. They are not depicted at all on the monument, unless one assumes that the unnamed Persians behind Darius happen to be two of them.[22] Balcer concludes, however, that the Behistun narrative is shaped, not only by the events and by the narrator's desire to justify Darius, but also by the ancient social structures and myths of the Persian people. Balcer's reminder not to read Behistun only as a Mesopotamian monument thus adds another important sociopolitical and mythological context for proper scholarly consideration of the inscription.

While Balcer sees the Behistun Inscription as an epic tale, Windfuhr sees it as a spell whereby the lie is dispelled, and truth is "spelled."[23] Windfuhr argues that the inscription is a speech act that creates a syllogism in which the acts and words of Darius are subsumed in the will of Ahuramazda and, as such, are by definition truth.[24] He finds the repeated references to the will of Ahuramazda and certain unusual numeric features, especially the repetition of the number 9, to be typical of spells.[25] In 76 paragraphs, Darius is mentioned 76 times, and Ahuramazda is also mentioned exactly 76 times.[26] Windfuhr also notes that, given the importance that the text places on the fact that all the events recorded in it occur in one year, one would also expect to find reference to the year in the structure of the text. By assuming that the original text ends with §67, he finds that these references exist in the fact that the length of the text is exactly $365\frac{1}{4}$ lines, and the first mention of the one year appears in the beginning of the conclusion in the 52nd paragraph.[27] To this he adds the observation that all Darius's and his father's

---

22. E. Schmidt (*Persepolis III: The Royal Tombs and Other Monuments* [Chicago: University of Chicago Press, 1970] 86) suggests that the first one was Gobryas, mentioned as one of the six (§68); however, there the identity of the other is not known. That only two are shown, without being identified, but all six are named in the text suggests that seeing these two as somehow representing the six is at best speculative.

23. Windfuhr, "Saith Darius," 265.

24. Ibid., 267.

25. Ibid., 265.

26. Ibid., 269. These and other figures mentioned by Windfuhr are based on the Old Persian text, and the patterns do not generally follow for the Elamite or Babylonian versions, though some do.

27. Ibid., 266. In §67 a warning against destroying the text does have a sound of finality, and the following material, crediting and invoking protection on the six followers and discussing the making and dissemination of the inscription, do read as an appendix. Whether they were afterthoughts and later additions as Windfuhr suggests is an open question; there is nonetheless a major structural division between §67 and §68.

major victories occur in months with equinoxes or solstices, while his allies' victories occur in odd months.[28]

Perhaps most striking, however, are the occurrences of the number 9 throughout the text. Windfuhr notes Darius is the 9th king in the family to reign, 9 provinces rebel, there are 9 rebel kings,[29] and 9 leaders oppose the rebels. Less convincing are Windfuhr's division of the 19 battles putting down the revolts into 9 sets and his creation of 9 sets of provinces out of the 23 that revolt.[30] The rhetorical significance of the repetition of 9 and other numeric features is not fully understood and warrants further study.

While, on one level, the inscription at Behistun is a royal inscription, proclaiming the works of a king, primarily in narrative form, Balcer and Windfuhr both show that this is only a superficial observation. Though some of Windfuhr's observations might be coincidental or contrived by him, he has made a number of important observations about the text that at the very least demonstrate that it is not a haphazard or plodding inscription of a boasting king but, in fact, a carefully crafted piece of literature. Balcer's demonstration of epic features shows that the narrative has layers beyond the strictly literal. A reading necessarily begins with an acknowledgment of the text as a royal inscription; however, the text invites us to look for other literary features without restricting our reading based on assumptions of genre.

Literary Features

There are a number of features of the text that suggest it is carefully written to establish the legitimacy of Darius's claim to the throne. His assertion is supported by a genealogical claim to the throne both di-

---

28. Ibid., 274–75.

29. The Scythian with the pointed hat was added later; however, it does not disrupt the count. Prior to its being added, there were 9 rebels in total, including the prostrate Gaumata. Afterward, there were 9 kings standing. Significantly, the rebel Ataimata (§71) is omitted from the last carving.

30. Ibid., 270–72. The challenge of the kind of mathematical analysis that Windfuhr does is determining at what point the calculations cease to be descriptive of the text and begin to be creations of their own, given that almost any set can generate a pattern, given sufficient ingenuity. In some cases, Windfuhr appears to have crossed this line. Dividing 19 battles and 23 provinces into sets of 9 requires a division between decisive and lesser battles, and leaves sets of only 1, 2, or 3 provinces per set. The more calculations and qualifications that Windfuhr makes, the less trustworthy his observation becomes. The number 3, and its square, the number 9, seem to have significance going back to the roots of the Indo-Aryan language family and can be traced through Iranian branches; see B. Keith, "Numbers (Aryan)," *Encyclopaedia of Religion and Ethics* 9.407–13.

rectly in the introduction, §1–4, and also implicitly elsewhere in the text. The narrative concerning the rebellions, §15–54, uses formulas in narrating the individual rebellions as well as arranging them in a geographical sequence that serves to reinforce the kingship of Darius. This is strengthened further by the use of *pasāva* as a means of slowing down or speeding up the narrative to control the impact of the chronology of the events. The next few paragraphs will develop the way that these various features work and lay a foundation for a specific study of characterization in the Behistun text, especially of Darius.

Genealogy and the Issue of Legitimacy

Darius's genealogical claim to the throne, stated explicitly in the opening sections, is based on his assertions that he was a member of the royal family and a descendant of kings, related to Cambyses, sharing Teispes as great-great-grandfather: "(There are) eight in my family who formerly have been kings; I am the ninth; (thus altogether) nine, now as ever, are we kings" (§4). The narrator deftly employs Darius's connection to Cyrus, avoiding any claim until §10, but then reasserting the claim five times to underscore the false claims of Gaumata and others (§§11, 13, 40, 52 twice). Without repeatedly stating Darius's claims to be related to Cyrus, the narrator evokes it by quoting the (false) claims of Gaumata to be a son of Cyrus and the other pretenders, at the same time discrediting them by showing the same claim of multiple individuals.

Notably, however, others living at the time held more immediate claims to the Persian throne; for example, Hystaspes, the father of Darius, who was still living at the time and even served Darius as a general (§35f).[31] The narrator bolsters Darius's claim, however, by declaring that he rescued the throne from the imposter Gaumata and that it was by the favor of Ahuramazda that he received his kingship: "There was no man, neither a Persian nor a Mede nor anyone of our family, who might have been able to despoil that Gaumāta the magus of the kingship. . . . I despoiled him of the kingship; by the favour of Ahuramazdā I became king; upon me Ahuramazdā bestowed the kingship" (§13). So, although Darius's genealogical claim to kingship is inferior to others', the intervention of Ahuramazda confirms the supremacy of his claim.

---

31. M. A. Dandamaev, *A Political History of the Achaemenid Empire* (trans. W. J. Vogelsang; Leiden: Brill, 1989) 107, 108; Briant, *From Cyrus to Alexander,* 110–11.

The inscription highlights the illegitimacy of Gaumata, and thus it also validates Darius's usurpation through its refutation of Gaumata's claims. According to the inscription, Gaumata the Magian had declared, "I am Smerdis, the son of Cyrus, the brother of Cambyses" (§11).[32] The Behistun text identifies this as a lie and reports that Cambyses had murdered his brother. Darius drives this point home by repeating the clause twice, almost word for word:

Pasāva:	Kabūjiya:avam:	Bardiayam:avāja:
yaθa:	Kabūjiya:	Bardiayam:avāja
		(§10; col. 1, lines 30–31)[33]

Kent's literal translation, "Afterwards, Cambyses slew that Smerdis. When Cambyses slew Smerdis," preserves much of the effect. *Pasāva*, translated 'afterwards', is effectively paralleled with *yaθa*, which is a subordinating conjunction introducing a temporal clause modifying the action of the following sentence, thus creating a syntactical separation, while at the same time functioning rhetorically in parallel with *pasāva*. The same structure is then repeated in lines 32 and 33 with reference to Cambyses' departure to Egypt. The placement of the second clause at the front of the sentence and the parallel wording are likely deliberate in order to emphasize the inaccuracy of Gaumata's claim and the absence of Cambyses, who could have prevented the corruption of the land and whose absence is essential for Gaumata's deception.[34]

Gaumata's claim to the throne is further refuted through the use of formulas and repetition in the narrative of the subsequent revolts. Behistun §11, which tells the story of Gaumata's rise, lays out a literary formula that serves as a template for the accounts of subsequent rebellions in §15–54. The formula, as found in this section, takes this form: "Afterwards, there was one man, [proper name] by name . . . he rose up. He lied to the people thus: 'I am [proper name].' Afterwards all the people became rebellious . . . and went over to him." The adaptation and creative use of this formula create a repetitive framework through-

---

32. The Old Persian name is Bardiya. Due to the influence of ancient Greek discussions, the name is usually translated 'Smerdis'.

33. I have arranged the phrases to highlight the parallels.

34. The clause can only appear here and at the end of the sentence it modifies (Kent, *Old Persian*, 96). It is found before the clause it modifies in 11 out of the 14 times that *yaθa* is used with reference to time in the Behistun Inscription (before in lines 1.31, 33, 73, 91; 2.22, 32, 52, 65; 3.3, 34; 4.5; and after in lines 1.27, 72, and 5.3). These are the only two occurences (col. 1, lines 30–31 and 32–33), however, in which the parallel structure seen here is thereby created.

out the narrative, the overall effect of which is to deemphasize and marginalize Gaumata's story.

Behistun §16 uses this formula to introduce two rebellions before either of them is resolved. In describing the first rebellion, by Açina, the narrator varies the formula by substituting the word "said" for "lied" and does not mention a name that Açina assumed; however, the second rebellion, by Nidintu-Bel, follows the formula fairly closely. The Old Persian relates §16 to the formula laid out in §11 more closely than Kent's translation suggests, because 'lied' in §11 and 'deceived' in §16 translate the same Old Persian word, *adurujiya*.[35] The rebellion of Martiya in Elam described in §23 follows the formula fairly closely, including the use of a false name. The most significant variation concerns the response of the people: "afterwards (it was) me [Darius] (that) the Elamites feared; they captured that Martiya who was their chief, and slew him." Still, even though the rebellion itself is quite different from a number of the others, the formula is present.

The rebellion of Ciçantakhma, introduced in §33, abbreviates the formula and does not claim a new name. An interesting exception to the formula is the rebellion of Frada, introduced in §38. The province rose up and, once in rebellion, appointed Frada as their ruler. Yet even here the formula is not abandoned but instead is adapted by rearranging the elements: "(There is) a country, Margiana by name, that became rebellious to me. (There was) one single man, Frāda by name, a Margian, —him they made (their) chief." In §24 the rebellion of Phaortes follows the formula with the omission of the explicit reference to lying; so also the rebellion of Vahyazdata, introduced in §40. The rebellion of Arkha, introduced in §49, restores the word "lied."

As the words and phrases of the formula are repeated over and over again in the narrative of each revolt, the revolts begin to sound alike, even with the variation, and each rebellion merges into a single narrative of a number of similar revolts, rather than a significant event worthy of notice on its own. This becomes especially pronounced with the rebellion of Arkha, who took the name Nebuchadnezzar, as did Nabintu-Bel, and Vahyazdata who took the name Smerdis. If the story of the rebellion of Gaumata seems incredible when the reader begins reading the Behistun Inscription, by the time the reader has finished,

---

35. These sections in the Old Persian are better translated by Schmitt than by Kent. Sukumar (*Old Persian Inscriptions*) translates the first 'thus deceived' and the second 'thus lied'; however, a much older translation (King and Thompson, *Sculptures and Inscription*) renders both 'lied'.

it seems to be just one of a number of similar rebellions, following the
usual pattern.[36]

Geography

The arrangement of the rebellions is based for the most part on geography, but, as Windfuhr notes, this arrangement involves several
geographical skips, which effectively break the provinces into groups
by discussing revolts in one region, then discussing revolts in another
region some distance away.[37] The list of rebellious provinces in §6 gives
the impression that the entire empire from one end to the other rose up
in rebellion, yet the narrative of rebellions focuses on those that are
nearer, in Persia and Media, the Iranian Plateau and Central Asia, and
Elam and Babylonia, rather than those in more distant locales, in
Egypt, Arabia, and Cappadocia.[38] Windfuhr observes further schema-
tization of the provinces, noting that there are 11 provinces to the west
of Persia and 11 provinces to the east of Persia.[39] Additionally, the first
two rebellions, Nabintu-Bel in Babylon and Açina in Elam (§16–20),
are both close to Persia, in lands more historically connected to Persia,
as are the last two, Vahyazdata in Persia and Arkha in Babylon (§40–
51), while the rebellions between them are further away, significantly
to the north. This creates a sense of imminent danger and immediacy
that contrasts with but also reinforces, even heightens, the literary effect of the summary of revolts in §6.

Chronology and Narrative Time

In addition to geographical arrangement, the Behistun Inscription
makes use of pacing and a temporal arrangement to highlight Darius's
achievements. It is very important to the narrator that all these events
happened in one year—implicitly revealed by dating events only by
the month and day and not by the year; and explicitly revealed by stating it five times (§52, 56, 57, 59, 62). In every case where it is explicitly

---

36. There is the possibility that the repetition indicates that Gaumata set the whole
mass of rebellions in motion, the former being connected to the latter through the mention of Gautama in §16. However, §14 gives a clear sense of closure to the Gaumata affair.
Furthermore, the use of *yaθa* with *pasāva* reinforces the temporal and causal separation;
the Lie was actually in the land before Gaumata acted (§10).

37. Windfuhr, "Saith Darius," 271. Geographical order was noted by Poebel, "Chronology," 149, 150 n. 13, 154; R. Hallock, "The 'One Year' of Darius I," *JNES* 19 (1960) 36;
L. Depuydt, "Evidence for the Accession Dating under the Achaemenids," *JAOS* 115
(1995) 196.

38. Briant, *From Cyrus to Alexander*, 115.

39. Windfuhr, "Saith Darius," 271.

stated, the narrator attributes the year's events to the favor of Ahura-mazda.

Windfuhr observes that the dating of key events is geometrically significant if the year is viewed as a circle. Gaumata's revolt, assumption of kingship, and death occur just before the spring equinox, at the summer solstice, and just after the fall equinox, respectively.[40] In contrast, Darius's main feats—seen by Windfuhr as the slaying of Gaumata, the defeat of Nidintu-Bel in Babylon, and the defeat of Phraortes in Media—occur just after the fall equinox, just after the winter solstice, and just after the spring equinox.[41] While the key events of Gaumata are in the summer months, the key events of Darius, forming a similar pattern, are in the winter months. The key events of his allies do not occur in months that have a solstice or an equinox. Thus, the key events in Darius's reign form a triangle that is a mirror of the triangle created by charting the key events of Gaumata.[42]

In addition to the absolute or calendric chronology, the narrator also orders the narrative through careful pacing of the action, primarily through the use of the Old Persian word *pasāva*. This word is an adverb, defined by Kent as 'after that, afterwards'.[43] Most of the occurrences of *pasāva* are found at Behistun. Although it may be assumed that this is simply because Behistun contains the vast majority of the narrative text surviving in the Old Persian corpus, a close look at the word's distribution within the text of Behistun reveals that its use reflects rhetorical consideration.

In the introduction and conclusion of Behistun (§1–9, 55–70), there is only 1 occurrence of the word. The opening narrative portions contain the word, the Gaumata episode (§10–14) having 10 occurrences in 5 sections, or 1 in 37 words (most frequently in the first 2 sections with 8 occurrences, or 1 occurrence per 18 words). The first two rebellions, in Babylon and Elam (§15–20), have 11 occurrences in 6 sections, or 1 in 19 words. The epilogue (§71–74) contains 7 occurrences in 4 sections, or 1 in 24 words. These sections average 1.8 occurrences per section, or 1

---

40. Ibid., 272–73.

41. Ibid., 274.

42. Ibid., 275–76. Windfuhr pushes the data much further, but his elaboration on these events beyond what is mentioned here appears to be forced, in my opinion, because it involves a suspiciously high number of calculations to create—among other things, a cross that has only three points represented. The sequence of the months was first elaborated by Arno Poebel, "The Names and the Order of the Old Perisan and Elamite Months during the Achaemenian Period," *AJSL* 55 (1938) 130–41.

43. Kent (*Old Persian*, 197) lists here all occurrences of the word.

occurrence of *pasāva* in every 24 words; in contrast with the rest of the narrative (§21–54), which averages less than 1.3 occurrences per section, or 1 in every 39 words (43 in 34 sections).

The narrative of the rebellion of Gaumata is very carefully paced. The first section (§10), which narrates the rise of the lie in the land, has 5 occurrences of *pasāva* in 70 words (a frequency of 1 in 14). It begins with Cambyses on the throne, then removes him to Egypt, sees his brother Smerdis slain, the people corrupt, and the lie covering the land. This section is the catastrophic setting for the next section (§11), which narrates the rise of Gaumata and the death of Cambyses. Here there are 3 occurrences of *pasāva*, a frequency of 1 in 35 words. The rise of Darius, by contrast, is discussed in some detail, bringing it to great prominence. There are only 2 occurrences of the word *pasāva* in the remaining 3 sections, or 230 words, of the opening narrative.

The frequent occurrences of the adverb *pasāva* drive the action forward, while its absence, including as a result of an increase in detail presented in the narrative, tends to slow the pace of the action. The repetition of the adverb is effectively used to create a sense of heightened drama in the events surrounding Darius's confrontation with Gaumata and the first rebellions in Elam and Babylon. It is also used to give the impression of fast action in the epilogue (§71–76), which has the highest density of use of the word *pasāva* in the inscription and describes the suppression of 2 revolts in a two-year period as opposed to 9 revolts suppressed in the previous year. The narrator is apparently seeking to create a sense of fast action, even when the facts are contrary.

Conversely, in the period between the first 2 rebellions in Babylon and Elam (§15–20) and the final rebellions in Persia and Babylon (§21–54), the word *pasāva* is used with much less frequency. It may have been important to the narrator to lengthen this sequence of events in order to put distance between the two Babylonian rebellions, because 2 rebellions in close succession in the same place would raise embarrassing questions about how successfully it was in fact put down. The use of *pasāva* combined with the spatial and geographical features create a sense that Darius dealt quickly with Gaumata and, even though he was immediately surrounded on all sides by rebellion, he quickly and decisively dealt with the first rebellions in Babylon and Elam. Between the first and the second set of rebellions, the scribe narrates the rebellions in other parts of the empire, avoiding the term *pasāva* in order to slow the action and to create the rhetorical separation. When Darius returns, he deals with the rebellions in Babylon and Persia at his leisure and, as reflected by the frequent use of *pasāva* again, quickly and decisively deals with rebellions in Elam and Scythia. In this way, the scribe expands and collapses narrative time, even in tension with the preserved chronology, for ideological purposes.

Characterization

Before looking more closely at Darius, we must consider other characters in the text to understand Behistun's narrative techniques. The people of each province as a collective group form a character to which the text of Behistun attributes choice and agency. That they are not merely an extension of the leaders, following and doing their will, can be seen from the times in which they act independently. So, in §22, Martiya rose up in Elam and said, "I am Imani, king in Elam." Rather than follow him, however, the Elamites favor Darius: "afterwards (it was) me (that) the Elamites feared; they captured that Martiya who was their chief and slew him." Conversely, the province of Margiana rose up without a leader and appointed one afterward. The inscription reads, "(There is) a country, Margia by name, that became rebellious to me. (There was) one single man, Frāda by name, a Margian—him they made (their) chief" (§38). This is especially significant for understanding the initial events in Cambyses' reign that led to the trouble. Behistun §10 reads, in part, "When Cambyses had set out for Egypt, after that the people became disloyal and Falsehood grew greatly in the land, both in Persia as well as in Media and the other countries." The trouble begins with the people, and then the lie grows in the land. The responsibility for the start of the problem belongs to the people, not to Gaumata, who is not introduced until §11.

The liar kings are flat characters, for whom very little detail is given, either individually or as a group. Significantly, however, their lineage is given as a means of certain identification and sometimes also for narrative purposes. There are two instances in which the liar king is not of the people he tries to rule, though he claims to be: Gaumata, a Median, who claims to be the son of Cyrus, and thus a Persian (§11, §52); and Arakha, an Armenian, who claims to be Nebuchadrezzar, and thus a Babylonian (§49, §52).[44] Except in the first occurrence, which reads, *martiya maguš āha Gaumāta nāma* ('there was one man, a magus, Gaumata by name') every single mention of Gaumata reads *Gaumāta : hya : maguš* ('Gaumata the magus'). Gaumata the Magian is identified as a Mede in the Babylonian version, but his identity as a Magian,

---

44. Martiya is not counted among these because, while he was living in Persia when he claimed to be king of Elam, it is not explicitly stated that he was Persian (§22).

which precluded him from the cult of Ahuramazda, is of primary significance, given the emphasis on the connection between Darius and Ahuramazda.[45] Arakha's father follows, unusually, after his nationality, *martiya Araxa nāma Arminiya, Halditahya* ('[There was] one single man, Arakha by name, an Armenian, son of Haldita' §49), thus giving emphasis to his nationality. This additional level of lying makes the lie inherent in rebellion all the more heinous.

There is very little information given about the rebel kings, except the identifying information and, in a few cases, the nature of their punishment. The most serious threat to Darius was from Phraortes, as reflected in the length of the narrative about him, the number of provinces involved in his rebellion, and the severity of the punishment.[46] Nevertheless, he is only named 7 times in the 11 sections, in contrast to only one of the generals sent against him, Dadarshi, who is named 8 times—4 generals being named 20 times altogether. Exceptionally, Gaumata is characterized as ruthless and brutal, inspiring the people's fear of him, "(since) he used to slay in great number the people who previously had known Smerdis" (§13). However, in a world in which opponents were routinely slaughtered by kings, this may have been expected, the intended focal point being the fear of the people in contrast to the bravery of Darius.[47]

While Darius's generals are named (in contrast to the generals of the false kings), there is little information provided about them. They act on the will of Darius, and their victory is his. Behistun §25 is typical. The general is introduced simply as "my vassal," is made chief, and is

---

45. Tuplin, "Darius' Accession," 231–32. Handley-Schachler studied the distribution of the *lan* ritual in administrative texts and noted from these texts that there is no association between the magi and Ahuramazda worship, and in fact that there was no individual associated with both. The religion of the magi specifically seemed to exclude the worship of foreign (non-Median) gods such as Ahuramazda (M. Handley-Schachler, "The *Lan* Ritual in the Persepolis Fortification Texts," in *Studies in Persian History: Essays in Memory of David M. Lewis* (ed. M. Brosius and A. Kuhrt; Leiden: Nederlands Instituut voor het Nabije Oosten, 1988) 199–200.

46. Phraortes occupies 11 chapters, or 80 lines, compared with an average of 2.5 paragraphs or 15.75 lines (average calculated, excluding longest and shortest). For the historical reality, see Dandamaev and Lukonin, *Culture and Social Institutions*, 120; Dandamaev, *Political History*, 118–20; Briant, *From Cyrus to Alexander*, 119.

47. This point would be self-evident in the Babylonian text: Darius kills 100,111 foes (Dandamaev, *Political History*, 128; citing R. Schmitt, "Zur babylonishen Version der Bistunün-Inschrift," *AfO* 27 [1980] 108; Josef Wiesehöfer, *Ancient Persia from 500 BC to 650 AD* [New York: Tauris, 1996] 18). Interestingly, this statistic is carefully omitted from the Persian text, perhaps because the implied threat was not considered necessary among Darius's own people as it was among the conquered Babylonians.

given a direct command, which he obeys. The description of the victory, "Ahuramazdā brought me aid; by the favor of Ahuramazdā my army defeated that rebellious army utterly," attributes it to Darius and Ahuramazda alone. The chiefs never act on their own initiative and, in fact, twice they cannot finish the job and must wait for Darius to arrive (§28, 30).

The character of Ahuramazda is difficult to discern, because it is difficult in the Behistun text to separate Darius and Ahuramazda as characters. While they are clearly separate entities, their actions are so intertwined that one cannot be defined apart from the other. On the one hand, everything Darius achieves is "by the favour of Ahuramazdā" who "brought me aid." In the narrative, the first act of Darius, after the account of the actions of Gaumata in deceiving the people and stealing the kingdom from the family of Cyrus, is to beseech the help of Ahuramazda (§13), setting up all future action as a response to this request. Almost every act of Darius is as an agent of Ahuramazda. On the other hand, at no point does Ahuramazda ever act except through Darius. It is even because of Darius's character that Ahuramazda and the other gods aid him: "because I was not disloyal, I was no follower of Falsehood, I was no evil-doer, neither I nor my family, (but) I acted according to righteousness" (§63).

The most complex character in the text is Darius himself, although he is far from fully developed. His descriptions of himself point merely to his virtue, as noted above, without any indication of personal limits or faults. His punishment of the rebels is proof of his virtue, despite our modern perception of barbarity. He boasts that "the man who was loyal, him I treated well, who was disloyal, him I punished severely" (§8), and "the man who strove for my (royal) house, him I treated well, who did harm, him I punished severely" (§63). These two statements are part of the summaries of his actions that form an inclusio around the narrative, and Darius repeats the idea in his charge to future kings: "You, whosoever shall be king hereafter—the man who shall be a follower of Falsehood, or (the man) who shall be an evil-doer, to those may you not be friendly, (but) punish them severely" (§64).

The text is written in the first-person voice of Darius, each paragraph being introduced with the phrase *θāti : Dārayavauš : xšâyaθiya* ('Proclaims Darius, the King'). Thus the whole narrative unfolds from a single point of view and, in fact, the whole world is seen from just one, all-important perspective, that of Darius. The narrator, by associating Darius with Ahuramazda and opposing the lie, implies that all he says and does is truth, so his self-descriptive statements reflect this.

The character Darius says, "because I was not disloyal, I was no follower of Falsehood, I was no evil-doer, neither I nor my family, (but) I
acted according to righteousness." Darius goes on to explain, "the man
who strove for my (royal) house, him I treated well, who did harm,
him I punished severely" (§63). These statements presuppose that Darius is tautologically good. To oppose Darius is itself a moral wrong and
to cooperate a moral good. Further, Darius's instructions concerning the
Behistun text, and his blessings on readers and curses on those who do
not promote it serve to make this text sacred, as if the words of Darius
are truth because they are the words of Darius. Windfuhr notes that,
through the inscription, "Darius' kingship, his deeds, and thought-
word-speech act of the inscription, [become] part of the cosmic truth of
Ahuramazda, with the conclusion that this truth, if not the King of
Kings, has to be protected."[48]

Darius is portrayed as recognizing that the events he describes are
incredible, as is clearly indicated in §56–58, which is sometimes seen
as an implicit acknowledgment that not everyone believed Darius's
claims to the throne.[49] This leads the modern reader who has otherwise not questioned the inscription to think that Darius "doth protest
too much."[50] However, it seems unlikely that Darius (or the scribes
who composed the text of Behistun) would believe that the incredulity
of a skeptic could be swayed merely by asserting that what was written was truth. Rather, Darius's recognition of the incredulity of the
hearer is best seen in his recognition of the incredible nature of the
story itself. The character of Darius is presented as being incredulous
at this amazing story. Combined with the constant repetition that the
acts were done with the aid or by the favor of Ahuramazda, the narrator suggests that Darius himself wonders at what Ahuramazda has
done through him. This is further reinforced by his frequent uses of
the passive voice, allowing the character or Darius to distance himself
from the action. He says, for example, "This (is) what has been done by
me in . . ." (§34, 37, 39, 44, 48, 51), and "the country became mine" (§37,
39, 48, 71, 74). Darius did not come into his kingdom by great might or
brilliant strategy but by the will of Ahuramazda, because he was a vir-
tuous person who did not follow the lie (§63). The narrator builds Darius up by portraying him as pious, chosen by Ahuramazda, and aided
by Ahuramazda in a way that leaves even Darius in humble awe.

48. Windfuhr, "Saith Darius," 265.
49. Wiesehöfer, *Ancient Persia*, 14.
50. Olmstead, "Darius and His Behistun Inscription," 397.

While Darius is portrayed as achieving many feats that only a king could achieve, these and all that he accomplishes are portrayed as supernatural events in which Darius is used to restore the right order of the universe. In §18, Nidintu-bel makes his stand at the Tigris, and the rough waters of the Tigris form a defensive line that Darius overcomes through creativity. In §19, however, it is the river that carries away the bodies of Darius's opponents. Briant notes that such authority over natural cycles was one aspect of royal power. Nevertheless, this is the only instance in the text where Darius even comes close to exhibiting supernatural power.[51] The only claim of the text is that Darius sought to correct the wrong done to his house by Gaumata, a wrong that no one else was willing or able to right. This model fits well with Balcer's description of the Indo-European epic hero: "Above all, it is the god(s) who represent the force of ultimate moral order and, therefore, causes the hero intruder as the victorious new king to rise from his personal interests to the final more important duty to his state."[52] Consequently, one of the major purposes of the Behistun monument is to show Darius's ascension to the throne as a supernatural event, not the result of his own will or personal prowess.

Summary

As Root notes, "the impact of the Behistun monument upon the traveler along the road to Ecbatana was conveyed solely by the sculpture"[53] and, as such, invites a reading of the text in light of the monument.[54] The core message of the image is expressed visually and is timeless, removed from a specific historical context.[55] While Ahuramazda is the smallest image on the monument, the squareness and detailing on the wings and tail feathers provide it with a heaviness that offsets the smallness and draws attention to this image.[56] Darius himself, while off center, is the largest object and thus a key focal point.[57] He appears more interested in the divine than in the things of this

---

51. Briant, *From Cyrus to* Alexander, 239. Pursuit and entrapment may also be considered strategy, but the lack of detail with which they are described argues against reading them as strategy.
52. Balcer, "Ancient Epic Conventions," 262.
53. Root, *King and Kingship*, 193.
54. The fact that the text was copied and distributed, as demonstrated by the existence of the Aramaic version, does not negate this.
55. Cindy Nimchuk, *Darius I and the Formation of the Achaemenid Empire: Communicating the Creation of an Empire* (Ph.D. diss., University of Toronto, 2001) 13.
56. Ibid., 16, 17.
57. Ibid., 11.

world.[58] The image of Ahuramazda is positioned above the rest of the figures, which are all on a horizontal plane, suggesting that the god is above this world. However, the representation of Ahuramazda is not entirely above Darius; rather, Darius's eyes are level with the bottom of the god's disk.[59] Nimchuk argues that Darius's posture is not one of worship but of beckoning, of summoning forward, while Ahuramazda provides Darius not only with kingship but with the rebels.[60] The relationship between Darius and Ahuramazda is a unique, reciprocal relationship.[61]

The text of the Behistun monument echoes the message of the images through a number of narrative techniques and provides a historical justification and context. Through repetition and the use of formulas, the narrator establishes that the acts of Gaumata in pretending to be Smerdis were unexceptional and were copied by other pretenders. The material is arranged and developed to highlight Darius's speed in putting down the rebellions and to deemphasize problems such as the temporal proximity of the Babylonian rebellions. It also minimizes how long it took him to put down two rebellions in years two and three. In the text, Darius is the only character with any significant depth, yet even so, he is flatter than our curiosity might like. It is difficult to separate his character from Ahuramazda, because all his acts are aided by Ahuramazda who, in turn, only acts through Darius. In the text, as in the monument, Darius and Ahuramazda are in a uniquely reciprocal relationship that makes the speech-act of Darius the truth of Ahuramazda.

Considering the presentation of Darius at Behistun provides clues to the way that the Persians saw kingship. Behistun presents Darius as the central focus of the narrative world. The whole narrative is communicated through the voice of Darius, and his actions alone achieve significant results. While Darius is never confused with Ahuramazda, no act of Darius is achieved without the aid of Ahuramazda. Conversely, Darius is never described as following direction, and the text, even while distancing these acts from Darius through the passive voice, presents the acts as though they are at the initiative of Darius himself. While his acts are always completed through the aid of Ahuramazda in ways

58. Ann Farkas, "The Behistun Relief," in *Cambridge History of Iran*, vol. 2: *The Median and Achaemenian Periods* (ed. Ilia Giershevitch; Cambridge: Cambridge University Press, 1985) 828.
59. Nimchuk, "Darius and Formation," 17.
60. Ibid., 15. See also Root, *King and Kingship*, 188–90.
61. Nimchuk, "Darius and Formation," 17.

that amaze even Darius himself, once he gives Darius the kingship, Ahuramazda seems to facilitate but not direct. Darius as king becomes the focal point of the narrative world and the primary agent, acting by the power of Ahuramazda but according to his own will. We may conclude, then, that the Persian king was intimately and reciprocally involved with the god, being given the kingship and supported by divine aid. The absence of the voice of Ahuramazda to Darius, directly or even through a prophetic character, may suggest that the Persian king was less directed than one might expect.[62]

Haggai: Orientation

In the previous section, this essay took a literary approach to the Behistun Inscription, reading it as a narrative. This approach allows the reader to draw conclusions about how the characters are developed, specifically how Darius, the ruler of the community that produced the text, is characterized. Through this narrative approach, insight was gained into the way the Persians understood kingship. Similarly, a narrative reading of the book of Haggai will allow an analysis of the development of the characters, specifically the characterization of Zerubbabel, offering a glimpse into the way the community of Yehud saw kingship.

Perhaps no book in the Bible is as closely tied to a single event and a single time as is the book of Haggai. By assigning the oracles to dates within the 2nd year of the reign of Darius the king, the narrative frame of the book of Haggai invites the reader to read the book against the background of the events occurring within this year. The occasion for the book of Haggai, as distinct from the occasion of the oracles themselves, is not known with certainty.[63] One dominant theme of the book

---

62. It would be profitable to compare and contrast this idea of kingship with the conceptions of the Egyptians, Assyrians, and Neo-Babylonians, as well as kingship ideas found in the Avestas and other Indo-Iranian sources; however, this is beyond the scope of this current study.

63. Early efforts to date the book did not look past the date formula (J. Calvin, *Commentaries on the Twelve Minor Prophets* [trans. J. Owen; Edinburgh: Calvin Translation Society, 1848] 4.317–32; S. R. Driver, *An Introduction to the Literature of the Old Testament* [New York: Scribners, 1914] 343–44; G. Robinson, *The Twelve Minor Prophets* [New York: Doran, 1926] 140; P. Bloomhardt, "The Book of Haggai," in *Old Testament Commentary* [ed. H. Alleman and E. Flack; Philadelphia: Muhlenberg, 1948] 870; S. Edgar, *The Minor Prophets* [London: Epworth, 1962] 47). Later scholars came to recognize a distinction between the prophecies of Haggai and the book as a whole, written during Haggai's lifetime or shortly thereafter, probably before the completion of the temple (O. Eissfeldt, *The*

is the reestablishment of the old social institutions. The theme of building the temple, which is seen by Boda as the defining theme of the
book,[64] is an obvious reminder to the people that the priesthood has
been reestablished, but more importantly, it points to the restoration of
royalty. The role of Haggai the prophet in the building of the temple is
also significant and points to the restoration of the prophetic office. But
if the nation was reestablished, the priesthood restored, and the temple
rebuilt, where was the promised king on David's throne? A narrative
reading of Haggai suggests that, though only a governor, Zerubbabel
can be seen as a partial fulfillment of that promise, pointing to a future
complete fulfillment.

Genre

While it is tempting to read the book of Haggai as a collection of oracles, there is reason to believe that a better approach is to read the
book as a whole as a prophetic narrative. In the book of Haggai, there
can be heard both the voice of the prophet and the voice of a narrator.[65]
Floyd's extensive study demonstrates that the two voices are not easily
separated and that, in addition to being a collection of prophecies, one
can also read Haggai as a prophetic narrative.[66] The superscriptions
differ from those of other prophetic books in that they are complete

Old Testament [trans. P. R. Ackroyd; New York: Harper & Row, 1965] 488; R. K. Harrison,
Introduction to the Old Testament [Grand Rapids: Eerdmans, 1969] 947; R. Mason, *The
Books of Haggai, Zechariah and Malachi* [Cambridge: Cambridge University Press, 1977]
413–21; B. Childs, *Introduction to the Old Testament Scripture* [Philadelphia: Fortress, 1979];
D. Petersen, *Haggai and Zecharia 1–8: A Commentary* [OTL; Philadelphia: Westminster,
1984] 37–38; R. Smith, *Micah–Malachi* [WBC 32; Waco, TX: Word, 1984] 148; P. C. Craigie,
"Micah, Nahum, Habakkuk, Zephaniah, Zephaniah, Haggai, Zechariah, and Malachi,"
in *Twelve Prophets* [ed. J. C. L. Gibson; Daily Study Bible; Philadelphia: Westminster, 1985]
2.135–36; P. Verhoef, *The Books of Haggai and Malachi* [Grand Rapids: Eerdmans, 1987] 10;
P. Redditt, *Haggai, Zechariah, Malachi* (NCB; Grand Rapids: Eerdmans, 1995) 11–12).
J. O'Brien believes that the book was written years after the temple was complete (*Habakkuk, Zephaniah, Haggai, Zechariah, Malachi* [Abingdon Old Testament Commentary;
Nashville: Abingdon, 2004] 136–37).
    64. M. Boda argues that each pericope of Haggai can be associated with the early
stages of ritual used in the reconstruction of temples in the ancient Near East, and the
book itself with the foundation-laying ("From Dystopia to Myopia: Utopian [re]visions
in Haggai and Zechariah 1–8," in *Utopia and Dystopia in Prophetic Literature* [ed. Ehud Ben
Zvi; Publications of the Finnish Exegetical Society 92; Helsinki: Finnish Exegetical Society, 2006] 242). He had argued earlier for the separation of Haggai from Zech 1–8 in his
"Zechariah: Master Mason or Penitential Prophet," in *Yahwism after the Exile* (ed. R. Albertz and B. Becking; Studies in Theology and Religion 5; Assen: Van Gorcum, 2003) 53.
    65. Redditt, *Haggai*, 11.
    66. Michael H. Floyd, "The Nature of Narrative and the Evidence of Redaction in
Haggai," *VT* 45 (2004) 474.

sentences, and the oracles themselves, in their entirety, are the direct object of the verb אמר.[67] Petersen argues persuasively that the book of Haggai is "an apologetic history that uses prophetic oracles as its source" but is itself a narrative.[68] Sweeney also observes that Haggai is a prophetic narrative that uses three "narrative date formulas" to structure the book into three sections.[69] The book of Haggai can be understood as a piece of historiography with a message of its own for a historical context sometime after the date given for the prophecies.

Character Analysis

Through the oracles of the LORD that come to Haggai, the narrator drives the plot of the book and creates characters. By defining the role of Zerubbabel, the narrator creates community identity in Yehud. The narrator of Haggai confronts the hard reality of Persian domination in the first verse. In contrast to the normal Hebrew dating formula in historiography covering the monarchic period, which dates events to the reign of a Judean or Israelite king, the opening words of Haggai date the first oracle to the second year of Darius, the king. Brown suggests this would be the necessary default in the absence of a reigning Jewish king.[70] However, the narrator could have dated the oracles by the year that Zerubbabel was in office, could have at least specified that Darius was the king of Persia, as Ezra does with Cyrus (Ezra 1:1), or could have omitted the word מלך as in Zechariah (1:1, 1:7, but contrast 7:1). Darius most commonly refers to himself as 'Darius, the king' *Dārayavauš xšāyaθiya*, which would best be translated into Hebrew by דריוש המלך. There is a clear recognition that the king is Darius, and no effort is made to distance or isolate the reader from this reality. The continued subjugation to Darius was a challenge to the theology of the Davidic covenant, and the narrator's reference to it in the first verse minimizes the role of Zerubbabel as a leader in the community.

However, the very structure of the book suggests that Haggai is saying something about Zerubbabel and kingship. The theme of building or rebuilding a temple is always associated strongly with kingship.

---

67. Ibid., 476.
68. Petersen, *Haggai*, 32–36 (quotation from p. 36). He cites N. Lohfink, "Die Gatung der 'Historischen Kurzgeschichte' in den letzen Jahren von Juda und in der Zeit des Babylonischen Exils," *ZAW* 90 (1978) 319–47.
69. M. A. Sweeney, *The Twelve Prophets, II: Micah, Nahum, Habakkuk, Zephaniah, Haggai, Zechariah, Malachi* (Berit Olam; Collegeville, MN: Liturgical Press, 2000) 532.
70. W. P. Brown, *Obadiah through Malachi* (Westminster Bible Companion; Louisville: Westminster John Knox, 1996) 122.

Riley notes that, in the ancient Near Eastern world, the king "was responsible for the building and maintenance of the national temples."[71]
A common pattern in temple-building stories throughout the Near
East was that they began either with a god commanding a king to
build a temple or a king seeking permission to build a temple.[72] For Riley, the role of temple builder, shared between David and Solomon, is
a dominant theme in the Chronicler's development of David, Solomon,
and the rest of the Davidic Dynasty.[73] The book of Haggai, while it begins with a foreign king, ends, as Brown notes, with the promise of a
new kingdom.[74] Zerubbabel is called פחת יהודה 'governor of Yehud', a
title that gives him leadership over the community of Yehud, while
carefully avoiding calling him king.[75] Nevertheless, the narrator
quickly begins to reshape, if not altogether undermine the image of
subjugation through the characterization of Zerubbabel, who is also
called by the end of the book עבדי ('my servant'), a title with potentially royal connotations. Indeed, from the beginning of the book, he is
called זרבבל בן־שאלתיאל 'Zerubbabel, son of Shealtiel' (1:1, 12, 14; 2:2,
23), which identifies him as a descendant of David[76] and assures the
community that the promise made to David can be renewed in his
descendants.[77]

Through the early portions of the book, Zerubbabel is not treated as
a separate character. The initial prophecy is addressed to both him and
Joshua (1:1). Zerubbabel, Joshua and the people respond in obedience
(1:12), and the LORD stirs up the spirits of Zerubbabel, Joshua, and the
people (1:14). The first statement directed to Zerubbabel alone is fol-

71. William Riley, *King and Cultus in Chronicles* (JSOTSup 160; Sheffield: Sheffield
Academic Press, 1993) 37.

72. Victor Hurowitz, *I Have Built You an Exalted House* (JSOTSup 115; Sheffield: Sheffield Academic Press, 1992) 143.

73. Riley, *King and Cultus*, 60.

74. Brown, *Obadiah through Malachi*, 131.

75. Redditt notes that פחה does not seem to have a technical meaning in the Hebrew
Bible despite its use in the Persian records for a specific office (Redditt, *Haggai*, 6). Zerubbabel clearly has the political leadership of Yehud at this time, but how his office fits into
the Persian hierarchy remains unclear.

76. 1 Chronicles 3:17–19 identifies Zerubbabel as the son of Pedaiah, brother of
Shealtiel, and son of Jeconiah, son of Jehoiakim, the king. While there is confusion between Ezra, Nehemiah, and Haggai on the one hand and Chronicles on the other hand,
both sides agree that Zerubbabel is a descendant of David through the royal line. On the
text-critical and exegetical issues, see further Gary N. Knoppers, *I Chronicles 1–9* (AB 12;
New York: Doubleday, 2004) 320–36.

77. Robert T. Siebeneck, "The Messianism of Aggeus and Proto-Zacharias," *CBQ* 19
(1957) 316.

lowed by almost identical statements to Joshua, then to the people (2:4), and is within the context of a prophecy that is directed to all three (2:2). It is noteworthy, however, that the order in which the three are mentioned is consistent in every occurrence, with Zerubbabel heading the list, followed by Joshua the high priest, and then the people.

The culmination of the book completes the shift, as Hag 2:21–22 resonates with language from earlier traditions of Scripture, especially throne language. The royal theme in 2:20–23 contrasts with the recognition of the kingship of Darius in 1:1. The language of the oracle in 2:21–22 and its immediate context provides compelling evidence for a royal interpretation. The opening words of the oracle, אני מרעיש 'I am shaking', suggest the direct act of God and a coming battle. The use of רעש in the Hiphil is elsewhere associated with the appearance of the LORD in both revelation and battle (Ps 60:2[4]; Job 39:20; Isa 14:13; Ezek 31:16; Hag 2:6, 7).[78] The participle indicates imminent action, and so is translated in the NRSV 'I am about to shake'.[79] The phrase occurs first in v. 6, where it is connected with the phrase "once again, in a little while."

In v. 21 the action, initiated by the participle, is expanded with a series of three first-person verbs: והפכתי ('I will overthrow'), והשמדתי ('I will destroy'), and והפכתי ('I will overthrow'). The root הפך, used twice here, from which והפכתי is derived, is also used of Sodom and Gomorrah (Gen 19:21, 25) and is regularly used of God's total and instantaneous destruction (e.g., Jer 20:16).[80] Similarly הפך, used elsewhere of God's judgment of the nations (Gen 19:21, 25; Deut 29:22; Isa 1:7–9; Jer 20:16; Amos 4:11; Lam 4:6), here depicts the total destruction of the power bases of the nations, including political, economic, and military power.[81] The reference to the overthrow of chariots and horses at once looks back to the destruction of the Egyptian army and ahead to the destruction of the nations. Petersen, following Sauer, notes that the language concerning the overthrow of thrones and ruin of nations strongly reflects the language of Ps 2, 110—both royal psalms—and Ps 100, associated directly with David in the prescript.[82]

---

78. Mark J. Boda, *Haggai/Zechariah* (NIV Application Commentary; Grand Rapids: Zondervan, 2004) 124.

79. For use of the participle in Hebrew, see Christo H. J. van der Merwe, Jackie A. Naudé, and Jan H. Kroeze, *A Biblical Hebrew Reference Grammar* (Biblical Languages: Hebrew 3; Sheffield: Sheffield Academic Press, 1999) 162; B. K. Waltke and M. O'Connor, *An Introduction to Biblical Hebrew Syntax* (Winona Lake, IN: Eisenbrauns, 1990) 627; Pieter Verhoef, *Haggai and Malachi*, 143.

80. Boda, *Haggai/Zechariah*, 162; Verhoef, *Haggai and Malachi*, 143.

81. Ibid., 143–44.

82. Petersen, *Haggai*, 100.

The phrase ביום ההוא 'on that day' serves to connect the events described in v. 22 with the coming events of v. 23. Significantly, the phrase is positioned outside the oracle itself, actually appearing before the introductory נאם־יהוה צבאות. It acts as a transition from the general predictions of vv. 21–22 to the very specific prediction of v. 23, and evokes the coming day when the LORD's enemies will be destroyed and salvation will be brought to the Jews.[83] In fact, Siebeneck suggests that it is only inasmuch as Zerubbabel is connected with the continuation of the Davidic Dynasty that he can be connected with universal dominion.[84]

Finally, in v. 23 the phrase אקחך זרבבל בן־שאלתיאל עבדי 'I will take you, Zerubbabel son of Shealtiel, my servant' uses the verbal root לקח, which is commonly used in similar constructions concerning election of a Davidic king.[85] While the language is eschatological, Zerubbabel is addressed within the narrative directly as a living person, creating expectations for him within his lifetime. The cumulative force of all these word pictures and allusions is that Zerubbabel is at least the partial fulfillment of God's promise to David.

Rose, however, has difficulty seeing Zerubbabel as a royal character. He points out that the messianic vocabulary used of Zerubbabel is not exclusively messianic. He demonstrates that the term עבד 'servant' with a pronoun referring to God, is used in a rich variety of contexts, including prophets, stewards, and even groups, such as the prophets or the nation of Israel.[86] However, of the 80 examples that Rose gives for individuals (by far the larger group), some 40 refer to David himself, and 12 refer to Moses. After a similar study of the root בחר 'choose' with God as the agent (chosen by God), he concludes that these terms are not specifically associated with kingship.[87] Once again the dominant association of בחר, with God as agent, is with David. While the effect of associating Zerubbabel with Moses, David, and the other great leaders of Israel may not be specifically intended to call him king, the

83. Ibid., 102; Boda, *Haggai/Zechariah*, 163.

84. Siebeneck, "Messianism of Aggeus," 318.

85. Petersen, *Haggai*, 103. Petersen concedes that this is a very common verb and can hardly be read as a technical term referring to the election of a Davidic king. Nonetheless, he believes that its use here in the midst of other language related to the Davidic throne is significant. He does not cite any examples.

86. W. H. Rose, *Zemah and Zerubbabel: Messianic Expectations in the Early Postexilic Period* (JSOTSup 304; Sheffield: Sheffield Academic Press, 2000) 210–11.

87. Ibid., 212, 215.

association definitely creates very high expectations for him.[88] The association specifically with David connects Zerubbabel with the expectation in Yehud that the community would be permanently and securely established with a descendant of David on the throne.[89]

More problematic for a royal view of Zerubbabel is that the image of the signet ring is not what one might expect. The sentence "I will . . . make you like a signet ring" (2:23) contrasts the position of Zerubbabel with that of Jehoiachin, of whom the LORD said, "even if King Coniah son of Jehoiakim of Judah were the signet ring on my right hand, even from there I would tear you off" (Jer 22:24). Rose argues that the image of the signet ring in Jer 22:24 and Hag 2:23 represents something that is intimately valued,[90] contrasting with an image of the giving of the signet ring as a symbol of the delegation of authority and power in Gen 41:40–42, and Esth 3:10–11 and 8:2.[91]

In contrasting similar passages, such as Ps 2:8–9; 110:1, 5; and Isa 45:1, Rose notes a number of elements of the Davidic promise that are missing in Haggai's oracle to Zerubbabel.[92] He is never called the LORD's anointed. He is never promised autonomous rule. The LORD never says that the other nations will submit to him. In short, Rose notes, Haggai does not call Zerubbabel מלך because Haggai does not see Zerubbabel as becoming king.[93]

With similar implications, though in a slightly different vein, John Kessler seeks to disconnect the prophecies in Hag 2 from the immediate historical context and from the historical person of Zerubbabel, seeing the prophecy as eschatological.[94] Boda also notes the possibility

---

88. Difficulty arises in discussing the royal expectations of Zerubbabel as a result of the overlap with the concept of the Messiah. Boda argues that there are at least four definitions in modern biblical studies. The views vary on the issue of time (is the Messiah contemporary with the text, a person in the near future, or an eschatological person) and the social role of the Messiah (M. Boda, "Figuring the Future: The Prophets and the Messiah," in *Messiah* [ed. S. Porter; McMaster New Testament Studies; Grand Rapids: Eerdmans, 2007] 36–38). This essay considers only the expectation that Zerubbabel would take on a royal role as a result of the promise to David, not to what degree his role was messianic.

89. As seen, for example, in 1 Chr 17:8–14; Jer 33:19–26; Ezek 37:24–28.

90. Rose, *Zemah*, 238.

91. As noted by Rose, ibid., 219.

92. Ibid., 241.

93. Ibid., 243.

94. J. Kessler, "The Shaking of the Nations: An Eschatological View," *JETS* 30 (1987) 160–63; idem, *The Book of Haggai: Prophecy and Society in Early Persian Yehud* (VTSup 91; Leiden: Brill, 2002) 234–39.

that Haggai was using the name Zerubbabel to speak of his descendants and cites precedence in the Hebrew Bible; however, he gives no
examples of this, aside from David himself.[95]

Perhaps Haggai, by connecting the hope of the renewed Davidic
kingship with the contemporary situation in the person of Zerubbabel,
is pointing to a new understanding of the Davidic line in which the office can be filled by someone who cannot be called מֶלֶךְ. On this theory,
the author of the book of Haggai is clearly connecting the promise of
the Davidic covenant with Zerubbabel. In fact, the author of Haggai
sees Zerubbabel as a prefigure that assures the reader that God's final
promise will be fulfilled. The partial fulfillment now points to the complete fulfillment yet to come: "The present pitiable condition of the
remnant was no cause of despair, for even as the Messias would rise
from a lowly condition, so would the remnant. Zorobabel, the restored
descendant of David, was but a prelude to the messianic age."[96]

While Yehud did not enjoy preexilic independence, things had definitely changed in the transition from Babylonian to Persian rule. The
precise organization of the Jewish people and their relationship to the
Persian Empire remains unclear; however, Yehud seems to have been
a province within the satrapy of Abar-nahara.[97] Numismatic discov-
eries and a Babylonian legal text both point strongly to the conclusion
that Yehud was a separate province within Abar-nahara with a certain
degree of autonomy and was not subordinate to Samaria:[98] "Each

---

95. Boda, *Haggai/Zechariah*, 167.

96. Siebeneck, *The Messianism of Aggeus*, 312–28.

97. Briant, *From Cyrus to Alexander*, 487, 488.

98. The degree and nature of the autonomy is unclear due to ambiguous terminology
in the primary texts and a degree of fluidity of boundaries and lines of authority in the
ancient world. For recent discussion, see M. W. Stolper, "The Governor of Babylon and
Across-the-River in 486 B.C.," *JNES* 48 (1989) 283–305; E. Stern, "New Evidence on the
Administrative Division of Palestine in the Persian Period," in *Centre and Periphery: Proceedings of the Groningen 1986 Achaemenid History Workshop* (ed. H. Sancis-Weerdenburg
and A. Kuhrt; Leiden: Nederlands Instituut voor het Nabije Oosten, 1990) 221–26; Wiesehöfer, *Ancient Persia*, 59–62; J. Weinberg, *The Citizen-Temple Community* (JSOTSup 151;
Sheffield: JSOT Press, 1992); H. G. M. Williamson, "Judah and the Jews," in *Studies in Persian History: Essays in Memory of David M. Lewis* (ed. P. Briant et al.; Achaemenid History
11; Leiden: Nederlands Instituut voor het Nabije Oosten, 1998) 145–63; C. Carter, *The
Emergence of Yehud in the Persian Period: A Social and Demographic Study* (JSOTSup 294;
Sheffield: Sheffield Academic Press, 1999) 279; D. Janzen, "Politics, Settlement, and
Temple Community in Persian-Period Yehud," *CBQ* 64 (2002) 490–510; J. Cataldo, "Persian Policy and the Yehud Community during Nehemiah," *JSOT* 28 (2003) 240–52; Dandamaev, "Neo-Babylonian and Achaemenid State Administration"; J. W. Wright, "Remapping Yehud: The Borders of Yehud and the Genealogies of Chronicles," in *Judah and
the Judeans in the Persian Period* (ed. Oded Lipschits and Manfred Oeming; Winona Lake,

province remained an independent socio-economic region with its own social institutions and internal structure; with its own local laws, customs, traditions, systems of weights and measures, and monetary systems."[99]

Although the governors of the provinces were carefully watched, they seem to have enjoyed a large degree of autonomy in internal affairs, provided they paid their taxes and did not rebel. The rebellions in other parts of the world would have had the effect of distracting the attention of the monarch from Yehud, because the impressive yet limited resources of the monarchy would be invested in settling troubled areas. This distraction would have given the community of Yehud more autonomy, because the eyes of the king were looking elsewhere. This was further accompanied by a rising prosperity, as can be seen by growth in the population during this time.[100] Carter concludes that, while Yehud was a small and under-populated community with little resources, it nevertheless had financial resources coming from outside that made it both more viable and more significant than pure statistics suggest.[101] The very literary activity of the community suggests a level of resources above subsistence. The narrator of Haggai, by shifting the character of Zerubbabel from a minor role as the governor of a province to a more significant role as "my servant" (Hag 2:23), constructs the vitality and whatever freedom they were experiencing as the partial fulfillment of the Davidic promise. Although Zerubbabel could not be called מֶלֶךְ, Haggai proposes that the community was nevertheless led by a royal figure.

For the Yehudite people, there was only one king—not Darius but the LORD.[102] However, because direct rule by God as king was difficult to sustain on an institutional level, human kings acted as mediators.[103]

IN: Eisenbrauns, 2006) 67–89; J. Maxwell Miller and John Hayes, *A History of Ancient Israel and Judah* (2nd ed.; Louisville: Westminster John Knox, 2006) 522–23.

99. Dandamaev and Lukonin, *Culture and Social Institutions*, 97.

100. Carter (*The Emergence of Yehud*, 226) notes a 42% growth in population in Benjamin and a 63% growth in Judah from the Persian I to the Persian II period. (In his introduction [p. 27], he divides the two periods roughly at 450 B.C.E. For a somewhat different perspective on demographic developments, see Oded Lipschits, *The Fall and Rise of Jerusalem: Judah under Babylonian Rule* [Winona Lake, IN: Eisenbrauns, 2005] 154–81.)

101. Carter, *Emergence of Yehud*, 294.

102. R. de Vaux, *Ancient Israel*, vol. 1: *Social Institutions* (Toronto: McGraw-Hill, 1965) 110.

103. W. Brueggemann, *Theology of the Old Testament* (Minneapolis: Fortress, 1997) 600–601. This fits well with L. L. Grabbe's assertion that the kings were also priests: *Priests, Prophets, Diviners, Sages: The Portrayal of Priests, Prophets and Other Religious Specialists in the Latter Prophets* (Valley Forge, PA: Trinity Press International, 1995) 23.

The authority of the king was not his own; instead, he acted as a servant of the LORD, an agent for the salvation of the people. The role of king as savior, ensuring the welfare of the people and the prosperity of the land, was critical in the understanding of kingship.[104] To the extent that Zerubbabel fulfilled these roles, he was de facto king of Yehud, even if the title belonged to Darius.

Summary

The concept of the king as a mediator endured into the exilic period, through the Davidic covenant, as a future hope. Working within this theological framework, Haggai was able to point to Zerubbabel as a Davidic royal figure, foreshadowing the fulfillment of the promises to David. The autonomy of Yehud within the Persian system would have given Zerubbabel the latitude needed to exercise political power for the transformation and rehabilitation of the community. Ultimately, a governor, at any level and in any system, is an agent acting on behalf of and with the authority of another. A governor has little or no independent authority of his own. Similarly a signet ring is but an agent, a means by which the authority of its owner is exercised. In the first verse of Haggai, Darius is recognized as king, but the book shifts its emphasis to the royal role of Zerubbabel, "my servant." For the Davidic promises to be fulfilled, it is not necessary that Zerubbabel be king. It is necessary that the LORD be king and Zerubbabel be his servant. And for the community, whether they are led by a "governor" or by someone the LORD calls "my servant" makes a tremendous difference in the way that they understand themselves.[105]

Conclusion

If the key element of royal ideology for the narrator of Haggai is not sovereign rule but divine agency on the part of the community, then Haggai and Behistun have much in common. As has been shown, Darius is not portrayed as seeking kingship as an end in itself but, rather, as a means of restoring his family's kingdom with the aid and favor of the divine. The result of this divine aid is that Darius finds himself king, sovereign over the provinces through an act of Ahuramazda that

---

104. De Vaux, *Institutions,* 110.

105. This essay has not examined the relationship between the Persian or Yehudite ideas of kingship and the ideas of the other ancient Near Eastern cultures. While such a study would be profitable, to compare and contrast properly either the Persian or the Yehudite ideas of kingship with the kingship ideas of other cultures would take more space than is here available.

even he himself finds incredible. In the same way, Zerubbabel, though not named king and without any real hope of becoming king, is a servant of the LORD on behalf of his people.

However, while the narrative of Behistun uses the motif of divine aid as a means of highlighting the piety of Darius, whose voice alone is presented by the narrator, Zerubbabel remains silent throughout the book. He is treated as a separate character only at the end and as a recipient of a divine oracle. This is not presented as something that Zerubbabel desires but as divine fiat, the prophetic proclamation of the word of the LORD. The LORD is a much more active character in Haggai than Ahuramazda is in Behistun. The narrative of Haggai is carried entirely by the prophetic word, which is initiated by the LORD. In contrast, the narrative in Behistun is carried by the word of Darius, and Ahuramazda never acts except through Darius. In the prophetic narrative, the plot is carried through the word of the LORD proclaimed by the prophets, and characters are shaped by what the LORD says about them. In contrast, in the Behistun Inscription the king speaks, and his character is defined by what he says and how he says it. The choice of genre, which determines voice, is itself an act of characterization on the part of the narrator. Nevertheless, in both texts the divine is the source of the ruler's authority. In both texts, human rulers are ultimately subjects of divine agency.

There is a surprising commonality between the two different texts of Behistun and Haggai. This essay has shown that the text of Behistun is carefully crafted to portray Darius as having been given the throne through a wondrous act of Ahuramazda; he finds himself the agent of divine purpose. Similarly, I have shown that, within the context of the Persian Empire, in which it would be almost impossible to claim independence or kingship, Zerubbabel is carefully presented as the partial fulfillment of the divine promise to David and functioning as a royal figure. Again, Zerubbabel does not seek this but is used as a divine agent by the LORD for his community.

There are, on the other hand, significant contrasts between the two texts. The voice of the LORD heard in Haggai does not have a parallel in Behistun; and Zerubbabel is silent in Haggai, in contrast to the voice of Darius in Behistun. Zerubbabel is a servant responding to the voice of his LORD, while Darius, notwithstanding his dependence on the favor of Ahuramazda, acts of his own accord. The Persian idea of kingship as revealed in Behistun is thus in some ways very similar to the concept of kingship revealed in Haggai but also quite different in a number of important ways.

The Diaspora in
Zechariah 1–8 and Ezra–Nehemiah:
The Role of History, Social Location,
and Tradition in the Formulation of Identity

JOHN KESSLER
Tyndale Seminary

Introduction:
The Emergence of Diverse Yahwistic Communities
in the Achaemenid Period

Over the course of the seventh and sixth centuries B.C.E., the geographical contours of the worship of Yahweh underwent a highly significant transformation. At the beginning of this period, Yahwistic worship was geographically quite circumscribed. Its practitioners were to be found in the Levant almost exclusively confined to the kingdoms of Israel and Judah. Through the impact of the Assyrian invasions and deportations in the Levant during the late seventh century[1] and similar activity by the Babylonians in the early sixth century, as well as other forms of voluntary emigration (perhaps for mercenary service or other economic reasons),[2] significant Yahwistic communities came to exist in various locations of the ancient Near East outside the province of

---

1. On this, see B. Oded, "Observations on the Israelite/Judaean Exiles in Mesopotamia during the Eighth–Sixth Centuries B.C.E.," in *Immigration and Emigration within the Ancient Near East: Festschrift E. Lipiński* (ed. K. van Lerberghe and A. Schoors; OLA 65; Leuven: Peeters, 1995) 205–12; idem, "The Settlements of the Israelite and Judean Exiles in Mesopotamia in the 8th–6th Centuries B.C.E.," in *Studies in Historical Geography and Biblical Historiography Presented to Zecharia Kallai* (ed. G. Galil and M. Weinfeld; VTSup 81; Leiden: Brill, 2000) 91–103.
2. See, for example, P. Garelli, "Les déplacements de personnes dans l'empire assyrien," in *Immigration and Emigration in the Ancient Near East: Festschrift E. Lipiński* (ed. K. van Lerberghe and A. Schoors; Leuven: Peeters, 1995) 79–82; H. Limet, "L'émigré dans la société mésopotamienne," in ibid., 165–79.

Yehud, principally in Egypt, Mesopotamia, and the surrounding regions of the Levant.[3]

Alongside these often economically stable communities, as other recent studies using various methodologies have shown, the province of Yehud experienced significant population decline and severe economic difficulty.[4] Several biblical texts reflect attempts to grapple with this situation when the temple still lay in ruins, and no officially sanctioned community was resident in Jerusalem.[5] However the officially authorized return to Jerusalem by a portion of the exiled population, espe-

---

3. See the surveys in S. Japhet, "People and Land in the Restoration Period," in *Das Land Israel in biblischer Zeit* (ed. G. Strecker; Göttingen: Vandenhoeck & Ruprecht, 1983) 103–25; J. Kessler, "Persia's Loyal Yahwists: Power Identity and Ethnicity in Achaemenid Yehud," in *Judah and the Judeans in the Persian Period* (ed. O. Lipschits and M. Oeming; Winona Lake, IN: Eisenbrauns, 2006) 91–121. For the principal textual evidence for these communities, see B. Porten, *The Elephantine Papyri in English: Three Millennia of Cross-Cultural Continuity and Change* (Documenta et Monumenta Orientis Antiqui 22: Leiden: Brill, 1996); F. M. Cross, "Papyri of the 4th Century B.C. from Dâliyeh," in *New Directions in Biblical Archaeology* (ed. D. N. Freedman and J. Greenfield; Garden City, NY: Doubleday, 1969) 45–69; idem, "A Report on the Samaria Papyri," in *Congress Volume: Jerusalem 1986* (ed. J. A. Emerton; VTSup 40; Leiden: Brill, 1986) 17–26; A. Lemaire, "Der Beitrag idumäischer Ostraka zur Geschichte Palästinas im Übergang von der persischen zur hellenistischen Zeit," ZDPV 115 (1999) 12–23; idem, "Les inscriptions palestiniennes d'époque perse: Un bilan provisoire," *Transeu* 1 (1989) 87–104; idem, *Nouvelles inscriptions araméennes d'Idumée au Musée d'Israel* (Suppléments à Transeuphratène 3; Paris: Gabalda, 1996); L. E. Pearce, "New Evidence for Judeans in Babylonia," in *Judah and the Judeans in the Persian Period* (ed. O. Lipschits and M. Oeming; Winona Lake, IN: Eisenbrauns, 2006) 399–412; F. Joannès and A. Lemaire, "Trois tablettes cunéiformes à onomastique ouest-sémitique," *Transeu* 17 (1999) 17–34; M. D. Coogan, *West Semitic Personal Names in the Murašu Documents* (HSM 7; Missoula, MT: Scholars Press, 1976); M. W. Stolper, *Entrepreneurs and Empire: The Murašu Archive, the Firm and Persian Rule in Babylonia* (Istanbul: Nederlands Historisch-Archaeologisch Instituut Istanbul, 1985).

4. In both the *Murašu* and *al-Yahudu* texts (see n. 3), the Yahwistic community consists largely of tenant farmers, who live in moderate prosperity and stability. On the population of Yehud and its general situation, see C. E. Carter, *The Emergence of Yehud in the Persian Period* (JSOTSup 294; Sheffield: Sheffield Academic Press, 1999); O. Lipschits, "Achaemenid Imperial Policy, Settlement Processes in Palestine, and the Status of Jerusalem in the Middle of the Fifth Century B.C.E.," in *Judah and the Judeans in the Persian Period* (ed. O. Lipschits and M. Oeming; Winona Lake, IN: Eisenbrauns, 2006) 19–52; idem, "Demographic Changes in Judah between the Seventh and Fifth Centuries B.C.E.," in *Judah and the Judeans in the Neo-Babylonian Period* (ed. O. Lipschits and J. Blenkinsopp; Winona Lake, IN: Eisenbrauns, 2003) 323–76; idem, *The Fall and Rise of Jerusalem: Judah under Babylonian Rule* (Winona Lake, IN: Eisenbrauns, 2005) 134–84.

5. On this, see especially R. Albertz, *Israel in Exile: The History and Literature of the Sixth Century B.C.E.* (Leiden: Brill, 2004); J. Middlemas, *The Templeless Age: An Introduction to the History, Literature and Theology of the "Exile"* (Louisville: Westminster John Knox, 2007).

cially the rededication of the Jerusalemite temple,[6] raised burning questions: What was the relationship between homeland and Diaspora? How would Yahwism now conceptualize the relationship between its population in Jerusalem and Yehud, and those who were scattered abroad? How would the religious traditions of an earlier age cope with the existence of strong and stable communities located far from Jerusalem and its rebuilt temple? Central to all these questions was the interface between geography and identity. Simply put, was a return to the ancestral homeland a core element in Yahwistic identity, or was it negotiable? Was the Diaspora to be viewed as a brief, temporary aberration, or was it to be embraced as a new reality? Could the newly reconstituted community in Yehud and its rededicated temple be viewed as one among many centers of Yahwistic expression, or must they be the sole manifestation of it?[7]

In this essay, I will examine the response to questions of this sort in two significant bodies of Persian-period literature: Zech 1–8, on one hand, and Ezra–Nehemiah, on the other. I will analyze the significantly different approaches taken to the question of the Diaspora in these texts and suggest certain historical and socioreligious factors that may have contributed to the change in perspective from one to the other.

The Diaspora in the Perspective of Zechariah 1–8

The literary history of Zech 1–8 is a complex history and cannot be discussed in detail here.[8] For the purposes of this study, however, I underline the following four points. First, despite the complex redactional

---

6. The biblical text portrays an initial edict to return as having been given by Cyrus in 538 B.C.E. followed by the emigration of groups of limited number. The rebuilding and rededication of the temple are portrayed as occurring in 520 and 515, respectively (Hag 1:1–2:19; Ezra 6:15). This material has been subjected to extensive discussion (e.g., B. Becking, "'We All Returned as One!': Critical Notes on the Myth of the Mass Return," in *Judah and the Judeans in the Persian Period* [ed. O. Lipschits and M. Oeming; Winona Lake, IN: Eisenbrauns, 2006] 3–18). Ideological shaping in the texts notwithstanding, I find no reason to reject this general chronological framework. For a different approach, which situates the rebuilding of the temple in the time of Nehemiah, see D. V. Edelman, *The Origins of the 'Second' Temple: Persian Imperial Policy and the Rebuilding of Jerusalem* (London: Equinox, 2005).

7. Among the various discussions of this issue, see J. R. Phillips, "Zechariah's Vision and Joseph in Egypt: An Ancient Dialogue about Jewish Identity," *Conservative Judaism* 53 (2000) 51–61. See my discussion below on Phillips's approach to Zech 1–8 (n. 88 below).

8. I view Zech 1–8 as a distinct literary entity, separate from (albeit related to) Zech 9–14, Haggai, and Malachi. The limits of this essay preclude a discussion of these matters here.

process through which the text took its present shape, Zech 1–8 can be viewed as consisting of two major blocks of material: (1) a Sermonic Framework consisting of 1:1–6; 7:1–8:23; and (2) a Visionary-Oracular Complex consisting of 1:7–6:15. Second, it is generally agreed that, while both sections reflect complex literary development and contain both earlier and later material, the Sermonic Frame represents the work's last major compositional stage.[9] The date of this final redaction is ascribed by some to the time around 515 B.C.E.,[10] by others to the late sixth or early fifth century,[11] and by others to the mid- to late fifth century.[12] I personally favor a dating of the materials from the late sixth to mid-fifth centuries (with the possible exception of 8:20–23).[13]

Third, while significant portions of the material contained in Zech 1–8 likely date to various moments early in the period, this material has been subject to ongoing reflection.[14] Fourth, Zech 1–8 reflects a Yehudite rather than a diasporic perspective.[15] Zion is the central point

---

9. W. A. M. Beuken, *Haggai–Sacharja 1–8: Studien zur Überlieferungsgeschichte der frühnachexilischen Prophetie* (SSN 10; Assen: Van Gorcum, 1967); D. L. Petersen, *Haggai and Zechariah 1–8* (OTL; London: SCM, 1985) 124; P. L. Redditt, *Haggai, Zechariah, Malachi* (NCB; Grand Rapids: Eerdmans, 1995) 40–43.

10. C. L. Meyers and E. M. Meyers, *Haggai, Zechariah 1–8* (AB 25b; Garden City, NY: Doubleday, 1987) xlv.

11. S. Amsler, A. Lacoque, and R. Vuilleumeier, *Aggée–Zacharie 1–8, Zacharie 9–14, Malachi* (Commentaire de l'Ancien Testament 11C; Geneva: Labor et Fides, 1988) 63; A. Petitjean, *Les oracles du proto-Zacharie: Un programme de restauration pour la communauté juive après l'exil* (Études Bibliques; Paris: Gabalda / Louvain: Imprimerie Orientaliste, 1969) 440; W. Rudolph, *Haggai, Sacharja 1–8, 9–14, Malachi* (Kommentar zum Alten Testament 13/4; Gütersloh: Gütersloher Verlagshaus, 1970).

12. P. R. Ackroyd, *Exile And Restoration: A Study of Hebrew Thought of the Sixth Century B.C.* (OTL; Philadelphia: Westminster, 1968) 152; Beuken, *Haggai–Sacharja 1–8*; R. J. Coggins, *Haggai, Zechariah, Malachi* (OTG; Sheffield: JSOT Press, 1987) 31.

13. Lipiński views 8:20–23 as a much later addition, stemming from the late Persian or Hellenistic period, due to its use of the pilgrimage motif (E. Lipiński, "Recherches sur le livre de Zacharie," *VT* 20 [1970] 25–55, esp. pp. 42–46). This possibility will be considered further below (see also Petitjean, *Les oracles du proto-Zacharie*, 419–38). Mason also views 8:20–23 as distinct from the preceding material (R. A. Mason, *Preaching the Tradition: Homily and Hermeneutic after the Exile* [Cambridge: Cambridge University Press, 1990] 233).

14. T. Chary, *Aggée-Zacharie, Malachie* (Sources bibliques; Paris: Gabalda, 1969) 43. Chary observes that the older material, "is not an immutable, monolithic piece. It is, rather, the property of the community that meditates on it and completes it as new religious needs arise" (translation mine).

15. This is not to deny that the scope of the text includes the Babylonian and broader Diaspora population, indeed the whole cosmos. Redditt (*Haggai, Zechariah, Malachi*, 42) argues on the basis of 2:10–17[2:6–13] that the visions and accompanying oracles were formulated in Yehud and sent back to Babylon. Thus the exiles were the "original audience to whom the visions were directed." See also Petitjean, *Les oracles du proto-Zacharie*,

from which the world is viewed or to which the world comes. Thus Zech 1–8 may be read as a textual unity comprising ongoing theological reflection in Yehud at various moments from the late sixth to late fifth centuries and possibly beyond.

In a recent study, I have sought to demonstrate that both the Sermonic Frame and the Visionary-Oracular Complex speak from the perspective of an implied narrative continuum with respect to Israel's historical experience.[16] Briefly put, in both sections the underlying assumption is that the people of Yahweh, consisting of the inhabitants of the northern and southern kingdoms, have ignored Yahweh's word through his prophets. As a result Yahweh became exceedingly angry and dispersed them among the nations to the east and west, most significantly to Babylon. Encouraging signs at the time of the prophet's proclamation in the second year of Darius were to be seen in the people's response to Zechariah's word, the return of some members of the community to Yehud, and the purification of the temple and its priesthood. Zechariah 1–8 presents the prophet's words as being spoken to a community that exists in two primary geographical realms: people who had already returned to the homeland and those still in the Diaspora. However, despite these hopeful beginnings, the narrative still awaits the "final act," which will bring it to completion. Central to this culmination is the return to Zion by the remaining members of the Diaspora. This theme pervades both the Sermonic Frame and the Visionary-Oracular complex, which, as we have noted, both likely underwent significant rereading and ongoing reflection.[17]

127–28. Petitjean sees the purpose of 2:10–17 as being "to support the return-from-exile movement."

16. J. Kessler, "Diaspora and Homeland in the Early Achaemenid Period: Community, Geography and Demography in Zech 1–8," in *Approaching Yehud: New Approaches to the Study of the Persian Period* (ed. J. Berquist; Semeia Studies 50; Atlanta: Society of Biblical Literature, 2007) 137–66. In this paper, I will not enter into great detail regarding the positions I take on various critical and exegetical issues in Zech 1–8, since these have largely been defended in my earlier work. The reader may consult my discussion of the relevant passages there.

17. On the redaction and ongoing rereading of the prophetic texts in Yehud, see the extensive work of Ehud Ben Zvi, especially "Beginning to Address the Question: Why Were Prophetic Books Produced and 'Consumed' in Ancient Yehud," in *Historie og konstruktion: Festskrift til Niels Peter Lemche* (ed. M. Miller and T. L. Thompson; Forum for Bibelsk Eksegese 14; Copenhagen: Københavns Universitet, 2005) 30–41; idem, *Signs of Jonah: Reading and Rereading in Ancient Yehud* (JSOTSup 367; London: Sheffield Academic Press, 2003); idem, "Studying Prophetic Texts against Their Original Backgrounds: Preordained Scripts and Alternative Horizons of Research," in *Prophets and Paradigms: Essays*

Within this implied narrative continuum, matters of geography play a critical role. Geographical designations serve as highly significant markers of identity and ultimate destiny. In a profound way, they define the people of Yahweh in terms of where they are, where they have come from, and where they ultimately will be. A brief survey of the various passages in Zech 1–8 that focus on geographical designations reveals how central the theme of geographical situation is to the identity of the people of Yahweh. Setting aside the more general terms that link the community to specific territories in an indirect way,[18] we find that several explicitly territorial/geographical designations are used with reference to the community's identity and experience (past, present, and future). These include: "Judah and Jerusalem" (1:12), "Judah, Israel, and Jerusalem" (2:2[1:19]), "the land of Judah" (2:4[1:21]), "scattered to the four winds" (2:10[6]), "the north" (2:10[6]), "Babylon" (2:11[7]), "Judah and Jerusalem" (2:16[12]), "the land of the north" (6:6–8), "the golah" (6:10), "those from afar" (6:15), "Jerusalem, the cities of Judah, the Negeb and Shephelah" (7:7), "the house of Israel and the house of Judah" (8:13; "my people living in the east and the west" (8:7), "Judah and Jerusalem" (8:15), and "a man of Judah" (8:23). The most significant geographical terms are clearly "Zion" (1:14, 17; 2:11[7]; 2:14[10]; 8:2–3) and, especially, "Jerusalem" (1:12, 14, 16–17; 2:2[1:19]; 2:6[2], 8[4], 16[12]; 3:2; 7:7; 8:3, 4, 8, 15, 22).

All of this geographical emphasis is focused on the concept of the return to Judah and Zion/Jerusalem. This theme is driven home in pericope after pericope. In Zech 1:7–17, impatience with the current political status quo is expressed via the angel's complaint regarding the report that declared that all the world was found to be at peace (1:11–12). In response, the oracle in 1:13–17 declares that the situation will radically change. The critical element in this change is Yahweh's return to Zion.[19] This return will radically alter the demographics in the land. Yahweh's cities overflow with prosperity (1:17, תְּפוּצֶינָה עָרַי מִטּוֹב). The nature of this prosperity, with its demographic component will unfold as the text progresses.

---

in Honour of Gene M. Tucker (ed. S. B. Reid; JSOTSup 229; Sheffield: Sheffield Academic Press, 1996) 125–35; idem, "The Urban Centre of Jerusalem and the Development of the Literature of the Hebrew Bible," in *Urbanism in Antiquity: From Mesopotamia to Crete* (ed. W. E. Aufrecht, N. A. Mirau, and S. W. Gauley; JSOTSup 244; Sheffield: JSOT Press, 1997) 194–209.

18. These would include the terms "your ancestors" (1:2, 6), "all the people of the land" (7:5), and "the remnant of this people" (8:6, 11, 14–15)

19. The reference is to either his imminent or recent return. See the commentaries and the summary in my "Diaspora and Homeland," 153 n. 51.

In the second night vision (2:1–4[1:18–21]), the question of the exile is taken up by means of reference to the "horns that have scattered Judah, Israel and Jerusalem."[20] In 2:4[1:21] the stage is set for the undoing of this scattering through the activity of the "smiths," who will 'terrify' (Hiphil of חרד) the "horns," and ultimately 'cast them down' (Hiphil of ירה). The reference here is to the imminent destruction of the Gentile powers that dominate Judah, have scattered its inhabitants, and are detaining them in exile.

The third vision and its oracles 2:5–17[1–13] further this theme of the dismantling of the power of the horns by describing the results of the horns' demise. This may be seen in Zech 2:4–9[1–5], which describes the glorious, ultimate destiny of Jerusalem. Through the image of a measuring line, the text describes the overflowing of Jerusalem's population "like a village without walls because of the multitude [רב] of people and animals in it" (2:8[4]). The oracle in 2:10–17[6–13] indicates the source of much of this population. Exiled Judeans, described in 2:11[7] as 'Zion who resides in Babylon' (צִיּוֹן הַמָּלְטִי יוֹשֶׁבֶת בַּת־בָּבֶל),[21] are urged to flee to Zion (2:10–11[6–7]) and join Yahweh, who dwells in its midst (2:14[10]).

What is more, many Gentile nations will follow suit and join themselves to Yahweh and become his people 2:15[11]. The theme of the repopulation of the land is also taken up in the prophetic-symbolic action of 6:9–14. Here various members of the Diaspora who have returned to Yehud provide the silver and gold from which crowns are made. Especially significant here is the fact that just as these individuals have supplied precious materials from beyond Yehud for the creation of items of great material and symbolic worth for the community, so in the future, the dispersed members of the community[22] will return and provide the needed resources for the rebuilding of the temple.[23] The theme of the land's repopulation is taken up again in 7:1–8:23, a section belonging to the Sermonic Framework, as we have seen. Zechariah 7:7 looks back to a time when Jerusalem, the towns around it, the Negeb, and the Shephelah were 'inhabited and prosperous' (יֹשֶׁבֶת וּשְׁלֵוָה). Due to the

---

20. The allusion to Israel here likely implies the conquests of both Assyria and Babylon. On the text-critical and historical issues here, see M. J. Boda, "Terrifying the Horns: Persia and Babylon in Zechariah 1:7–6:15," *CBQ* 67 (2005) 22–41.

21. On the use of Zion here, see Petitjean, *Les oracles du proto-Zacharie*, 105–7.

22. Following the widely held reading of "those who are far off" as Diaspora Jews.

23. The oracle in this section was delivered either at a point early in the Persian period, before the arrival of Zerubbabel and a significant cohort, or it refers to another act of rebuilding. For the former, see M. J. Boda, *Haggai, Zechariah* (NIV Application Commentary; Grand Rapids, MI: Zondervan, 2004) 336. For the latter, Meyers and Meyers, *Haggai, Zechariah 1–8*, 364.

obstinate attitude of the people, however, the land's inhabitants were scattered among the nations (7:14). However, this situation would ultimately only be temporary. Zechariah 8:1–8 describes the future repopulation of Jerusalem in great detail. Once again Yahweh insists that it is his return to Zion that provides the basis for its repopulation (8:3 cf. 1:16; 2:14[10]).

An idyllic portrait of Jerusalem's peaceful and populous future follows in 8:4–5. The elderly will lean on their staffs, and the young will play carelessly[24]—a picture of ongoing peace and freedom from fear (note the absence of fear expressed by the expression וְאֵין מַחֲרִיד in Mic 4:4; cf. Lev 26:6; Deut 28:26; Isa 17:2; Jer 7:33; 30:10; 46:27; Ezek 34:28; 39:26; Nah 2:12[11]; Zeph 3:13). Verses 7–8 indicate the source of this population: Yahweh will deliver his people from the east and west and bring them to dwell in Jerusalem. The use of east and west here may be a merism referring to the totality of the Diaspora, or it may be an explicit reference to both the Egyptian and the Babylonian communities.[25] Ultimate peace and rest are achieved because Yahweh's people will have returned to his land, and he will once again dwell with them, and they will be his people, and he, their God (8:3, 8).

In 8:20–23, which concludes Zech 1–8, the theme of the future of Jerusalem is once again taken up, though a rather different note is struck. The text works from the perspective of the Gentile inhabitants of many cities, and many peoples and strong nations (עַמִּים רַבִּים וְגוֹיִם עֲצוּמִים; cf. Mic 4:1–5; Isa 2:1–4) who go up (הלך, בוא), to entreat the favor (חלה את־פני) of Yahweh and seek him (בקשׁ). This language is clearly rooted in the traditions of the nations' pilgrimage to Zion (cf. Mic 4:1–5; Isa 2:1–4; Zech 14:16–18).[26] The journey of the nations to Jerusalem is occasioned by the activity of an אִישׁ יְהוּדִי, probably used here with reference to an ethnic Judean who is en route to Jerusalem himself, although the reason for his travel (return to dwell in Jerusalem or pilgrimage to Jerusalem) is not revealed.[27] Thus the emphasis in

---

24. For an analysis of the various elements of the scenario, see Ackroyd, *Exile and Restoration*, 212.

25. Meyers and Meyers, *Haggai, Zechariah 1–8*, 418; Ackroyd, *Exile and Restoration*, 213.

26. Cf. M. D. Knowles, *Centrality Practiced: Jerusalem in the Religious Practice of Yehud and the Diaspora in the Persian Period* (Archaeology and Biblical Studies 15; Atlanta: Society of Biblical Literature, 2006) 80.

27. See Esth 2:5 and Lipiński, "Recherches sur le Livre de Zacharie," 42–43. Note also the discussion in H. Schmid, "Die 'Juden' im Alten Testament," in *Wort und Wirklichkeit: Studien zur Afrikanstik und Orientalistik* (ed. B. Benzing, O. Bocher, and G. Mayer; Meisenheim am Glan: Hain, 1976) 17–29, esp. p. 25. Schmid maintains that the context here

this pericope seems to be on the motif of pilgrimage to Jerusalem by the Gentiles, rather than on the return of the Diaspora, as elsewhere in Zech 1–8. This would bear out the suggestion that 8:20–23 constitutes a separate perspective.[28]

In sum then, the joint concepts of the return of the Diaspora and the repopulation of Jerusalem loom exceedingly large in Zech 1–8. From the perspective of Zech 1–8, the Diaspora is quite simply the visible manifestation of the people's rebellion and Yahweh's judgment. It originated in the people's unwillingness to obey the word of Yahweh, which resulted in his scattering of them (7:11–14). The Diaspora's existence is thus fundamentally anomalous. This is profoundly reflected in 2:12[7], where "Zion" is seen as dwelling in Babylon. The comment of Petitjean captures this anomaly and ambiguity. He states: "The use of Zion to designate the deportees in Babylon serves to place the dramatic situation created by the exile in stark relief. Israel has been snatched away from its land and from the religious center that Yahweh has assigned to his people—Jerusalem and the hill of Zion. Put another way, Zion is no more in Zion."[29] As such then, given the return of Yahweh to dwell in Jerusalem and the possibility for a return on the part of the former inhabitants of the northern and southern kingdoms, our prophet and his editor(s) can see absolutely no future for the Diaspora in any form. All will return, and all will dwell in the land.[30]

The Diaspora in the Perspective
of Ezra–Nehemiah

When we turn to Ezra–Nehemiah, a very different picture of the Diaspora emerges. The historical and redactional questions regarding these texts are legion. For our present purposes, it is sufficient to say that, despite some recent attempts to view this work as a product of the

---

is eschatological, and the Judean in question is returning to dwell in Yehud. This, however, is to read 8:23 in the light of passages such as Zech 2:6–12[10–14] and Isa 60, which feature a definitive return of the Diaspora. However, as Mason and Lipiński suggest (see n. 28) and the parallels with Isa 2 and Mic 4 indicate, the passage probably reflects a later moment, one in which Gentiles join Jewish pilgrims in their journey to Jerusalem.

28. Lipiński, "Recherches sur le livre de Zacharie," esp. pp. 42–44; Mason, *Preaching the Tradition*, 233.

29. Petitjean, *Les oracles du proto-Zacharie*, 106. Translation mine.

30. For an evaluation of the idealistic nature of this vision of the future and its tradition-historical roots, see my "Diaspora and Homeland," esp. pp. 157–66.

Hellenistic age, a mid- or late fourth-century date is still widely held.[31] In any case, it may be argued that whatever the date of the latest redaction, the substance of the text reflects Persian-period concerns.[32] We noted above that the perspective of Zech 1–8 is rooted in an implied narrative continuum, according to which the return of the exiles and the passing out of existence of the Diaspora is the endpoint. In Ezra–Nehemiah the reader also encounters an underlying narrative continuum; however, it is one in which the Diaspora plays quite a significantly different role. The narrative motif appears in two ways: first in the events narrated in the texts themselves, and second, in the words spoken by characters in the narration. Let us examine these in turn.

Regarding the events narrated in Ezra–Nehemiah, there is a recurring motif[33] of pious members of the Babylonian Diaspora returning to Yehud to fulfill important purposes, specifically with regard to the rebuilding of the temple, the restoration of true worship, the rebuilding of cities and towns, and the undertaking of religious reforms.[34] Thus in the first unit, Ezra 1–6, in response to Yahweh's stirring, Cyrus issues a decree encouraging members of Yahweh's people to "go up"[35] to Jerusalem to build his house (Ezra 1:1–3). Much discussion surrounds the issue of whether the allusion to the "men of their place" (1:4) who financially support the returnees refers to Jews who remain or to Gen-

---

31. *Hellenistic age*: L. Grabbe, "The 'Persian Documents' in the Book of Ezra: Are they Authentic?" in *Judah and the Judeans in the Persian Period* (ed. O. Lipschits and M. Oeming; Winona Lake, IN: Eisenbrauns, 2006) 531–70. *Fourth century*: H. G. M. Williamson, *Ezra, Nehemiah* (WBC 16; Waco, TX: Word, 1985) xxxv–xxxvi.

32. J. Blenkinsopp, *Ezra–Nehemiah: A Commentary* (OTL; Philadelphia: Westminster, 1988) 38.

33. On Ezra 1–Neh 7 as three "chapters" with similar motifs, see Williamson, *Ezra, Nehemiah*, xlix. Note also the structural analysis of B. Porten, "Theme and Structure of Ezra 1–6: From Literature to History," *Transeu* 23 (2002) 27–44.

34. In the present essay, I cannot discuss the process of reframing that resulted in the conviction that Babylonian Diaspora constituted the "holy seed" and "true Israel." On this matter, see E. Ben Zvi, "Inclusion in and Exclusion from 'Israel' in Post-Monarchic Biblical Texts," in *The Pitcher Is Broken: Memorial Essays for Gösta W. Ahlström* (ed. S. W. Holloway and L. K. Handy; JSOTSup 190; Sheffield: Sheffield Academic Press, 1995) 95–149; S. Japhet, "The Concept of the 'Remnant' in the Restoration Period: On the Vocabulary of Self-Definition," *From the Rivers of Babylon to the Highlands of Judah: Collected Studies on the Restoration Period* (Winona Lake, IN: Eisenbrauns, 2006) 432–49.

35. Hebrew וַיַּעַל. This use of *aliyah* language contrasts with the verbs יָשַׁב and בוא, which are used in Zech 1–8 for a return to dwell in Jerusalem (Zech 2:8[4]; 6:10, 15; 8:4, 8). While 8:22 does employ בוא, the use of הלך in 8:21, 23 (הלך is used nowhere else in Zech 1–8 for the return to Zion) and the general perspective of this oracle witnesses to the difference between its ideological orientation and the rest of Zech 1–8; cf. pp. 126–127 above.

tile neighbors. While the matter is by no means easy to decide, with Williamson and many others I favor the former position.[36] If this is the case, the Diaspora members are viewed as standing in solidarity with the returnees, despite their remaining behind.[37]

Thus certain members of the Babylonian golah, whose spirits God had stirred, prepared to return to Jerusalem to build its temple (1:5). They were further aided in this by their Gentile neighbors, who also gave them silver and gold, and by King Cyrus, who handed over to the exiles the temple vessels that Nebuchadnezzar had taken (1:5–11). Ezra 2 continues with an extensive list of these individuals from the captivity (Heb. שְׁבִי; cf. Ezra 2:1; 3:8; 8:35; 9:7; Neh 1:3; 7:6; 8:17), who were exiled (Hiphil of גלה; cf. Ezra 2:1; 4:10; 5:12; Neh 7:6) by Nebuchadnezzar and were now 'going up' (Heb. עלה; cf. Ezra 1:5, 11; 2:1, 59; 7:6, 7, 28; 8:35; Neh 7:6, 61; 12:1, 31) and returning (Heb. שׁוב; cf. Ezra 2:1; 6:21) to Jerusalem and Judah (2:1, 70). Ezra 3:1–13 relates that these returnees reconsecrated the altar, celebrated Sukkot, began regular offerings and the rebuilding of the temple, and reinstituted the proper offices of the temple personnel. This was done despite the terror (3:3) and opposition (4:5, 6–24) of the peoples of the land,[38] with whom they eschewed any association (4:1–4).

Despite some initial delays as a result of this opposition during the reign of Cyrus (Ezra 4:24), the temple building was resumed and completed and rededicated in the reign of Darius (5:1–15). The narrative culminates in the celebration of the Passover by the entire community,

---

36. E. J. Bickerman, "The Edict of Cyrus in Ezra 1," *JBL* 65 (1946) 249–75, esp. p. 259; S. Japhet, "Postexilic Historiography: How and Why?" *From the Rivers of Babylon to the Highlands of Judah*, 307–30, esp. p. 318 n. 29; Williamson, *Ezra, Nehemiah*, 14–15. See also L. C. Allen and T. S. Laniak, *Ezra, Nehemiah, Esther* (NIBCOT 9; Peabody, MA: Hendrickson / Carlisle: Paternoster, 2003) 17–18. Allen and others decide the matter on the analogy of the exodus traditions in which the Egyptian neighbors of the departing Israelites offer them silver and gold as they leave Egypt (Exod 11:2). Notice, however, that in the Exodus passage, people who give gifts are the neighbors (רֵעַ), whereas in Ezra 1:4, the reference is to the אַנְשֵׁי מְקֹמוֹ. This phrase is used frequently in Ezra–Nehemiah for fellow Israelites (Ezra 2:2, 22, 23, 27, 28;10:9; Neh 3:2, 7, 22; 4:23; 7:7, 26–33; 11:6; cf. also 1 Chr 4:12 and widely in Chronicles). I note in passing that this tradition obtains in the widespread naming of synagogues in the New World with reference to the origins of their founders; thus for example, the *Anshe Minsk* synagogues in Manhattan and Toronto.

37. There can be no doubt that the implied narrative in Ezra–Nehemiah presupposes that not all the community returned, because the Diaspora members will go on to play significant roles later in the story.

38. On the chronological and literary questions regarding this section, see Williamson, *Ezra, Nehemiah*, 57–60.

with special direction given by the priests and Levites (6:19–22).[39] It should be noted that in Ezra 1–6, after 1:11, the scene shifts entirely to Jerusalem and Yehud. No further mention is made of the people who remained in Babylon. Similarly, aside from the allusion in 6:21, reference to any orthodox Yahwists who may have remained in the land and whose existence is discernible from various other biblical texts[40] is studiously avoided.

The book's next major section, chaps. 7–10, repeats this basic structure of the departure from Diaspora and return to Yehud of a select group of faithful Yahwists, with the support of their co-religionists who remained in the east. Ezra 7 begins this theme with the person of Ezra. Various epithets and qualifiers are used to describe his piety, orthodoxy, and fitness to undertake needed religious direction and reform of the community in Yehud. He is accorded an extensive priestly genealogy, linking him back as far as Aaron (7:1–5). He is described as a "ready scribe" in the law of Moses that Yahweh, the God of Israel, had given (7:6).[41] His journey proves successful due to "the gracious hand of his God" (7:9). Again, to underline his piety and orthodoxy, Ezra is said to have "set his heart" to "seek" the law of Yahweh to do it, and to teach its statutes and ordinances in Israel (7:10).[42] No explanation is given about how he came to possess this knowledge and exper-

---

39. Ezra 6:21 probably reveals that the exclusion of the Yehudite remainees was not as all encompassing as the rest of Ezra presents it. The text bears witness to a modality of inclusion whereby the remainees could be "counted" as members of the golah community. On the strategies of exclusion and inclusion in Persian-period literature, with bibliography, see my "Persia's Loyal Yahwists," esp. pp. 107–12.

40. On this matter, see the classic studies of the period: Ackroyd, *Exile and Restoration*; E. Jannssen, *Juda in der Exilszeit: Ein Beitrag zur Frage der Entstehung des Judentums* (FRLANT 69; Göttingen: Vandenhoeck & Ruprecht, 1956).

41. The word מָהִיר in this case probably means 'skillful' or 'wise'. Similarly, the scribe is one who is competent to understand and teach the law. See Williamson, *Ezra, Nehemiah*, 92. Williamson also discusses the historical issues involved in the reference to the "law of Moses." Whatever the historical referents may be, Ezra is being presented as a pious, devout, and supremely orthodox Yahwist.

42. 'Set his heart' הֵכִין לְבָבוֹ; compare the similar expression, שִׂים לֵב, in Hag 1:5, 7. 'Seek' דרשׁ. Note the frequent use of this verb for piety in Chronicles (e.g., 1 Chr 10:13–14; 16:11; 22:19; 28:8; 2 Chr 12:14; 14:4; 19:3). 'The law of Yahweh . . . statutes and ordinances' אֶת־תּוֹרַת יְהוָה וְלַעֲשֹׂת וּלְלַמֵּד בְּיִשְׂרָאֵל חֹק וּמִשְׁפָּט. This description is couched in typical Deuteronomistic phraseology. On the use of Priestly and Deuteronomistic traditions in the Babylonian and Persian periods, see M. J. Boda, "Confession as Theological Expression: Ideological Origins of Penitential Prayer," in *Seeking the Favor of God*, vol. 1: *The Origins of Penitential Prayer in Second Temple Judaism* (ed. M. J. Boda, D. K. Falk, and R. A. Werline; Early Judaism and Its Literature 21; Atlanta: Society of Biblical Literature, 2006) 21–50.

tise in the law, but it probably proceeds from the narrator's assumption that this knowledge remained intact and uncorrupted among the Diaspora members who instructed him in it.

The following section (7:11–21) further emphasizes Ezra's qualifications for his role, and his piety. He is described as a priest and scribe learned in matters of the commandments of Yahweh and his statutes for Israel (7:11). This perspective is carried on through Artaxerxes' letter. There Ezra is referred to as a priest and scribe of the law of the God of heaven (7:12).[43] The text furthermore takes pains to note that Ezra's specific role is to inquire regarding the situation in Jerusalem and Judah vis-à-vis the law of God and to bring royal gifts for the temple (7:14; cf. 8:25–30). The king further commends Ezra to the treasurers in *Abar Nahara* using the term "scribe of the law of God" (7:21). He also gives Ezra the mission of instructing all the Yahwists in the province in matters of obedience to the "law of your God and law of the King," via the appointment of local magistrates, on pain of severe punishment for disobedience (7:26).[44]

The culminating testimony to Ezra's orthodoxy and piety in this section is his own prayer in 7:27–28. In it another side of Ezra is shown. He is not only a scribe and teacher of the law, as evidenced in the descriptions of him but also a pious Yahwist who displays gratitude and dependence on Yahweh, as well as joy at the prospect of the beautification of the temple. A similar perspective is manifested in Ezra's rejection of royal protection for his journey, his concern for Yahweh's reputation before the king, and his proclamation of a fast in order to seek divine protection en route (8:21–23). It is apposite at this point to reiterate the fact that, despite the larger framework of the book's

---

43. Williamson, following de Vaux, views the term "priest and scribe of the law of the God of heaven" as a reference to an official role in the Persian Empire (R. de Vaux, "Les décrets de Cyrus et de Darius sur la reconstruction du temple," *RB* 46 [1937] 29–57; Williamson, *Ezra, Nehemiah,* 100). This presupposes that the Artaxerxes letter in this case reflects Persian usage, rather than a Yahwistic theological overlay. Either way, Ezra is being commended as a skilled and faithful Yahwist.

44. On the specifics of what this entailed, and the diverse historical issues it raises, see G. N. Knoppers, "An Achaemenid Imperial Authorization of Torah in Yehud?" in *Persia and Torah: The Theory of Imperial Authorization of the Pentateuch* (ed. J. W. Watts; SBLSymS 17; Atlanta: Society of Biblical Literature, 2001) 115–34; H. H. D. Mantel, "The Dichotomy of Judaism during the Second Temple," *HUCA* 44 (1973) 55–87; R. North, "Civil Authority in Ezra," in *Studi in onore di Eduardo Volterra* (Milan: Giuffrè, 1971) 377–404; H. G. M. Williamson, "Exile and After: Historical Study," in *Faces of Old Testament Study* (ed. B. T. Arnold; Grand Rapids, MI: Baker, 1999); idem, "Judah and the Jews," in *Studies in Persian History: Essays in Memory of David M. Lewis* (ed. A. Kuhrt; Achaemenid History 11; Leiden: Nederlands Instituut voor het Nabije Oosten, 1998) 145–63.

insistence that it was people whose spirits Yahweh had stirred up who left for Jerusalem at an earlier time (Ezra 1:5), this does not translate into a critique of individuals who remained. Ezra, a product of the community that remained in the east, is a picture of Yahwistic piety in his honoring of the law and temple and his humble dependence upon Yahweh.[45]

The theme of pious Yahwists returning to Yehud is expanded to include others who will accompany Ezra on his journey. The king thus grants permission for those of the people of Israel who freely offer themselves to return to Jerusalem (7:13).[46] Thus Ezra stands at the head of a group of Israelites, including priests and Levites, singers and doorkeepers, who left their fellows (7:7)[47] and 'went up' (עלה, 7:6–7) from Babylon to Jerusalem, leaving in the first month and arriving five months later (7:8). However, this departure does not presuppose that Ezra took with him all of the remaining Yahwists in the east. In 7:16 we find an allusion to the offerings of the people who do not go but choose to remain (cf. 1:4). Similarly, in 7:28, Ezra gathers "from Israel"[48] certain leaders to accompany him to Jerusalem.

As was the case in Ezra 1–6, following a list of those who returned (8:1–20, cf. 2:1–63), and various details regarding the transport of the offerings for the temple (8:24–30, cf. 2:64–70), the rest of the narrative of Ezra 7–10 switches its focus of attention to the situation in Yehud and to the activities of Ezra and his companions there. Special attention is devoted to the separation of the returnees from other communities, especially heterodox and unfit Yahwists, and the preservation of "a holy seed" (Ezra 9–10). No further mention is made of any interchange between homeland and Diaspora.

The same perspective and motif repeats itself, although in an abbreviated fashion, in the next "chapter" of Ezra–Nehemiah, Neh 1–7.[49]

---

45. Clines appropriately comments, "It must have been difficult for those [who returned] not to imagine themselves more dedicated to the will of God than those who remained behind in Babylon. But from [their] descendants . . . came the two great leaders of the Judean community"; D. J. A. Clines, *Ezra, Nehemiah, Esther* (NCB; London: Marshall, Morgan and Scott, 1984) 107.

46. Reading מן partitively—that is, 'from among'. 'Who freely offer themselves' כָּל־מִתְנַדֵּב. The root denotes willingness and choice; see *HALOT* נדב (671b).

47. The word מן here should also be understood partitively, indicating 'some of'.

48. 'Assembled leading men in Israel to go with me' וָאֶקְבְּצָה מִיִּשְׂרָאֵל רָאשִׁים לַעֲלוֹת עִמִּי. Again מן is to be taken partitively.

49. On the literary shape of the final form of the narrative, see Allen and Laniak, *Ezra, Nehemiah, Esther* 6–8; Williamson, *Ezra, Nehemiah*, xxxix–xliv. On the more inclusive stance toward non-exiled Judeans here, see Japhet, "Concept of the "Remnant,"" esp. p. 438.

Once again we begin with a Yahwist, Nehemiah, whose orthodoxy and piety are revealed through his reaction to the sorry state of Jerusalem (1:2–2:8). Upon learning of this terrible state of affairs, his piety, like Ezra's, is manifested through his sitting, weeping, mourning, and fasting before God (1:4). This is followed by an account of his prayer of penitence and request for God's grace before the Persian king (1:5–11).[50] His piety is similarly revealed through his sad appearance at the royal court (2:2), his concern for the fate of his ancestral home (2:3–5), and his attribution of his success before the king to the hand of God (2:8). He requests that he be sent to Jerusalem by the king (2:5). His request is granted, and the text moves immediately to his arrival there (2:10).

The rest of Neh 1–7 is concerned with similar matters to those in Ezra 1–6 and 7–10: opposition from without (Neh 2:10, 19; 4:1–3, 7; 6:1–14) and reformation of the internal life of the community (Neh 5:1–13; 7:1–5). The motif of a Diaspora member returning to put things right also reappears near the climax of Ezra–Nehemiah, in Neh 13:4–9.[51] Once again, left to itself the community in Yehud exhibits a failure to maintain the proper boundaries of sanctity and is guilty of fraternizing with the enemy. This is seen through Eliashib's allowing Tobiah to use a storeroom in the temple (normally used for holy objects and tithes) for his own personal belongings. Once again the situation is resolved via a reformer from the east, in the person of Nehemiah, who has been called away and subsequently returns.[52] He remedies the situation by expelling Tobiah and his goods, reconsecrating the temple chamber, and restoring it to its proper use.

As was the case with Ezra, no explanation is given for the origins of Nehemiah's piety or orthodoxy. It is assumed, however, that the necessary knowledge to inform these qualities was present and available to him in the east. Furthermore, as in the Ezra narrative, the reader is probably meant to assume that this knowledge has been faithfully and meticulously preserved and passed down, despite the geographical and chronological distance that separated the Babylonian/Elamite Diaspora from its geographical roots. It must be acknowledged that unlike the "returns" in Ezra 2 and 7–8, Neh 1–7 and 13:4–9 do not

---

50. Penitential prayer has received significant attention in recent years. See M. J. Boda, D. K. Falk, and R. A. Werline, eds., *Seeking the Favor of God*, vol. 1: *The Origins of Penitential Prayer in Second Temple Judaism* (Early Judaism and Its Literature 21; Atlanta: Society of Biblical Literature, 2006).

51. On the literary structuring of Neh 12:44–13:14, see Williamson, *Ezra, Nehemiah*, 380–84.

52. On the historical matters here, see ibid., 382–33.

portray Nehemiah as returning with other Yahwists or divulge any details regarding others who may have remained in the east. Nevertheless, the description of the arrival of Hannai and his companions in Susa (Neh 1:2), bringing news of Jerusalem's state to Nehemiah seems to presuppose that these individuals have come not simply to see Nehemiah. Rather, they are returning to a larger community of which they had formerly been a part.[53]

In sum then, the narrative portions of the books of Ezra and Nehemiah present Diaspora-Homeland relations in the following terms. The Diaspora consists of a larger group of Yahwists who have been exiled to the east. Certain members of this group, whose hearts Yahweh has stirred, leave and move permanently to Yehud. Various members of this group carry out the restoration of several aspects of civil and religious life in Yehud, frequently occupying highly significant roles. They depart with the support of their communities in the Diaspora. The returnees, especially Ezra and Nehemiah, are portrayed as orthodox Yahwists who are qualified to undertake the leadership of the community in Yehud. Although not explicitly stated, we should assume that these individuals are fit for their roles because they have been schooled in the law of Moses, that is to say, "orthodox" Yahwism, which was preserved in the community in Babylon and restored to Yehud through the golah returnees.[54] This is in contradistinction to all other Yahwists, who do not qualify as heirs of the community of old.[55] The narrative nowhere criticizes the Diaspora members who remain in the east and is utterly silent regarding the future return of the Diaspora.

53. The normal place of residence of these individuals and the reason for their contact with Nehemiah is not specified. Williamson (*Ezra, Nehemiah,* 171) suggests the possibility that they may have come from Yehud as an official delegation "specifically to request that [Nehemiah] press the Jewish case at court." Similarly, M. Boda (personal communication) suggests that imperial support for Yehud may have waned in the later years of the empire. Thus the community in Yehud sent delegates to the east to reinforce ties with the Babylonian remainees and through them to have influence at the imperial court. These suggestions, though speculative, fit well with my own understanding of the golah returnees as a "Charter Group" (on which, see below). I am grateful to M. Boda for his suggestions here and at various points in the present study.

54. On the interpretive role of this group, see Williamson, *Ezra, Nehemiah,* xxxix.

55. This continuity is especially symbolized through Ezra's bringing of the temple vessels back to Jerusalem (Ezra 7:19). On the importance of the temple vessels, see P. R. Ackroyd's older but programmatic essay, "The Temple Vessels: A Continuity Theme," in *Studies in the Religion of Ancient Israel* (ed. H. Ringgren et al.; VTSup 23; Leiden: Brill, 1972) 166–81. On the temple-vessel theme in Chronicles, see G. N. Knoppers, "Treasures Won and Lost: Royal (Mis)appropriations in Kings and Chronicles," in *The Chronicler as Author* (ed. M. P. Graham and S. L. McKenzie; JSOTSup 263; Sheffield: Sheffield Academic Press, 1999) 181–208.

A second perspective may be found within the reported speech of the various protagonists at various moments in the narrative described above, chiefly in the prayers of its key figures. Like Zech 1–8, these prayers attribute the destruction of Jerusalem and exile of its citizens under Nebuchadnezzar to the people's rejection of Yahweh's ways (Ezra 5:11–12; 9:7, 13; Neh 1:6–9; 9:29–37). The extended prayers in Ezra 9 and Neh 9 serve as vehicles for the expression of the community's understanding of its present circumstances and its hopes for the future.[56] Thus Ezra's prayer in Ezra 9 affirms that, despite some encouraging beginnings (referred to in 9:8–10), especially the presence of a remnant in the land (9:8, 13), the effects of the exile have not yet come to an end.[57] This is seen in Ezra's words to the effect that "until this day" the community of Yahweh (and here he likely refers to both the Babylonian golah and the returnee community already in Jerusalem)[58] continues to be at the mercy of foreign kings and subject to captivity, pillage, and shame (9:7). Even the restoration community of repatriates is viewed as "slaves in bondage" (9:8–9).

In the logic of the prayer, the community in Yehud is seen as the manifestation of Yahweh's favor (9:8). This favor is especially manifested in his activity in influencing Israel's Persian overlords to permit the rebuilding of the Jerusalemite temple (9:9). The mention of the rehabilitation of temple and city here constitutes the apex of Yahweh's gracious activity (in contrast to Zech 1–8, where the Diaspora's return to Zion constitutes the culmination). It therefore appears that in this context the primary significance of the presence of the restoration community in Yehud lay in its role as an exemplary, pristine, and holy community, able to implement fully Yahweh's statutes (especially in cultic matters) and to care for the temple and holy city (perhaps as an emerging pilgrimage site for the Diaspora). No mention is made of the

---

56. On the provenance of the prayers and their literary history, see below. Whatever their origin, they are redactionally used as a means of expressing the community's self-understanding and religious expression.

57. See Williamson (*Ezra, Nehemiah*, 128) for the view that the prayer here was specifically composed for its present context, as well as bibliography on contrary positions. Note especially the phrase לְהַשְׁאִיר לָנוּ פְּלֵיטָה 'left us a remnant' in 9:8. On this expression, see Japhet, "Concept of the "Remnant, 439–41"; Williamson, *Ezra, Nehemiah*, 135. The aspects of Ezra's prayer that allude to the effects of the exile not yet being at an end are very similar to the perspective in sections of Zech 1–8, where the community perceives itself to be on the cusp of the end of the "seventy years" of exile, signaled by the destruction of Babylon and return of the exiled population; see esp. Zech 1:12–17; 2:10–16[6–12]; 7:5.

58. Cf. Williamson, *Ezra, Nehemiah*, 135.

return of all the Diaspora members to dwell in a small and impoverished Yehud.

A very similar perspective may be seen in the prayer of confession
in Neh 9:6–37.[59] This passage recognizes that, although the nation
merited total annihilation for its sins, Yahweh's judgment was not absolute, and in his mercy a remnant was left (9:16–31). Yet, despite this
gracious restraint, the situation of this remnant in the land is miser-
able. The community is described as subject to foreign control of the
fruit of its own labor as well as the offering of its animals and the produce of the land (9:36–37). Thus, despite being permitted to return to
the land,[60] the people are "slaves . . . in great distress" (9:36–37). Most
telling however, is the reference to the ongoing oppression as occurring 'because of our sins' בְּחַטֹּאותֵינוּ; v. 37). This stress on the ongoing
punishment despite restoration lies at the heart of the prayer. The logic
is that, because the community still labors in slavery and oppression,
Yahweh has not fully pardoned; thus prayer is needed. The prayer culminates in the request that Yahweh not view the community's distress
as insignificant (9:32) but forgive and grant relief from the oppressive
aspects of Persian rule (9:32; 36–37). The prayer contains no explicit expression of hope regarding the future of the Diaspora.[61] The closest allusion to any future return to the land is found in 9:35–36, which refers

---

59. For a detailed examination of Neh 9 from the perspective of tradition criticism,
see M. J. Boda, *Praying the Tradition: The Origin and Use of Tradition in Nehemiah 9* (BZAW
277; Berlin: de Gruyter, 1999). On the specific matter of the attitude toward Persian rule
in Neh 9, with bibliography and a nontraditional solution, see M. Oeming, " 'See, We Are
Serving Today' (Nehemiah 9:36): Nehemiah 9 as a Theological Interpretation of the Persian Period," in *Judah and the Judeans in the Persian Period* (ed. O. Lipschits and M. Oeming;
Winona Lake, IN: Eisenbrauns, 2006) 571–88.

60. Does the prayer in Neh 9 assume a dispersion and subsequent return? Much depends on one's view of the date of its formulation. If, with Boda, we see it as a product of
the early Persian period, reflecting both the remainees and returnees together, then exile
and partial return may be implied (Boda, *Praying the Tradition*, 190–95). If, however, we
assume that the prayer was an expression of non-exiled Yahwists in the Babylonian period, concepts of that sort would be foreign, and the reference would be simply to the
disobedience of the ancestors once in the land and the subsequent judgment. See
H. G. M. Williamson, "Structure and Historiography in Nehemiah 9," in *Proceedings of
the Ninth World Congress of Jewish Studies*, Panel Sessions: *Bible Studies and Ancient Near
East* (ed. M. Goshen-Gottstein and D. Assaf; Jerusalem: Magnes, 1988) 117–32. In any
case, for the final editor's purpose, the context of dispersion and return is to be assumed
(see Williamson, *Ezra, Nehemiah*, 309).

61. The absence of any explicit mention of the return of the Diaspora is striking, especially if, as Boda argues, the prayer originally stems from the earliest moments of the restoration, when expectations were more lively (Boda, *Praying the Tradition*, 193–96). Was
this element of the tradition suppressed when it was incorporated into its later context?

to Yehud as "the spacious and fertile land that you gave our ancestors so that they might eat its fruit and goodness." Yet even this contains no explicit mention of a full return of the Diaspora.

In sum then, in Ezra–Nehemiah, both in the events narrated and in the reported speech of its principal characters, the Babylonian/Elamite Diaspora is viewed as the locus and repository of orthodox Yahwism. At various moments, leaders and groups move from Diaspora to homeland in fulfillment of Yahweh's purposes. However at no point is there any critique of the people who remain, nor is there any reference to Yahweh's imminent intervention, the end of the Diaspora, and a full return to Zion. This stands in stark contrast to Zech 1–8, a text which, like many other earlier traditions (e.g., Hos 11:10–11; Isa 43:5; chap. 60; Jer 30:10; 31:8; 46:27; cf. also Tob 14:1–7), forcefully expresses the hope of the full return of the exiles. Ezra–Nehemiah's silence regarding the present status and ultimate future of the Diaspora is highly remarkable.

Toward the Acceptance of the Diaspora as an Authentic Expression of Yahwism

We are thus confronted with two distinct visions of homeland and Diaspora. In the first, manifested in Zech 1–8, which reflects the perspectives of the late sixth to mid-fifth centuries, the Diaspora is a fundamentally aberrant phenomenon—a manifestation of the brokenness of the relationship between Yahweh and his people. As such, no other destiny is feasible than its ultimate dissolution by a full and definitive return to Zion on the part of all Diaspora members. The foundational narrative continuum in it is thus: sin > judgment > dispersion > partial return to the land > cataclysmic intervention of Yahweh > full return and end of Diaspora.

Ezra–Nehemiah, which reflects the ideological preoccupations of the fourth century, presents a rather different view. It shares with Zech 1–8 the view that the people of Yahweh are the individuals who are genealogically related to the former inhabitants of the land and who through their own rebellion incurred the wrath of Yahweh and were consequently exiled from it. However, here the perspective diverges. Unlike the Zecharian perspective, wherein the exiles will be gathered "from the east and the west" (Zech 8:7), here the Diaspora is limited to the Babylonian/eastern Diaspora, and the land is viewed as empty.[62]

---

62. Ezra 6:21 and Neh 1:1–3 are more inclusive; see Japhet, "Concept of the Remnant," esp. p. 438.

No other Yahwists retain any theological significance. The golah group has preserved the true knowledge of Yahweh and constitutes the "holy seed"—the Yahwists who are the repository of Yahweh's earlier promises and the new kernel from which he will bring forth a New People to establish in the land. And although a portion of the eastern Diaspora members had returned to the land, they experienced suffering and servitude. From this position of suffering and distress, they confess their sins and pray for forgiveness and relief from the oppression of their overlords. The scenario in Ezra–Nehemiah may thus be presented as: sin > judgment > dispersion > skimming off of a portion of the exiles and their resettlement in Babylon/Elam > return of a portion of these to the land > oppression in the land > prayer for relief in the land. The silence in Ezra–Nehemiah regarding the future of the remainder of the returnees' co-religionists in the east is striking and profound. This is especially true in light of the fact that this group was conceived of as the matrix of the returnee community, the one location where the true knowledge of Yahweh was kept alive, and the place from which the community's most important leaders emerged to reform it when it was in dire danger of losing its way.[63]

What is to be made of this silence, and what does it imply? In one response to this question, Sara Japhet has suggested that this omission reflects the theological insignificance of these eastern remainees:

> The position of Ezra–Nehemiah on the most fundamental issues of identity and continuity is characterized by a view of partial and restricted connection with the past. In terms of identity the book professes a distinct definition of "we," the community in which Israel's existence and survival is represented. This is the community of the "Exile," the people from Judah, Benjamin and Levi who came to settle in Judah. Ezra–Nehemiah displays no interest in the fortunes of the Diaspora as such. The Jews of the Diaspora are referred to primarily as a "source" of returnees . . . and financial means.[64]

While it is quite accurate to say that Ezra–Nehemiah focuses its attention on the returnee community in the land, our analysis above indicates that in Ezra–Nehemiah the Babylonian remainee community is portrayed as playing a highly significant role. Thus I believe it to be unlikely that the framer of Ezra–Nehemiah views them with utter disinterest and consigns them to the same oblivion as the ten northern tribes and the Judean remainees. Given the prevalence of hopes for the

---

63. See P. R. Bedford, "Diaspora: Homeland Relations in Ezra–Nehemiah," *VT* 52 (2002) 147–65, esp. pp. 152–56.

64. Japhet, "Postexilic Historiography," esp. p. 318.

return of the Diaspora, the absence of any such discussion must be rooted in other motives.

Bedford has proposed an alternative interpretation. He suggests that the omission of the theme of a universal return in Ezra–Nehemiah is rooted in Diaspora-homeland relations.[65] Bedford uses a colonial model to describe these relations.[66] In this model, the returnees are an extension or "colony" of the Diaspora community who have been sent to resettle the homeland.[67] Bedford then goes on to argue that the emphasis on strict separation from the nondeported population in Ezra–Nehemiah reflects, at least in part, a concern on the part of the people who remained in Babylon to protect their status and influence in Yehud. Such control was particularly threatened due to the growing links between the non-exiled Yahwists and the returnees, giving the former group growing leverage in the power balance in Yehud. [68] Thus for Bedford, the Babylonian remainees continued to exert control over the social, religious, and political dimensions of life in Yehud. Bedford's analysis has much to commend it. He is correct in his emphasis on the profoundly significant religious role that is played by members of the Diaspora community (Joshua, Zerubbabel, Sheshbazzar, Ezra, and Nehemiah). He notes that the role of these individuals is especially important in the narratives about the work of Ezra and Nehemiah, who successfully intervene in contexts where the local leadership has let the situation go astray and seems incapable of correcting it without assistance from the Babylonian Diaspora.

However, Bedford's reconstruction may be open to question at two significant points. The first concerns the high degree of contact that he appears to presuppose between homeland and Diaspora. Close, frequent contact would be necessary if the Babylonian remainees were to exercise the kind of "hands-on" control assumed by Bedford. Is close contact demonstrable? Various biblical texts do allow us to glimpse some contact between homeland and Diaspora (e.g., Jer 29; 51:59–60; Zech 2:10–17[6–13]; Ezek 24:1–2; 26–27; 33:21; Neh 1:2–3; 6:9–15).[69]

---

65. Bedford, "Diaspora: Homeland Relations."

66. He states, "[I]n Ezra–Nehemiah the community of repatriates is not in a position to develop an identity independent of its parent Diaspora community . . . the two form a single people, albeit in an unequal relationship of parent community and colony" (Bedford, "Diaspora: Homeland Relations," 158).

67. Ibid., 159.

68. Ibid., 161–63.

69. On this, see B. Oded, "Exile-Homeland Relations during the Exilic Period and Restoration," in *Teshurot LaAvishur: Studies in the Bible and the Ancient Near East, Hebrew and Semitic Languages* (ed. M. Heltzer and M. Malul; Tel-Aviv: Archaeological Center,

Nevertheless, it is impossible to extrapolate to what degree these passages represent regular or exceptional contacts.

The second objection concerns the degree of dependence manifested by the golah returnees toward their co-religionists in the east with regard to leadership and polity. Oded comments,

> Bedford justifiably emphasizes the continuing connections and unequal interdependence between homeland and exile. . . . Nevertheless it goes beyond the evidence and is even hazardous to conclude, "as a colony of the Babylonian exiles, the community of repatriates remained dependent on the Diaspora for leadership and for instruction in religious culture and practice."[70]

To this may be added the fact that Ezra–Nehemiah does not appear to portray Ezra and Nehemiah as acting as agents for a broader Diaspora community, but rather as individuals acting on their own initiative. Similarly there are no examples within the narrative of Ezra–Nehemiah of the Babylonian Diaspora community, which had its own inner governance structures,[71] exercising the kind of managerial control over the Repatriate community that would be done in a full-blown "colonial" context (as in the colonization practiced by European powers).

In an earlier study, I proposed the model of the "Charter Group" as a means of describing homeland-Diaspora relations, as well as relations between the returnees and remainees in Yehud.[72] There, I argued that as an "enfranchised, geographically transplanted elite" or "Charter Group" the golah returnees functioned in quasi-independence from their region of origin. Thus, while depending on the Persian crown for official authorization, and being still connected to the Babylonian remainees for religious and financial support, the golah returnees nevertheless developed their own distinct identity. In this way, the returnees manifested both connectedness and independence vis-à-vis the east. For a variety of reasons, I believe this model to be a useful point of departure for the analysis of the golah in Yehud.[73] Nevertheless, whether

---

2004) 153–60; idem, "The Judean Exiles in Babylonia: Survival Strategy of an Ethnic Minority," in *For Uriel: Studies in the History of Israel in Antiquity Presented to Professor Uriel Rappaport* (ed. M. Mor et al.; Jerusalem: Zalman Shazar Center, 2005) 53–76.

70. Oded, "Exile-Homeland Relations," esp. p. 157 n. 14.

71. Idem, "Observations on the Israelite/Judaean Exiles"; idem, "Settlements."

72. Kessler, "Persia's Loyal Yahwists."

73. My use of the Charter Group model is essentially heuristic, and I in no way seek to explain the behavior of the golah on the basis of the model. The essence of my comparison is to note the similarities and differences in the functioning of elites who move from one context and assume a position of dominance, especially with the ongoing support

Bedford's proposal of more direct influence is taken, or a proposal assuming less direct involvement, such as my own, is adopted, I believe it to be more likely that the silence in Ezra–Nehemiah regarding the future of the Babylonian Diaspora is due to a growing willingness to entertain the notion of the Diaspora as an ongoing reality than it is a blatant writing off of the eastern Diaspora as theologically irrelevant.

This being the case, what might explain this willingness to entertain the concept of an ongoing Diaspora and a multicentric Yahwism in the mid-fourth century, when a concept of this sort was eschewed a century earlier? What led, on one hand, to an urgent expectation of the end of the Diaspora, and to an accommodation to its ongoing existence, on the other? It seems that we have here an excellent example of the influence of historical realities and social location on the appropriation of religious tradition. Clearly both Zech 1–8 and Ezra–Nehemiah know and to a greater or lesser extent bear the marks of the principal theological streams of the late-monarchic and Babylonian periods, especially Deuteronomism, Priestly traditions, and Zion theology.[74] All three streams demonstrate a special interest in the land, Jerusalem, and its temple. Deuteronomism views the land as Yahweh's supreme gift and its loss the profoundest of tragedies. The future hope (at least in some strands of the Deuteronomistic tradition)[75] consists of a return to the land (Deut 30:1–10). Priestly traditions focus on the ritual necessities for the ongoing dwelling of Yahweh with his people and in certain texts anticipate the future dwelling of Yahweh in the land with his people, who will have returned to him (Lev 26:42–45; Ezek 36:22–32; 37:21–22; chaps. 40–48). Zion theology likewise stresses Yahweh's choice

---

and authorization of a power base in the home region. Especially significant to my approach is the official recognition of the golah returnee community by the Persian Crown and the status which that recognition consequently gave to the returnees vis-à-vis other local Yahwists in Yehud. I similarly emphasize the ongoing sense of connectedness, on the part of the golah returnees, to their home communities in the east.

74. On theological streams in the Persian period, see the programmatic essay of O. H. Steck, "Theological Streams of Tradition," in *Tradition and Theology in the Old Testament* (ed. D. A. Knight; Philadelphia: Fortress, 1977) 183–214. On the theological streams in Haggai, Zech 1–8, and Ezra–Nehemiah, see Boda, "Confession as Theological Expression: Ideological Origins of Penitential Prayer"; idem, *Praying the Tradition*; J. Kessler, *The Book of Haggai: Prophecy and Society in Early Persian Yehud* (VTSup 91; Leiden: Brill, 2002); Mason, *Preaching the Tradition*; idem, "The Purpose of the 'Editorial Framework' of the Book of Haggai," *VT* 27 (1977) 413–21; J. A. Tollington, *Tradition and Innovation in Haggai and Zechariah 1–8* (JSOTSup 150; Sheffield: Sheffield Academic Press, 1993).

75. See J. G. McConville, "1 Kings VIII 46–53 and the Deuteronomic Hope," *VT* 42 (1992) 67–79.

of Zion as his dwelling place and the holiness and centrality of the city and land (Pss 2:6; 9:12[11]; 46; 48; 74:2; 78:68; Isa 2:3; 8:18; 12:6; Joel 2:1).

Many of the prophetic traditions rooted in Zion theology feature the concept of a total return to Zion on the part of dispersed Israel and a pilgrimage to Zion by the nations of the world (Isa 2; Mic 4; Isa 60; Zech 14). The early restoration was a time of great geopolitical shifts in Mesopotamia and the Levant. The fall of Babylon to the Persians (539 B.C.E.), the conquest of Egypt by Cambyses (525 B.C.E.), the political struggles before and just after the accession of Darius (522–21 B.C.E.) seem to have created an atmosphere of intense eschatological expectation. Haggai 2:6–9 and Zech 2:10–18[6–10] are saturated with the expectation of an imminent intervention of Yahweh that would disrupt the present world order, bring judgment on first Babylon then all the nations of the world, and propel the exiles in all locations back to Yehud.[76] The language of "shaking," "trembling," and "waving the hand,"[77] all of which provoke terror in humankind and perturbations in the cosmos, is especially significant here. It is therefore completely understandable that the community in Yehud should deduce from the intersection of their own theological traditions and the course of world events that a dramatic intervention was at hand—one that would bring to naught all Gentile power, and reunite Yahweh and the totality of his people in his land (cf. also Hag 2:6–9, 20–23; Ezek 37–39; 40–48; Isa 40–55; 56–66).

In Ezra–Nehemiah, by contrast, this sort of eschatological expectation has been profoundly muted.[78] The stresses on the empire posed by Egypt and Greece were likely felt only to a very limited degree in Yehud.[79] The Persian rulers were well entrenched, and the political climate was quite stable. It is frequently noted that this ongoing and

---

76. On this, see Japhet, "Postexilic Historiography," esp. p. 317; Kessler, *The Book of Haggai*, 173–95, 222–42; idem, "The Shaking of the Nations: An Eschatological View," *JETS* 30 (1987) 159–66.

77. 'Shaking' רעש, Ezek 38:20; Joel 2:10; 4:16[3:16]; Nah 1:5; Hag 2:6–7, 21. On the distinctive uses of this verb with a personal versus impersonal object, see my *Book of Haggai*, 176–80. 'Trembling' רגז, Isa 64:2; Jer 50:34; Joel 2:10; 'fearing' חרד, Isa 19:16; 41:5; Ezek 26:16, 18; 30:9; 32:10; Hos 11:10–11; Zech 1:21. 'Waving the hand' נוף יד, Zech 2:13[9]; Isa 11:15; 19:16.

78. Japhet, "Postexilic Historiography," 314–15; J. G. McConville ("Ezra–Nehemiah and the Fulfillment of Prophecy," *VT* 36 [1986] 205–24) argues that this eschatological restraint should not be taken as a complete renunciation of eschatological hopes. See my discussion of the deferral of hope of a full return below.

79. Lipschits, "Achaemenid Imperial Policy," esp. pp. 35–40.

durable political reality probably led to the rereading of the earlier expectations regarding an imminent intervention of Yahweh. What is not so often observed is that, along with this diminution of eschatological expectation in the circles reflected in Ezra–Nehemiah and Chronicles (clearly there is ongoing eschatological reflection as evidenced in texts such as Zech 9–14 and Joel), there was a corresponding revision of earlier notions regarding the return of the Diaspora. This revision resulted in the minimization of earlier hopes regarding the return of the Diaspora and a growing acceptance of the possibility of the more multicentric form that Yahwism now took.[80] This is not to say that Ezra–Nehemiah necessarily reflects a total loss of all hope of a future return to the land. The reference to Yehud as the "land as promised to the ancestors" (Neh 9:36) along with the various Deuteronomistic traditions present in the text indicate that many of the older Deuteronomistic ideals still survived, and many of these traditions, as we have seen, feature an ultimate return to the land. However in Ezra–Nehemiah, if this hope has not been *forgotten*, it has certainly been *deferred*. Those returning to Yehud are seen as acting out of their own volitional response to the urging of Yahweh (Ezra 1:1–4; 7:13), and no critique is made of individuals who stay behind. It therefore appears that the concepts of the collapse of the Diaspora and the full return to Zion have been implicitly thrust forward to an indefinite future.[81] The historical realities of an impoverished and geographically reduced territory (when compared with pre-587 Judah), a well-established Diaspora, and a militarily secure Persian Empire contributed significantly to this reframing of the tradition.

Ezra–Nehemiah's implicit acceptance of the ongoing existence of the eastern Diaspora as a legitimate expression of Yahwism is also explicable on the basis of social and theological location—specifically, the impact of the belief that the Babylonian golah was the sole guardian of Yahweh's revelation and the kernel out of which the future of the nation would come forth. It is noteworthy that Ezra–Nehemiah's definition of the remnant as exclusively Jews who had been exiled to the east and returned was not an innovation. It reformulated an ongoing conflict within Yahwistic circles that began in the late sixth century regarding which group was to be considered the true heirs of the

---

80. Petersen, *Haggai and Zechariah 1–8*, 119–20.
81. See also the arguments from prophetic traditions in McConville, "Ezra–Nehemiah," passim.

promises and, especially, the land. This conflict is evident in the "good and bad figs" metaphor in Jer 24 and the debate over descent from Abraham and possession of the land in Ezek 11:14–21 and 33:23–29.[82] Thus, even during the Babylonian period, within certain circles the Babylonian Diaspora was identified as Yahweh's chosen and preserved community apart from any decision to return, because no return was possible. All of this probably stemmed from a growing self-perception on the part of the eastern Diaspora that they were an elect community, destined for the preservation and continuation of Yahweh's purposes in the world.[83] Thus a foundational conviction regarding the Babylonian community as an elect and faithful remnant was already in existence before the fifth and fourth centuries B.C.E.

Furthermore, as we have seen, not all the eastern Diaspora members are portrayed as returning, and there is no critique of the spirituality of those who remained behind. The golah returnees in Yehud likely retained connections with their relatives who stayed in the east. This may be seen, in part, by the extensive interest in genealogy in evidence in the period.[84] This being the case, it is highly unlikely that the community who returned viewed themselves as the sole locus of authentic Yahwism, to the exclusion of their relatives and friends back in the east.[85] Nor—given the political context of the fourth century, specifically the fact that the longed-for eschatological intervention of Yahweh had not arrived—would they be likely to view the ongoing presence in the east of these fellow members of their community as theologically irrelevant. Rather, despite their focus on the return to Yehud and the community there, it is more likely that they would continue to regard their extended community in the east as an expression of faithful Yahwism. This perspective on the Diaspora is clearly evi-

---

82. As Japhet notes, however, the remnant terminology is not used in these texts (Japhet, "Concept of the "Remnant," esp. p. 422).

83. The variations and transformation of this motif within the deuteronomic and Deuteronomistic traditions (such as Deuteronomy, Jeremiah, and 1–2 Kings, despite their differences at various points) is striking. We begin with kings and nobles who exploit and ruin the population (Jer 19–23; 2 Kgs 24). These are exiled to Babylon (Jer 52; 2 Kgs 24) and become the good figs (Jer 24). On this, see C. Seitz, "The Crisis of Interpretation over the Meaning and Purpose of the Exile: A Redactional Study of Jeremiah xxi–xliii," *VT* 35 (1985) 78–97; idem, *Theology in Conflict: Reactions to the Exile in the Book of Jeremiah* (BZAW 176; Berlin: de Gruyter, 1989).

84. On this, see Oded, "Judean Exiles in Babylonia," esp. pp. 64–65.

85. On the importance of family connections between homeland and Diaspora, see ibid., 68–69.

dent in texts such as Esther, Daniel, and Tobit, as well as other passages depicting Jews in high positions in Gentile kingdoms.[86] What is more, as suggested above, the self-understanding of the golah returnees may have included a vision of their special and exemplary role vis-à-vis the Diaspora. As a holy community gathered around the Jerusalemite temple, they were in the unique position of being able fully to enact the requirements of the law of Yahweh, especially laws of a cultic nature. Thus they could view themselves as something of a "proxy community" representing and anchoring[87] the religious life and identity of their fellow Yahwists in the Diaspora. Furthermore they could maintain and service the holy city and its temple in its emerging role as a pilgrimage center.

In sum then, we have in the varying perspectives on Diaspora in Zech 1–8 and Ezra–Nehemiah an illustration of the power of historical circumstance and socioreligious location to shape tradition, and then the power of these reshaped traditions to construct identity. Questions concerning the relationship between homeland and Diaspora have marked Jewish experience from the Persian period to our own.[88] Furthermore, issues regarding the reframing of traditions formulated in the heat of eschatological expectation in light of later situations of ongoing stability are issues that have profoundly marked and molded both Judaism and Christianity.

---

86. Bedford, "Diaspora: Homeland Relations," esp. pp. 163–65.
87. Perhaps something of this concept underlies the metaphor of the 'tent peg' (יתד) in Ezra 9:8.
88. Phillips, "Zechariah's Vision and Joseph in Egypt." While I disagree with Phillips's assessment of Zech 1–8's view of diasporic religious practice, her essay does, nevertheless, raise significant issues regarding the dynamics of Jewish religious expression, ancient and modern.

Ethnicity, Genealogy, Geography, and Change: The Judean Communities of Babylon and Jerusalem in the Story of Ezra

GARY N. KNOPPERS
The Pennsylvania State University

In his recent book, Shaye Cohen provocatively declares that "Jewishness, like most—perhaps all—other identities, is imagined; it has no empirical, verifiable reality to which we can point and exclaim, 'This is it!' Jewishness is in the mind."[1] Confronting the challenges of defining Jewish identity in antiquity, Cohen draws attention to the subjectivity involved in attempting to pinpoint a community's distinctive attributes. Ethnologists sometimes speak of ethnicities as "imagined communities," because they believe that ethnicities are very much shaped, if not defined, by persons (not always people within the communities themselves) who want them to exist and believe that they do so.[2]

To complicate matters, the cultural and organizational traits of groups may shift and develop over time. Indeed, what characteristics make an identifiable group is a matter of dispute among sociologists and ethnographers. Some stress practical concerns, such as common customs, habits, food-ways, styles of clothing, institutions, religious practices, and languages, while others stress broader ideological concerns, such as a group's attachment to a particular land, a sense of shared history, collective values, a common notion of group destiny, and a unique understanding of cultural distinctiveness. Yet others emphasize the definition of boundaries, whether mental or physical, setting one group apart from another and the maintenance (or redefinition) of these boundaries over time.[3] On a literary level, a given

---

1. S. J. D. Cohen, *The Beginnings of Jewishness: Boundaries, Varieties, Uncertainties* (Hellenistic Culture and Society 31; Berkeley: University of California Press, 1999) 5.
2. The work to which Cohen (ibid.) refers is: B. R. Anderson, *Imagined Communities: Reflections on the Origin and Spread of Nationalism* (rev. ed.; London: Verso, 1991).
3. So, for example, F. Barth, *Ethnic Groups and Boundaries* (Boston: Little, Brown, 1969).

writer may attempt to defend a group's identity, redefine this group's identity in a certain way, or play on competing definitions of identity. In the story of Ezra, one encounters not one but two imagined Israelite communities.[4] One group, a relatively new community, is centered in the large city of Babylon, while another resides far away in the ancestral homeland of Judah. The native community receives the bulk of attention in the book, but the diasporic community drives the action.[5] The narratives about Ezra—his background, his journey to Judah, and his interventions in the Jerusalem community—raise some interesting issues about developing notions of Judean ethnicity and community identity in the international context of the Achaemenid Empire. One is dealing with multiple and overlapping relationships between Yahwistic groups located in widely different geographic areas. In most cases of interactions between related communities geographically set apart, the community rooted in the ancestral land would represent the established community, and the diasporic community would represent a colony or dependent community, but in Ezra these roles are in many ways reversed.

In this essay, I would like to read against the grain and focus on the eastern Diaspora, specifically the Babylonian community, and its ongoing relations to the community in Yehud.[6] The lineage of Ezra, the conception of his mission, the narrative about his travels back to his homeland, and his public reading of the Torah may be set against the background of the stories about earlier returns from the eastern Diaspora during the reigns of Cyrus and Darius I (Ezra 1–6). The focus of this essay will not be on Ezra 7–10 (1 Esd 8:1–9:36) and Neh 8 (cf. 1 Esd 9:37–55) as a whole, since recent monographs have devoted considerable attention to the form, structure, and compositional history of these

---

4. Or, one community geographically dispersed in at least two completely different contexts. Please see further below.

5. H. G. M. Williamson, *Ezra, Nehemiah* (WBC 16; Waco, TX: Word, 1985) xliv–lii; T. C. Eskenazi, *In an Age of Prose: A Literary Approach to Ezra–Nehemiah* (SBLMS 36; Atlanta: Scholars Press, 1988); T. Willi, *Juda – Jehud – Israel: Studien zum Selbstverständnis des Judentums in persischer Zeit* (Forschungen zum Alten Testament 12; Tübingen: Mohr, 1995); P. R. Bedford, *Temple Restoration in Early Achaemenid Judah* (Journal for the Study of Judaism Supplement 65; Leiden: Brill, 2001); idem, "Diaspora: Homeland Relations in Ezra–Nehemiah," *VT* 52 (2002) 147–65; R. G. Kratz, *Das Judentum im Zeitalter des Zweiten Tempels* (Forschungen zum Alten Testament 42; Tübingen: Mohr-Siebeck, 2004).

6. In what follows, I will take Ezra 7–10 and Neh 8 as a starting point, but occasionally I will pay some attention to the witness of 1 Esdras, especially when its text and sequence differ from those of the MT.

curious and complicated texts.[7] My focus will be limited to addressing certain questions raised by the ancestral lineage of Ezra, the introduction to his mission, his journey, and his expounding the Torah (Ezra 7:1–10, 27–28; 8:1–20; Neh 8:1–18).[8] In what follows, I would like to stress two related points. First, I will argue that the Ezra narrative advocates a form of Judean identity that is trans-temporal and international in scope. Second, I will argue that the Ezra story promotes an intergenerational process of Judean identity (re)formation that reshapes the homeland community according to mores developed and cultivated in the Diaspora.

The Genealogy of Identity:
Introducing the Person and Mission of Ezra

The brief transitional remark "'and after these things' [ואחר הדברים האלה], during the reign of Artaxerxes, king of Persia" (Ezra 7:1), introducing the person and lineage of Ezra, may be classified as quite an understatement.[9] The temporal transition marks a period of some 57

---

7. D. Böhler, *Die heilige Stadt in Esdras a und Esra–Nehemia: Zwei Konzeptionen der Wiederherstellung Israels* (OBO 158; Freiburg: Universitätsverlag / Göttingen: Vandenhoeck & Ruprecht, 1997); J. Pakkala, *Ezra the Scribe: The Development of Ezra 7–10 and Nehemia 8* (BZAW 347; Berlin: de Gruyter, 2004); J. Wright, *Rebuilding Identity: The Nehemiah-Memoir and Its Earliest Readers* (BZAW 348; Berlin: de Gruyter, 2004); S. Grätz, *Das Edikt des Artaxerxes: Eine Untersuchung zum religionspolitischen und historischen Umfeld von Esra 7,12–26* (BZAW 337; Berlin: de Gruyter, 2005); R. G. Kratz, *The Composition of the Narrative Books of the Old Testament* (trans. J. Bowden; London: T. & T. Clark, 2005) 49–86. There are serious disagreements among these scholars, but they all argue for a complicated history of composition. Even if one takes issue with some of their presuppositions, analyses, and conclusions, they have successfully pointed to a number of stresses and strains in the text.
8. For the judicial aspects of the much-discussed rescript (Ezra 7:14, 25–26), see my contribution to the Ephraim Stern Festschrift (forthcoming).
9. The classification of periods and the lacunae in coverage are significant but constitute subjects in and of themselves. See S. Japhet, "Composition and Chronology in the Book of Ezra–Nehemiah," in *Second Temple Studies 2: Temple and Community in the Persian Period* (ed. T. C. Eskenazi and K. H. Richards; JSOTSup 175; Sheffield: JSOT Press, 1994) 189–216; eadem, "Periodization between History and Ideology II: Chronology and Ideology in Ezra–Nehemiah," in *Judah and the Judeans in the Persian Period* (ed. O. Lipschits and M. Oeming; Winona Lake, IN: Eisenbrauns, 2006) 491–508. Following the traditional chronology of Ezra (458 B.C.E.) and Nehemiah (445 B.C.E.), there is a gap of 13 years from the time of Ezra's mission (Ezra 7:1; 458 B.C.E.) to the time of Nehemiah's arrival (Neh 1:1; 2:1; 445 B.C.E.). An editorial attempt has been made to overcome this segmentation by placing the two together for the reading of the Torah and the celebration of Sukkot, narrated in Nehemiah (Neh 7:73b–8:18; cf. 1 Esd 9:37–55) but pertaining to the time of Ezra. If one wishes to place Ezra after Nehemiah, as some do, the work would still display a

years since the dedication of the temple under Zerubbabel and Jeshua with which the previous narrative concludes (Ezra 6:19–22).[10] In the context of the book, not only has the historical period shifted from the late sixth to the mid-fifth century B.C.E., but the geopolitical scene has also shifted from postexilic Judah to a diasporic setting some 1,600 km away in Babylon. This change in venues is significant, because it points to the coexistence of Yahwistic communities in two different parts of the Persian Empire.[11]

Ties of birth, ties of blood, and ties to an ancestral land are three of the many ways by which a writer may seek to define ethnic identity. In this respect, it is relevant that the writers choose to employ a lengthy linear genealogy, immediately following the introductory chronological marker, to introduce the person of Ezra, his priestly pedigree, and his line of work.[12] The ascending lineage of Ezra 7:1–5 places Ezra in

---

major lacuna from 430 B.C.E. (the approximate end of Nehemiah's second mission) to 398 B.C.E. (the estimated year of Ezra's coming to Yehud in the reign of Artaxerxes II): Williamson, *Ezra, Nehemiah,* xxxix–xliv; J. Blenkinsopp, *Ezra–Nehemiah: A Commentary* (OTL; Philadelphia: Westminster, 1988) 139–44. In either reading of the chronology involved in dating the missions of Ezra and Nehemiah, there are very significant gaps in the coverage of the postmonarchic period: G. Knoppers, "Periodization in Ancient Israelite Historiography: Three Case Studies," in *Periodisierung und Epochenbewusstein in der antiken Geschichtsschreibung* (ed. J. Wiesehöfer; forthcoming).

10. Another important shift in scenes involves the introduction to Nehemiah. His story also begins in the eastern Diaspora (Neh 1:1–2), where he resides in the fortress of Susa as a cupbearer to the king. As with Ezra, Nehemiah professes a keen sense of solidarity with the people of Judah and Jerusalem, in spite of the great geographical distance that separates him from them.

11. Among the relevant pieces of extrabiblical evidence, one may refer to the recently discovered cuneiform references to *āl-Yāhūdu* 'the town of Judah', probably in the Babylon-Borsippa region: F. Joannès and A. Lemaire, "Trois tablettes cunéiformes à l'onomastique ouest-sémitique," *Transeu* 17 (1999) 17–34; D. S. Vanderhooft, "New Evidence Pertaining to the Transition from Neo-Babylonian to Achaemenid Administration in Palestine," in *Yahwism after the Exile: Perspectives on Israelite Religion in the Persian Era* (ed. R. Albertz and B. Becking; Assen: Van Gorcum, 2003) 219–25; L. E. Pearce, "New Evidence for Judeans in Babylonia," in *Judah and the Judeans in the Persian Period* (ed. O. Lipschits and M. Oeming; Winona Lake, IN: Eisenbrauns, 2006) 399–411. From an ethnographic standpoint, one should also refer to the use of the term *yĕhûdîn* to refer to the members of the Elephantine colony (e.g., AP 6.3–10; 8.2; 10.3). The Judean communities of Egypt are not referred to, however, either in Ezra–Nehemiah or in 1 Esdras.

12. The genealogy is introduced into the text through the literary technique of repetitive resumption, from עזרא in Ezra 7:1 to עזרא הוא in Ezra 7:6. I am not as confident as a variety of scholars are that many, if not most, of the lists and genealogies in Chronicles, Ezra, and Nehemiah are later additions to the text. Genealogies were used in the classical world, for example, to address questions about the pedigree and relations (or non-relations) among the characters discussed in literary narratives; G. N. Knoppers,

some illustrious company—Hilkiah, Zadok, Phinehas, Eleazar, and others—before concluding with the relevant figure of the authoritative Sinaitic age, "the chief priest [הכהן הראש] Aaron" (Ezra 7:5).[13] Like the founding father (Aaron), Ezra had never actually lived in the land, at least up to this point.[14] The genealogy establishes Ezra's credentials as a priest, even though Ezra is not called a chief priest himself.[15]

The statement about pedigree serves multiple functions. To begin with, the family tree indicates that priestly lineages were maintained even in the Diaspora. The great distance of the exiles from the Jerusalem temple does not lead to the dissolution of priestly succession in the Babylonian Judean community. Residing in a cosmopolitan city far from Jerusalem in Judah, the expatriate Ezra is a direct descendant of a distinguished series of Aaronide priests who had served at the First Temple. The length of the lineage is itself important, because most genealogies from the ancient Near Eastern world extend to just a few generations. The content of the genealogy thus establishes his pedigree, status, and ancestral roots in the land.

---

1 Chronicles 1–9 (AB 12; New York: Doubleday, 2004) 245–65. The inclusion of genealogical material adds depth and definition to the surrounding narratives. Hence, the judgment as to whether a genealogy or a list represents a later addition to a given narrative text should be handled on a case-by-case basis. The presumption should not be that a genealogy or list is intrusive simply because it appears within a narrative context.

13. The lemma of the MT may also be translated 'the first priest': D. W. Rooke, *Zadok's Heirs: The Role and Development of the High Priesthood in Ancient Israel* (Oxford Theological Monograhs; Oxford: Oxford University Press, 2000) 169–70. See also 1 Esd 8:2, *prōtou hiereōs* 'first priest' or 'chief priest'. J. W. Watts discusses the importance of the Aaronide pedigree for a variety of priestly dynasties that served in the Yahwistic temples of the postexilic era: "The Torah as the Rhetoric of Priesthood," in *The Pentateuch as Torah: New Models for Understanding Its Promulgation and Acceptance* (ed. G. N. Knoppers and B. M. Levinson; Winona Lake, IN: Eisenbrauns, 2007) 319–31.

14. The issues involved in the classification of the priests and Levites as well as the history of their relationships in postmonarchic times are much debated: J. Schaper, *Priester und Leviten im achämenidischen Juda: Studien zur Kult- und Sozialgeschichte Israels in persischer Zeit* (Forschungen zum Alten Testament 31; Tübingen: Mohr Siebeck, 2000) 162–308. See also the essay by Mark Leuchter in this volume.

15. He is, however, repeatedly referred to as 'chief priest' (*ho archiereus*) in 1 Esd 9:39, 40, 49. In the work of Josephus (*Ant.* 11.121), which is dependent on 1 Esdras, Ezra is referred to as a 'chief priest' (*prōtos hiereus*), residing in Babylon. For an argument that Ezra was actually a high priest, see K. Koch, "Ezra and Meremoth: Remarks on the History of the High Priesthood," in *"Sha'arei Talmon": Studies in the Bible, Qumran, and the Ancient Near East Presented to Shemaryahu Talmon* (ed. M. Fishbane and E. Tov; Winona Lake, IN: Eisenbrauns, 1992) 105–10. Interestingly, Josephus, drawing on his main source (1 Esdras), speaks of Ezra functioning as a 'chief priest' (*prōtos hiereus*) in Babylon at the same time as Joiaqim was functioning as a 'high priest' (*archiereus*). On this curiosity, see J. VanderKam, *From Joshua to Caiaphas: High Priests after the Exile* (Minneapolis: Fortress, 2004) 45–46.

The importance of Ezra's lineage for understanding his identity can
be viewed from another vantage point. The particular configuration of
his immediate ancestors is significant and requires some commentary.
The genealogist does not mention any Neo-Babylonian or Persian-
period predecessors for Ezra. The text lists Ezra's most immediate predecessor as Seraiah, son of Azariah.[16] This means that there is over a
century between the time of Ezra and that of his most recent priestly
predecessor.[17] Family trees can be highly selective and telescopic in
character and thus skip over what genealogists consider to be insignificant generations.[18] Genealogists can choose to omit people whom they
consider to be embarrassing or malefic characters.

Given the existence of these sorts of typical genealogical conceits, it
is useful to study what the lineage contains and what it lacks (or
omits). The books of Kings and Jeremiah mention that Seraiah was the
"chief priest" at the time of the second Babylonian deportation of 586
B.C.E. (2 Kgs 25:18, 21//Jer 52:24, 27).[19] Seraiah was captured and executed in that same year by the Babylonians at Riblah (2 Kgs 25:18–
21//Jer 52:24–27). The author of the long priestly genealogy in Chronicles speaks of Jehozadak as the successor to Seraiah, but mentions that
Jehozadaq was banished to Babylon, when "Yhwh exiled Judah and Jerusalem by the hand of Nebuchadnezzar" (1 Chr 5:41).[20] Jehozadak, in
turn, is mentioned in Haggai (1:1, 12, 14; 2:2, 4), Zechariah (6:11), and
elsewhere in Ezra (3:2, 8; 5:2; 10:18) as the father of Jeshua, the high
priest in the early postexilic period. The connection to Jehozadak, and
ultimately to Aaron, legitimates Jeshua's priesthood and, by implica-

---

16. MT and LXX Ezra 7:1, as well as 1 Esd 8:1 and 2 Esd 1:3, have "Seraiah." The
name is lacking in both Josephus (*Ant.* 10.153) and 1 Chr 9:10–11, but not in Neh 11:11.
The fact that Josephus speaks of a sequence of 18 high priests in First Temple times but
provides only 17 specific names (*Ant.* 10.152–153; 20.231) seems to confirm the likelihood
of a haplography. See further my *I Chronicles 1–9*, 496. On the ill fate of Seraiah, 'the chief
priest' (כהן הראש), see 2 Kgs 25:18–21//Jer 52:24–27.
17. One branch of the family led by Jeshua returned to Jerusalem in the late sixth
century, while a collateral branch of the family presumably chose to remain in Babylon.
18. Especially middle generations. The first and last names appearing in lineages are
usually the most significant: R. Wilson, *Genealogy and History in the Biblical World* (Yale
Near Eastern Researches 7; New Haven, CT: Yale University Press, 1977).
19. The fact that Ezra appears as a "son" of Seraiah may explain the rabbinic tradition that situates him in the exilic period and renders him a contemporary of Zerubbabel
(*Cant. Rab.* 5:5).
20. See further my "Relationship of the Priestly Genealogies to the History of the
High Priesthood in Jerusalem," in *Judah and the Judeans in the Neo-Babylonian Period* (ed.
O. Lipschits and J. Blenkinsopp; Winona Lake, IN: Eisenbrauns, 2003) 109–33.

tion, the priesthood of his Persian-period successors.[21] The familial an-
cestry furnished for Ezra thus indicates that Ezra was consanguineous
with the priests serving at the Jerusalem temple. The different lines of
descent, as they are presented in select biblical settings, may be compared in this context. The testimony of Josephus may also be relevant.[22]

As the comparative table (table 1, p. 154) demonstrates, Ezra's lineage bypasses the generations covered by all of the high priests of the
exilic and early postexilic ages. At first glance, one might say that this
is perfectly understandable, because Ezra and his immediate predecessors reside in Babylon and not in Jerusalem. However, there may be
more to the story than that. In the case of Ezra, his genealogical proximity to Seraiah (with no mention of intervening ancestors of his line
in Babylon) underscores his close connection to the preexilic succession
of priests in Judah. The link with the First Temple lineage is vital, because it provides Ezra with a pedigree that is as stellar as that of Jeshua
and his successors in Jerusalem. Both are ultimately tied to the same
priestly family tree, and both have undergone the experience of living
in exile.

The appearance of a lengthy Aaronide lineage for Ezra is thus no ac-
cident. As Ezra's mission evolves, he and his confederates will do
battle with a number of elite families in Jerusalem, including priestly
and Levitical families, over the issue of intermarriage with foreign
women (Ezra 9:1–10:1–44). One of the priestly families that becomes
involved in this crisis is none other than the family of Jeshua *ben* Joza-
dak (Ezra 10:18). Members of Jeshua's family are listed first among the

---

21. In table 1, I am placing Ezra in the time of Eliashib, not in the earlier time of
Joiakim. Admittedly, this is somewhat arbitrary, because the the writers of the Ezra narrative do not disclose (perhaps deliberately) who was functioning as high priest during
the time of Ezra. On Joiakim, see Neh 12:10, 12–13, 26; Jdt 4:6, 8; Josephus, *Ant.* 11.121,
158 (cf. 1 Esd 5:5; Bar 1:7). In the reconstruction of F. M. Cross, Eliashib (II) was born
around 495 B.C.E., while his son Joiada (I) was born around 470 B.C.E.: "A Reconstruction
of the Judean Restoration," *JBL* 94 (1975) 4–18 (= *Int* 29 [1975] 187–203); idem, *From Epic
to Canon: History and Literature in Ancient Israel* (Baltimore: Johns Hopkins University
Press, 1998) 151–72. If so, Eliashib II would most likely be the high priest during the
times of both Ezra and Nehemiah. His successor, Joiada, would be too young to be serving as high priest in the mid-fifth century.

22. The lists of priests appear chiefly in two contexts (*Ant.* 10.152–53; 20.224–34).
Only the latter discussion deals with the beginning of the postmonarchic period. The
references to the other high priests must be gleaned from scattered comments in other
settings: Joiakim (*Ant.* 11.121); Eliashib (11.158); Joiada (11.297); Jonathan (11.297); Jaddua (11.302); Onias (11.347). Josephus speaks of a succession of 15 high priests, beginning
with Jeshua until the time of Antiochus Eupator at the beginning of the Hasmonean era
(*Ant.* 20.234).

Table 1. Ezra's Lineage: Genealogies Compared

1 Chr 5:27–41	Ezra 7:1–5	Josephus	Neh 12:10–11	Neh 12:22[a]
Levi				
Kohath				
Amram				
Aaron	Aaron			
Eleazar	Eleazar			
Phinehas	Phinehas			
Abishua	Abishua			
Bukki	Bukki			
Uzzi	Uzzi			
Zerahiah	Zerahiah			
Meraioth	Meraioth			
Amariah				
Ahitub				
Zadok		Sadokos		
Ahimaaz		Achimas		
Azariah		Azarias		
Johanan		Iōramos		
Azariah	Azariah	Iōs		
Amariah	Amariah	Axiōramos		
Ahitub	Ahitub	Phideas		
Zadok	Zadok	Soudaias		
		Iouēlos		
		Iōthamos		
		Ourias		
		Nērias		

a. The list of priestly names in MT (and LXX) Neh 12:22 is problematically introduced by the phrase, הלוים בימי אלישיב ('The Levites in the days of Eliashib'). Text-critical solutions vary. Given the appearance of the participle (כתובים) later in the verse, followed by the clause 'heads of the ancestral houses and the priests' (ראשי אבות וכהנים), W. Rudolph reconstructs: "The heads of the ancestral houses of the priests in the days of Eliashib," *Esra und Nehemia* (Handbuch zum Alten Testament 20; Tübingen: Mohr, 1949) 194. Blenkinsopp (*Ezra–Nehemiah*, 333) thinks that the present introduction to v. 22 is a gloss influenced by the introduction to v. 23 ('The sons of Levi, heads of ancestral houses, were recorded . . .'), and so he omits הלוים. Also assuming that the beginning of v. 22 is a corruption influenced by the introduction to v. 23, A. H. J. Gunneweg emends the text to read 'The priests in the days of Eliashib', in *Nehemia* (Kommentar zum Alten Testament 19/2; Gütersloh: Mohn, 1987) 151. The NJPS translation presents another possibility, "The Levites and the priests were listed by heads of clans in the days of Eliashib." Williamson basically maintains the reading of the MT, understanding the reference to the Levites as pertaining to the form of social organization (families) recorded for both the Levites (v. 23) and the priests in this specific instance (*Ezra, Nehemiah*, 356, 364).

Table 1. Ezra's Lineage: Genealogies Compared (cont.)

1 Chr 5:27–41	Ezra 7:1–5	Josephus	Neh 12:10–11	Neh 12:22ᵃ
		Ōdaias		
Shallum	Shallum	Salloumos		
Hilqiah	Hilkiah	Elkias		
Azariah	Azariah	Azaros		
Seraiah	Seraiah			
Jehozadaq		Iōsadakos		
		Iēsous	Jeshua	
		Iōakeimos	Joiakim	
	Ezra	Eliasibos	Eliashib	Eliashib
		Iōdas	Joiada	Joiadaᵇ
		Iōannes	Jonathanᶜ	Johanan
		Iaddous	Jaddua	Jaddua
		Onias		

b. In the short list of Neh 12:23, Johanan is mentioned as a son of Eliashib. Compare Jehohanan *ben* Eliashib in Ezra 10:6 (*Iōanan* in 1 Esd 9:1, but *Iōannes* in Josephus, *Ant.* 11.147). The matter is complicated by the question of whether the priest(s) named Eliashib who appears in the stories about control of certain temple chambers (Ezra 10:6; Neh 13:4) is a high priest (Rooke, *Zadok's Heirs*, 169–70). But Rudolph (*Esra und Nehemia*, 203–4), Williamson (*Ezra, Nehemiah*, 151–54, 386), and Blenkinsopp (*Ezra–Nehemiah*, 189–90, 336–41) think not. On Joiada, see, e.g., Neh 12:10–11, 22; 13:28 (cf. Ezra 10:6; Neh 12:23; 13:28; Josephus, *Ant.* 11.297 [Iōdas]). VanderKam provides a useful discussion of the issue of high-priestly succession in the postexilic period (*From Joshua to Caiaphas*, 43–99).

c. In the genealogy of Neh 12:10–11 (and in Josephus, *Ant.* 11.297), Jonathan succeeds Joiada, while in the list of Neh 12:22, Johanan is mentioned after Joiada. In the view of VanderKam, Jonathan is a copyist's error for Johanan (*From Joshua to Caiaphas*, 55). The issue is important and may be related to two other questions. The first is whether the author of Neh 12:22 intends his list to function as a genealogical sequence. The names in Neh 12:22 are connected to the reign of Darius the Persian (הפרסי דריוש על־מלכות). Presumably, given the occurrence of the final name, Jaddua, the reference is to Darius III (Codomannus). It may be, as some have argued, that the preposition (על) can sometimes carry the force of 'to' or 'up to' (= אל) in Late Biblical Hebrew: A. Kropat, *Die Syntax des Autors der Chronik verglichen mit der seiner Quellen: Ein Beitrag zur historischen Syntax des Hebräischen* (BZAW 16; Giessen: Alfred Töpelmann, 1909) 41–42. See also the recent work of D. Marcus (עזרא ונחמיה [*Ezra and Nehemiah*] [Biblia Hebraica Quinta 20; Stuttgart: Deutsche Bibelgesellschaft, 2006] 47*). W. F. Albright ("The Date and Personality of the Chronicler," *JBL* [1921] 113), followed by J. M. Myers (*Ezra, Nehemiah* [AB 14; Garden City, NY: Doubleday, 1965] 195, 198–99) emends the text to מעל (the initial *mêm* having been lost after כהנים) and connects this phrase with what follows in v. 23, pertaining to the time of Johanan, son of Eliashib. More plausible is the proposal of Rudolph, who argues for a haplography (*homoioarkton*) and reconstructs, '*al sēper dibrê hay-yāmîm 'ad* 'upon the scroll of chronicles up to [the time of Darius the Persian]' (*Esra und Nehemia*, 194). The second question involves whether the genealogy of Neh 12:10–11 is, as almost all commentators suppose, a high-priestly succession in genealogical dress. The matter deserves much closer scrutiny, but this is not the context in which to pursue it.

priestly families who elect to divorce their foreign wives (Ezra 10:19). Ezra's position on intermarriage and the position of the community at large was to hold sway over a prominent, perhaps the prominent, priestly dynasty in Jerusalem.[23] Apparently, the ties that bind are very strong. The fact that Ezra's family had been in exile for some six generations, from the time of the early sixth century to the time of the mid-fifth century, has no ill effect on his ability to influence the course of events in his homeland. Indeed, one could argue that, because Ezra is a recent arrival from Babylon and a direct appointee of the Persian king, he has an edge over his priestly kin, who had been repatriated some generations earlier.[24]

The narrative introduction provides further information about 'this Ezra' (הוּא עֶזְרָא). He was a scribe, "skilled in the Torah of Moses, which Yhwh the God of Israel had given" (Ezra 7:6). Ezra was thus a scholar, rather than a scribe in a narrow or limited sense (for example, a clerk or a copyist).[25] This particular priest was not simply literate in the sense of being able to handle temple records, receipts, legal deeds, and so on, but an expert in what the writers of Ezra–Nehemiah present as the foundational document or sacred constitution of their people.[26] Ezra may live some 1,600 km away from Jerusalem, but he identifies with Israel and the Torah that the God of Israel had given to his people. The story presupposes, of course, that the community in Babylon had a Torah scroll and that Ezra (and others) not only read (or recited) it but also made a point of studying it.

---

23. The importance of Jeshua can be seen by his place at the forefront of a number of different lists and genealogies dealing with the postexilic age in Ezra–Nehemiah (Ezra 2:2//Neh 7:7; Ezra 2:6//Neh 7:11; Ezra 3:8//Neh 12:1, 10–11, 26). The time of Zerubbabel and Jeshua (not of Sheshbazzar and his generation—Ezra 1:8; 5:14–16) is presented as of primary importance, probably because the temple was rebuilt and dedicated during the tenure of Zerubbabel and Jeshua.

24. It is telling that in the communal covenant (אֲמָנָה) of Neh 10, the stipulations of which include a commitment not to intermarry (Neh 10:31), the name of the high priest is noticeably missing. J. Liver points out that some six priestly names found in Neh 12:1–21, most notably some belonging to the prominent Jedaiah lineage (cf. Ezra 2:36–39), are not found among the signatories to the corporate pledge in Neh 10:1–40 (*Chapters in the History of the Priests and Levites* [Jerusalem: Magnes, 1968] 35–42 [Hebrew]).

25. K. van der Toorn, *Scribal Culture and the Making of the Hebrew Bible* (Cambridge: Harvard University Press, 2007) 78–82.

26. The presentation is at some variance with the presentation of Ezra in the rescript (esp. 7:12, 14, 21) as a Persian-appointed official sent by the imperial court to conduct an inquiry in Judah and Jerusalem or implement a set of legal decrees. It is quite possible that the present form of the book conflates two different images of Ezra in early Judean tradition (Blenkinsopp, *Ezra–Nehemiah*, 136–57).

The point about Torah study relates to the kind of religiosity that could or could not be practiced in an exilic setting. Ethnographers point out that the typical practices of a group at a certain time should not be interpreted as innate, ineffable, and immutable indications of permanent identity.[27] Members of a given ethnicity may change their behaviors in response to shifting political, cultural, or social circumstances. This is not to discount the commonly cited factors of shared myths, social structures, ancestral ties, languages, religious institutions, political associations, and so forth in helping to define a people. Rather, the choice and content of these sorts of indices may be modified to meet new social, political, religious, or economic challenges. Group identity may be reframed and renegotiated in different times and settings.[28]

Residing in Babylon over the generations, the Judean community had to make a number of adjustments. Ezra's immediate priestly predecessors were not able to serve at the Jerusalem temple, yet they could maintain a priestly succession as if they still had access to the temple.[29] Members of the Diaspora could not easily journey to the Jerusalem sanctuary to bring offerings there, but they could send gifts and tribute

---

27. O. Patterson, "Context and Choice in Ethnic Allegiance: A Theoretical Framework and Caribbean Case Study," in *Ethnicity: Theory and Experience* (ed. N. Glazer and D. P. Moynihan; Cambridge: Harvard University Press, 1975) 308; M. G. Brett, "Interpreting Ethnicity" in *Ethnicity and the Bible* (ed. M. G. Brett; Leiden: Brill, 1996) 3–22.

28. See Cohen, *The Beginnings of Jewishness*, 1–10; J. L. Berquist, "Constructions of Identity in Postcolonial Yehud," in *Judah and the Judeans in the Persian Period* (ed. O. Lipschits and M. Oeming; Winona Lake, IN: Eisenbrauns, 2006) 53–66; L. C. Jonker, "Reforming History: The Hermeneutical Significance of the Books of Chronicles," *VT* 57 (2007) 21–44; idem, "Textual Identities in the Books of Chronicles," and the additional references cited in these essays.

29. My assumption is that the Babylonian Judeans did not have their own temple. Some scholars have viewed the reference to "the place [הַמָּקוֹם] Casiphia" in Ezra 8:17 as indicating the existence of a Yahwistic sanctuary in Babylon. But an allusion, absent other evidence, is not much to go on (G. N. Knoppers, "'The City Yhwh has Chosen': The Chronicler's Promotion of Jerusalem in the Light of Recent Archaeology," in *Jerusalem in Bible and Archaeology: The First Temple Period* [ed. A. Killebrew and A. Vaughn; SBLSymS 18; Atlanta: Society of Biblical Literature, 2003] 320 n. 55). B. A. Levine argues on the basis of Ezek 20:27–29, 32–44 that sacrificial worship of Yhwh was, in fact, deemed to be illicit in the Babylonian Judean community ("The Next Phase in Jewish Religion: The Land of Israel as Sacred Space," in *Tehillah le-Moshe: Biblical and Judaic Studies in Honor of Moshe Greenberg* [ed. M. Cogan, B. L. Eichler, and J. H. Tigay; Winona Lake, IN: Eisenbrauns, 1997] 245–57). In this context, the oracle of Ezek 20:40 is telling: "For on my holy mountain, on the lofty mountain of Israel—declaration of the Lord Yhwh—there, the entire house of Israel, all of it, will worship me in the land. There I shall accept them and I shall seek your contributions and your choicest gifts in all your sacred things."

to the temple (Ezra 1:4, 6; 7:16; 8:25–30). Given Ezra's geographical location, it would not be feasible for Ezra to offer sacrifices at the Jerusalem temple. Nevertheless, he is able to study sacrifices in the book that
prescribes how sacrifices are to be offered (Ezra 7:10–11). When facing
the challenge of embarking on a long, unguarded journey from their
encampment by the Ahava River to Jerusalem, Ezra and his compatriots do not resort to bringing offerings to the nearest sanctuary. Rather,
Ezra proclaims a fast and seeks out the deity (ונבקשה מאלהינו על־זאת),
who becomes the object of entreaties by Ezra and his party (Ezra 8:21–
23).[30] In these and other ways, the authors of Ezra–Nehemiah highlight
a certain kind of piety that is especially appropriate to an exilic setting
but need not be exclusive to that setting.[31]

*Teaching and Practicing Torah
in the Homeland*

Although the genealogy situates Ezra in a long succession of priests
who served for centuries at the temple and before that at the tabernacle, the narrative introduction stresses Ezra's skill as a scribe of the
Torah.[32] Reflecting this bipartite introduction, Ezra receives in a number of cases the dual title 'the priest, the scribe' (הכהן הספר) in the rescript and story to follow.[33] But it is his expertise in "matters of the

---

30. On the phenomenon of preparatory fasts in late biblical literature, see also Esth
4:15–16; 2 Chr 20:3; Jer 36:9.
31. I. Eph'al discusses a variety of other adjustments the Judean community could
make in a Babylonian context: "The Babylonian Exile: The Survival of a National Minority in a Culturally Developed Milieu," in *Gründungsfeier am 16. Dezember 2005* (Centrum
Orbis Orientalis; Göttingen: Akademie der Wissenschaften, 2006) 21–31.
32. The rescript, however, underscores his ties to the highest echelon of the central
Achaemenid government (Ezra 7:12–14, 25–26).
33. Ezra 7:11 (///1 Esd 8:8), 12 (///1 Esd 8:9), 21(///1 Esd 8:19); Neh 8:9 (///1 Esd 9:49
["high priest and reader"]); 12:26. As simply a priest, see Ezra 10:10 (the title is lacking
in 1 Esd 9:7), 16 (///1 Esd 9:16). Ezra is first introduced as a scribe in Ezra 7:6 (/// 1 Esd 8:3).
For the name *Ezra* accompanied by the title of scribe, see Neh 8:1 (cf. 1 Esd 9:39 "priest
and reader"), 8:4 (cf. 1 Esd 9:42 "priest and reader of the law"), 8:13; 12:36. For the proper
name, absent any titles, see Ezra 7:1 (///1 Esd 8:1), 7:10 (///1 Esd 8:7), 7:25 (///1 Esd 8:23);
10:1 (///1 Esd 8:88), 10:2 (///1 Esd 8:89), 10:5 (///1 Esd 8:92), 10:6 (///1 Esd 9:1), 1 Esd 9:7; Neh
8:5 (///1 Esd 9:45), 6 (///1 Esd 9:46). The range and different combinations of Ezra's titles
are discussed at some length by Pakkala (*Ezra the Scribe*, 42–44), who regards the use of
the dual title as reflecting one of the latest layers in the development of the Ezra text.
This is quite possible, but the situation may be more complicated, given the likelihood of
haplography (*homoioarkton*) in the transmission of the text (הכהן הספר). For this reason, I
am not as inclined as Pakkala is to disregard the witness of 1 Esdras (9:39 [cf. Neh 8:1];
9:42 [cf. Neh 8:4]), when it has a form (or a modified form) of the dual title in the two instances in which Ezra–Nehemiah reads only one of the two titles ("scribe").

commandments of Yhwh and his statutes concerning Israel" (Ezra 7:11) that stands out.[34]

Indeed, when the omniscient narrator speaks of Ezra's ambition, he states that Ezra "set his heart to seek out [לדרוש] the Torah of Yhwh to observe [לעשת] and to teach [ללמד] statute and custom in Israel" (Ezra 7:10).[35] Ezra envisions his task upon his return as residing not so much in the narrow sacerdotal realm, offering sacrifices or helping to administer the temple, as in the realm of education and law, practicing and teaching Torah in his ancestral homeland. Moreover, his desire is not narrowly construed as teaching law to his fellow scribes at the temple. Rather, his ambition is broadly construed as teaching "statute and custom in Israel." In other words, the fact that Ezra and his priestly forefathers have not been able to officiate and offer sacrifices at the Jerusalem temple for a number of generations is not the driving force leading him to journey to his ancestral land. The declaration is particularly striking, because in pentateuchal legislation, officiating at the altar, offering sacrifices, and safeguarding the sanctity of the sanctuary are deemed to be central duties of priests (Exod 28:43; 29:1–46; 30:1–38; Lev 1:1–7:38; 8:14–9:24; Num 18:1–8).

To be sure, there are a few texts in Deuteronomy that mention priestly instructions. Before Israel is to go to war, a priest is supposed to address the troops (Deut 20:1–3). The pedagogical duties of the sacerdocy may also be assumed in the so-called law of the king (Deut 17:14–20) insofar as the Torah scroll that the king is obliged to study is in the possession of the Levitical priests (Deut 17:18). In one of his last actions, Moses writes down "this Torah" and gives it to the priests and instructs the priests and all the elders of Israel so that they might read and teach "this Torah" every seven years (Deut 31:9–13). Finally, in the poem of Deut 33:1–29 (the "Blessing of Moses"), teaching (יורו) Yhwh's instructions to Israel (תורתך לישראל) is one of the major functions of the tribe of Levi (MT Deut 33:10a), along with offering sacrifices (Deut 33:10b).[36] There are also passages in the prophets, especially in the

---

34. It is this expertise and skill, rather than the care and offering of sacrifices, that is celebrated in later tradition (e.g., *b. B. Bat.* 15a, 21b–22a; *b. Qidd.* 69a–b; *b. Sanh.* 21b; *b. Sukk.* 20a; *t. Sanh.* 4:7; *y. Meg.* 1:9). See further G. Porten, "Ezra in Rabbinic Literature," in *Restoration: Old Testament, Jewish, and Christian Perspectives* (ed. J. M. Scott; Journal for the Study of Judaism Supplement 72; Leiden: Brill, 2001) 305–33.

35. On the specialized use of the verb דרש, see my *I Chronicles 10–29* (AB 12A; New York: Doubleday, 2004) 524.

36. The pedagogical duties of the priests and Levites are also mentioned in some late narrative texts (e.g., 2 Chr 17:7–9; *Jub.* 31:13–17). In one of the rabbinic texts written

works of the later prophets, that speak, whether derisively or more positively, of requesting instruction (תורה) from the priests (Jer 18:18; Ezek 7:26; Hag 2:11; Mal 2:6–7). Hosea 4:6 speaks of Yhwh's rejecting the priest(hood), because "you have forgotten [תשכח] the teaching [תורת] of your God." The writer of Ezek 22:26 has Yhwh declare that the priests "have violated [חמסו] my instruction" (תורתי; cf. Zeph 3:4).

Nevertheless, in the legislation dealing with priests in the Pentateuch, the sacerdotal obligation to provide instruction in Torah is a relative rarity. In the section of Deuteronomy containing the laws pertaining to public officials (Deut 16:18–18:22), the stipulations governing Levitical priests (Deut 18:1–8) mention the duty "to stand [and] to serve [לשרת] in the name of Yhwh," that is, to serve at the central altar (Deut 18:5, 7). These stipulations pertaining to the support and duties of the Levitical priests do not mention teaching. Speaking on behalf of the deity is a responsibility of the prophets (Deut 18:15–22). The prophet that Yhwh will raise up is to be the successor to Moses (Deut 18:15–18). "If anyone should fail to heed the words he speaks in my [Yhwh's] name, I myself will hold him accountable" (Deut 18:19).

The transformations appearing in the book of Ezra ironically mean, among other things, that although Ezra the priest dedicates his life to teaching Torah to his compatriots so that they may apply Torah to their own lives, the Torah he is advancing mentions such a pedagogical role for priests only in a few of its Deuteronomic (or Deuteronomistic) portions.[37] In the case of Ezra, the wish to study and teach "the command-

---

about Ezra, Ezra is praised for his choice of training, because Torah study is deemed to be superior to temple worship (*b. Meg.* 16b).

37. Given that the stipulations alluded to in Ezra 9:1–2 involve Deuteronomic law and other aspects of the Ezra narrative presuppose Priestly stipulations, my assumption is that the Torah text referred to in the story of Ezra includes both Priestly and Deuteronomic elements. If, as some argue, the Torah of Ezra was primarily Priestly in character, the content of this more limited code would undermine the positive legal basis for Ezra's teaching mission. The secondary literature on the issue of the nature of Ezra's Torah is voluminous. See recently, S. Mowinckel, *Studien zu dem Buche Ezra–Nehemia*, vol. 3: *Die Esrageschichte und das Gesetz Moses* (Skrifter utg. av det Norske videnskaps-akademi i Oslo 2; Hist.-filos. Klasse n.s. 7; Oslo: Universitetsforlaget, 1965) 124–41; U. Kellerman, "Erwägungen zum Esragesetz," *ZAW* 80 (1968) 373–85; R. Rendtorff, "Esra und das Gesetz," *ZAW* 96 (1984) 165–84; A. H. J. Gunneweg, *Esra* (Kommentar zum Alten Testament 19/1; Gütersloh: Gütersloher Verlagshaus Mohn, 1985) 118–27; Williamson, *Ezra, Nehemiah*, 88–106; Blenkinsopp, *Ezra–Nehemiah*, 152–57; Kratz, *Das Judentum*, 6–22; I. Kalimi, *Zur Geschichtsschreibung des Chronisten: Literarisch-historiographische Abweichungen der Chronik von ihren Paralleltexten in den Samuel- und Königsbüchern* (BZAW 226; Berlin: de Gruyter, 1995) 128; Willi, *Juda – Yehud – Israel*, 91–101; T. Veijola, *Moses Erben: Studien zum Dekalog, zum Deuteronomismus und zum Schriftgelehrtentum* (BWANT 149; Stuttgart: Kohlhammer, 2000) 224–40; Becking, "The Idea of *Thorah*," 277–86.

ments of Yhwh and his statutes concerning Israel" (7:11) is, however, paramount. This evidence not only suggests that the definition of what it means to be a Judean (or an Israelite) has shifted in the Diaspora but also that (in Ezra's view) the Judeans residing in the homeland may profit from undergoing some aspects of this sort of shift themselves.[38]

Ethnicity, Geography, and Community Identity

At this point in the discussion, it may be helpful to pause and consider some controverted questions of identity, religion, and ethnicity. Within the first few lines of the Ezra narrative, one is introduced to two Judean groups coexisting in the mid-Persian period in two completely separate geographic locales. Judaism has become an international religion. One group is centered in Jerusalem in one part of the patrimonial territory of Israel, while another, consisting of expatriates, resides far away in one of the major centers of Mesopotamia. Neither community enjoys political hegemony. Both comprise but very small parts of an immense Achaemenid Empire. In spite of the great distance between them and the two different geographical regions of which they are a part, each exhibits a very similar social-religious structure consisting of Israelites (understood to be laypeople), priests, Levites, singers, gatekeepers, and temple servants (Ezra 7:7).[39] This common social structure is maintained over several generations with little development. At least, this seems to be a valid inference from the nearly identical social classification of the people who returned to Jerusalem under Zerubbabel and Jeshua—Israelites, priests, Levites, singers, gatekeepers, temple servants, sons of Solomon's servants (Ezra 2:1–70//Neh 7:6–72a)—and the

---

38. For the sake of clarity, I refer to the residents of the exilic communities as Judeans. The text of Ezra often refers to them as "the children of the exile" or simply as "Israel(ites)." In employing the latter usage, the writers of Ezra are not unique: H. G. M. Williamson, "The Concept of Israel in Transition," in *The World of Ancient Israel: Sociological, Anthropological, and Political Perspectives* (ed. R. E. Clements; Cambridge: Cambridge University Press, 1989) 119–42; S. S. Scatolini Apóstolo, "On the Elusiveness and Malleability of 'Israel,'" *Journal of Hebrew Scriptures* 6 (2006) 1–27. See further below.

39. The system of categorization is all the more intriguing when one considers that the books of Kings and Jeremiah do not depict preexilic Judah as having the same societal makeup: K. L. Sparks, *Ethnicity and Identity in Ancient Israel* (Winona Lake, IN: Eisenbrauns, 1998). To be sure, there is some, but by no means complete, overlap between the presentation of Chronicles (which largely depicts the time of the monarchy) and the presentation of Ezra–Nehemiah insofar as both books speak of priests, Levites, gatekeepers, and singers, but most commentators believe that the authors of Chronicles are largely engaging and (re)configuring the social makeup of the postexilic society of their own time and projecting this picture, to a significant extent, onto the period of the monarchy.

people who returned under Ezra—Israelites, priests, Levites, singers, gatekeepers, and temple servants (Ezra 7:7; 8:1–20).[40]

Both groups also exhibit similar kinship structures, the בית אבות ('ancestral houses'), marking units that are larger than families but smaller than tribes.[41] This social organization of the people into ancestral houses is attested in Chronicles, Ezra–Nehemiah, and certain parts of the Priestly work. To be sure, the בית אבות have been subject to much discussion over the past few decades, with scholars disagreeing about the size and precise configuration of these kinship or quasi-kinship units.[42] The issue does not have to be resolved in the context of the present discussion. Rather, it is enough to say that the בית אבות appear as social entities within both the Judean community in Babylon and the Judean community centered in Jerusalem.

Residents of the two communities share a number of important ethnic markers: the same languages (Hebrew and Aramaic), the same bloodlines, similar traditions, and common ties to a particular ancestral territory.[43] This evidence suggests that in the view of the authors of Ezra–Nehemiah the Yahwistic communities in Jerusalem and Babylon shared much in common and developed up to a certain point in parallel fashion during the postexilic period.

At first glance, the similar social-religious makeup of the two communities may seem absolutely remarkable, but it is not. In the narrative world of Ezra–Nehemiah, the Judean residents of the province of

40. Although the 'gatekeepers' (השערים) are mentioned in Ezra 7:7, they do not appear in the list of Ezra 8:1–20.

41. J. P. Weinberg, "Das Bēit ʾĀbōt im 6.-4. Jh. v. u.Z.," *VT* 23 (1974) 400–414; P.-E. Dion, "The Civic-and-Temple Community of Persian Period Judaea: Neglected Insights from Eastern Europe," *JNES* 50 (1991) 281–87; J. Blenkinsopp, "Temple and Society in Achaemenid Judah," in *Second Temple Studies 1: Persian Period* (ed. P. R. Davies; JSOTSup 117; Sheffield: JSOT Press, 1991) 22–53; B. A. Levine, "The Clan-Based Economy of Ancient Israel," in *Symbiosis, Symbolism, and the Power of the Past: Canaan, Ancient Israel, and Their Neighbors from the Late Bronze Age through Roman Palaestina—Proceedings of the Centennial Symposium, W. F. Albright Institute of Archaeological Research and American Schools of Oriental Research, Jerusalem, May 29–31, 2000* (ed. W. G. Dever and S. Gitin; Winona Lake, IN: Eisenbrauns, 2003) 445–53. H. G. M. Williamson argues, however, that one can discern within the development of Ezra–Nehemiah some changes in familial structure: "The Family in Persian Period Judah: Some Textual Reflections," in *Symbiosis, Symbolism, and the Power of the Past*, 469–85.

42. A brief discussion of relevant scholarship with additional references may be found in my *I Chronicles 10–29*, 616–17.

43. A. D. Smith, *The Ethnic Origins of Nations* (Oxford: Blackwell, 1986); R. H. Thompson, *Theories of Ethnicity: A Critical Appraisal* (New York: Greenwood, 1989); Brett, "Interpreting Ethnicity," 9–20.

Yehud are actually repatriates from Babylon, Judeans who elected to return to the land of their ancestors in the late sixth century during the reigns of Cyrus the Great and Darius I (Ezra 1–3). One could thus argue that such strong similarities are only to be expected between the two groups. The very terms used to describe the Judean residents— בני הגולה 'the children of the exile' (Ezra 4:1; 6:19–20; 8:35; 10:7, 16), העלים משבי הגולה 'the ones who came up from the captivity of the exile' (Ezra 2:1//Neh 7:6), and הגולה 'the exile(s)' (Ezra 1:11; 9:4; 10:6)—reinforce this impression.[44] When divorce proceedings are later convened during the time of Ezra's visit to deal with the problem of mixed marriages, the convocation is referred to as the 'assembly of the exile' (קהל הגולה; Ezra 10:8, 12–16).[45] In short, the very terms employed to refer to the Judean community underscore the links between this community and the community in Babylon.[46] The nomenclature used ("the children of the exile") underscores dislocation as the cardinal feature in shaping the group's self-definition. The reference to the experience of exile becomes determinative in distinguishing between insiders and outsiders.[47]

The Israel of Ezra is geographically dispersed. The various people who identify with the name of Israel may all profess an attachment to the land of Israel, but only some actually reside there. Indigeneity is no longer a criterion for Israelite identity. The term *Israel* has taken on significant ethnic and religious overtones. When Ezra later speaks of his taking strength and assembling "leaders from Israel [ראשים מישראל] to go up with me" to Jerusalem (Ezra 7:28), he is speaking of fellow expatriates and not of people in his homeland.

---

44. The reference to the בני גלותא in Ezra 6:16 is also relevant. On the references to the hendiadys שארית ופליטה 'surviving remnant' (Ezra 9:14), the 'remnant' (פליטה; 9:8, 13, 15), and other terms for the community in the penitential prayer of Ezra, see M. J. Boda, *Praying the Tradition* (BZAW 277; Berlin: de Gruyter, 1999) 68–70.

45. The mention of the 'assembly of God' (קהל האלהים) in the time of Nehemiah (13:1) is also worth noting. In this case, the writers are quoting from the "Book of Moses," that is, from Deut 23:4–7.

46. The situation is more complex in the so-called Nehemiah memoir, because Nehemiah often refers to his constituents as '(the) Judeans' (היהודים): G. N. Knoppers, "Nehemiah and Sanballat: The Enemy Without or Within?" in *Judah and the Judeans in the Fourth Century B.C.E.* (ed. O. Lipschits, G. N. Knoppers, and R. Albertz; Winona Lake, IN: Eisenbrauns, 2007) 305–31.

47. I speak of a "reference to the experience of exile," because most of the people that Ezra would be dealing with in mid-fifth-century Yehud would not have experienced exile themselves. Most of these compatriots would be at least a couple of generations removed from the return under Sheshbazzar and the later return under Zerubbabel and Jeshua.

The same point can be seen from another perspective. Ethnographers point out that some groups exhibit a clear sense of the self and the "other," actively defining their own identities by articulating both their own *ethnos* and what they are not—the *ethnē* that are their opposites.[48] In the case of Ezra, those who are neither repatriates nor their descendants are referred to as 'the people of the land(s)' (עם/עם הארץ הארצות) or 'the peoples of the land(s)' (עמי הארץ/עמי הארצות).[49] The very choice of nomenclature is important, indicating that residence in the land of Israel is no longer either a necessary or a sufficient criterion of Israelite identity.[50]

We have been discussing the depiction of the Judeans in Ezra as a transtemporal, international entity. The nomenclature referring to the people and the nomenclature referring to their God are identical, regardless of whether one is speaking of dislocated Israelites or of relocated Israelites. The use of such similar terminology is important, yet it does not tell the full story. It does not address the diachronic presentation of corporate life in Yehud over several generations. The book of Ezra–Nehemiah depicts snippets of time in the history of postexilic Judah from the late sixth century to the end of the fifth century. When Ezra and his compatriots elect to travel to Yehud in the mid-fifth cen-

---

48. In detail, see E. Ben Zvi, "Inclusion in and Exclusion from Israel as Conveyed by the Use of the Term 'Israel' in Post-Monarchic Biblical Texts," in *The Pitcher Is Broken: Memorial Essays for Gösta W. Ahlström* (ed. S. W. Holloway and L. K. Handy; JSOTSup 190; Sheffield: Sheffield Academic Press, 1995) 99–145. For the Greco-Roman realm, see J. Hall, *Ethnic Identity in Greek Antiquity* (Cambridge: Cambridge University Press, 1997); I. Malkin, "Introduction," in *Ancient Perceptions of Greek Ethnicity* (ed. I. Malkin; Cambridge: Harvard University Press, 2001)1–28; B. Isaac, *The Invention of Racism in Classical Antiquity* (Princeton: Princeton University Press, 2004).

49. See, for instance, Ezra 3:3; 4:4; 9:1, 2, 11; 10:2, 11; Neh 9:24, 30; 10:29, 31, 32. Compare עמי התעבות האלה 'these abominable peoples' (Ezra 9:14); גוי־הארץ 'nations of the land' (Ezra 6:21); כל הגוים אשר סביבתנו 'all the nations that surround us' (Neh 6:16). L. S. Fried distinguishes between the 'the people of the land(s)' (עם־הארץ/עם הארצות), that is, the Judeans who remained in the land from the time of the Babylonian and Egyptian exiles, and 'the peoples of the land(s)' (עמי הארץ/עמי הארצות), that is, the surrounding nations: "The *ʿam-hāʾāreṣ* in Ezra 4:4 and Persian Imperial Administration," in *Judah and the Judeans in the Persian Period* (ed. O. Lipschits and M. Oeming; Winona Lake, IN: Eisenbrauns, 2006) 123–45. There is a distinction of this sort in preexilic texts, but I am not so confident that one can maintain the distinction in the postexilic text of Ezra–Nehemiah. See Willi, *Juda – Jehud – Israel*, 11–17; and also the earlier discussion of S. Talmon, "The Judaean *ʿam haʾareṣ* in Historical Perspective," in the *Fourth World Congress of Jewish Studies, 1: Papers* (Jerusalem: World Union of Jewish Studies, 1967) 71–76.

50. D. Rom-Shiloni discusses the influence of Ezekiel on the mentality found in Ezra–Nehemiah: "Ezekiel as the Voice of the Exiles and Constructor of Exilic Ideology," *HUCA* 76 (2006) 1–45.

tury, almost six decades have elapsed since the time of the dedication of the temple under Zerubbabel and Jeshua.

Interestingly, the authors of Ezra–Nehemiah do not present the on-going life of the Judean communities of Babylon and Yehud in a static manner. Quite the contrary, there is a historical progression in the narration of the returns under Sheshbazzar, Zerubbabel and Jeshua, and Ezra. To be sure, there is a stress on obedience to the Torah in Ezra 1–6. The narrators refer, for example, to the "Torah of Moses" as an authoritative writing in connection with the sacrifice of burnt offerings at the Jerusalem altar (Ezra 3:2–3). The celebration of the Festival of Sukkot is said to occur 'as it is written' (כככתוב; Ezra 3:4). But, as we have seen, there is a new element introduced into the story when the authors depict the arrival of Ezra, the scribe, "skilled in the Torah of Moses," in Jerusalem (Ezra 7:6–9), because this scholar "set his heart to seek out the Torah of Yhwh to observe and to teach law and custom in Israel" (Ezra 7:10).[51]

In the narration of Ezra's work in Jerusalem, the task of publicly teaching the Torah stands out. Perhaps the parade example is Ezra's reading from the "scroll of the Torah of Moses by which Yhwh charged Israel" in front of the assembly gathered before the Water Gate (Neh 8:1–8). The communal nature of this undertaking is stressed: "The ears of all the people were [directed] to the scroll of the Torah" (Neh 8:3). But the pedagogical task involves more than reading. The Levites, who read from the scroll, are "making [it] distinct [מפרש] and giving the sense [שום שכל] so that they [the people] understood [ויבינו] the reading" (Neh 8:8; cf. v. 12). Moreover, the occasion is presented as a solemn one. The people are repeatedly told not to mourn or weep, as they come to grasp the force of the texts read to them, because "this day is holy to Yhwh your God" (Neh 8:9; cf. v. 11). In the narrative that follows, the community translates its learning into practice, when the people observe Sukkot (Neh 8:13–18). "The entire assembly, those who had returned from the captivity, constructed booths and resided in the booths, for they had not done so since the days of Joshua, son of Nun" (Neh 8:17).[52] Each day, during the celebrations, Ezra read to them from "the scroll of the Torah of God" (Neh 8:18).

---

51. See also B. Becking, "Law as Expression of Religion (Ezra 7–10)," in *Yahwism after the Exile: Perspectives on Israelite Religion in the Persian Era* (ed. R. Albertz and B. Becking; Assen: Van Gorcum, 2003) 18–31.

52. The incomparability statement is remarkable in light of the earlier assertion that the celebration of Sukkot in the time of Zerubbabel and Jeshua was conducted "as is written" (Ezra 3:4a). The claim made about this earlier celebration may relate directly,

Ezra's instructing the people in the Torah along with the people's concerted observance of the stipulations found in the Torah scroll are clearly presented as highlights of his work back in the homeland. But the kind of public reading of the Torah that one finds in connection with the observance of Sukkot is not unique. Another public reading of the Torah by the Levites involves the Israelites' public confession of sins (Neh 9:1–3), which introduces the long Levitical prayer (9:4–37). The confession of the people's sins and the sins of their ancestors leads, in turn, to the public formulation of a detailed covenantal 'pledge' (אמנה; Neh 10:1–40). Nehemiah, the leaders, the priests and Levites, the ancestral heads, and the rest of the people all swear an oath in writing "to follow the Torah of God, which was given through Moses the servant of God, and to take care to observe all of the commandments of Yhwh our God, his customs and statutes" (Neh 10:1, 30). In the case of the 'pledge' (אמנה), one written document validates the authority of another (the Torah), even if a number of the commitments of the communal covenant extend beyond the commandments found within the Torah.[53]

One of the important aspects of the presentation of Ezra's story, even as this story becomes linked to Nehemiah's, is the stress laid upon the public reading of, the popular assent given to, and the broad implementation of Torah stipulations within the community.[54] Here, one can see the desire felt by the editors of the book to integrate the story of Ezra into the larger framework of the story of Nehemiah, because the public proclamation and explication of Torah statutes is not an emphasis in the so-called memoir of Nehemiah. The point of the story goes beyond one in which the law is being conceived of as an authoritative written text implemented by select leaders, as in the time of Zerubbabel and Jeshua. There is an additional dimension to the commitment given to the Torah in the Ezra narrative in that the Torah

---

however, to the schedule and number of the daily burnt offerings (Ezra 3:4b), whereas the latter statement has to do with all of the people actually constructing booths and residing in them (Neh 8:13–17). For the specific citation base of each text, see K. L. Spawn, *As It Is Written and Other Citation Formulae in the Old Testament: Their Use, Development, Syntax and Significance* (BZAW 311; Berlin: de Gruyter, 2002) 97–101, 212–17.

53. Rudolph, *Esra und Nehemia,* 172–81; D. J. A. Clines, "Nehemiah 10 as an Early Example of Early Jewish Biblical Exegesis," *JSOT* 21 (1981) 111–17; Williamson, *Ezra, Nehemiah,* 320–40; Blenkinsopp, *Ezra–Nehemiah,* 308–19; David A. Glatt-Gilad, "Reflections on the Structure and Significance of the *'amānāh* (Neh 10,29–40)," *ZAW* 112 (2000) 386–95.

54. For the view that Neh 8 should be read as an integral part of the larger Nehemiah narrative, see B. Becking, "The Idea of *Thorah* in Ezra 7–10: A Functional Analysis," *Zeitschrift für altorientalische und biblische Rechtsgeschichte* 7 (2001) 273–85.

comes to be recited and enacted in a public setting.[55] Laymen, lay-women, and children all participate in the exercise (Neh 8:2–3, 7–8) in conformity with one of the directives found in Deuteronomy (31:9–13). The parties who later 'cut a covenant' (כרתים אמנה) include not only the governor, gatekeepers, singers, and temple servants, but also their wives, sons, and daughters, "all who know (and) understand" (Neh 10:1–29). Yet another public reading from the scroll of Moses serves as a prelude to separation of "everything foreign from Israel" (Neh 13:1–3).[56] Public lectures, group discussions, and the practice of authoritative writings thus affirm the authority of the Torah for the ongoing life of the repatriated community.[57]

Conclusions

In standard scholarly treatments of community identity in Ezra–Nehemiah, an emphasis is placed on the narrowing down of the concept of Israel to apply only to the exiles and their descendants. Whereas some postmonarchic texts, such as Chronicles, broadly employ the term *Israel* to designate anyone who is a resident of the kingdoms of Israel and Judah or who is a biological descendant of the eponymous ancestor Jacob/Israel, the writers of Ezra–Nehemiah restrict the usage of the term *Israel* to apply to the Judahite deportees to Babylon and their seed. There is much value in recognizing this distinction and in coming to terms with the manner in which different writers (re)define Israel during the Persian and Hellenistic periods.[58]

---

55. As J.-L. Ska observes, certain texts within the Pentateuch underscore the relevance of written law and the authority that this legislation is to have for the larger community: "From History Writing to Library Building: The End of History and the Birth of the Book," in *The Pentateuch as Torah: New Models for Understanding Its Promulgation and Acceptance* (ed. G. N. Knoppers and B. M. Levinson; Winona Lake, IN: Eisenbrauns, 2007) 145–69. J. Schaper explores the process whereby legal and other important texts were published and confirmed in the community, "The 'Publication' of Legal Texts in Ancient Judah," in *The Pentateuch as Torah*, 225–36.

56. The number of public readings is stressed by M. W. Duggan (*The Covenant Renewal in Ezra–Nehemiah (Neh 7:72b–10:40): An Exegetical, Literary, and Theological Study* [SBLDS 164; Atlanta: Society of Biblical Literature, 2001] 108).

57. In these instances, one can discern a transition not so much from the oral to the written as from the written to the oral: G. N. Knoppers and P. B. Harvey, "The Pentateuch in Ancient Mediterranean Context: The Promulgation of Local Lawcodes," in *The Pentateuch as Torah: New Models for Understanding Its Promulgation and Acceptance* (ed. G. N. Knoppers and B. M. Levinson; Winona Lake, IN: Eisenbrauns, 2007) 105–41.

58. So also in the prophetic writings. See, e.g., R. G. Kratz, "Israel in the Book of Isaiah," *JSOT* 31 (2006) 103–28.

Far less attention has been devoted, however, to how the nomenclature employed in Ezra, although restrictive in one sense is open-ended
in another sense. The usage of 'the children of exile' (בני הגולה) for 'Israel' (ישראל) authorizes a transformation in the nature of the Judean
people from a people that is restricted to a certain land in the southern
Levant to one that operates in different lands. In my essay, I have argued for a dynamic and complex view of identity formation in the
story of Ezra that attempts to take into account the transtemporal and
international nature of the Israelite people. Ezra is not only a story of
the gradual reconstitution of the formerly exiled Judean people in Jerusalem and Yehud but also a story of the establishment and confirma-
tion of productive long-term relations between the Judean community
of Babylon and the Judean community of Yehud. The identification of
the exiles with Israel is thus not simply a slight against the Judeans
who remained in the land during the Neo-Babylonian era but also a
privileging of the Diaspora in the continuing history of the Judean
people. That the usage remains in place, even though several generations of returnees have lived in the land by the time Ezra arrives in Jerusalem suggests the primacy of the exilic designation as a symbol
uniting the two communities. Indeed, the continuation of this usage
over many generations by the authors/editors of Ezra–Nehemiah, who
lived centuries after the first return, perpetuates a liminal state for the
people residing back in the homeland. The returnees living back in
their ancestral territory derive their primary identity neither from
their homeland nor from their eponymous ancestor but from their ancestral links to the Diaspora.

This intergenerational dynamic, which privileges the accomplishments of expatriates in the ongoing history of their ancestral common-
wealth, points to a shortcoming of the standard approach, which
focuses simply on the rebuilding of institutions in Yehud. Many scholars have construed the *Leitmotiv* of Ezra–Nehemiah to be the successful
institution of a theocracy in Yehud.[59] Accepting the fact of Persian im-

---

59. So, e.g., M. Noth, *Überlieferungsgeschichtliche Studien: Die sammelnden und bearbei-
tenden Geschichtswerke im Alten Testament* (Tübingen: Max Niemeyer, 1943) 171–80; Rudolph, *Esra und Nehemia*, xxvii–xxx; idem, *Chronikbücher* (Handbuch zum Alten Testament 21; Tübingen: Mohr, 1955) xviii–xxiv; K. Galling, *Die Bücher der Chronik, Esra,
Nehemia* (Das Alte Testament Deutsch 12; Göttingen: Vandenhoeck & Ruprecht, 1954) 14–
17; O. Plöger, *Theokratie und Eschatologie* (WMANT 2; Neukirchen-Vluyn: Neukirchener
Verlag, 1959) 50–58; J. M. Myers, *I Chronicles* (AB 12; Garden City, NY: Doubleday, 1964)
lxxviii–lxxx; idem, *Ezra–Nehemiah*, liii–lxii. E. M. Dörrfuss points to a number of serious
conceptual problems with this longstanding view, both with respect to its definition and

perial rule, the community concentrates on reconstituting itself after
the disaster of the Babylonian deportations. When the people return to
Judah and Jerusalem, rebuild the temple, and remove everything foreign from Jerusalem, the Judean community becomes the divinely ordained and divinely governed society it was supposed to be.[60] In this
view, the perspective of Ezra–Nehemiah (or of Chronicles-Ezra-Nehemiah, for that matter) is fundamentally un-eschatalogical, if not anti-
eschatological, in nature.[61] Given the fact that Israel has been restored,
there is no longer any need for fundamental change.

Nevertheless, the writers of Ezra–Nehemiah can only celebrate the
accomplishments of Sheshbazzar, Zerubbabel, Jeshua, Ezra, and Nehemiah if they have accepted the ongoing fact of the Judean dispersion.[62]
For the "children of the exile" to provide repeatedly an active stimulus
to the life of the "children of the exile" residing in the homeland, there

---

to theocracy's being set in opposition to eschatology: *Mose in den Chronikbüchern: Garant
theokratischer Zukunftserwartung* (BZAW 219; Berlin: de Gruyter, 1994) 18–118.

60. Of course, as R. Albertz observes, the restoration was only in name, because the
Davidic monarchy was not returned to its former position of power in the community: *A
History of Religion in the Old Testament Period, 2: From the Exile to the Maccabees* (OTL; Lou-
isville: Westminster John Knox, 1994) 437–54; idem, "The Thwarted Restoration," in *Yah-
wism after the Exile: Perspectives on Israelite Religion in the Persian Era* (ed. R. Albertz and
B. Becking; Assen: Van Gorcum, 2003) 1–17.

61. The view of common authorship for Chronicles-Ezra-Nehemiah, predominant in
the nineteenth and first half of the twentieth century, has been much questioned in recent scholarship: S. Japhet, "The Supposed Common Authorship of Chronicles and Ezra–
Nehemiah Investigated Anew," *VT* 18 (1968) 338–71; eadem, *The Ideology of the Book of
Chronicles and Its Place in Biblical Thought* (Beiträge zur Erforschung des Alten Testaments und des antiken Judentum 9; Frankfurt am Main: Peter Lang, 1989); H. G. M. Wil-
liamson, *Israel in the Books of Chronicles* (Cambridge: Cambridge University Press, 1977);
T. Willi, "Late Persian Period Judaism and Its Conception of an Integral Israel according
to Chronicles," in *Second Temple Studies 2: Temple and Community in the Persian Period* (ed.
T. C. Eskenazi and K. H. Richards; JSOTSup 175; Sheffield: JSOT Press, 1994) 146–62;
Knoppers, *I Chronicles 1–9*, 73–100. But it does not appear that such a separation of
Chronicles from Ezra–Nehemiah would affect the conclusions of these earlier scholars
that the work (more narrowly construed as the book of Ezra–Nehemiah) is all about the
establishment of a theocracy in Jerusalem and Judah.

62. At least for the period under view. In this context, it is relevant that some passages in Ezra (9:7–9) and Nehemiah (9:32, 36–37) speak of the exile as an ongoing phenomenon, in spite of the returns of some of the Babylonian captives back to Yehud. See,
further, P. R. Ackroyd, *Exile and Restoration: A Study of Hebrew Thought of the Sixth Century
B.C.* (OTL; Philadelphia: Westminster, 1968) 232–56; Williamson, *Ezra, Nehemiah*, 134; Albertz, *History of Religion*, 454–58. B. C. Gregory discusses the possible connections between these texts in Ezra–Nehemiah and related motifs in Third Isaiah, "The Postexilic
Exile in Third Isaiah," *JBL* 126 (2007) 475–96.

must be a longstanding diasporic community.[63] The writers allow that the religious practices of the two groups, given their different locations—one with a temple in their midst and the other with a temple in another land—must differ to some degree. Members of the Babylonian Judean community must be largely content with supporting Jerusalem, the Jerusalem temple, and its clergy at a distance, whereas the Judeans residing within Yehud and its environs must frequent the temple itself. Judaism has become an international religion, but the religious practices of the "children of the exile," who live in different international settings, are not and cannot be completely identical.

The stance of the Ezra narrative toward community identity has to do with more than an acceptance of the international nature of the Judean people. The writers also endorse the adoption of certain practices developed in other lands as helpful for the community in Yehud. Transformations that have taken place in the Diaspora as a key to community survival are deemed to be relevant for the people in the homeland as well.[64] To cast the story of Ezra conservatively as one of restoration is, therefore, misleading in some important respects. The writers of the Ezra story promote a set of behaviors that largely did not exist either in the monarchy or, for that matter, in early postexilic times.[65] The communal public readings and discussions of the Torah, the priestly and Levitical instruction of the laity in the Torah, and the public divorce and dispossession proceedings against those involved in mixed marriages are all cases in point. In the presentation of Ezra–

---

63. See further my "Construction of Judean Diasporic Identity in Ezra–Nehemiah," in _Judah and the Judeans: Negotiating Identity in an International Context_ (ed. O. Lipschits, G. N. Knoppers, and M. Oeming; Winona Lake, IN: Eisenbrauns, forthcoming). The pattern sketched in the book of Ezra–Nehemiah is not unique but endures in subsequent centuries. In a later age, the importance of the eastern Diaspora for the Judean community in the southern Levant is evident in the efforts of the _Tannaim_, the _Amoraim_, and later the _Savoraim_ and the _Gaonim_ in compiling, organizing, and editing the Babylonian Talmud, a monumental work that becomes one of the "Sources" of Judaism.

64. The inconclusive ending of the book (Neh 13:4–31) in which Nehemiah battles against a variety of problems (e.g., Sabbath observance, insufficient support for the Levites, intermarriage) also indicates that the community in Yehud has not yet achieved full restoration. Rather than depicting a society that has achieved all of its goals, the writers of Ezra–Nehemiah depict a society that is called to work toward further renewal.

65. One could hold that a number of Ezra's actions are called for in different portions of the Pentateuch; but, even so, the point is that these mandates are implemented in Ezra's time. The reforms of Josiah during which the king reads "all of the words of the covenant scroll" to all of the people assembled from Judah and Jerusalem constitute a preexilic precedent for one of Ezra's actions (2 Kgs 23:1–3), but this Josianic initiative, as presented in Kings, is a unique venture.

Nehemiah, these phenomena appear as welcome developments, but they are also new developments.[66] With the mission of Ezra, the Torah takes on a broader role within provincial life.

The same phenomenon can be viewed from another angle within the larger compass of the community's history. In the narration of Ezra–Nehemiah, the passage of time is not entirely kind to the repatriates and their descendants in Yehud. Indeed, the very mission of Ezra suggests a need in the homeland.[67] In the age of Ezra, some of the expatriates become repatriates to reform the previously repatriated expatriates. The story of Ezra is, therefore, as much a justification of the ongoing relevance of the Babylonian Judean community and the positive contributions it makes to the refashioning of the homeland community as it is a story about the internal social and religious development of Yehud. The historical dynamic depicted in the book authorizes a role both for Judeans residing in the Diaspora and for diasporic Judeans residing in Yehud to play in the ongoing development of the Israelite people.

---

66. The point about obedience to the Torah is stressed by Josephus in his retelling of Ezra's mission (*Ant.* 11.141–58); L. H. Feldman, "Restoration in Josephus," in *Restoration: Old Testament, Jewish, and Christian Perspectives* (ed. James M. Scott; Journal for the Study of Judaism Supplement 72; Leiden: Brill, 2001) 231–41.

67. A point also emphasized by Bedford, "Diaspora: Homeland Relations," 157–58.

Ezra's Mission and the Levites of Casiphia

MARK LEUCHTER

Temple University

According to the historical picture presented in the book of Ezra–Nehemiah, a Jewish priest of Zadokite heritage named Ezra was charged by the royal Persian authorities to return from Babylon to supervise the civil dynamics of the community in his national homeland of Yehud sometime in the mid-fifth century B.C.E.[1] This was part of a larger mission that bestowed on Ezra the authority of royal emissary over the entire satrapy of Transeuphrates of which Yehud was only one part, and it is here where scholars have found difficulty in reconciling the biblical presentation of Ezra with the implications of his larger mission. On the one hand, Ezra's priestly lineage is strongly emphasized within the tradition (Ezra 7:1–5), as are his qualifications as a proficient exegete of the Mosaic Torah (Ezra 7:6, 10). However one chooses to identify the Mosaic Torah tradition in the mid-fifth century,[2] the identification of Ezra as a skilled and qualified interpreter

---

1. Some scholars date Ezra's mission to 398 B.C.E., during the reign of Artaxerxes II; see D. Rooke, *Zadok's Heirs: The Role and Development of the High Priesthood in Ancient Israel* ([Oxford: Oxford University Press, 2000] 153–54 n. 6) for an overview of scholarly views on this date and other options; L. S. Fried, "You Shall Appoint Judges: Ezra's Mission and the Rescript of Artaxerxes," in *Persia and Torah: The Theory of Imperial Authorization of the Pentateuch* (ed. J. W. Watts; SBLSymS; Atlanta: Scholars Press, 2001) 63–89; J. Schaper, "The Temple Treasury Committee in the Time of Nehemiah and Ezra," *VT* 47 (1997) 201; S. M. Olyan, "Purity Ideology in Ezra–Nehemiah as a Tool to Reconstitute the Community," *Journal for the Study of Judaism* 35 (2004) 14. The traditional date of 458 B.C.E., however, can be defended (Rooke herself adopts this date in *Zadok's Heirs*, 155). See R. C. Steiner, "The *mbqr* at Qumran, the *episkopos* in the Athenian Empire, and the Meaning of *lbqr'* in Ezra 7:14: On the Relation of Ezra's Mission to the Persian Legal Project," *JBL* 120 (2001) 628–30; J. Blenkinsopp, *Ezra–Nehemiah* (OTL; Louisville: Westminster John Knox, 1988) 144.
2. For diverse options of identifying the Mosaic "Torah" at this time, see T. C. Römer and M. Z. Brettler, "Deuteronomy 34 and the Case for a Persian Hexateuch," *JBL* 119 (2000) 401–19; J. Blenkinsopp, "Was the Pentateuch the Civic and Religious Constitution of the Jewish Ethnos in the Persian Period?" in *Persia and Torah* (ed. J. W. Watts; SBLSymS; Atlanta: Scholars Press, 2001) 56–59.

and administrator of its contexts would facilitate his authority over the Jews of Yehud as outlined in the Artaxerxes Rescript in Ezra 7:12–26.[3] However, the Rescript also identifies him as an authority over the entire satrapy of Transeuphrates (vv. 25–26). If Ezra's primary responsibility was to establish socioreligious standards among the Jews of Yehud according to the Mosaic Torah (Ezra 7:14), why is he charged with setting ostensibly secular administrators over the entire satrapy of Transeuphrates (Ezra 7:25–26)?[4]

One could reasonably argue that, as a member of the Zadokite elite in Babylon, Ezra not only would have possessed a good priestly education but also would have obtained skills within the Persian administrative superstructure.[5] But if this is the case—that is, if he carried dual responsibilities that brought together his duties as a Persian official and a Zadokite priest—why do the redactors of Ezra–Nehemiah keep Ezra at a relative distance from the inner hierarchy of the Jerusalem priesthood?[6] Ezra's Zadokite (or, better, Aaronide) lineage is remem-

---

3. Some scholars view the Rescript as generally authentic due to diplomatic language therein that is equally at home in other Persian diplomatic correspondence; see Steiner, "The *mbqr* at Qumran," 623–24. Steiner makes a strong case for the authenticity of Ezra's mission, though the Rescript itself (while likely inspired by an actual diplomatic charge or document) is constructed for its present literary context. For an overview, see A. C. Hagedorn, "Local Law in an Imperial Context: The Role of the Torah in the (Imagined) Persian Period," in *The Pentateuch as Torah: New Models for Understanding Its Promulgation and Acceptance* (ed. G. N. Knoppers and B. M. Levinson; Winona Lake, IN: Eisenbrauns, 2007) 69–71.

4. This is the reading of the charge offered by L. S. Fried ("You Shall Appoint Judges," 63–89). Though Ezra's actual mission likely consisted of responsibilities other than the appointment of secular Persian administrators (as will be argued below), Fried's evidence does place the language of the Rescript in a larger political context that gives the impression of this sort of role for Ezra.

5. See esp. D. S. Vanderhooft, "New Evidence Pertaining to the Transition from Neo-Babylonian to Achaemenid Administration in Palestine," in *Yahwism after the Exile: Perspectives on Israelite Religion in the Persian Era* (ed. R. Albertz and B. Becking; Assen: Van Gorcum, 2003) 234.

6. I use the term *redactors* here for purposes of clarity in relation to the writers and editors who oversaw the penultimate shaping of the materials in Ezra–Nehemiah. It is clear, however, that the book emerged over a long period of time with successive waves of redaction adding new layers of discourse and commentary. For a full discussion, see J. L. Wright, *Rebuilding Identity: The Nehemiah Memoir and Its Earliest Readers* (BZAW 348; Berlin: de Gruyter, 2004). Furthermore, G. N. Knoppers argues for a later hand at work in Ezra 1–3, writing with an eye to 1–2 Chronicles (*I Chronicles 1–9* [AB 12; New York: Doubleday, 2003] 96–100). Though Wright's case for Ezra 1–6 as a response to an early stratum of the Nehemiah corpus is compelling (*Rebuilding Identity*, 338–39), the evidence that Knoppers marshals suggests subsequent reworking within these chapters. See also R. C. Steiner ("Bishlam's Archival Search Report in Nehemiah's Archive: Multiple

bered and credited,[7] as are his concerns with temple ritual, but this pertains primarily to his fitness as a Persian royal representative (Ezra 7:15–19) and his charge to bring the temple in line with imperial interests. Considering the paramount role of the Zadokite priesthood in the civil and religious life of Second Temple Judaism, it would be fitting for him to be portrayed in a manner consistent with this form of leadership,[8] yet this is not the case. What is known of Zadokite priestly social convention is not reflected in Ezra's behavior.[9] Possessing Zadokite priestly heritage does not automatically lead to priestly behavior or participation in an active priesthood, especially when the person is separated from the Jerusalem cult;[10] this is certainly Ezra's background upon receiving his Persian commission. It is curious, however, that in the Ezra Memoir only Ezra appears as a suitable candidate for the office of high priest (Ezra 7:5), and no other such candidate receives note; yet, upon reaching Jerusalem, there is little to point to Ezra's incorporation into the active temple priesthood, despite the influence in the religious life of Yehud this would have afforded.[11] Ezra's Zadokite

---

Introductions and Reverse Chronological Order as Clues to the Origin of the Aramaic Letters in Ezra 4–6," *JBL* 125 [2006] 674–76), who notes that an early stratum of material in Ezra 4–6 would have been drawn from Nehemiah's archive and that this material would have been incorporated into a later and larger literary context. Steiner's discussion points to a significant portion of material originating in Nehemiah's own time.

7. The genealogy in Ezra 7:1–5 ends with Aaron; Rooke sees this as a statement on Ezra's fitness to serve as high priest, though she also recognizes that this is not developed within the Ezra Memoir, with Ezra serving more as a second Moses than a second Aaron (*Zadok's Heirs*, 164–165). The emphasis is directed to the exodus/wilderness era for purposes other than matters concerning the high priesthood; see below.

8. For detailed examinations of the influence and social role of the Zadokite priesthood in the Second Temple period, see J. W. Watts, *Rhetoric and Ritual in Leviticus: From Sacrifice to Scripture* (New York: Cambridge University Press, 2007), esp. pp. 142–72; G. Boccaccini, *Roots of Rabbinic Judaism: An Intellectual History from Ezekiel to Daniel* (Grand Rapids, MI: Eerdmans, 2002) 49–72.

9. So also G. N. Knoppers, "An Achaemenid Imperial Authorization of Torah in Yehud?" in *Persia and Torah* (SBLSymS; Atlanta: Scholars Press, 2001) 121 n. 28.

10. See B. Schwartz, "A Priest out of Place: Reconsidering Ezekiel's Role in the History of the Israelite Priesthood," in *Ezekiel's Hierarchical World: Wrestling with a Tiered Reality* (ed. S. L. Cook and C. L. Patton; SBLSymS; Atlanta: Scholars Press, 2004) 61–71. Schwartz's observations regarding Ezekiel are applicable to Ezra with respect to his status before returning to Jerusalem.

11. Especially intriguing here is that the Artxerxes Rescript employs deuteronomic language, and Ezra's own activity is described with deuteronomic terminology (see below for a full discussion), and it is in Deuteronomy where a Levite who comes to Jerusalem from elsewhere is empowered to join the priesthood at the temple (Deut 18:6–8). Though Ezra is a Zadokite, the P traditions that this priestly group authored and advocated loosely identify the descendants of Aaron as a Levitical subset, as does Ezekiel

heritage is obviously not ignored, but it does not receive much in the way of extensive elaboration.

Whoever the historical Ezra was and whatever the specifics of his activity in Transeuphrates and/or Yehud, the redactors have chosen *not* to portray Ezra as an active member of the Zadokite priesthood (or, for that matter, deal with the priesthood as any sort of influential political group).[12] It is true that the phrase "Ezra the priest" may be found throughout the Ezra material in Ezra–Nehemiah, but it is counterbalanced by the phrase "Ezra the scribe," often in literary proximity. Even the ritual reading of the Torah in Neh 8—the outstanding event in the legacy of Ezra's career—takes places beyond the precincts of the temple.[13] The phrase "Ezra the priest" may well play on Ezra's Zadokite lineage roots, but its pairing with the phrase "Ezra the scribe" and his overall distance from the conventions of the priestly office suggest that the redactors wish to qualify Ezra's priesthood in a manner distinct from extant Zadokite typologies.[14]

Here, we must direct our attention to a brief passage regarding the initial stages of Ezra's mission. Ezra 8:15–19 tells us of an interruption

---

(Ezek 44:15). Ezra could have certainly capitalized on the window left open by the deuteronomic legislation and assumed an active priestly position in Jerusalem, or the redactors of the Ezra materials could have done so in their presentation of Ezra. See Rooke, *Zadok's Heirs*, 164.

12. Ibid., 168.

13. Scholars of course remain strongly divided on the origins, purpose, and historicity of this episode. For representative perspectives, see H. G. M. Williamson, *Ezra, Nehemiah* (WBC; Waco, TX: Word, 1985) 283; J. Pakkala, *Ezra The Scribe: The Development of Ezra 7–10 and Nehemiah 8* (BZAW; Berlin: de Gruyter, 2004) 177–78; W. M. Schniedewind, *How the Bible Became a Book: The Textualization of Ancient Israel* (New York: Cambridge University Press, 2004) 183–84; Rooke, *Zadok's Heirs*, 152. With J. L. Wright ("Writing the Restoration: Compositional Agenda and the Role of Ezra in Nehemiah 8" in Mark Leuchter, ed., "Scribes before and after 587 B.C.E.: A Conversation," *Journal of Hebrew Scriptures* 7 [2007] Article 10, 25–29 [http://www.jhsonline.org]) but against the majority opinion, I see Neh 8 as being composed specifically for its current context and not as being dislodged from an original Ezra corpus; see also D. Kraemer ("On the Relationship of the Books of Ezra and Nehemiah," *JSOT* 59 [1993] 80–83), whose examination supports this view. As I argue herein, however, the traditions in the so-called Ezra Memoir (Ezra 7–10) have themselves undergone a redactional stage related to the Nehemiah material, and it seems very likely that Neh 8 was composed and obtained its position within the Nehemiah corpus in dialogue with the redaction of the Ezra Memoir. That the chapter was composed with an awareness of the larger Ezra–Nehemiah corpus links it to a redactional category shared with the Artaxerxes Rescript in Ezra 7, which also appears to know the later Ezra–Nehemiah corpus; see Hagedorn, "Local Law," 71.

14. It is also relevant that the phrase "Ezra the priest" is used only sparingly in Ezra–Nehemiah, whereas "Ezra the scribe" is used quite often. See Kraemer, "Ezra and Nehemiah," 83.

in Ezra's travels from Babylon to Yehud for the purposes of recruiting additional support. We learn that, upon noticing the paucity of Levites in his retinue, Ezra calls upon the Levites of the Mesopotamian city of Casiphia to join him in his return to the homeland:

> And I gathered them together to the river that runs to Ahava; and there we camped three days; and I viewed the people, and the priests, and found there none of the sons of Levi. Then sent I for Eliezer, for Ariel, for Shemaiah, and for Elnathan, and for Jarib, and for Elnathan, and for Nathan, and for Zechariah, and for Meshullam, chiefs; also for Joiarib, and for Elnathan, teachers. And I commanded them [to go to] Iddo the chief at Casiphia, the [sacral] place; and I placed in their mouths words to speak to Iddo and his brothers, the Netinim[15] at Casiphia, the [sacral] place, to bring to us ministers for the house of our God. And they brought to us by the good hand of our God a man of reason from the sons of Mahli, the son of Levi, the son of Israel; and Sherebiah, with his sons and his brothers, eighteen; and Hashabiah, and with him Jeshaiah from the sons of Merari, his brothers and their sons, twenty.[16]

Though we are provided with several details here regarding these Levites, they raise as many questions as they do answers. We are told that they are situated in Casiphia, but there is debate over what was significant about this city or what is meant by referring to it twice as a '[sacral] place' (מקום). Moreover, while we are informed that these Levites have a 'chief' (ראש) by the name of Iddo, the nature of this title is ambiguous. Is Iddo a familial head of an extensive Levite kinship group akin to a ראש בית אבות, or is his title more political or sacral in nature?[17] Finally, the text does not tell us about the ideological predilections of these Levites or the features of their training at Casiphia. We may assume that Levite status carried a degree of traditional socio-religious authority that would have broadened the scope of Ezra's mission for the Jewish residents of Yehud (though not for the Gentile populations of Transeuphrates), but there were certainly Levite groups

---

15. Williamson emends the MT from אל אדו אחיו הנתינים to אל אדו ואחיו והנתינים (*Ezra*, 113), drawing a distinction between Iddo's Levite brothers and the 'temple servants' (נתינים). This reading is possible considering the identification of נתינים as temple servants elsewhere in Ezra–Nehemiah, but this may also be a rhetorical nuance deployed to harmonize the distinct role of Iddo's Levite kin at Casiphia (see below) with the larger interests of Ezra–Nehemiah.

16. In this essay, translations are my own, based in part on the JPS translation.

17. On the בית אבות, see H. G. M. Williamson, "The Family in Persian Period Judah: Some Textual Reflections," in *Symbiosis, Symbolism, and the Power of the Past: Canaan, Ancient Israel, and Their Neighbors from the Late Bronze Age through Roman Palaestina* (ed. W. G. Dever and S. Gitin; Winona Lake, IN: Eisenbrauns, 2003) 472–78.

already in the homeland from whom Ezra could have recruited supporters.[18] Why these Levites, and what is the relationship to the characterization of Ezra and his mission?

The Background to Exilic Levitical Ideology

Our first task is to consider the distinction between the Levites of Casiphia and those already in Yehud by the mid-fifth century and having
some part in the temple cult. The biblical record identifies the Levites
of the respective returns of Sheshbazzar and Zerubbabel as drawn
from the exilic community, an important hallmark of postexilic sacral
legitimacy.[19] There is every reason to believe that Ezra did make use of
the Levites whose ancestors returned during these earlier periods;
they would have held important temple-based responsibilities that
Ezra would certainly have exploited during his tenure as overseer of
royal policy in the province. In addition to this, however, these Levites
serve a ritualistic function, because Ezra's delegation from Mesopotamia to Yehud functions as a sort of second exodus and wandering
through the wilderness.[20] The mission required its own faculty of both
Aaronide priests and Levites to complete the ritual rehearsal of the
construction of the cultic faculty in the exodus/wilderness period.[21]

---

18. Considering the connection of Levites to specific hinterland clan/kinship groups
and the persistence of many of these groups in Judah during the Neo-Babylonian period,
this remains very likely. See P. D. Hanson, *The Dawn of Apocalyptic* ([Minneapolis: Fortress, 1975] 226–27), for a discussion of Levites who remained in Judah during the exilic
period. See also my " 'Prophets' and the 'Levites' in Josiah's Covenant Ceremony" (*ZAW*,
forthcoming) for the regional kinship affiliations of Levitical groups. However, the social
and thus religious conditions of these groups were severely affected by the Babylonian
destruction and conquest of Judah and Jerusalem, which would create significant rifts in
the Levite traditions of the remnant community versus those of the eastern Diaspora.
For a full examination of the socioeconomic disruption suffered even by those who were
not led into Babylonian captivity, see O. Lipschits, *The Fall and Rise of Jerusalem: Judah under Babylonian Rule* (Winona Lake, IN: Eisenbrauns, 2005) 258–71.
    19. See esp. P. R. Bedford, "Diaspora: Homeland Relations in Ezra–Nehemiah," *VT* 52
(2002) 147–65.
    20. K. Koch, "Ezra and the Origins of Judaism," *JSS* 19 (1974) 173–97 (esp. p. 184);
Rooke, *Zadok's Heirs*, 164; Williamson, *Ezra*, 93.
    21. Both Chronicles and Ezra–Nehemiah appear to present Levites as full members
of the Zadokite temple establishment (see, among others, Boccaccini, *Roots of Rabbinic Judaism*, 71) in contrast to the distinctions made by Ezekiel (e.g., Ezek 44); see S. L. Cook,
"Innerbiblical Interpretation in Ezekiel 44 and the History of Israel's Priesthood," *JBL*
114 (1995) 193–208; see also G. N. Knoppers, "Hierodules, Priests or Janitors? The Levites
in Chronicles and the History of the Israelite Priesthood," *JBL* 118 (1999) 49–72. As I will
demonstrate below, however, the rhetorical nuances of the redactors of Ezra–Nehemiah
reveal the affiliation of some Levites such as those of Casiphia with traditions that are

Thus new Levites had to be recruited to the cause in order to round out Ezra's mission as more than just a Persian administrative project. Like the consecration of the Levites in the exodus/wilderness traditions, the Levites brought on board by Ezra had to be consecrated for the task while en route to the promised land.[22]

That the Levites of Casiphia were recruited by Ezra after his departure allows them to qualify as Levites consecrated during the ritualized second period of wilderness wandering. However, the reference to Casiphia as their place of residence requires additional consideration, and we may ask why Casiphia, in particular, was selected as the locale where suitable Levites could be found. Some scholars conclude that Casiphia is an unknown locale but have suggested that it was a cultic or administrative center, the name of which reflects the processing of imperial taxes (from the root *ksp* 'silver/currency').[23] Though this might at first glance apply to the Akkadian name for the city (*kassappa/i*), the name is in fact derived from the old Assyrian *kaštappum* and can be positively located between Calah and Assur.[24] This location would have made Casiphia a prime location to settle deportees in the Neo-Assyrian period, which saw the deportation of many northern Israelites between 732–721 B.C.E. and then a significant number of southern Judeans in 701 B.C.E.[25] Neo-Assyrian archives show that many Israelite deportees were not settled in remote regions but instead were incorporated into well-developed urban locations and administrative hubs for the royal court.[26] As one location of this sort, Casiphia would

---

either openly critical of the Zadokite establishment or that attempt to homogenize the Zadokite lineage into a broad Levitical social miasma.

22. This would explain why the Levites of Casiphia were recruited only after Ezra and his band of supporters already began their mission. The precedent tradition that Ezra seems to follow here is that of Exod 32:26–29, where Levites are consecrated to serve YHWH following the Golden Calf episode. This episode takes place only after the designation of the Aaronides as curators of the tabernacle (Exod 27:21; chaps. 28–29; 30:30), akin to Ezra's enlistment of Zadokite [Aaronide] personnel to his mission and their confreres already serving in the rebuilt Temple in Jerusalem.

23. Williamson, *Ezra*, 117; Blenkinsopp, *Ezra–Nehemiah*, 165.

24. K. Deller, "aB Kaštappum, mA Kaltappu, nA Kassapa/i," *Nouvelles assyriologiques brèves et utilitaires* 1990, no. 4 (pp. 61–62).

25. 2 Kings 17:6 suggests as much with respect to the northern deportees of 732–721 B.C.E., and many administrative documents reveal West-Semitic settlement in this region that would certainly have included Israelites and Judeans (Grant Frame, personal correspondence). See K. L. Younger Jr., "The Deportation of the Israelites," *JBL* 117 (1998) 201–27.

26. M. Leuchter, "A King like All the Nations: The Composition of I Samuel 8,11–18," *ZAW* 117 (2005) 548–52; Younger, "Deportation."

have been a hub of exilic Israelite life from the late eighth century onward; successive waves of deportations would have reinforced its profile as a major center of Diaspora Jewish life in Mesopotamia by the
mid-fifth century.[27]

It would be in urban environments such as this that Israelite religion during the exile would have been transformed in a number of
ways. Deutero-Isaiah's condemnation of Mesopotamian idol production presupposes that this was an activity with which his audience was
intimately familiar and in which they themselves engaged.[28] Yet idol
production fell within the jurisdiction of priesthoods and temples,
hallmarks of well-developed urban centers.[29] That Deutero-Isaiah's response to this pervasive cultural force is expressly literary is significant. Ezekiel's similar oracles against idolatry from earlier in the exile
are preserved in literary form but presented as oral proclamations and
delivered in oral contexts;[30] Deutero-Isaiah's oracles, by contrast, do
not carry oral qualities but emulate scribal, literate forms as a principal
element in their rhetoric of opposition.[31]

It is doubtlessly the case that the members of the Zadokite priesthood were highly literate and capable of functioning in scribal capaci-
ties.[32] However, Zadokite scribal qualifications and agenda must be
seen in distinction to the agenda of the Shaphanide scribal circle that
wielded enormous influence in the Josianic period (as well as during the
exile) and that developed in a unique fashion in distinction to the older

27. Many scholars correctly note that Judeans deported during the Neo-Babylonian
period amalgamated with Israelites and Judeans already in settled in Mesopotamia from
earlier periods of captivity. For an overview, see P. Barmash, "At the Nexus of History
and Memory: The Ten Lost Tribes," *Association for Jewish Studies Review* 29 (2005) 229–32.

28. M. S. Smith, *The Origins of Biblical Monotheism: Israel's Polytheistic Background and
the Ugaritic Texts* (Oxford: Oxford University Press, 2001) 180–93 (especially p. 192).

29. Ibid., 180–93. See also Thorkild Jacobsen, "The Graven Image," in *Ancient Israelite
Religion* (ed. P. D. Miller et al.; Philadelphia: Fortress, 1987) 15–31.

30. For the orality of Ezekiel's rhetoric, see Schwartz, "A Priest Out of Place";
M. Odell, "You Are What You Eat: Ezekiel and the Scroll," *JBL* 117 (1998) 242–43; M. A.
Sweeney, "Ezekiel: Zadokite Priest and Visionary Prophet of the Exile," in *Society of Biblical Literature 2000: Seminar Papers* (SBLSP; Atlanta: Society of Biblical Literature, 2000)
728–51.

31. See esp. B. D. Sommer (*A Prophet Reads Scripture: Allusion in Isaiah 40–66* [Stan-
ford: Stanford University Press, 1998]), who identifies the literary subtlety of Deutero-
Isaiah's compositional style.

32. See most recently K. van der Toorn, *Scribal Culture and the Making of the Hebrew
Bible* ([Cambridge: Harvard University Press, 2007] 82–89), for the temple as a locus of
education and scribal activity and the literacy of the Zadokite priesthood.

bastions of the Jerusalem establishment.[33] It is the Shaphanide group that is best understood as the core of the Deuteronomistic movement, which possessed a lineage and outlook wholly different from the Zadokites.[34] The rift between Zadokite and Shaphanide-Deuteronomistic (or "Levite"; see below) scribal methods, values, and sacred curricula only broadened during the course of the exile; respective views regarding Deuteronomy are a revealing barometer, with the Shaphanide-Deuteronomistic group expanding its significance and the Zadokites consistently setting limits on its viability.[35]

All of this must bear upon our views concerning the scribal tradition characterizing the Levites of Casiphia. The scribal process itself—both textual composition and the exegesis of earlier traditions—became a potent devotional act during the exile, offering on the one hand an alternative to the foreign cultic practices surrounding Israelites living in Mesopotamia and on the other an avenue away from the discourse that still placed the Zadokite priests at the top of the pecking order. The Jeremiah tradition attests to this in two ways, both by elevating the status of scribes to the equivalent level of (but in distinction to) prophets and by associating the cultic term מקום with exilic scribal activity.[36]

What is notable here is that the Jeremiah tradition characterizes its scribal characters as Levites and speaks broadly to Levite interests, developing ideas already embedded within earlier deuteronomic tradition. Deuteronomy related rural Levites to the Jerusalem temple as

---

33. The aphorism lying beneath Jer 18:18 provides insight into the relationship between the Zadokite priesthood and other literate/administrative groups associated with the royal institutions of Jerusalem.

34. For a full discussion, see my *Josiah's Reform and Jeremiah's Scroll: Historical Calamity and Prophetic Response* (Hebrew Bible Monographs 6; Sheffield: Sheffield Phoenix, 2006) 50–58; J. A. Dearman, "My Servants the Scribes: Composition and Context in Jeremiah 36," *JBL* 109 (1990) 417–21; J. R. Lundbom, *Jeremiah 1–20* (AB 21A; New York: Doubleday, 1999) 92; Schniedewind, *How the Bible Became a Book*, 149–57. See also M. Weinfeld, *The Place of the Law in the Religion of Ancient Israel* ([VTSup 100; Leiden: Brill, 2004] 80–94) for the socioreligious differences between the Zadokite (P) literature and the deuteronomic tradition.

35. See Levinson, "Manumission of Hermeneutics"; S. W. Hahn and J. S. Bergsma, "What Laws Were 'Not Good'? A Canonical Approach to the Theological Problem of Ezekiel 20:25–26," *JBL* 123 (2004) 217; M. Leuchter, "Why Is the Song of Moses in the Book of Deuteronomy?" *VT* 57 (2007) 299–300.

36. M. Leuchter, "The Temple Sermon and the Term מקום in the Jeremianic Corpus," *JSOT* 30 (2005) 93–109; idem, *The Polemics of Exile in Jeremiah 26–45* (New York: Cambridge University Press, 2007) esp. chap. 6.

local agents/exegetes of central law and religion,[37] and the Jeremiah tradition develops this Levite characteristic independently from the temple institution pursuant to the prophet's own objections to the failings of this institution (Jer 7:1–15; chaps. 8–10). Scribal activity took on pseudocultic dimensions; centers of scribal activity could thus be qualified with cultic language to carry forward the authority of literary processes that now rivaled and replaced temple-based authority.[38] These considerations can be sensed within the Casiphia episode, especially in Ezra 8:17. The city is twice identified as a מקום; the repetition calls attention not only to the special status of Casiphia but also to the meaning of the term מקום itself in this context. While it was likely a center for prayer and study, Casiphia would not have been a "cult" site housing a temple or shrine structure.[39] The exilic development of both the Jeremiah tradition and Deuteronomy effectively eliminated the need for these structures or priesthoods to staff them (Jer 31:31–34; Deut 30:11–14), and the ideology in both cases is heavily steeped in Levitical thought.[40] Casiphia would have thus obtained the qualifications of a מקום not due to the erection of a shrine or sanctuary but due to serving as a locus of Levite scribal activity and teaching.[41]

---

37. Idem, "'The Levite in Your Gates': The Deuteronomic Redefinition of Levitical Authority," *JBL* 126 (2007) 417–36.

38. See idem (*Polemics of Exile*, 156–65) for an example of a Shaphanide-Levite argument for sacral authority in contrast to Zadokite tradents.

39. Pace Williamson, *Ezra*, 117.

40. Leuchter, *Polemics of Exile*, 182–84.

41. With many scholars, I see the Deuteronomistic and Jeremianic materials as primary repositories of Levitical thought and tradition. When considering the history of Israelite religion in the preexilic period, we should not reduce the diversity of Levite ideas to a single stream of tradition, because it appears that disparate religious concepts characterized the variety of rural priestly groups down to the Josianic period. Nevertheless, it is during this same period that the architects of the Deuteronomistic literature sought to homogenize these different priestly groups under a united Levitical banner (see my "'Prophets' and the 'Levites'") shaped in large part by the Shaphanide scribal party in Jerusalem, who themselves very likely possessed Levite heritage. The Jeremiah tradition, which spans both the Josianic period and the exilic and also involved significant Shaphanide contributions, continued this task and appears to have been rather successful with respect to the Levites exiled to Mesopotamia. We are thus justified in seeing the Levites of Casiphia as falling under the umbrella of the Deuteronomistic and Jeremianic traditions, which set the standard for Levite interests and discourse during the exilic period. For more detailed discussions of these matters, see J. C. Geoghegan, *The Time, Place and Purpose of the Deuteronomistic History: The Evidence of "Until This Day"* (Brown Judaic Studies; Providence: Brown University Press, 2006); idem, "Until This Day and the Pre-Exilic Redaction of the Deuteronomistic History," *JBL* 122 (2003) 201–27; Leuchter, *Polemics of Exile*, 166–76.

Viewing Casiphia and its Levites in this way invites new understandings of the otherwise ambiguous terms and figures mentioned in
Ezra 8:15–19. We may conjecture that Iddo's designation as ראש relates
to his position as a leader of this Levitical guild; this sort of leadership
is sensed among similar guilds in the preexilic and exilic literature
(1 Sam 10:13; cf. 19:20; Jer 35:4). The term also intimates a typological
connection with Ezra 7:5, where Aaron is similarly depicted, thereby
suggesting the fitness of these Levites to join Ezra's delegation. However, because Ezra is strongly identified as a scribe as well (Ezra 7:6
and other places), the scribal role of this group and their leadership is
emphasized. The identity of the Levites of Casiphia as נתינים is not as
'temple servants' in this context but as devotees of a scribal tradition,
and the word denotes their membership in this guild.[42] It is indeed the
case that their projected position in Jerusalem relates to temple service,
but this need not have been exclusively or even primarily cultic in nature. It is clear from Persian-era compositions and compiled literary
works that Levites carried pedagogical, scribal, and administrative
roles both in and beyond Jerusalem,[43] which invariably would have
been connected to the temple as the central hub of the Yehudite socioreligious world.[44] All of these roles would have required teaching
skills, whether as mediators of written scriptural tradition, dissemina-
tors of Zadokite religious policy, or local agents of Persian authority.

"Levitical" Rhetoric in the Ezra Corpus

The aforementioned idea receives attention within the account of Ezra's
recruitment of these Levites in Ezra 8:17; the previous verse specifies
that Ezra's emissaries to Casiphia were themselves teachers (v. 16) and
therefore suggests that teaching was a chief concern for the Levites
that he sought to recruit.[45] Ezra's selection of teachers as emissaries is a

---

42. So also Williamson's discussion regarding the discrepancy between the *Kethiv*
and *Qere* (*Ezra*, 113) and the possible translation as 'devoted' (p. 36). See, however, his
translation on p. 112.

43. M. S. Smith, "The Levitical Compilation of the Psalter," *ZAW* 103 (1991) 258–63;
Knoppers, "Imperial Authorization," 124; Leuchter, "Levite in Your Gates," 433 n. 64.

44. Jeffrey Stackert notes that this is already presupposed in the exilic and early postexilic Zadokite literature, where Zadokites minister to YHWH, while Levites minister to
the people, indicating a distance from the cult (*Rewriting the Torah: Literary Revision in
Deuteronomy and the Holiness Legislation* [Ph.D. dissertation, Brandeis University, 2006]
271, 277–78).

45. The term in question in 8:16 is מבינים, which carries wisdom connotations. This,
however, is also consistent with Levitical tradition; see Smith, *Origins of Biblical Monotheism*, 182–83.

calculated strategy, because it establishes a certain common ideological ground between the Levites already with Ezra and the Levites of Casiphia. Indeed, the engagement of one group with figures sharing some sort of typological connection boasts a venerable history in biblical tradition and the ancient world more generally. Sennacherib's agent, the Rabshakeh, addresses the population of Jerusalem in Hebrew, pointing to his own background as an Israelite.[46] The Josianic literature conceived of prophets in a similar regard, representing the interests of the royal establishment to rural Levite groups throughout the hinterland.[47] Thus it is fitting that Ezra 8:17 employs language that recalls Deuteronomy when elaborating upon Ezra's charge to his emissaries to Casiphia:

> *Ezra 8:17*: I commanded them [ואצוה אותם][48] . . . and I put in their mouths words to speak [ואשימה בפיהם דברים] to Iddo and his brothers.

> *Deut 18:18*: I will put my words in his mouth [ונתתי דברי בפיו], and he shall speak to them all that I shall command him [אצונו].[49]

The manner in which Ezra 8:17 refers to Deuteronomy is especially "scribal" in nature. Not only does the author qualify the scribes' eventual role in Jerusalem with the שרת terminology that Deuteronomy had earlier used to characterize Levitical scribal activity,[50] he also reverses the lexemes of Deuteronomy:

> *Ezra 8:17*: ואצוה אותם ואשימה בפיהם דברים

> *Deut 18:18*: ונתתי דברי בפיו ודבר עליהם את כל אשר אצונו

Here, then, is an example of Seidel's law of intertextual citation that characterizes the scribal invocation and reuse of source material.[51] The redactors of Ezra–Nehemiah responsible for this text want to make certain that the parallel to Deuteronomy is overt. The theopolitical implications of this parallel are, of course, dramatic: YHWH commands

---

46. For this proposal, see M. Cogan and H. Tadmor, *II Kings* (AB 11; Garden City, NY: Doubleday, 1988) 230.

47. Leuchter, "Song of Moses," 312–14; idem, "The 'Prophets' and the 'Levites'."

48. Williamson reconstructs from the *Kethiv* as 'and I sent them' (ואוצאה), though the *Qere* (ואצוה) is to be preferred based on the remaining features of the verse (see the ensuing discussion).

49. One is also reminded of Jer 1:9 in this regard: "And YHWH said to me, 'Behold, I have put my words in your mouth'" (נתתי דברי בפיך).

50. Leuchter, "Levite in Your Gates," 425.

51. For a discussion of this scribal device, see B. M. Levinson, *Deuteronomy and the Hermeneutics of Legal Innovation* (New York: Oxford University Press, 1997) 18–20.

and places the word in the mouth of the prophet; Ezra commands and places the word in the mouth of his emissaries. If these verses were conceived to establish a tit-for-tat development of the deuteronomic dynamic, then Ezra would appear to be deified, but the redactors of Ezra–Nehemiah are less interested in the details of a systematic theology and more concerned with overall rhetorical effect.[52] By using both deuteronomic terminology and Jeremianic concepts in this way, the redactors suggest that Ezra's mandate is consistent with the ideological tradition preserved by the Levites of Casiphia.

The Ezra–Nehemiah corpus does not restrict this rhetorical strategy to the brief episode of Ezra 8:15–20. As many scholars have noted, the Artaxerxes Rescript in Ezra 7 also characterizes Ezra's mission in Deuteronomically-inflected terms:[53]

> *Ezra 7:25*: And you, Ezra, according to the wisdom of your God that is in your hand, appoint magistrates and judges [מני שפטים ודינים] who may judge all the people (די להון דינים לכל עמא] that are in Transeuphrates.

> *Deut 16:18*: Judges and magistrates [שפטים ושטרים] shall you establish in all your gates that Yнwн your God gives you, tribe by tribe; and they shall judge the people [ושפטו את העם] with righteous judgment.

Scholars often point to these and other lexical/linguistic features as evidence that the Artaxerxes Rescript is not an authentic document. This perspective argues that it is highly unlikely that a Persian king (or the Persian court scribes) would evidence familiarity with a text such as Deuteronomy and that the formal structure of the Rescript is not consistent with other Achaemenid diplomatic documents.[54] This criticism is justified, but in this case, it is actually beside the point; as elsewhere, the redactors of Ezra–Nehemiah are interested in rhetorical

---

52. T. Veijola discusses the strong deuteronomic connections in the Ezra tradition ("The Deuteronomistic Roots of Judaism," in *Sefer Moshe: The Moshe Weinfeld Jubilee Volume — Studies in the Bible and the Ancient Near East, Qumran, and Postbiblical Judaism* [ed. C. Cohen, A. Hurvitz, and S. M. Paul; Winona Lake, IN: Eisenbrauns, 2004] 459–78), though his analysis suggests Deuteronomy's direct effect on Ezra and does not consider the rhetorical implications of the redactors' use of the deuteronomic discourse.

53. Hagedorn, "Local Law," 72; Blenkinsopp, "Constitution," 53–54. The language is properly at home in royal administrative contexts; see M. Weinfeld, "Judge and Officer in Ancient Israel and in the Ancient Near East," *Israel Oriental Studies* 7 (1977) 65–88.

54. L. Grabbe, "The Law of Moses in the Ezra Tradition: More Virtual Than Real?" *Persia and Torah* (SBLSymS; Atlanta: Scholars Press, 2001) 93–94; D. Janzen, "The 'Mission' of Ezra and the Persian Period Temple Community," *JBL* 119 (2000) 619–43. Nevertheless, Hagedorn makes the point that the Rescript was written by someone who was generally familiar with Persian official correspondence ("Local Law," 71).

and hermeneutical resonance and not historical accuracy.[55] Just as Ezra's language in 8:17 casts his recruitment of the Levites of Casiphia in a Levitical light, so also the language in Ezra 7:25 is formulated to make the entire program of Persian-sponsored administration in Transeuphrates resonate at this same frequency. Thus, as the Rescript continues and establishes parity between Persian law and Jewish law (v. 26),[56] the implication is that Persian administrators such as Ezra are indeed acting in good faith and supporting the superstructure of their own ancient native traditions, which would also have been cultivated by exilic Levites.

A certain continuity in the chain of political command is thus established when we read the Artaxerxes Rescript in dialogue with the account of the recruitment of the Levites of Casiphia. Within the hermeneutical context of Ezra–Nehemiah, Ezra is charged in deuteronomic terms by Artaxerxes, and the Levites are charged in deuteronomic terms by Ezra. In this case, carrying out the will of the king (as entrusted to Ezra) is indeed to carry out the mandates of Deuteronomy in good Levitical spirit, both theologically and politically,[57] as Persian administrative positions become typologically equivalent to Levitical administrative roles. In fact, the sequential implications of Ezra's recruitment of the Levites bears this out: if the depiction of Ezra's delegation is patterned on the exodus/wilderness traditions, then the Persian legal authority with which Ezra is charged is set parallel to the Sinaitic law with which Moses is charged. Considering the Levitical responsibility in Deuteronomy to teach and administer that law (Deut 16:18–20; 31:9–13), the characterization of Ezra as a second Moses and his Persian mission as a second Sinaitic enterprise paves the way for the Levites of Casiphia to expand their traditional roles to include the promulgation of Persian imperial interests.[58]

---

55. This does not discount the possibility or even the likelihood that the Rescript is based on an authentic document or that an authentic document has been heavily reworked into the present form of the Rescript. Steiner's position that the Rescript is authentic is difficult to sustain ("The *mbqr* at Qumran," 623–24), but his arguments support the existence of an authentic prototype underlying or inspiring the current text. See also Blenkinsopp ("Constitution," 53–54) for the value of cautiously mining the Rescript for historical information.

56. The parity between Persian and local divine law expressed in v. 26 is consistent with the Persian diplomatic/administrative practice of supporting local traditions and institutions of leadership in the service of the Empire, but this should not lead to the assumption that the Pentateuch or any actual collection of Jewish law was literally understood to be the same as imperial law (Hagedorn, "Local Law," 71).

57. So also Blenkinsopp, "Constitution," 55–56.

58. See below.

Ezra's Prayer and the Invocation of Prophecy

The Ezra–Nehemiah corpus carries this rhetorical argument even further when we take a closer look at Ezra's prayer in Ezra 9:6–15. Though
the prayer takes up the discourse of Zadokite expiation,[59] it is equally
shaded by Levitical discourse of the Jeremiah-Deuteronomistic variety.
Ezra's concerns with pollution and purity are couched in the *Heilsgeschichte* form, replete with an emphasis on the exodus, the abomina-
tions of the fathers, the ignoring of YHWH's servants the prophets, and
persistent variations on the redactional formula "until this day," which
appears throughout the Deuteronomistic literature and the book of
Jeremiah (cf. 2 Kgs 17:7–23; Jer 11:1–17; 25:1–13).[60] The variety of hard-
ships recounted in the prayer (בחרב בשבי ובבזה ובבשת) not only conforms to Deuteronomistic threats of the same ilk,[61] it recalls Jeremiah's
repeated threats of punishment that Judah will face for ignoring his
words (see esp. Jer 15:2; 24:10).

The prayer's concern with illegitimate marriages is especially relevant here. Ezra's overall concern with these marriages is influenced
both by Deuteronomy and by Priestly ideas,[62] but the manner in which
the problem is communicated weighs in more closely on the deuteronomic end of the spectrum, taking up the rhetoric of Deut 24:4, a passage also concerned with the institution of marriage:[63]

> *Ezra 9:11b*: the land [הארץ] that you go to possess [לרשתה][64] is an unclean
> land through the uncleanness of the peoples of the lands, through their
> abominations [בתועבתיהם] wherewith they have filled it from one end to
> another with their filthiness [בטמאתם].

---

59. B. Becking, "Law as Expression of Religion (Ezra 7–10)," *Yahwism after the Exile*
(ed. R. Albertz and B. Becking; Assen: Van Gorcum, 2003) 29. See also the detailed discussion of the prayer's terminology in dialogue with diverse lexical trends regarding holiness and the expiation of impurity by Olyan, "Purity Ideology."

60. For a full discussion of "until this day," see Geoghegan, *Deuteronomistic History*,
passim.

61. Williamson, *Ezra*, 134.

62. Becking, "Law," 29.

63. Olyan discusses the crosscurrents in Ezra's prayer that are drawn from a variety
of sources including Deuteronomy, as often noted by other commentators, such as Deut
7:3–4 and 23:4–9 ("Purity Ideology," 3–5), though Deut 24:1–4 tends to go unnoticed in
this regard.

64. The switch in terminology from נחלה in Deut 24:4 to לרשתה in Ezra 9:11b is relatively minor and still retains the essential idea of the deuteronomic source; similar minor
variants occur in other citations of Deuteronomy (see immediately below). The phenomenon is inherent to scribal memorization of sources and the inadvertent variants that
emerge from the rewriting of these sources; see D. M. Carr, *Writing on the Tablet of the
Heart: Origins of Scripture and Literature* (New York: Oxford University Press, 2005).

> *Deut 24:4*: Her former husband, who sent her away, may not take her again to be his wife, for she has been defiled [הטמאה]; for that is abomination [תועבה] before YHWH; and you shall not cause the land [הארץ] to sin that YHWH your God gives your for an inheritance [נחלה].

The lexical congruence here is unmistakable, but we must note that Ezra 9:10–11a introduces this unit by identifying it as "commandments" communicated by YHWH's "servants the prophets." Though the concept of commandments supported by YHWH's "servants the prophets" is of course Deuteronomistic, the language of Deut 24:4 occurs prominently only in Jeremiah:

> *Jer 2:7*: I brought you into a land of fruitful fields, to eat the fruit thereof and the good thereof; but when you entered, you defiled [ותטמאו] my land [ארצי], and made my heritage [נחלתי] an abomination [תועבה].

> *Jer 16:18*: because they have defiled [חללם][65] my land [ארצי]; they have filled mine inheritance [נחלתי] with the carcasses of their detestable things and their abominations [תועבותיהם].

Ezra's prayer also plays on Jeremiah's repeated metaphor of the cessation of joyous marriage and separation from life in the land as a punishment for covenantal abrogation (Jer 7:34; 16:9; 25:10). In particular, Ezra 9:12 takes up the language of Jer 29:6–7, which notably addresses life away from the land:

> *Ezra 9:12*: Now therefore do not give your daughters to their sons [לבניהם ובנתיכם אל תתנו], neither take their daughters for your sons [ובנתיהם אל תשאו לבניכם] nor seek their peace [ולא תדרשו שלומם].

> *Jer 29:6–7*: take wives for your sons [קחו לבניכם נשים], and give your daughters to husbands [ואת בנתיכם תנו לאנשים] . . . and seek the peace of the city [העיר ודרשו את שלום].

Jeremiah 29 goes on to speak of eventual restoration to the homeland after the period of captivity in Babylon comes to an end (Jer 29:10); Ezra's dissolution of the foreign marriages is reformulated according to Jeremiah's language, suggesting that the conditions of exile will only end and the promise of restoration will only happen when these illegitimate marriages are nullified.[66]

---

65. The substitution of the טמא terminology with חללם is another example of the aforementioned scribal process of the introduction of minor variants; see n. 64.

66. For the engagement of prophecy in Ezra–Nehemiah, see J. G. McConville, "Ezra–Nehemiah and the Fulfillment of Prophecy," *VT* 36 (1986) 205–24 (though McConville concludes that Ezra–Nehemiah cites prophecy to emphasize anti-Persian sentiments).

Most commentators view Ezra's dissolution of these marriages as a historical event, but it is clear that the redactors of Ezra–Nehemiah have attempted to portray it as a step toward the fulfillment of prophecy. That the prophecy in question is Jeremiah's and that the prayer in Ezra 9 is saturated with Jeremianic and Deuteronomistic terminology reinforces the other similar flourishes resulting from the redactors' design. Ezra 9, in fact, evidences the highest concentration of these flourishes in the entire Ezra corpus; it constitutes a climax in the rhetorical presentation of Ezra as standing in the exilic Levitical traditions.

The Purpose of the Levitical Rhetoric in the Ezra Corpus

The redactors of Ezra–Nehemiah have gone to great lengths to create a memory of Ezra as an ideological colleague of the Levites that he recruited from Casiphia. Their traditions are transplanted into the account of Ezra's own activity with great care; whatever the historical Ezra may have accomplished is now refracted through a "Levitical" lens.[67] The interpolation of Neh 8, an Ezra narrative,[68] into the Nehemiah corpus reinforces his association with the Deuteronomistic Torah tradition that would have been more closely associated with the Levites that Nehemiah supports, as opposed to the sacrifice/temple orientation we encounter in the Ezra corpus.[69] This helps to create equivalency between Torah and temple throughout Ezra–Nehemiah,[70] but it also contributes to the rhetorical shaping of the character of Ezra

---

67. The same redactional strategy was applied to the account of Josiah's reign. See especially L. A. S. Monroe ("A Pre-exilic 'Holiness' Substratum in the Deuteronomistic Account of Josiah's Reign," in M. Leuchter, ed., "Scribes before and after 587 B.C.E.: A Conversation," *Journal of Hebrew Scriptures* 7 [2007] Article 10, 42–53 [http://www.jhsonline .org]), who sees an exilic Deuteronomistic revision of a Zadokite "Holiness" narrative within the account of Josiah's reign and reform. Geoghegan's model of a preexilic Deuteronomistic redaction of records from Josiah's account provides an alternative model in terms of dating this redaction to the late preexilic period (Geoghegan, "Until This Day," 225–27) though this does not nullify Monroe's observations regarding the older substratum in the account.

68. There are good grounds, however, for viewing Neh 8 as separate from the Ezra corpus and composed for its current context (as discussed above). See Wright, "Writing the Restoration," 27–29; Kraemer, "Ezra and Nehemiah," 80–83.

69. Williamson (*Persian Period History*, 274–76) is no doubt correct that Nehemiah's interest in the temple is as a pragmatist rather than an interest born out of deep commitment to its mythosacral system.

70. T. C. Eskenazi, "The Structure of Ezra–Nehemiah and the Integrity of the Book," *JBL* 107 (1988) 649–50.

specifically. In both cases, a revision of earlier traditions more concerned with distinctively Priestly concepts brought it in line with Levitical ideology.[71]

It is therefore very likely that, while Ezra did indeed recruit Levites from Casiphia, his interest in their scribal/exegetical skill was secondary to his desire to ritualize his mission. As the corpus continues in the Nehemiah section, however, our attention is drawn away from the temple and its ritual function and directed to the community beyond its precincts and the role of the Levites therein.[72] Nehemiah's support of Levites beyond the temple and the extent of his own lay-authority hardly follow the lead of Ezra's original temple-based concerns in Yehud, and one may easily see how a Zadokite critique might be lodged against this.[73] Infusing the Ezra tradition with Levitical overtones emphasizing extra-temple ideas, however, would allow for Nehemiah to appear to faithfully "continue" Ezra's mission.

All of this tells us a great deal about the redactors of Ezra–Nehemiah, their intended audience, and the traditions they inherited. The redactors were well versed in Levitical modes of discourse, though this does not necessarily mean that these redactors were themselves Levites.[74] It may be the case that the redactors constituted a mediating party standing somewhere between the Zadokites and the Levites who had, until the mid-fifth century, stood in tension with each other since the exilic period (if not earlier).[75] The retention of temple-centered

---

71. Here I differ in opinion from Wright, who views the purpose of Ezra 7–8 as similar to Ezra 1–6—that is, as part of a literary balancing of the book to countermand the impact of the Nehemiah Memoir (*Rebuilding Identity*, 338–39; idem, "Writing the Restoration," 25). Both units of text, he observes, deal more with temple than with Torah, and in this he is certainly correct. But as demonstrated in the foregoing discussion, the redactors have taken up the traditions regarding Ezra's mission in Ezra 7–8 (as well as chaps. 9–10) and produced a literary unit that mediates between the temple-centrism of Ezra 1–6 and the account of Nehemiah's governorship and the opportunities afforded to the Levites therein. There is a marked absence of Levitical rhetoric (as defined in the present study) in Ezra 1–6 in comparison with what we encounter in the Ezra Memoir.

72. Wright, "Writing the Restoration," 27–29.

73. So also ibid., 25.

74. Pace K. Min, *The Levitical Authorship of Ezra–Nehemiah* (JSOTSup 409; London: T. & T. Clark, 2004).

75. For a full discussion, see my *Polemics of Exile*, 152–65. There is ample evidence to suggest the existence of such a party even within the ranks of the Jerusalem priesthood, as history demonstrates the evolution and fragmentation of Zadokite thought and subgroups. See especially S. M. Olyan, "Exodus 31:12–17: The Sabbath according to H or the Sabbath according to P and H?" (*JBL* 124 (2005) 201–9) for evidence of developments within the priesthood in relation to the Zadokite Holiness School.

concerns in the Ezra corpus suggests that the redactors were themselves supporters of the temple's ritual vitality, and the overall structure of Ezra–Nehemiah establishes it as equally important to the Torah
process facilitated by the Levites in Neh 8.[76] However, the redactors
appear to support Nehemiah's sociotheological outlook, replete with
the convening of the community for a covenant ceremony (Neh 8) and
its investiture of Levites as important social mediators beyond the temple precincts (Neh 11 and 13). Nehemiah's initiatives are repeatedly
justified by his own appeal to scriptural precedent rather than any interest in Zadokite priestly authority.[77] This no doubt resulted from his
official status within the Persian imperial administration, but it also
constituted a sidelining of the traditional Zadokite socioreligious leadership that Persia had earlier supported and whose perspectives Ezra
had evidently espoused as well.[78]

At the same time, the redactors have not eschewed the historical
resonances of Ezra's mission that must have drawn from and reinforced his own Zadokite heritage. Ezra's concern with the temple cult
and matters of communal purity would have been a top priority to a
Zadokite priest such as himself and indeed to the entire Zadokite establishment.[79] His activity in Yehud may well have established a standard for ideology and behavior in Jewish communities elsewhere.
There is no reason to doubt that Ezra was in fact empowered to enforce
Zadokite law among Jews throughout Transeuphrates as part and parcel of his responsibilities as an agent of the Persian royal court.[80] The
term תורה indeed functions as a symbol of Zadokite values throughout
the Ezra corpus,[81] and it is this value system that Ezra is charged with
promulgating throughout the Jewish world of Transeuphrates. There

---

76. Eskenazi, "The Structure of Ezra–Nehemiah," 649–50.

77. Knoppers, "Imperial Authorization," 132.

78. Ibid., 133; Fried, "Judges," 85–88. Jacob Wright notes, for example, that Nehemiah is characterized in a somewhat prophetic manner (see especially the ריב terminology that he repeatedly employs), taking to task the priesthood for its failings (H. Wiley,
"Review of L. L. Grabbe and A. O. Bellis, ed., *The Priests in the Prophets: The Portrayal of
Priests, Prophets and Other Religious Specialists in the Latter Prophets*," *Review of Biblical Literature*, http://www.bookreviews.org [2005]).The door for this is opened by the presentation of Ezra's own mission as part of the fulfillment of Jeremiah's earlier prophetic
oracles (see above).

79. See the discussion by Kraemer, "Ezra and Nehemiah," 80–83.

80. Williamson, *Ezra*, 103–5; Rooke, *Zadok's Heirs*, 165.

81. Becking, however, views the Ezra material as being fourth-century ideological
discourse rather than preserving authentic memories of Ezra's actual mission ("Law,"
22–24).

is good reason to believe that Ezra would have viewed this as an attainable goal. The documents from Elephantine deriving from one generation after Ezra testify to the fact that Jewish communities surrounding Yehud deferred to the authority of the Jerusalem priests, and it is very likely that this deference obtained in earlier periods as well.[82]

Thus, while the Artaxerxes Rescript credits Ezra with executive dominion over the entire satrapy of Transeuphrates, the view that Ezra was actually commissioned to deal with the Jewish communities of this area provides the most likely reconstruction of his actual mission.[83] Consonant with the concerns of the Ezra corpus, the focus of his mission would have been Yehud itself and, considering the Persian practice of using native leaders and traditions to influence local populations, Ezra's mission was probably not unique. Following the social and military disruptions of only a few years earlier,[84] other emissaries of the Persian court were probably deployed to the same satrapy to address their own kin populations within their respective home provinces. The dispersed nature of the Jewish communities, however, would have demanded special consideration in this regard, requiring Ezra to address communities beyond the boundaries of Yehud—ergo, the memory of his authorization to address the satrapy of Transeuphrates, as preserved within the Rescript.

Though the redactors of Ezra–Nehemiah remembered and retained dimensions of Ezra's Zadokite heritage and outlook, they projected new characteristics onto their literary presentation, first looking to the perceptions about him that they inherited. The memory of Ezra as following a ritual pattern from the exodus/wilderness traditions would have served to reinvigorate the authority of the Jerusalem temple and its Zadokite faculty upon Ezra's arrival in Yehud and simultaneously establish it as consistent with the Persian imperial universe. Thus, while Ezra was a scribe in the Persian governmental sense of the term,[85] he was empowered administratively to capitalize on his Zado-

---

82. Blenkinsopp, "Constitution," 52. See also Rooke, *Zadok's Heirs*, 174, 181, 183. Rooke discusses evidence from both Ezra–Nehemiah and the Elephantine documents that reveals a similar picture of the sociopolitical place of the Zadokite priesthood in Jerusalem from the mid- to late fifth century, which suggests that the deference shown to the Jerusalem priesthood in the Elephantine papyri on matters of cult reflects a longer-running relationship between communities.

83. Williamson, *Ezra*, 103–5; Blenkinsopp, *Ezra–Nehemiah*, 151; pace Fried, "Judges," 88–89.

84. Blenkinsopp, "Constitution," 54.

85. See the classifications in van der Toorn, *Scribal Culture*, 82–89.

kite lineage and qualifications. Ezra was charged with reestablishing Zadokite socioreligious hegemony among the Jewish communities in Transeuphrates by affirming the temple community in Yehud as a faithful bastion of Persia's imperial presence and interests. The early stratum of material in the Ezra corpus casts him in the same role that Moses plays in P—a facilitator of the Zadokite cultic and theological system—only now, this system is empowered as much by Artaxerxes as by YHWH (Ezra 7:26).

The redactors of Ezra–Nehemiah seized on the hermeneutical window opened by both the recruitment of the Levites of Casiphia and the casting of Ezra as a second Moses of the P variety. Whereas Ezra's "scribal" status had originally pertained to the imperial administrative sense of the term, the redactors channeled this historical echo in a new direction. The account of the recruitment from Casiphia was redacted to highlight the scribal tradition of Torah exegesis that had been fostered by exilic Levites emulating the Jeremianic-Deuteronomistic paradigm, and the records of Ezra's own words and deeds were similarly shaped. The literary Ezra thus becomes a scribe in the *Schriftgelehrter* sense of the term, balancing his Zadokite affiliations with (exilic) Levitical discourse and praxis. The redactors transformed the earlier image of Ezra as a P-type Moses into a D-type Moses: an exegete, teacher, covenant mediator, and lawgiver.

Within the literary world of Ezra–Nehemiah, this sets a precedent for Nehemiah's support of the Levites and his move away from the temple cult as consistent with both divine and royal will, despite the likely dissent of the Zadokite priesthood.[86] The primary audience for

---

86. Kraemer notes this thematic dimension in the book of Nehemiah, especially in the Levitical prayer of Neh 9, where the *Heilsgeschichte* form emphasizes the teaching of Torah: "this history includes the giving of Torah to Moses at Mt. Sinai *for the first time in any such biblical historical review*; the Temple is ignored completely" ("Ezra and Nehemiah," 79; emphasis in the original; see also Wright, *Rebuilding Identity*, 337). So also Kraemer's observation regarding the citation of Deut 23:4–5 in Neh 13:1–3; in the book of Nehemiah, "the scribe has superseded the priest" (p. 85). As discussed in the present study, the redactors of the Ezra corpus have attempted to temper this priestly emphasis with Levitical-scribal rhetoric, but the original priestly valences have survived in the present text with enough force for the shapers of the Nehemiah material to counterbalance them as per Kraemer's observations.

Watts (*Ritual and Rhetoric*, passim) makes a convincing case for the rhetoric of Leviticus as advancing a purely Zadokite (or Aaronide) agenda of authority. It is tempting to see the shaping of Leviticus and perhaps the entire Pentateuch (which, in its current form, favors Zadokite/Aaronide interests) as a response to the ideas advanced through the redaction of Ezra–Nehemiah. I hope to address this matter in greater detail in a subsequent publication.

Ezra–Nehemiah may have been the general Yehudite population, but
the target of the redaction of Ezra–Nehemiah was the Zadokite priesthood active in the Jerusalem temple. The redactors of Ezra–Nehemiah
created a work that presented an interpretation of recent history that
compromised the exclusive authority of the Zadokites, who would
have initially benefited from Ezra's primary imperial interests via his
support of the temple's social status within the Jewish world of Yehud
and Transeuphrates. The redacted version of Ezra–Nehemiah, by contrast, shapes the memory of Ezra in a manner that is reminiscent of his
original mission but emphasizes very different aspects of the proto-
canonical scriptural tradition in the Jewish world.[87] The shape of Ezra–
Nehemiah ultimately supports an argument for a broader scope of
political and religious leadership, one in which Zadokite theology had
to function in tandem with other literary and exegetical methods and
values.

Whatever the sociological tensions that gave rise to and emerged
from the redaction of Ezra–Nehemiah, the end result is a new social
typology constructed within the text. The literary character of Ezra
emerges as a composite mediator who represents the genuine interests
of Israel's two great priestly traditions, one mythosacral (Zadokite),
the other sociosacral (Levite),[88] balancing both with imperial duties.
The rifts between groups are blurred as a result of this, following similar impulses within Deuteronomy regarding the elimination of clan divisions.[89] In both cases, adherence to law and the superstructure of the
government hierarchy defines what it means to be a Jew, irrespective
of geographical location or lineage tradition. The literary Ezra is a man
for all seasons, a hermeneutical resource from which other traditions
of leadership may draw inspiration and to whom they may appeal for

---

87. By the mid- to late fifth century, the Jeremianic/Deuteronomistic literature was
regarded as essential to the religious literary corpus but had been subjected to different
traditions of reading and interpretation by Levite-Deuteronomistic groups on one side
and Zadokites on the other. One instructive example is the Zadokite use of Jer 34 in the
development of the Holiness Code (H). See my "Manumission Laws in Leviticus and
Deuteronomy: The Jeremiah Connection," *JBL* 127 (2008) 635–53. For a fuller analysis of
the H author's revision of the Deuteronomic manumission legislation and its polemical
purpose, see Levinson, "Manumission of Hermeneutics."
88. See Weinfeld, *The Place of the Law*, 80–94; E. Regev, "Priestly Dynamic Holiness
and Deuteronomic Static Holiness," *VT* 51 (2001) 243–60.
89. B. Halpern, "Jerusalem and the Lineages in the Seventh Century BCE: Kinship and
the Rise of Individual Moral Liability," *Law and Ideology in Monarchic Israel* (ed. B. Halpern
and D. W. Hobson; JSOTSup 124; Sheffield: Sheffield Academic Press, 1991) 75.

authority and legitimacy.[90] It may be for this reason that later tradition ascribes to Ezra the promulgation of the entire Pentateuch, a literary work that accomplishes within its chapters what Ezra is said to manifest through his actions, namely, the unification of once mutually exclusive textual traditions and the mediation of different socioreligious interests.[91]

---

90. H. Mantel may therefore be correct in seeing in Ezra the beginnings of the Pharisee/Sadducee sectarian division, as ideological categories of experience eclipsed traditions defined by priestly lineage ("The Dichotomy of Judaism in the Second Temple Period," *HUCA* 44 [1973] 55–87).

91. Blenkinsopp, "Constitution," 59–61. On the one-time mutually exclusive nature of these law codes, each of which represented different intellectual and religious perspectives, see Levinson, "Manumission of Hermeneutics"; Stackert, *Rewriting the Torah*, 283–86.

Textual Identities in the Books of Chronicles: The Case of Jehoram's History

LOUIS JONKER

Stellenbosch University

Introduction

In recent years, increasing interest has been expressed in the issue of identity formation in the Persian-period Yehud. The theme of the present book and the seminar on which it is based bears witness to this fact. Self-identification, community identity, and ethnicity in Judahite/Yehudite historiography are the key points of departure and have influenced Chronicles scholarship. Many studies of the past decade and more focus on or discuss aspects of identity formation in the Yehudite community.[1] When Siedlecki, for example, discusses the circumstances surrounding the origin of Chronicles in the late Persian (or possibly early Ptolemaic) Empire, he remarks: "The question of Judahite identity is necessarily a precarious one in this situation."[2]

This interest in identity formation in Chronicles is in line with what Willi has described as a shift away from studies concentrating on the

---

1. See, e.g., P. R. Davies, "Defending the Boundaries of Israel in the Second Temple Period: 2 Chronicles 20 and the 'Salvation Army,'" in *Priests, Prophets, and Scribes: Essays on the Formation and Heritage of Second Temple Judaism in Honour of Joseph Blenkinsopp* (ed. E. Ulrich et al.; JSOTSup 149; Sheffield: JSOT Press, 1992) 43–54; T. Willi, *Juda – Jehud – Israel: Studien zum Selbstverständnis des Judentums in persischer Zeit* (Forschungen zum Alten Testament 12; Tübingen: Mohr Siebeck, 1995); J. E. Dyck, "The Ideology of Identity in Chronicles," in *Ethnicity and the Bible* (ed. M. G. Brett; Leiden: Brill, 1996) 89–116; idem, *The Theocratic Ideology of the Chronicler* (Leiden: Brill, 1998); A. Siedlecki, "Foreigners, Warfare and Judahite Identity in Chronicles," in *The Chronicler as Author: Studies in Text and Texture* (ed. M. P. Graham and S. L. McKenzie; JSOTSup 263; Sheffield: Sheffield Academic Press, 1999) 229–66; J. L. Berquist, "Constructions of Identity in Postcolonial Yehud," in *Judah and the Judeans in the Persian Period* (ed. O. Lipschits and M. Oeming; Winona Lake IN: Eisenbrauns, 2006) 53–66.

2. Siedlecki, "Foreigners, Warfare and Judahite Identity," 229. See also p. 232: "(T)he question of identity is generally held to be of crucial importance for the formation and stabilization of the Judahite/Jewish community during the Persian and Hellenistic periods."

historical value of Chronicles toward studies focusing on the under-standing of the unique theology and method of Chronicles.[3] It is within this development that many studies on the rhetoric of Chron-icles should also be situated.[4] The issue of identity formation emerges mostly in the studies that focus on the rhetorical intention or prag-matic function of Chronicles.

Jon Berquist has, however, indicated that not all of these studies on identity formation in Chronicles proceed from the same presupposi-tions about identity.[5] In his contribution in the Lipschits and Oeming volume, *Judah and the Judeans in the Persian Period*, he expresses the need for clarity about the identity of the Judeans mentioned in the title of the volume. To do so, he says, one must focus on the scholarly uses of the concept of identity. On this point Berquist registers a theoretical shortcoming in our present and past studies on this issue: "Studies in ancient Judaism have rarely addressed this question [that is, theoreti-cal reflection on the issue of identity] . . . , even though the larger field of cultural studies has concentrated on identity as a major problem for scholarship."[6]

In order to identify the different and diverging assumptions under-lying our present scholarship on identity formation in Achaemenid Ye-hud, Berquist discusses five modes of scholarship on this issue. First, he mentions the identification of identity as ethnicity, understood as

---

3. T. Willi, "Zwei Jahrzehnte Forschung an Chronik und Esra–Nehemia," *Theologische Rundschau* 67 (2002) 70.

4. See, e.g., M. A. Throntveit, *When Kings Speak: Royal Speech and Royal Prayer in Chronicles* (Atlanta: Scholars Press, 1987); R. K. Duke, *The Persuasive Appeal of the Chroni-cler: A Rhetorical Analysis* (JSOTSup 88; Sheffield: Almond, 1990); R. Mason, *Preaching the Tradition: Homily and Hermeneutics after the Exile* (Cambridge: Cambridge University Press, 1990); W. Riley, *King and Cultus in Chronicles: Worship and the Reinterpretation of History* (JSOTSup 160; Sheffield: JSOT Press, 1993); E. M. Dörrfuss, *Mose in den Chronik-büchern* (Berlin: de Gruyter, 1994); B. E. Kelly, *Retribution and Eschatology in Chronicles* (JSOTSup 211; Sheffield: Sheffield Academic Press, 1996); Dyck, *Ideology of Identity*; idem, *Theocratic Ideology*. See also my own contributions, *Reflections of King Josiah in Chronicles: Late Stages of the Josiah Reception in 2 Chr 34f.* (Gütersloh: Gütersloher Verlag, 2003); idem, "The Rhetorics of Finding a New Identity in a Multi-religious and Multi-ethnic society: The Case of the Book of Chronicles," *Verbum et Ecclesia* 24 (2003) 396–416; idem, "The Cushites in the Chronicler's Version of Asa's Reign: A Secondary Audience in Chron-icles?" *Old Testament Essays* 19 (2006) 863–81; idem, "Reforming History: The Hermeneu-tical Significance of the Books of Chronicles," *VT* 57 (2007) 21–44; idem, "Refocusing the Battle Accounts of the Kings: Identity Formation in the Books of Chronicles," in *Behut-sames Lesen: Alttestamentliche Exegese im Gespräch mit Literaturwissenschaft und Kulturwis-senschaften* (ed. S. Lubs et al.; Leipzig: Evangelische Verlagsanstalt, 2007) 245–74.

5. Berquist, *Constructions of Identity*.

6. Ibid., 54.

"members of an extended family, sharing lineage and descent, and measurable by genealogy. Such identity is objective; it is innate from birth."[7] According to him, this is the "classic assumption of early and modern scholarship." He identifies certain weaknesses of this assumption, two of which are: (1) "ethnicity is essentially a modern concept and does not fit well with descriptions of the premodern world," and (2) "such theories ignore too much of the biblical textual evidence."[8]

In a second mode, identity is seen "as a matter of nationality or of connection to some other political organization."[9] Apart from the fact that "such a theory of identity import(s) assumptions about the modern nation-state and its theory of unitary sovereignty within measurable boundaries, it negates one of the things we know to be most significant about this period from the biblical and epigraphical records: identity was not restricted to the environs of Jerusalem but related to places such as Elephantine, Samaria, Babylon, and even al-Jahuda."[10]

A third approach, according to Berquist, connects identity with religion. According to this model, Judean identity is reduced to the Yahwistic cult. Berquist argues, however, "that we must understand Judean identity as something distinct from religion. The biblical texts portray the error of such an oversimplification, in that not all of the Judeans understood themselves as sharing a single religion. In fact, there was substantial disagreement about who was properly obedient to the faith."[11] The above approaches are fairly static and top-down; that is, "they develop easy criteria for our discernment about identity, but they are unlikely to reflect how ancient Judeans thought of themselves."[12]

A fourth (more flexible and bottom-up) model therefore stands in contrast to the models discussed above. In this model, according to Berquist, identity is described from the perspective of role theory "as a description of how individual people take on distinct roles in society, integrating functions and self-understandings."[13] Although this model provides a more dynamic perspective on the interactions within any society that contribute to identity formation, it does not (according to Berquist) escape the dangers of essentialism ("the assumption that

---

7. Ibid.
8. Ibid.
9. Ibid., 56.
10. Ibid.
11. Ibid., 57.
12. Ibid., 58.
13. Ibid.

roles define all of life or render behavior definite and predictable, as if roles determined a person's essence")[14] and functionalism ("which assumes that society is the sum total of the additive roles undertaken by its participants").[15] Berquist therefore suggests that "scholarship of Achaemenid Judah should ally itself with newer historiographic methods, such as the postmodern direction that also seeks to avoid functionalism."[16]

He therefore identifies a fifth model, which also represents his own point of view: "Postmodernism and the Mathematics of Chaos."[17] He takes his point of departure from postmodern historiographies, which "tend to emphasize the inherent instability of any system or society."[18] This leads him to the following conclusion:

> Simply put, the categorizing of identity as religious, national, or ethnic is a response to the wrong question. Identity refers to the pattern that multiple forces produce. Each point is fluid and changing. . . . This approach transforms the previous questions about ethnicity, nationality, and religion as defining identity. No longer are such identities seen as fixed and static categories, but as continuing *processes* [italics his]. We must speak not of identity but of identity formation.[19]

Although aspects of Berquist's work could be criticized,[20] he has helped us at least with the following theoretical insights:

1. We should not underestimate the complexity of the matter when investigating identity formation in Achaemenid Yehud. Multiple forces cooperated in this process.
2. We should therefore not describe identity formation in static terms but should allow for the dynamic of the process in our descriptions.
3. Our attempt should not be to reconstruct something concrete that existed in Achaemenid Yehud—namely, the identity of the Judeans. Apart from the fact that identity is fluid and cannot be pinpointed in a specific phase, our sources also do not allow these kinds of reconstructions.

---

14. Ibid., 59.
15. Ibid.
16. Ibid.
17. Ibid.
18. Ibid.
19. Ibid., 63.
20. For example, Berquist's designation *"Postcolonial* Yehud" in the title of his contribution is debatable. When speaking of Yehud during the Achaemenid Period (as he does), one should instead speak of *colonial* existence. Did Berquist perhaps, in his application of *postcolonial* criticism, allow the description of his method to become a designation of this phase in Yehud's history?

4. Identity should not be described as something homogeneous (such as ethnic, religious, political, etc.). We should, rather, proceed from the presupposition of multiple (or hybrid) identities.
5. We should focus on a description of the traces of identity formation that are evinced in our sources.

My intention in the remainder of this contribution is to show how recent developments in the field of social psychology can assist us in this pursuit. I contend here that particularly the notion of "textual identities" developed in social psychology could help us toward a more adequate understanding of the relationship between identity formation and literary sources, such as biblical documents. In the next section, I will therefore provide a short overview of recent developments in this field, and I will explore the usefulness of the notion *textual identities*. In a subsequent section, I will analyze the Jehoram narrative in Chronicles (2 Chr 21:2–22:1)—in synoptic comparison with the Vorlage in 2 Kgs 8—in order to test the hypothesis that the notion of "textual identities" could help us achieve a more adequate understanding of the dynamics of identity formation in the books of Chronicles.

Can Social Psychology Be of Any Assistance?

In an unfortunately still-unpublished dissertation, Jan Bosman has shown the value of gleaning insights and theoretical models from social psychology in his discussion of the oracles concerning the nations as a witness to the social-identity formation process in the book of Nahum.[21] He is well aware of "the dangers of reductionism, positivism, determinism and relativism in the 'marriage'" of literary and sociological investigation, "not to mention the danger of the modernistic biases of the interpreters to impose their own modern and Western experiences on to the world of ancient Israel."[22] He nevertheless contends with Lester Grabbe[23] that social studies could at least contribute to the study of the Old Testament on four levels: (1) "we see new possibilities and approaches to familiar texts"; (2) "we can now interrogate the texts and try to find answers to questions that were not necessarily viewed as important questions by the ancient authors/editors or audiences";

---

21. See J. P. Bosman, *Social Identity in Nahum: A Theological-Ethical Enquiry* (D.Th. diss., University of Stellenbosch, 2005).

22. Ibid., 45.

23. See L. L. Grabbe, *Priests, Prophets, Diviners, Sages: A Socio-Historical Study of Religious Specialists in Ancient Israel* (Valley Forge, PA: Trinity Press International, 1995) 15.

(3) "we have models that we can test against the biblical data"; and
(4) "by way of analogy we have cross-cultural comparisons that help to
fill in gaps in the biblical data."[24]

With Bosman I would like to explore the potential contribution of
social psychology to our discussions on identity in ancient Yehud. In
this section I will provide a short overview of developments in the
field. Two subareas of social psychology that are of particular interest
for our discussions on identity formation are social identity theory
(SIT) and self-categorization theory (SCT).[25] The social identity theory
that was developed by Henri Tajfel and colleagues at the University of
Bristol in the 1970s and 1980s "offers an explanation for minimal intergroup bias, and also a broader statement of how relationships between
real-world groups relate to social identity."[26] Social identity "is the individual's knowledge that he or she belongs to certain social groups
together with the emotional and value significance of the group mem-
berships. Social identity affects and is affected by intergroup relationships. The theory aims to explain the uniformity and coherence of
group and intergroup behavior as mediated by social identity."[27]

Categorization plays an important role in social identity theory.
Group membership is often based on certain principles of belief ac-

---

24. Bosman, *Social Identity in Nahum*, 47.

25. See also my *Reforming History*, 32–36, where I have argued similarly and where I
have illustrated the usefulness of social-psychological insights with reference to the
Chronicler's Hezekiah narrative. The following works also provide summaries of these
theories: D. Abrams, "Social Identity, Psychology of," in *International Encyclopedia of the
Social and Behavioral Sciences* (ed. N. J. Smelser and P. B. Baltes; Amsterdam: Elsevier,
2001) 21.14306–9; M. A. Hogg and D. Abrams, "Social Identity and Social Cognition: Historical Background and Current Trends," in *Social Identity and Social Cognition* (ed.
D. Abrams and M. A. Hogg; Oxford: Blackwell, 1999) 1–25; D. Bar-Tal, "Group Beliefs as
an Expression of Social Identity," in *Social Identity: International Perspectives* (ed. S.
Worchel et al.; London: Sage, 1998) 93–113; C. Fraser and B. Burchell, eds., *Introducing Social Psychology* (Oxford: Polity, 2001); M. A. Hogg, "Social Identity Theory," in *The Blackwell Encyclopedia of Social Psychology* (ed. A. S. R. Manstead and M. Hewstone; Oxford:
Blackwell, 1995) 555–60; idem, "Intragroup Processes, Group Structure and Social Iden-
tity," in *Social Groups and Identities: Developing the Legacy of Henri Tajfel* (ed. W. P. Robinson;
Oxford: Butterworth-Heinemann, 1996) 65–93; M. A. Hogg and D. Abrams, "Intergroup
Behavior and Social Identity," in *The Sage Handbook of Social Psychology* (ed. M. A. Hogg
and J. Cooper; London: Sage, 2003) 407–31; R. Stainton Rogers et al., *Social Psychology: A
Critical Agenda* (Cambridge: Polity, 1995); J. C. Turner, "Henri Tajfel: An Introduction," in
Social Groups and Identities: Developing the Legacy of Henri Tajfel (ed. W. P. Robinson; Ox-
ford: Butterworth-Heinemann, 1996).

26. Abrams, *Social Identity*, 14306.

27. Ibid.

cording to which group members act.[28] Self-categorization theory (developed by Turner) therefore extends social identity theory by describing the way that social identity regulates behavior. Hogg summarizes this as follows:

> When we categorize others as in-group or out-group members we accentuate their similarity to the relevant prototype—thus perceiving them stereotypically and ethnocentrically. When we categorize ourselves, we define, perceive, and evaluate ourselves in terms of our in-group prototype, and behave in accordance with that prototype. Self-categorization produces in-group normative behavior and self-stereotyping, and is thus the process underlying group behaviour.[29]

In terms of the motivation behind these processes of self-categorization, different possibilities are mentioned in the literature (not all of them without criticism). Among other things, Brewer discusses the following motivational theories: (1) common fate (in which perceived interdependence among individual members of a collective is seen as the defining characteristic of a social group); (2) self-esteem (in which individual members maintain a positive self-esteem by means of the group's successes and achievements); (3) self-verification (in which people are motivated to belong to a group in order to reduce uncertainty; and clarification of group membership, adherence to group norms, and associating positive group features with the self are ways to achieve this); and (4) optimal distinctiveness (in which two powerful social motives are held in balance: the need for inclusion, which is satisfied by assimilation of the self into larger collectives, and the opposing need for differentiation, which is satisfied by distinguishing the self from others).[30]

In recent years, however, reactions from within social psychology have transformed the field significantly. As a reaction against (what Stainton Rogers et al. call) the "reification" of personhood and identity, there has been a turn to the notion of textuality.[31] De Fina et al. mention that "(r)esearch on language and identity has experienced an unprecedented growth in the last ten years. The time when scholars in

---

28. See Bar-Tal's discussion of group beliefs as an expression of social identity. He defines group beliefs "as convictions that group members (a) are aware that they share, and (b) consider as defining their 'groupness'" (Bar-Tal, *Group Beliefs*, 94).

29. Hogg, *Social Identity Theory*, 559.

30. See M. B. Brewer, *Intergroup Relations* (2nd ed.; Philadelphia: Open University Press, 2003) 36–39. See also M. A. Hogg, "Intergroup Relations," in *Handbook of Social Psychology* (ed. J. Delamater; New York: Kluwer, 2003) 479–502.

31. See Rogers et al., *Social Psychology*, 44.

the field needed to advocate for the centrality of language in the study of identity . . . seems far away indeed."[32] They then continue to provide an overview of the developments in research on discourse and identity that have become widely accepted. The first development that they mention is social constructionism, which provides a very basic way of thinking about identity:

> the assumption (is) that identity is neither a given nor a product. Rather, identity is a process that (1) takes place in concrete and specific interactional occasions, (2) yields constellations of identities instead of individual, monolithic constructs, (3) does not simply emanate from the individual, but results from processes of negotiation and entextualization . . . that are eminently social, and (4) entails discursive work.[33]

The last point is explained in the following way: "identity is a process that is always embedded in social practices . . . within which discourse practices . . . have a central role. Both social and discourse practices frame, and in many ways define, the way individuals and groups present themselves to others, negotiate roles, and conceptualize themselves."[34]

The turn to textuality (in the postmodern sense of the word) is clear here. Stainton Rogers et al. also discuss this turn under the rubric "textual identities." They refer to the groundbreaking work of Harré in this regard, who "discusses how we craft out understandings of who we are . . . from out of the socially available pool of textual resources that are available in a given culture at a given time."[35] Shotter and Gergen expressed this notion as follows: "The primary medium within which identities are created and have their currency is not just linguistic, but textual: persons are largely ascribed identities according to the manner of their embedding within a discourse—in their own or in the discourse of others."[36]

A second field of development discussed by De Fina et al. is the analysis of processes of categorization and membership definition: "Recent approaches to categorization have highlighted the limitations of applying pre-established categorizations, emphasizing instead the locally occasioned, fluid and ever-changing nature of identity claims.

---

32. A. De Fina, D. Schiffrin, and M. Bamberg, eds., *Discourse and Identity* (Cambridge: Cambridge University Press, 2006) 1.

33. Ibid., 2.

34. Ibid.

35. Rogers et al., *Social Psychology*, 60.

36. J. Shotter and K. J. Gergen, eds., *Texts of Identity* (London: Sage, 1989) ix. See also J. Shotter, *Conversational Realities: Constructing Life through Language* (London: Sage, 1993).

... Thus identities are seen not as merely represented in discourse, but rather as performed, enacted and embodied through a variety of linguistic and non-linguistic means."[37]

A third trend in identity studies is the development of anti-essentialism. It is now emphasized that people and groups can "simultaneously assume voices that are associated with different identity categories, and that they can perform identities, that is, represent themselves as different from what their personal visible characteristics would suggest, therefore concluding that there is nothing given or natural about being part of a social category or group. The inadequacy of an essentialist notion of identity as being embodied in the 'self'" has been shown in recent research.[38]

A last development indicated by De Fina et al. is the increasing attention to the centrality of processes of indexicality in the creation, performance and attribution of identities:

> Indexicality is a layered, creative, interactive process that lies at the heart of the symbolic workings of language. The idea that signs are indexical goes beyond simple referential anchoring to encompass the ability of linguistic expressions to evoke, and relate to, complex systems of meaning such as socially shared conceptualizations of space and place, ideologies, social representations about group membership, social roles and attributes, presuppositions about all aspects of social reality, individual and collective stances, practices and organization structures.[39]

In my view, the turn toward "textual identities" in the social-psychological fields of social identity theory and self-categorization theory is a very important one.[40] This development could help provide new insights into the processes of identity formation in Second Temple Yehud on at least the following levels:

1. "Textual identities" emphasize the fluid, dynamic, and discursive nature of processes of identity formation.
2. This notion emphasizes the close interrelationship between the social environment within which a group exists, the textual resources that are available in the given culture, and the role that renewed textual construction plays in the process of identity formation.
3. It therefore provides us with a firmer theoretical basis for relating the issue of identity formation to our literary and textual sources.

---

37. De Fina, Schiffrin, and Bamberg, *Discourse and Identity*, 3.

38. Ibid.

39. Ibid., 4.

40. M. Whitebrook uses the term "narrative identities," in *Identity, Narrative and Politics* (London: Routledge, 2001).

4. It cautions us not only to take into account multiple motivational
    factors that could have contributed to self-categorization but also to
    view these motivational factors in a discursive framework.

It is clear from the above discussion that Berquist's recent contribution
to scholarship on identity formation in Second Temple Yehud is in line
with developments in social psychology, particularly social identity
theory and self-categorization theory. However, it is also clear that the
emphasis on "textual identities" in recent social-psychological research
could complement Berquist's views significantly. How these broadened
insights could assist us in identifying and describing the identity formation processes in Chronicles will now be illustrated with reference
to the Chronicler's version of Jehoram's history. Only one example from
Chronicles is discussed here because of the constraints of this essay.
One should, however, take into account the fact that the traces identified here should also be substantiated from the overall narrative construction of the book of Chronicles.[41]

An Illustration:
The Chronicler's Account of Jehoram's History
(2 Chronicles 21:2–22:1)

The Chronicler's Jehoram narrative[42] has not received much attention
in scholarly publications over the past two decades (apart from discussions in recent commentaries). Scholarly articles on this narrative have
focused mainly on the historical question of Jehoram's genealogy, suggesting alternative possibilities for the ambiguous biblical data and the
traditional interpretation that Jehoram was the son of Jehoshaphat,
king of Judah, and the father of Ahaziah (with Athaliah as mother [the
daughter of Ahab of Israel and Jezebel]).[43] Another article addresses
the question whether Jehoram of Judah and Jehoram of Israel were one

---

41. See also J. W. Wright, "The Fight for Peace: Narrative and History in the Battle
Accounts in Chronicles," in *The Chronicler as Historian* (ed. M. P. Graham, K. G. Hoglund,
and S. L. McKenzie; JSOTSup 238; Sheffield: Sheffield Academic Press, 1997) 150–77. In
another contribution, I widen the scope of my investigation to 2 Chr 10–36 to show how
the refocusing of the battle accounts of the Judahite kings functioned in the service of
identity formation in Chronicles (see "Refocusing the Battle Accounts").

42. The succession notes in 21:1 and 22:1 are taken as the conclusion of the respective
narratives. The account about Jehoram is therefore delimited here as 21:2–22:1.

43. See D. V. Etz, "The Genealogical Relationship of Jehoram and Ahaziah, and of
Ahaz and Hezekiah, Kings of Judah," *JSOT* 71 (1996) 39–53; W. B. Barrick, "Another
Shaking of Jehoshaphat's Family Tree: Jehoram and Ahaziah Once Again," *VT* 51 (2001)
9–25.

and the same king.[44] In this case as well, the biblical data are somewhat ambiguous. Still another study (the most recent to my knowledge) discusses the question of whether Elijah was indeed the author of the letter mentioned in 2 Chr 21:12–15.[45]

A contribution that in my view deserves more attention, however, is Christopher Begg's discussion of the heavy editorial changes that we witness in the Chronicler's version.[46] In his article, Begg argues that one should not necessarily postulate that the Chronicler's *Sondergut* was taken over from unknown and extrabiblical historical traditions. He proposes that the following could have been the reference points for the Chronicler's reconstruction of the Deuteronomistic narrative: "A) the influence of the Deuteronomistic 'Ahabite material' on the *Sondergut* in 2 Chronicles 21; B) the Chronicler's Asa and Jehoshaphat stories as inspiration for this special material; and C) the themes of 'exile and beyond' in their impact on the same."[47]

Although I find his proposals fresh and convincing, the "why" questions still remain. Why did the Chronicler make these editorial changes? Why did the Chronicler in Second Temple Yehud choose to present his Jehoram narrative in this particular fashion? I would like to relate these questions to our discussion on identity formation in Chronicles in the sections below. However, we should first of all read the

---

44. Strange suggests that "the Deuteronomist deliberately used every ambiguity in his sources and created a 'ghost' in Israel. He did so to avoid that any of the descendants of David should have had any part in the apostate and abominable kingdom of Israel." See J. Strange, "Joram, King of Israel and Judah," *VT* 25 (1975) 201.

45. See also the paper of Christine Mitchell presented at the 2006 CSBS meeting, "Writing/Elijah/Cursing: 2 Chronicles 21:11–20." During the preparation of my essay, however, her study was not yet available in print.

On Elijah, see R. E. Knuteson, "Elijah's little-known letter in 2 Chronicles 21:12–15," *BSac* 162 (2005) 23–32. He argues that Elijah was indeed the author of this letter. He comes to this conclusion after contending that Elijah was not taken to heaven but was removed by the Lord to another geographical location. There he was prompted by the Lord to write this letter to Jehoram. In my view, and from the perspective of an investigation into the identity formation processes witnessed in Chronicles, the question addressed by Knuteson is totally irrelevant. The historicity of this letter should not be the focus of our investigation; the function of the mentioning of Elijah in the Jehoram narrative should be the focus. See my discussion below. (On account of the similar content in the Elijah letter and the other *Sondergut* parts of the Chronicler's Jehoram narrative, one could assume that the letter was also written by the writer of the *Sondergut*.)

46. See C. T. Begg, "Constructing a Monster: The Chronicler's *Sondergut* in 2 Chronicles 21," *Australian Biblical Review* 37 (1989) 35–51. In his study, he builds on B. J. Diebner, "Überlegungen zum 'Brief des Elia' (2 Chr 21,12–15)," *Henoch* 9 (1988) 197–228.

47. Begg, "Constructing a Monster," 37.

Chronicler's text closely in synoptic comparison with the narrative in
2 Kgs 8 in order to recap the editorial changes that were made.[48]

Synoptic Comparison with the Vorlage (2 Kings 8)

The appendix shows the text of 2 Chr 21:2–22:1 in synoptic comparison with its Vorlage of 2 Kgs 8:16–24 (see pp. 215–217). Three types of
editorial change occur in this narrative: omissions, additions, and
changes.

Omissions from the Vorlage

The introductory remark in 2 Kgs 8:16 was omitted by the Chronicler. This is in line with the trend in 2 Chr 10–36 to omit the coordinat-
ing dating of the reigns of Judahite kings and their Israelite counterparts. The Israelite monarchy does not form the focus of the Chronicler's narrative. The northern kingdom and kings are mentioned only
when they impinge on the Judahite history.[49] Another omission in
Chronicles is the note in 2 Kgs 8:21d, which says that "the people fled
to their tents"—a note that indicates in the Deuteronomistic version
that Joram[50] of Judah lost the battle against the Edomites. A third
omission is the concluding phrase presented in 2 Kgs 8:23, which refers
to the annals of the kings of Judah as an additional source for the deeds
of King Joram. Although this typical remark is omitted in some instances in Chronicles, it is not a general trend.[51]

Additions to the Vorlage

The first addition is the account of Jehoram's fratricide (2 Chr 21:2–
4). Apart from the fact that this account provides new information that
is absent in 2 Kgs 8, this section also creates confusion about where this
actually happened: in Israel or in Judah? 2 Chronicles 21:2 suggests
that the brothers of Jehoram were all sons of Jehoshaphat, king of Is-

---

48. Time and space constraints do not allow a full exegetical study here. I will, however, focus on the aspects of the text that could possibly be related to a process of identity
formation.

49. See the Rehoboam narrative, in which Jeroboam of Israel features prominently as
a constant opponent in war. See also the Chronicler's Abijah narrative (with again Jeroboam of Israel as opponent), the Asa narrative (with Baasha of Israel as opponent), the
Jehoshaphat narrative (with Ahab of Israel as ally), the Ahaziah narrative (with Jehoram
of Israel as ally), the Amaziah narrative (with Joash of Israel as opponent), and the Ahaz
narrative (with Pekah of Israel as opponent).

50. Note that 2 Chr 21 uses the variant form of the name ("Jehoram") compared with
2 Kgs 8 ("Joram").

51. See, e.g., 2 Chr 13:22; 20:34; 25:26; 27:7; 28:6; 32:32; 33:18; 35:26; and 36:8, where
this phrase was retained.

rael.[52] Verse 3 mentions, however, that fortified cities in Judah were given to these brothers and that the kingship was given to Jehoram, who was the oldest son. After establishing his power, Jehoram then killed all his brothers and also some Israelite leaders (v. 4). In order to resolve this confusion in the text, some scholars emend "Israel" in v. 2 to read "Judah." Another suggestion is that "Israel" in v. 2 should not be taken as a reference to the northern kingdom but as the more general designation, which is used elsewhere by the Chronicler to refer to the southern and northern kingdoms (e.g., in the כל־ישראל expressions). Another possibility would be to see the phrase "king of Israel" in v. 2 as an attempt by the Chronicler to link the Jehoram narrative to the Ahabite line of the northern kingdom (which ran through Athaliah, the daughter of Ahab of Israel, who was married to Jehoram).[53] Whatever the case might be, we should not ignore the "blurring of the lines" between Judah and Israel that occurs here.

We find the next addition in 2 Chr 21:10c–11c. Here a theological motivation is provided for the Edomite (and Libnite) rebellion against Jehoram. The addition is introduced with a כי־phrase, and the theologically laden expression עזב את־יהוה is used to indicate the transgression. It continues in v. 11, indicating that Jehoram has built high places on the hills of Judah, that he has led the inhabitants of Jerusalem into adultery (the verb זנה is used), and that he has led Judah astray. The allusion to the Ahabite connection is clear here. The Edomite and Libnite rebellion now becomes a punishment for Jehoram's following of practices for which his northern in-laws were actually better known! The irony is furthermore that Jehoram is evaluated very negatively here (in line with the Deuteronomistic Vorlage) in terms of his Ahabite connection, although Jehoshaphat, his father, who went into alliance with Ahab of Israel, is evaluated positively. Again, the lines between Judah and Israel are blurred.

Elijah's letter in 2 Chr 21:12–15 presents another addition. The letter is called a מכתב and is introduced with the typical messenger formula "thus speaks Yahweh" (who is specified as "the God of David, your father").[54] Again, the accusation against Jehoram is that he has taken the

---

52. Although Jehoram is not mentioned by name in 21:2, the enclitic personal pronoun at the beginning of the verse refers back to the concluding remark of the previous royal narrative in 21:1, in which Jehoram is nominalized. See also the studies dealing with the genealogical difficulties presented by this text: e.g., Strange, "Joram"; Etz, "Genealogical Relationship"; Barrick, "Jehoshaphat's Family Tree."

53. See particularly Begg, "Constructing a Monster," on this view.

54. Begg indicates that this same word ("to stir up") is used in 2 Chr 36:22 in connection with Cyrus's proclamation. He (ibid., 49) argues that this is only one of the ways in

path of the Ahabites. A great plague will come over his people.[55] He himself will fall into severe sickness.

The themes in the letter are then taken up in the continuation of the Chronicler's *Sondergut* in 21:16–17 and 18–19b. Yahweh then "stirred up" the Philistines and Arabs (who were near the Cushites) against Jehoram and Judah, and they destroyed the palace and killed his sons (except Joahaz) and his wives (vv. 16–17).[56] After this, Yahweh struck (again נגף) Jehoram with a bowel sickness—in fulfillment of the prophecy in Elijah's letter (18–19b).

The last addition appears in 21:20a–b. After the change to the death notice in v. 19c and 20c (see discussion below), Jehoram's regnal details are repeated (from v. 5). This repetition forms an inclusio before and after Jehoram's reign.

Changes to the Vorlage

There are also a few instances in which the Chronicler has taken over the material of his Vorlage but has made changes to it.[57] The first significant change is in 21:7a–b. Whereas the Deuteronomistic Vorlage says that "Yahweh did not want to destroy Judah on account of David his servant," the Chronicler states that "Yahweh did not want to destroy the house of David on account of the covenant he had made with David." The change from "Judah" to "House of David" is significant in that it focuses attention on the continuation of the royal line of David instead of on the continuation of the Kingdom of Judah. The reference to the "covenant" probably invokes the memory of the promise made to David by Yahweh, spoken through Nathan the prophet (2 Sam 7).

---

which the Chronicler already opened a vision on the "exile and beyond" in the Jehoram *Sondergut*. He sees the relationship between these two verses as one of reversal: whereas the Elijah letter precedes Judah's destruction by a foreign coalition (the Philistines and Arabs), the Cyrus proclamation precedes the restoration of Judah.

55. The term used here, נגף, is often employed in the Chronicler's *Sondergut* as an indication of Yahweh's punishing actions. See 13:15, 20; 14:1; 20:15, 22, 29; 21:18.

56. The same verb, עור, is used here and in 2 Chr 36:22 (which indicates that the LORD "stirred up" Cyrus to write his proclamation).

57. Some of the changes (e.g., in 21:5a and 5c, and possibly also in 9a and 9c) are stylistic in nature and will not be discussed here. See, however, the text-critical discussion on 21:9c (compared with 2 Kgs 8:21c). It is suggested that an emendation should be made in 2 Kings to read "Edom struck him," instead of "he struck Edom." The addition of the suffix to the accusative marker could result in a possibility of this sort. This change will also fit better in the context in which the Edomites are indicated to be in rebellion "until this day." It therefore does not seem logical that Jehoram struck Edom. The opposite, that Edom struck him, fits more logically into the context.

The second extensive reworking can be found at the end of the narrative, in 21:19c–22b (with the exclusion of v. 20a–b—see the discussion above). The phrase in 2 Kgs 8:24a announcing the death of Joram as well as the burial notice in 8:24b were transformed in 2 Chr 21:19c/20c and 20d to indicate that there was no remorse about the death of Jehoram. The Chronicler specifically indicates that Jehoram was not buried in the usual way and certainly not together with the other kings. A clear distancing from Judah's king is created here.

The concluding phrase in 2 Kgs 8:24c, announcing the new king, Ahaziah, was also changed significantly. 2 Chronicles 22:1 indicates that the inhabitants of Jerusalem made Jehoram's youngest son, Ahaziah, king after him. The unusual incident of the youngest son's becoming king is explained in 22:1b by referring to the killing of all the other brothers in the battle against the Arabs. The Chronicler's account concludes then with a repetition of the accession formula but adds that Ahaziah became king over Judah.

Observations on Identity Formation

In my observations on the Chronicler's Jehoram narrative, I must latch onto the "why" question again. Why were these changes made? We may, as Begg has aptly done, refer to the intertexts that determined these changes. The question remains, however, what function these changes had in the discourse presented in Chronicles. I propose the following reading: in the Chronicler's Jehoram narrative, we see a Second Temple Jerusalemite community in the process of negotiating a new identity. This is done on at least two levels.

First, this community was trying to come to terms with the new postexilic reality, in which the boundaries between the south and the north were no longer defined in terms of two separate monarchies. Categorization could no longer be done in terms of the monarchic political realities, because those realities were now substituted by a common political fate as provinces under Persian imperial rule. This common fate motivated them to remember their continuity with their northern neighbor again—a continuity that was even testified in the crisscrossing of genealogical lines during the time of Jehoram.[58] In

---

58. Knoppers confirms the cultural continuity between Yehud and Samaria when he says: "Culturally speaking, Samaria and Yehud shared much in common. Indeed, in speaking of two separate provinces of Samaria and Yehud, one has to recognize that such a distinction is inherently an administrative and political one and not so much a cultural one." See G. N. Knoppers, "Revisiting the Samarian Question in the Persian Period," in

order to avoid a "blurring of the lines" between the Yehudite and Samarian communities in the postexilic period, Jehoram's narrative was a
rather useful story to tell. Assimilation with their "blood brothers"
from the north could have been a useful option in their postexilic reality (knowing that Samaria was a "larger, better-established, and con-
siderably more populous" province than Yehud).[59]

However, this narrative simultaneously witnesses to differentiation.
Although the lines between Judah and Israel, between Yehud and Samaria were blurred by the presentation of this narrative, the Jerusalemite community was also quite sure about the fact that the Davidic
line (not as political reality but as religious-theological reality) provided an assurance for the future. It was on account of Yahweh's covenant with David that they were not destroyed by the exile. The "ways
of their father David" therefore stand in sharp contrast to the "ways of
the Ahabites" of the north. A prophetic word put in the mouth of the
northern prophet Elijah, who was so prominent in the time of Ahab,
confirms this sort of message for the Jerusalemite community.[60] The
people of Jerusalem should differentiate themselves from the northern
religious ways.[61]

Judah and the Judeans in the Persian Period (ed. O. Lipschits and M. Oeming; Winona Lake,
IN: Eisenbrauns, 2006) 279.

59. Knoppers (ibid., 272–73) offers evidence from archaeology to make the following
point:

> The Jerusalem of the Achaemenid era has been described as a village with an adminis-
> trative center. In contrast, the Samaria of the Achaemenid era has been described as
> one of ancient Palestine's larger urban areas. If so, we are dealing not with a situation
> of comparability but with a situation of disparity. One regional center was substan-
> tially larger and wealthier than the other. The difference between the two provinces
> and their two capitals cannot but have affected the intelligentsia of Jerusalem. During
> the Achaemenid era, members of the Judean elite were not dealing with a depopulated
> outback to the north. Quite the contrary, they were dealing with a province that was
> larger, better-established, and considerably more populous than was Yehud.

60. The fact that a northern prophet is introduced here by the Chronicler to fulfill the
function of rebuking a southern king for following the northern religious ways seems
odd. Although the prophet is clearly portrayed as part of the in-group, he reminds the
king that the Jerusalemite community should differentiate themselves from the northern kingdom, which functions as the out-group. This "blurring of the lines" between Judah and Israel is in line with other tendencies in Chronicles, which I have described in
"Refocusing the Battle Accounts."

61. Knoppers ("Revisiting the Samaritan Question," 279) mentions that recent exca-
vations suggest that some sort of sanctuary or temple existed on Mt. Gerizim already
during the Persian period. He therefore remarks: "[T]his would only have added further
impetus for Jerusalem Temple scribes to authenticate the distinctive positions of their
city and shrine."

In this way, group belief is strengthened, and an in-group proto-type is presented. Behavior in accordance with this prototype is natu-rally suggested here. The Chronicler's Jehoram narrative is therefore a text that contributes to the Yehudite/Jerusalemite community's pur-suit of optimal distinctiveness.[62] Assimilation and differentiation with their northern "blood brothers" are in tension. Self-categorization takes place in terms of a group that in some instances could be considered an in-group but in other instances could be seen as an out-group.

A second level of identity negotiation could also be distinguished. The introduction of foreign peoples as opponents in this narrative fol-lows a pattern that also occurs in the rest of Chronicles.[63] In this spe-cific narrative, the Philistines and the Arabs (who are said to have lived near the Cushites) feature as opponents. They are stirred up by Yah-weh in order to punish Jehoram for his wicked ways. With Siedlecki, I see the inclusion of these foreign nations as an attempt to define Yehud "at the geographical margins of Judah."[64] But again, the relationship of Judah to these nations is vague: the Philistine-Arab alliance is por-trayed as the victors in their skirmish with Judah, destroying even the royal palace and family (with the exception of the youngest son). However, the Chronicler is also convinced that these nations were stirred up by Yahweh. These nations are different and foreign but are still under Yahweh's dominion. They act on behalf of Judah's God.

The addition of the Philistines and Arabs as opponents fits well into the Jehoram narrative, in which the Edomites already played a role. The Chronicler has taken over from his Vorlage the account of Edom's (and Libnah's) rebellion against Jehoram. However, an addition by the Chronicler (vv. 10c–11c) turns the Edomite rebellion into a punishment of Jehoram, because he has forsaken Yahweh, the God of his fathers. Already here we see the ambiguous role of a foreign nation, which is also portrayed in the later section on the Philistines and Arabs. It is

---

62. Knoppers (ibid.) indicates that "[a]ttempts at self-definition may have been nec-essary for some of the elite in Jerusalem precisely because of the similarities between the Yahwists living in the two territories. . . . [T]here was no unanimity among writers in Ye-hud about how to define Israelite identity, the community's institutions, and the people's relations to their neighbors." The point that I am making here from the perspective of self-categorization theory supports Knoppers's observation.

63. See "Refocusing the Battle Accounts," where I have described the battle accounts in 2 Chr 10–36.

64. Siedlecki, "Foreigners, Warfare and Judahite Identity," 231. See also J. W. Wright, "The Fight for Peace" and his "Remapping Yehud: The Borders of Yehud and the Gene-alogies of Chronicles," in *Judah and the Judeans in the Persian Period* (ed. O. Lipschits and M. Oeming; Winona Lake, IN: Eisenbrauns, 2006) 67–89.

certainly not a coincidence that Edom and Philistia/Arabia are mentioned in this narrative. Here we see again the Yehudite community in the process of differentiating themselves from their provincial neighbors—this time their southern neighbors Ashdod and Idumea. The Chronicler's Jehoram narrative admits to the fact that Yehud will probably never have power over its southern neighbors. However, there is no doubt in the Chronicler's mind that Yahweh controls this situation. And Yahweh's control reminds Yehud that they should walk in the ways of their father David. Yehud's self-categorization hinges not on political power but on cultic-religious purity.

The Chronicler's Jehoram account is a bold witness to Yehud's attempts to assimilate themselves into a new sociopolitical environment of provincial existence under Persian dominion. But simultaneously, the Yehudites want to differentiate themselves from others, indicating that their uniqueness lies in their being Yahweh's people.[65] For this purpose the available pool of historical traditions in the Second Temple period proved to be very appropriate material to work with. By using these historical traditions (the Deuteronomistic History in particular), the Jerusalemite elite could show their continuity with the heyday of their Davidic monarchy but also with the cultic traditions that were centered in the Jerusalem temple. However, by reforming these historical traditions, those Yehudites could entextualize their identity formation processes in the new present.

Conclusion

I have shown that Chronicles (the Jehoram narrative, in particular) may be read as literature that formed part of a process of identity formation. The sociopsychological notion of "textual identities" provided the theoretical basis for this reading. This reading emphasized that historical traditions were repeated not for the sake of reconstructing the past but for the sake of self-categorization in a new present. The edito-

---

65. Siedlecki ("Foreigners, Warfare and Judahite Identity," 266) comes to a similar conclusion when he says:

> Edom and the northern kingdom of Israel receive somewhat more attention than other neighbours of Judah during the divided monarchy. In the case of Israel, this may be explained by the problematic status of the northern kingdom, being at the same time similar and dissimilar to Judah. The northern kingdom represents Judah's 'alter-ego', the externalization of its own alienation from itself. Likewise, Edom is portrayed as Israel's brother in the genealogies. Thus, there exists a heightened degree of similarity between Judah and Edom or Israel, and hence a stronger need for Judah to define itself as separate from either one.

rial changes to these historical traditions were particularly significant in this regard. They witness a community coming to terms with their provincial existence under Persian imperial dominion—amidst other similar provinces to the north and the south. But they also witness the belief that constituted their uniqueness as group—namely, Yahwism practiced in Jerusalem in continuation of the Davidic covenant.

Appendix:
Parallel Accounts of Jehoram, King of Judah

Key

(----)	Not present in the other version
Single underline	Pluses in Chronicles compared with the other version
Double underline	Changes in Chronicles compared with the other version

2 Kings 8:16–24	*2 Chronicles 21:2–22:1a*
8:16a וּבִשְׁנַת חָמֵשׁ לְיוֹרָם בֶּן־אַחְאָב מֶלֶךְ יִשְׂרָאֵל וִיהוֹשָׁפָט מֶלֶךְ יְהוּדָה מָלַךְ יְהוֹרָם בֶּן־יְהוֹשָׁפָט מֶלֶךְ יְהוּדָה׃	(----)
(----)	21:2a וְלוֹ־אַחִים בְּנֵי יְהוֹשָׁפָט עֲזַרְיָה וִיחִיאֵל וּזְכַרְיָהוּ וַעֲזַרְיָהוּ וּמִיכָאֵל וּשְׁפַטְיָהוּ כָּל־אֵלֶּה בְּנֵי יְהוֹשָׁפָט מֶלֶךְ־יִשְׂרָאֵל׃
(----)	3a וַיִּתֵּן לָהֶם אֲבִיהֶם מַתָּנוֹת רַבּוֹת לְכֶסֶף וּלְזָהָב וּלְמִגְדָּנוֹת עִם־עָרֵי מְצֻרוֹת בִּיהוּדָה
(----)	b וְאֶת־הַמַּמְלָכָה נָתַן לִיהוֹרָם
(----)	c כִּי־הוּא הַבְּכוֹר׃
(----)	4a וַיָּקָם יְהוֹרָם עַל־מַמְלֶכֶת אָבִיו
(----)	b וַיִּתְחַזַּק
(----)	c וַיַּהֲרֹג אֶת־כָּל־אֶחָיו בֶּחָרֶב וְגַם מִשָּׂרֵי יִשְׂרָאֵל׃
17a בֶּן־שְׁלֹשִׁים וּשְׁתַּיִם שָׁנָה הָיָה בְמָלְכוֹ	5a בְּמָלְכוֹ יְהוֹרָם בֶּן־שְׁלֹשִׁים וּשְׁתַּיִם שָׁנָה
b וּשְׁמֹנֶה שָׁנִים מָלַךְ בִּירוּשָׁלָ͏ִם׃	b וּשְׁמוֹנֶה שָׁנִים מָלַךְ בִּירוּשָׁלָ͏ִם׃
18a וַיֵּלֶךְ בְּדֶרֶךְ מַלְכֵי יִשְׂרָאֵל	6a וַיֵּלֶךְ בְּדֶרֶךְ מַלְכֵי יִשְׂרָאֵל
b כַּאֲשֶׁר עָשׂוּ בֵּית אַחְאָב	b כַּאֲשֶׁר עָשׂוּ בֵּית אַחְאָב
c כִּי בַּת־אַחְאָב הָיְתָה לּוֹ אִשָּׁה	c כִּי בַּת־אַחְאָב הָיְתָה לּוֹ אִשָּׁה
d וַיַּעַשׂ הָרַע בְּעֵינֵי יְהוָה׃	d וַיַּעַשׂ הָרַע בְּעֵינֵי יְהוָה׃

2 Kings 8:16–24		2 Chronicles 21:2–22:1a	
וְלֹא־אָבָה יְהוָה לְהַשְׁחִית אֶת־יְהוּדָה לְמַעַן דָּוִד עַבְדּוֹ	19a	וְלֹא־אָבָה יְהוָה לְהַשְׁחִית אֶת־בֵּית דָּוִיד לְמַעַן הַבְּרִית	7a
(----)		אֲשֶׁר כָּרַת לְדָוִיד	b
כַּאֲשֶׁר אָמַר־לוֹ לָתֵת לוֹ נִיר לְבָנָיו כָּל־הַיָּמִים:	b	וְכַאֲשֶׁר אָמַר לָתֵת לוֹ נִיר וּלְבָנָיו כָּל־הַיָּמִים:	c
בְּיָמָיו פָּשַׁע אֱדוֹם מִתַּחַת יַד־יְהוּדָה	20a	בְּיָמָיו פָּשַׁע אֱדוֹם מִתַּחַת יַד־יְהוּדָה	8a
וַיַּמְלִכוּ עֲלֵיהֶם מֶלֶךְ:	b	וַיַּמְלִכוּ עֲלֵיהֶם מֶלֶךְ:	b
וַיַּעֲבֹר יוֹרָם צָעִירָה וְכָל־הָרֶכֶב עִמּוֹ	21a	וַיַּעֲבֹר יְהוֹרָם עִם־שָׂרָיו וְכָל־הָרֶכֶב עִמּוֹ	9a
וַיְהִי־הוּא קָם לַיְלָה	b	וַיְהִי קָם לַיְלָה (-)	b
וַיַּכֶּה אֶת־אֱדוֹם הַסֹּבֵיב אֵלָיו וְאֵת שָׂרֵי הָרֶכֶב	c	וַיַּךְ אֶת־אֱדוֹם הַסּוֹבֵיב אֵלָיו וְאֵת שָׂרֵי הָרֶכֶב:	c
וַיָּנָס הָעָם לְאֹהָלָיו:	d	(----)	
וַיִּפְשַׁע אֱדוֹם מִתַּחַת יַד־יְהוּדָה עַד הַיּוֹם הַזֶּה	22a	וַיִּפְשַׁע אֱדוֹם מִתַּחַת יַד־יְהוּדָה עַד הַיּוֹם הַזֶּה	10a
אָז תִּפְשַׁע לִבְנָה בָּעֵת הַהִיא:	b	אָז תִּפְשַׁע לִבְנָה בָּעֵת הַהִיא מִתַּחַת יָדוֹ	b
(----)		כִּי עָזַב אֶת־יְהוָה אֱלֹהֵי אֲבֹתָיו:	c
(----)		גַּם־הוּא עָשָׂה בָמוֹת בְּהָרֵי יְהוּדָה	11a
(----)		וַיֶּזֶן אֶת־יֹשְׁבֵי יְרוּשָׁלִַם	b
(----)		וַיַּדַּח אֶת־יְהוּדָה:	c
(----)		וַיָּבֹא אֵלָיו מִכְתָּב מֵאֵלִיָּהוּ הַנָּבִיא לֵאמֹר	12a
(----)		כֹּה אָמַר יְהוָה אֱלֹהֵי דָּוִיד אָבִיךָ	b
(----)		תַּחַת אֲשֶׁר לֹא־הָלַכְתָּ בְּדַרְכֵי יְהוֹשָׁפָט אָבִיךָ וּבְדַרְכֵי אָסָא מֶלֶךְ־יְהוּדָה:	c
(----)		וַתֵּלֶךְ בְּדֶרֶךְ מַלְכֵי יִשְׂרָאֵל	13a
(----)		וַתַּזְנֶה אֶת־יְהוּדָה וְאֶת־יֹשְׁבֵי יְרוּשָׁלִַם	b
(----)		כְּהַזְנוֹת בֵּית אַחְאָב	c
(----)		וְגַם אֶת־אַחֶיךָ בֵית־אָבִיךָ הַטּוֹבִים מִמְּךָ הָרָגְתָּ:	d
(----)		הִנֵּה יְהוָה נֹגֵף מַגֵּפָה גְדוֹלָה בְּעַמֶּךָ וּבְבָנֶיךָ וּבְנָשֶׁיךָ וּבְכָל־רְכוּשֶׁךָ:	14a
(----)		וְאַתָּה בָּחֳלָיִים רַבִּים בְּמַחֲלֵה מֵעֶיךָ	15a
(----)		עַד־יֵצְאוּ מֵעֶיךָ מִן־הַחֹלִי יָמִים עַל־יָמִים:	b

2 Kings 8:16–24	2 Chronicles 21:2–22:1a
(----)	16a וַיָּעַר יְהוָה עַל־יְהוֹרָם אֵת רוּחַ
(----)	הַפְּלִשְׁתִּים וְהָעַרְבִים אֲשֶׁר עַל־יַד
(----)	כּוּשִׁים:
(----)	17a וַיַּעֲלוּ בִיהוּדָה
(----)	b וַיִּבְקָעוּהָ
(----)	c וַיִּשְׁבּוּ אֵת כָּל־הָרְכוּשׁ הַנִּמְצָא
(----)	לְבֵית־הַמֶּלֶךְ וְגַם־בָּנָיו וְנָשָׁיו
(----)	d וְלֹא נִשְׁאַר־לוֹ בֵּן כִּי אִם־יְהוֹאָחָז
(----)	קְטֹן בָּנָיו:
(----)	18a וְאַחֲרֵי כָּל־זֹאת נְגָפוֹ יְהוָה בְּמֵעָיו
(----)	לָחֳלִי לְאֵין מַרְפֵּא:
(----)	19a וַיְהִי לְיָמִים מִיָּמִים וּכְעֵת צֵאת הַקֵּץ
(----)	לְיָמִים שְׁנַיִם יָצְאוּ מֵעָיו עִם־חָלְיוֹ
(----)	b וַיָּמָת בְּתַחֲלֻאִים רָעִים
23a וְיֶתֶר דִּבְרֵי יוֹרָם וְכָל־אֲשֶׁר עָשָׂה	(----)
הֲלוֹא־הֵם כְּתוּבִים עַל־סֵפֶר דִּבְרֵי	(----)
הַיָּמִים לְמַלְכֵי יְהוּדָה:	(----)
24a וַיִּשְׁכַּב יוֹרָם עִם־אֲבֹתָיו	c וְלֹא־עָשׂוּ לוֹ עַמּוֹ שְׂרֵפָה כִּשְׂרֵפַת
(----)	אֲבֹתָיו: (----)
(----)	20a בֶּן־שְׁלֹשִׁים וּשְׁתַּיִם הָיָה בְמָלְכוֹ
(----)	b וּשְׁמוֹנֶה שָׁנִים מָלַךְ בִּירוּשָׁלָיִם
(----)	c וַיֵּלֶךְ בְּלֹא חֶמְדָּה
b וַיִּקָּבֵר עִם־אֲבֹתָיו בְּעִיר דָּוִד	d וַיִּקְבְּרֻהוּ (----) בְּעִיר דָּוִיד
	וְלֹא בְּקִבְרוֹת הַמְּלָכִים:
c וַיִּמְלֹךְ אֲחַזְיָהוּ בְנוֹ תַּחְתָּיו:	22:1a וַיַּמְלִיכוּ יוֹשְׁבֵי יְרוּשָׁלַיִם אֶת־
	אֲחַזְיָהוּ בְנוֹ הַקָּטֹן תַּחְתָּיו
(----)	b כִּי כָל־הָרִאשֹׁנִים הָרַג הַגְּדוּד הַבָּא
	בָעַרְבִים לַמַּחֲנֶה וַיִּמְלֹךְ
(----)	c אֲחַזְיָהוּ בֶן־יְהוֹרָם מֶלֶךְ יְהוּדָה:

Reading and Rereading Josiah: The Chronicler's Representation of Josiah for the Postexilic Community

KENNETH A. RISTAU

The Pennsylvania State University

The Problem

In historical-, source-, and redaction-critical studies of the Hebrew Bible, Josiah king of Judah often occupies a pivotal place. Any student or scholar of biblical studies will know something of the enormous body of literature that exists on Josiah, as the key figure in theories of the historical development of the Israelite religion and the sources and development of the biblical text.[1] These studies, in large part, have their roots in work on the Deuteronomistic History and, more specifically, in the account of Josiah's reign in 2 Kgs 22–23. This account, particularly the reports of the finding of the book of the law (2 Kgs 22:8–9) and the extensive reforms (2 Kgs 23:1–25) that this find inaugurates, has captured the imagination of many scholars, who have since expanded their studies to look for Josiah in the prophetic writings and in other books of the Hebrew Bible.

Author's note: This essay is a revised excerpt from my M.A. thesis, *Reading and Re-reading Josiah: A Critical Study of Josiah in Chronicles*, written under the direction of Ehud Ben Zvi at the University of Alberta (2005). The thesis is available through ProQuest's Digital Dissertations and Theses and on my website, http://anduril.ca/.

1. See, e.g., the bibliographies in A. Laato, *Josiah and David Redivivus: The Historical Josiah and the Messianic Expectations of Exilic and Postexilic Times* (Coniectanea biblica: Old Testament 33; Stockholm: Almqvist & Wiksell, 1992) 378–403; M. A. Sweeney, *King Josiah of Judah: The Lost Messiah of Israel* (New York: Oxford University Press, 2001) 325–41. For many scholars, the reign of Josiah marks the apex of Israelite/Judean sociopolitical power and a watershed in the history of Yahwism and the biblical text, particularly as it relates to deuteronomic/Deuteronomistic theology and writings, the movement(s) towards centralization and monotheism in the cult, and even the beginnings of messianism.

Despite all of the work on Josiah, however, the story of Josiah in Chronicles has received comparatively little attention.[2] For example, in Sweeney's recent work, *King Josiah of Judah: The Lost Messiah of Israel*,

---

2. The rare exceptions are recent; see E. Ben Zvi, "Observations on Josiah's Account in Chronicles and Implications for Reconstructing the Worldview of the Chronicler," in *Essays on Ancient Israel in Its Near Eastern Context: A Tribute to Nadav Na'aman* (ed. Y. Amit et al.; Winona Lake, IN: Eisenbrauns, 2006) 89–106, an essay written by my graduate adviser, at least partially in response to my M.A. thesis (see author's note above); L. Jonker, *Reflections of King Josiah in Chronicles: Late Stages of the Josiah Reception in 2 Chr 34f.* (ed. C. Hardmeier; Gütersloh: Gütersloher Verlag, 2003), in which Jonker uses Hardmeier's pragmatic-rhetorical approach to analyze the chronological and temporal markers as a guide to understanding the communicative intent of the narrative; and C. Mitchell, "The Ironic Death of Josiah in 2 Chronicles," *CBQ* 68 (2006) 421–35.

The work that otherwise exists on the Chronicler's Josiah is primarily limited to historical-, tradition-, and source-critical inquiries of particular issues. In historical-critical studies, attention has tended to concentrate on evaluating the historicity of the Chronicler's alternative presentation of Josiah's reign and death vis-à-vis Kings, as exemplified by M. Cogan, "The Chronicler's Use of Chronology as Illuminated by Neo-Assyrian Royal Inscriptions," in *Empirical Models for Biblical Criticism* (ed. J. H. Tigay; Philadelphia: University of Pennsylvania Press, 1985) 197–210; and W. B. Barrick, *The King and the Cemeteries: Toward a New Understanding of Josiah's Reform* (VTSup 88; Leiden: Brill, 2002), who provides a comparative analysis of Josiah's reforms that, somewhat uncharacteristically, gives significant attention to the Chronicler's account.

In source-critical analysis, Williamson and Begg have engaged in a spirited exchange on the integrity of the Chronicler's report of Josiah's death, while Talshir has contributed to the discussion with a study of the three strata of the account of Josiah's death in Kings, Chronicles, and 1 Esdras; see C. T. Begg, "The Death of Josah in Chronicles: Another View," *VT* 37 (1987) 1–8; Z. Talshir, "The Three Deaths of Josiah and the Strata of Biblical Historiography (2 Kings xxiii 29–30, 2 Chronicles xxxv 20–25, 1 Esdras i 23–31)," *VT* 46 (1996) 213–36; H. G. M. Williamson, "The Death of Josiah and the Continuing Development of the Deuteronomic History," *VT* 32 (1982) 242–48; idem, "Reliving the Death of Josiah: A Reply to C. T. Begg," *VT* 37 (1987) 9–15. On Josephus's representation of Josiah and use of sources, including Chronicles, see C. T. Begg, "The Death of Josiah: Josephus and the Bible," *Ephemerides theologicae lovanienses* 64 (1988) 157–63. Using a tradition-historical approach rather than source-critical approach to this issue is especially S. Delamarter ("The Death of Josiah in Scripture and Tradition: Wrestling with the Problem of Evil?" *VT* 54 [2004] 29–60), who examines the death of Josiah in the Hebrew and Greek versions of Kings and Chronicles as well as its afterlives in "1 Esdras, Sirach, Josephus, 2 Baruch, the Old Latin, Jerome's Vulgate, the Syriac Peshitta, of 2Kgs, 2Chr and 1Esdr, the Targum to 2Chr, and various Rabbinic texts recorded in the Babylonian Talmud" (p. 29).

In tradition-historical analysis and studies of Israelite religion, the Chronicler's account of Josiah's Passover often figures prominently; see especially the contributions of E. Ben Zvi, "Revisiting 'Boiling in Fire' in 2 Chron. 35.13 and Related Passover Questions: Text, Exegetical Needs, Concerns, and General Implications," in *Biblical Interpretation in Judaism and Christianity* (ed. I. Kalimi and P. J. Haas; Library of Hebrew Bible/Old Testament Studies 439; London: T. & T. Clark, 2006) 238–50; M. A. Fishbane, *Biblical Interpretation in Ancient Israel* (Oxford: Clarendon, 1985) 137–43; L. Rost, "Josias Passa," in *Theologie in Geschichte und Kunst: Walter Elliger zum 65. Geburtstag* (ed. S. Herrmann and O. Söhngen; Witten: Luther Verlag, 1968); J. B. Segal, *The Hebrew Passover from the Earliest Times to*

there is a systematic analysis of the ideological perspectives on Josiah in the Hebrew Bible, and yet the Chronicler's two chapters on the king are almost completely ignored. In fact, Sweeney's work makes reference to 2 Chr 34–35 only in the context of the discussion on the Deuteronomistic History and then only briefly.[3] This tendency is typical of the work on Josiah by biblical scholars.[4] It seems likely that this results from a perception that the narrative in Chronicles is late and is a tendentious revision of the narrative in Kings that downplays Josiah.[5] Seen as derivative, the Josiah narrative in Chronicles is dismissed as unimportant and not very insightful. Although perhaps understandable, this is a mistake.

The Chronicler's representation of Josiah, while perhaps having limited value in reconstructing historical events (though even this is arguable), provides a window into the didactic and kerygmatic significance of his reign among Judeans of the fourth or third centuries B.C.E.[6] Reading and rereading the story of Josiah in Chronicles reveals a layered and sophisticated representation that reflects specific concerns and ideologies of a postexilic society.[7] In the interests of limiting

---

A.D. 70 (London: Oxford University Press, 1963); J. R. Shaver, *Torah and the Chronicler's History Work: An Inquiry into the Chronicler's References to Laws, Festivals and Cultic Institutions in Relation to Pentateuchal Legislation* (BJS 196; Atlanta: Scholars Press, 1989) 104–17.

3. Sweeney, *King Josiah*, 3–5.

4. See Laato (*Josiah and David Redivivus*, 329–30), for example, who hardly does much better than Sweeney, assigning a mere page to the "depiction of Josiah in Chr."

5. See Laato, for example (ibid.), who argues, "The Chronicler probably wanted to avoid an ideology (and eventual vicarious interpretation of Josiah's death) which used Josiah as a model because this would have conflicted with his views of retribution and messianic expectation; the righteous king must succeed."

6. By *Chronicler*, I mean the implied author of the book of Chronicles, excluding the book(s) of Ezra–Nehemiah, and as primarily reflected in the Masoretic text tradition. My analysis assumes that the Chronicler is responsible for the structure and presentation of the entire narrative, not only for deviations from the probable Vorlage of Samuel–Kings and any other sources, but also for the narrative that is copied/retained. In this essay, I also employ the term *Chronistic* to refer to a quality or characteristic of this author. See G. N. Knoppers, *I Chronicles 1–9: A New Translation with Introduction and Commentary* (AB 12; New York: Doubleday, 2004) 73–89; W. Riley, *King and Cultus in Chronicles: Worship and the Reinterpretation of History* (JSOTSup 160; Sheffield: Sheffield Academic Press, 1993) 17–20, for helpful overviews of the debate about the unity and disunity of Chronicles and Ezra–Nehemiah.

7. By using the term *rereading*, I am calling attention to the documented tendency among Judean scribes and priests to write, read, rewrite, and reread texts and so interpret and reinterpret the significance of these texts for particular communities. On this issue, see, e.g., E. Ben Zvi, *History, Literature and Theology in the Book of Chronicles* (London: Equinox, 2007);

the scope of the present analysis, I will focus primarily on the Chronicler's representation of Josiah's death and illustrate how the narrative conditions the community, or communities, of the text toward new sociopolitical and religious realities consistent with their loss of independence, experience(s) of exile and restoration, and the emergence of Persian governance.

The Restorer of Order

The positive evaluation of Josiah in 2 Chr 34:2 and 35:26–27 aligns Josiah with the good kings of the Davidic monarchy: David, Solomon, Abijah, Asa, Jehoshaphat, Uzziah, and Hezekiah.[8] In contrast to these other good kings in Chronicles, however, Josiah is not primarily a builder or a warrior. Instead, Josiah belongs to an ancient Near Eastern character type that Liverani identifies as "the restorer of order" or, more appropriately for the Chronicler, "the consummator of order."[9]

In his work, Liverani isolates several common ideological motifs and character types that permeate historiographical texts.[10] Paramount to understanding some of these motifs is "the characterization of time as cyclic," in which events are perceived as positive or negative and in which "all positive events" are temporally located in one period and "all negative events" are temporally located in another period.[11] From this characterization of time, a pattern emerges in numerous historiographical texts in which time moves in a cycle from good to bad to good. Making reference to "the reforms of Urukagina, the edict of Telipinu, . . . [and the edict] of Horemhab" as examples, Liverani situates the restorer of order at a specific point in this cycle:

> The happy past is pushed back into a more remote past, a veritable mythical age, and its function of ideal model of a corrected situation is underscored. The phase of corruption and chaos is over, i.e. moved from the present to a nearby past, just finished; while the second stage of

---

idem, *Micah* (FOTL 21B; Grand Rapids: Eerdmans, 2000); idem, *Signs of Jonah: Reading and Rereading in Ancient Yehud* (JSOTSup 367; London: Sheffield Academic Press, 2003).

8. There is no formal theological evaluation of Abijah, but the account of his reign is uniformly positive, and therefore I have included him in this list. There is also a subset of good kings who receive a more tempered theological evaluation by the Chronicler—that is, Joash (see 2 Chr 24:2) and Amaziah (see 2 Chr 25:2).

9. M. Liverani, "Memorandum on the Approach to Historiographic Texts," *Or* 42 (1973) 186. Liverani does not specifically identify Josiah as a character of this type but, as I will argue, this pattern does apply.

10. Ibid., 178–94.

11. Ibid., 187.

order and prosperity is moved ahead from the future to the present . . .
[or] the immediate future.[12]

The restorer of order is the subject or catalyst that promises the order
of an immediate future and goes on to inaugurate this order.

In large part, this is the situation in the Josiah narrative. The reign of
Amon (2 Chr 33:21–24) with its "corruption and chaos is over," and a
new king is made ruler by the people of the land (33:25). The intervention of the people of the land immediately suggests a reversal—a new
beginning rather than a succession—and thus signals the soon-to-be-
present "second stage of order and prosperity," a return to the model
past of Moses, David, and Solomon. Indeed, the opening regnal ré-
sumé (34:1–2) confirms the beginning of a good cycle. The program for
reform is inaugurated when Josiah begins to seek the god of his father
David in the eighth year (34:3) and continues with the many narrated
events that proceed from this. Especially in the Passover narrative, the
Chronicler repeatedly invokes the cultic authority of Moses, David,
and Solomon, which emphasizes this pattern of return and restoration.

Liverani's analysis, however, does not entirely explain the situation
in Chronicles or the character of Josiah.[13] In Chronicles, time is generally not cyclical; it is rhythmic.[14] Moreover, order exists independently
of any king, as a sort of "eternal Torah" to which the righteous are always subject and which the righteous strive to see fully realized.[15] The

---

12. Ibid., 187–88.

13. Of course, to be fair, this is not his intent.

14. I lean toward the recent work of S. Stern, *Time and Process in Ancient Judaism* (Oxford: Littman Library of Jewish Civilization, 2003), who argues that time in the Hebrew
Bible and ancient Judaism is process-related. Calendars and chronology do not measure
a transcendent time dimension, as in the classical world but, rather, coordinate processes. Thus, it is the predictable rhythm of these processes that serves to measure and
coordinate definite points in time. Moreover, these processes are inherently teleological
because the world is governed by an active god, who purposes events. Cf. E. Ben Zvi,
"About Time: Observations about the Construction of Time in the Book of Chronicles,"
Horizons in Biblical Theology 22 (2000) 17–31; M. Z. Brettler, "Cyclical and Teleological
Time in the Hebrew Bible," in *Time and Temporality in the Ancient World* (ed. R. M. Rosen;
Philadelphia: University of Pennsylvania Museum of Archaeology and Anthropology,
2004) 111–28; A. Momigliano, "Time in Ancient Historiography," in *Essays in Ancient and
Modern Historiography* (Middletown, CT: Wesleyan University Press, 1977) 179–204.

15. The concept of "eternal Torah" is a later, postbiblical development, but the trajec-
tory toward a concept of this sort can already be seen in the Chronicler's views of Torah
and the nature of the relationship between Yahweh and Israel. The Chronicler's view of
Torah is transcendent and immanent: transcendent insofar as it is rooted in Yahweh's
transcendence, and immanent insofar as it has been revealed to Israel in time and, since
that time, is always present in the life of Israel. This transcendence and immanence in-
spires the inchoate sense of "eternal Torah" in Chronicles.

Urzeit, therefore, is never completely idealized; instead, it is instrumentalized for use by subsequent generations.[16] Additionally, Josiah is not simply a restorer of order who attempts to see the Torah fully realized through the purge, the repairs, the covenant, and the Passover. His programme, aided by the finding of the book of the law, is presented by the Chronicler as another step toward a future realization of order that builds on and constantly transforms, rather than simply restores, the successes of the *Urzeit*—a process that the Chronicler invites readers to join, by way of Cyrus's edict in 2 Chr 36:22–23.

The End

The narrative of Josiah's death is found in 2 Chr 35:20–25/27. Significantly, the Chronicler's account of Josiah's reign prepares for this narrative in several ways. Even as the Chronicler foregrounds the restoration of the cult in 2 Chr 34:1–35:19, several motifs or subtexts emerge that contextualize and give deeper meaning to Josiah's death and augur the Judean exile within the world of the narrative.[17] The Chronicler's storytelling abilities are perhaps at their most rich and poignant as the dual ends of the Josiah narrative—that is, the restoration and transformation of the cult and Josiah's death—are negotiated with potent irony.

The Pall

A noticeable pall hangs over the Chronicler's account of Josiah's reign that strikes a dramatically different tone for the narrative than the tone that characterizes the narratives of the other good kings in Chronicles. This pall creates a sense of apprehension even amid the king's positive contributions to the religious life of Judah. The pall is palatable through the absence of the joy and blessing paradigms, the

---

16. On idealized vis-à-vis instrumentalized, see Jonker, *Reflections*, 33.

17. I am using the term *subtexts* here as defined by M. Riffaterre (*Fictional Truth* [Baltimore: Johns Hopkins University Press, 1990] xvii–xviii), who writes, "Symbolism raises the problem of the gap between the metalinguistic structure of its referentiality, the sequential telling of the story, and the hierarchy of esthetic values that make the novel into an artifact. What accounts for the bridging of the gap, it seems to me, is the presence of subtexts, texts within the text that are neither subplots nor themes but diegetic pieces whose sole function is to be vehicles of symbolism. They offer a rereading of the plot that points to its significance in a discourse closer to poetry than narrative . . . there is an unconscious of the text that works like the human unconscious. This unconscious of the text is represented by the symbolism of the subtext and by the intertext this symbolism mobilizes. Readers accede to it not by plumbing the innermost recesses of the psyche, but by following the clues of the text itself."

specter of exile, the finding of the book of the law, the encounter with Huldah, and the despondency of the king.

Of the chief characteristics of Chronicles, two that are central to the entire narrative are (1) joy in worship, celebration, and volitional giving and (2) Yahweh's blessings in response to the faithfulness of king and people. Over and again, the Chronicler calls attention to the joy of the people in worship, celebration, and volitional giving (1 Chr 12:41; 15:16, 25; 16:10, 31; 29:9, 17, 22; 2 Chr 6:41; 7:10; 15:15; 20:27; 23:13, 18, 21; 24:10; 29:30, 36; 30:21, 23, 25–26). Joy is present in the reigns of the majority of good kings and characterizes the people in nearly every major Yahwistic reform or festival. Similarly, the Chronicler makes repeated references to Yahweh's blessings upon either king or people commensurate with their faithfulness. These blessings may include produce, peace, victory over enemies, fertility, and restoration after exile. But, these are all strikingly absent from the Josiah narrative, even though the story evidently concerns one of Israel's greatest kings and consists of some of the most thorough and comprehensive reforms and the greatest ceremonies and festivals in the entire history of the monarchy. As Halpern writes,

> Simply, from David to Hezekiah, Chronicles regards and bestows abundance as a mark of divine favor . . . the motifs of nearness to god, of salvation, and of expansion, growth, and accumulation all merge into a single complex, characterized by the rest motif. . . . From Manasseh onward, the whole rest/prosperity/salvation complex disappears.[18]

Instead, it is the specter of exile and, in the Josiah narrative, the despondency of the king that hold the reader's attention.

Already in the account of the temple repairs, the Chronicler employs language that prefigures the exile. The phrases 'the rest of Israel' (שארית ישראל in 34:9) and 'the buildings that the kings of Judah destroyed' (הבתים אשר השחיתו מלכי יהודה in 34:11) reflect language that is a part of the discourse of exile.[19] Notably, the Chronicler attributes the

---

18. B. Halpern, "Sacred History and Ideology: Chronicles' Thematic Structure-Indications of an Earlier Source," in *The Creation of Sacred Literature: Composition and Redaction of the Biblical Text* (ed. R. E. Friedman; Berkeley: University of California Press, 1981) 40–41.

19. On the construction of Israel in Chronicles, see esp. R. Mosis, *Untersuchungen zur Theologie des chronistischen Geschichtswerkes* (Freiburg theologische Studien 92; Freiburg: Herder, 1973); H. G. M. Williamson, *Israel in the Books of Chronicles* (New York: Cambridge University Press, 1977); E. Ben Zvi, "Inclusion in and Exclusion from Israel as Conveyed by the Use of the Term 'Israel' in Postmonarchic Biblical Texts," in *The Pitcher Is Broken: Memorial Essays for Gösta W. Ahlström* (ed. S. W. Holloway and L. K. Handy; JSOTSup 190; Sheffield: JSOT Press, 1995) 95–149.

destruction of the temple buildings to "the kings of Judah," a totality
that potentially indicts Josiah along with the king's predecessors and,
in this way, creates a subtext that, while operating on one level to
present Josiah as a new temple builder like Solomon, also undercuts
and denies Josiah, and every Judean king, unvarnished recognition. [20]
The kings of Judah are destroyers even as they are builders and, even
as kingdoms unite and build up, the specter of exile threatens to dis-
perse and destroy them.

Similarly, the finding of the book of the law in 2 Chr 34:14–15 serves
the main narrative thread leading to the consummation of the cult,
while also concretizing justification for an exile.[21] One the one hand,
the book of the law is a symbol that foregrounds the discourse of covenant, precipitates the covenant-renewal ceremony, and informs the
exemplary performance of the Passover. Its important role is made
apparent by the references to the book in 34:30–31 and 35:12 and the
words of the book in 35:6. At the same time, it exposes the failure of
king and people to keep covenant, reflected by Josiah's contrition and
commission to seek out Yahweh in 34:19–21, and serves as the theological basis for an imminent cataclysm prophesied by Huldah in 34:22–28
(especially v. 24).

In Josiah's commission to seek out Yahweh (34:21), which follows on
the finding of the book, the specter of exile is invoked again. Josiah orders a group of officials to 'go and seek Yahweh on my behalf and on
behalf of those who remain in Israel and in Judahs (לכו דרשו את־יהוה
בעדי ובעד הנשאר בישראל וביהודה). The phrase 'those who remain in Israel and in Judah' (הנשאר בישראל וביהודה) echoes the earlier reference
to 'the rest of Israel' (שארית ישראל). The verbal root 'to remain' (שאר)
within the context of Chronicles, like its nominal שארית, is an ideologically nuanced word that conveys exilic connotations of a remnant.
Further, the Chronicler now explicitly draws Judah into the exilic dis-

---

20. In a simple, sequential, first reading, the phrase seems to refer to Josiah's predecessors but even so might indict Josiah up to his eighteenth year, when he finally takes
action. More importantly, however, the perspective of the implied author, who stands
outside time (or at least well after the events) of the entire history, and also the perspective of the reading community potentially broaden the application of this phrase to an
indictment of the entire monarchy.

21. By using the term *consummation* here and elsewhere, I do not mean to imply the
ultimate completion of the cult for all time but only its completion/perfection in the monarchic period, which serves as an ideal model for the inheritors of these traditions. The
Chronicler would, in my opinion, conceive of the cult in terms that required constant developments and transformation in light of contemporary events but also consistent with
past traditions.

course, so that Josiah seems to situate himself and the people in the exilic age; and, rather than seeking out Yahweh to prevent an exile, Josiah seeks Yahweh to abate that which has already started.

Huldah's prophecy in 2 Chr 34:22–28 actualizes the specter of exile prefigured in the account of the temple repairs and Josiah's speech. Prophecies of the post-Solomonic era in Chronicles conform to one of two generic types: they pronounce a judgment (2 Chr 12:5; 16:7–10; 18:16; 19:2–3; 20:13–17; 20:37; 21:12–15; 25:15–16) or provide Yahweh's perspective on an action contemplated or in process (2 Chr 11:3–4; 15:1–7; 18:19–22; 24:19–22; 25:7–9; 28:9–11). In relation to the book of the law, Huldah's prophecy confirms the message of the book; it pronounces a judgment.[22] The exile is transformed from specter to imminent judgment.

Huldah's prophecy also directly concerns Josiah's death. Through Huldah's voice, Yahweh says of Josiah, "Behold, I am gathering you to your fathers, and you will be gathered to your graves in peace [בשלום], and your eyes will not look on all the evil that I am bringing upon this place and upon its inhabitants" (34:28). The promise to Josiah is undeniably bittersweet, for the promise extends only to him and reiterates the judgment pronounced upon "this place" (that is, the temple or Jerusalem) and the people.

The last element of the narrative to contribute to the pall is the despondency of the king. Huldah's prophecy amplifies this element, which begins with the king's desperate response to the words of the book. In response to its words, the king tears his clothes (34:19). In Huldah's prophecy, Yahweh acknowledges that Josiah has not only torn his clothes but also wept before him (34:27). Both of these emotional outbursts are unique to Josiah in Chronicles; no other king displays such expressive repentance.[23] The outbursts are the antithesis of the Chronicler's tendency to accentuate positive, celebratory emotions in the reigns of good kings; that is, not only is the joy paradigm absent in the Josiah narrative, but it is replaced by a grief paradigm. Josiah is the king of tears, a portrayal that serves as a source of irony in the account of his death and eulogy.

---

22. The message is negative insofar as its threatens exile. However, insofar as it reveals the will of Yahweh and brings an awareness of sin, it is a positive message.

23. Athaliah tears her clothes in 23:13 but in an entirely different context and on entirely selfish grounds. It is also interesting to note that, in parallel accounts to Chronicles, Kings and Isaiah report that Hezekiah tore his clothes in response to Rabshakeh's taunts and wept when he became ill to the point of death (2 Kgs 19:1 // Isa 37:1 // 2 Chr 32:20; 2 Kgs 20 // Isa 38 // 2 Chr 32:24–26). Neither detail is, however, carried forward in this language by the Chronicler.

The Death of Josiah

The account of Josiah's death (2 Chr 35:20–23) is a particularly reso-
nant narrative with many intertextual allusions to his reign and the
rest of Chronicles. The overwhelming effect of this resonance is a
deeply ironic portrayal of Josiah's last days. The account announces the
consummation of the cult in the monarchic period but also augurs the
end of the Davidic monarchy in Judah and Israel. In this respect, the
narrative has unique importance within the world of Chronicles.

The initial after-clause of the death narrative, 'after all of this'
(אחרי כל־זאת), is a significant literary and ideological construction. The
after-clause is a relative temporal transition that, at the same time that
it produces discontinuity to introduce a new narrative also establishes
temporal or topical continuity between what precedes the narrative
and what proceeds from it. Readers are encouraged to read the text in
light of previous events and also regard subsequent events as successive or near-successive. Quite often, there is also an implied causality.

This construction appears 11 other times in Chronicles with primarily stylistic variations.[24] In 7 of the 11 occurrences, the device introduces a war report. In the Davidic narratives (1 Chr 18:1; 19:1; 20:4), the
repetition of the after-clause creates a sense of perpetual conflict and
expansion. On the one hand, this supports the characterization of David as a man of war (1 Chr 22:8) and, on the other, it dramatically actualizes Yahweh's covenant promise to David to subdue all his enemies
(1 Chr 17:10). By contrast, in the 4 cases in which it initiates a war report in the post-Solomonic era (2 Chr 20:1; 20:35; 32:1; 32:9), the after-
clause creates tension between the generally faithful acts of the king
that precede it and the threat against Israel posed by the onset of war.

The onset of war after a period of faithfulness appears, at least at
first, to be inconsistent with the Chronicler's tendency to ascribe immediate rewards for faithfulness; faithfulness should beget peace in
the world of Chronicles.[25] Japhet explains this inconsistency with re-

24. The occurrences and variations are: 'and it happened afterward' ויהי אחרי כן in
1 Chr 18:1; 19:1; 20:4; ויהי אחריכן in 2 Chr 20:1; 24:4), 'and afterward' ואחריכן in 2 Chr
20:35; ואחרי כן in 2 Chr 33:14), 'and it happened after' ויהי אחרי in 2 Chr 25:14), 'after these
deeds and faithfulness' אחרי הדברים והאמת האלה in 2 Chr 32:1), 'after this' אחר זה in 2 Chr
32:9), and 'and after' ואחר in 2 Chr 35:14).

25. The theme of immediate reward and punishment (or "immediate retribution") is
an undeniable component of the Chronicler's narrative; see, e.g., R. B. Dillard, "The Reign
of Asa (2 Chronicles 14–16): An Example of the Chronicler's Theological Method," *JETS*
23 (1980) 207–18; idem, "Reward and Punishment in Chronicles: The Theology of Immediate Retribution," *WTJ* 46 (1984) 164–72; S. Japhet, *The Ideology of the Book of Chronicles
and Its Place in Biblical Thought* (2nd ed.; Beiträge zur Erforschung des Alten Testaments

course to the idea of test; the invasion of Judah by foreign enemies after a period of peace is meant to challenge the professions of loyalty and commitment made by king and people in the previous narrative.[26] While this has some currency, it seems to me that Japhet's argument falters insofar as foreign invasions are never ascribed to Yahweh unless they are punishments (for example, 2 Chr 12:1–12), and the language of test is not explicitly used in any of these cases. Certainly, it might be tempting to infer that the Chronicler's theodicy naturally demands that it is Yahweh who directs events, but the absence of the language of test is a tougher dilemma to overcome. The language of test appears only twice in Chronicles: in the account of the queen of Sheba's visit to King Solomon to test him with difficult questions (2 Chr 9:1), and in the story of the Babylonian embassy's visit to Hezekiah, in which Yahweh is said to have left Hezekiah alone in order to test him (2 Chr 32:31). The absence of the language of test in the war reports suggests something else is likely at play in these narratives. If, in the case of the Davidic narratives, the after-clause points to Yahweh's covenant promise to David, perhaps there is a more explicit explanation for these conflicts in the text itself.

The first war report in the post-Solomonic era is the most natural place to find such an explanation as it sets the precedent for the subsequent narratives. This war report occurs in Rehoboam's reign and depicts Shishak's invasion (2 Chr 12:1–12). Although this war report shares the same *topos* of invasion by a foreign army, it is explicitly ascribed to the unfaithfulness of king and people; it is a punishment. When king and people are confronted by Yahweh's prophet, they humble themselves in the face of the threat and consequently Yahweh gives them some deliverance. Yahweh makes a pledge to king and people through the prophet: "They have humbled themselves. I will not destroy them. I will give to them a little reprieve and my wrath will not pour out against Jerusalem by the hand of Shishak. Instead they will be his servants and they will know my service and the service of the kingdoms of the lands" (2 Chr 12:7–8; cf. 2 Chr 9:26). This promise fundamentally alters the political dynamic in the post-Solomonic era

---

und des antiken Judentum 9; New York: Peter Lang, 1997) 150–98; S. L. McKenzie, *1–2 Chronicles* (Abingdon Old Testament Commentaries; Nashville: Abingdon, 2004) passim. The theme, however, is generally overstressed by its proponents. The Chronicler also advances the idea of transgenerational sin and even inexplicable events; see E. Ben Zvi, "A Sense of Proportion: An Aspect of the Theology of the Chronicler," *SJOT* 9 (1995) 37–51.

26. Japhet, *Ideology*, 191–98.

by conceding the historical reality of Judah's vassalage. Moreover, it seems almost certain by the plural 'kingdoms of the lands' (ממלכות הארצות) that the Chronicler presents the inauguration of a long-term political situation by which numerous foreign kings will rule the people. The passage also implies that this development is intended, not simply to make known to the people the service of Yahweh and the service of foreign kings, but the difference between them.

If the invasions by foreign kings in Chronicles are understood in light of this admission of Judah's vassal status, then, the invasions are not so much a test of king and people but an intended contrast of the preceding service of Yahweh, which yields success and blessings, with the proceeding service of the kingdoms of the lands, which threaten, pillage, destroy, and take away. Indeed, three of the remaining four occurrences of the after-clause (2 Chr 24:4; 25:14; 33:14), which do not initiate a war report, also convey similar contrasts between the consequences of fidelity and infidelity. As such, the after-clause in the account of Josiah's death immediately sets an ominous tone for the narrative. The Chronicler has conditioned readers to expect the possibility of an event in contrast to the preceding, positive events that will likely take the form of an invasion by a foreign king and is intended to demonstrate the difference between the service of Yahweh and the service of foreign kingdoms.

There is yet more significance to the after-clause, bound up in the intended referent 'all of this' (כל זאת). In the subordinate clause in apposition to the after-clause, the Chronicler clarifies that "all of this" refers to 'when Josiah had prepared the temple' (אשר הכין יאשיהו את הבית). This is a somewhat ambiguous referent. The Chronicler commonly identifies temple service as preparations for the temple itself. Therefore, by employing the key word 'to prepare' (כון) from the Passover narrative and placing this referent in literary proximity to that narrative, the Chronicler appears to refer to the Passover. The Chronicler may, however, be referring to the temple, rather than just the Passover, in order to encase in the referent all the events in Josiah's eighteenth year that began with the temple repairs. Additionally, there is finality to the preparations of the temple implied in the Passover evaluation and, indeed, the whole account of Josiah's reign; Josiah variously embodies the characters and authority of Moses, David, Solomon, and Hezekiah. Idolatry is purged (2 Chr 34:3–7), the temple is (re)built (2 Chr 34:8–13), the book of the law is present in the community (2 Chr 34:14–18), king and people are bound (again) in a covenant to Yahweh (2 Chr 34:29–33), and the whole service of (the house of) Yahweh is prepared for the greatest Passover in the entire history of the Davidic Dynasty (2 Chr 35:1–19). As such, amplified by 'all' (כֹּל), "all of this" might even envelop the entire cultic history as epitomized in Josiah's extensive preparations of the temple. In such a reading, this is the ultimate turning point in Chronicles. It signals a radical change in the purpose of the narrative, marking the final development of the cult in the monarchic period and, consequently, the terminus ad quem of Yahweh's promise, given through David to Solomon, never to fail or forsake the king until "all the work of the service of the temple of Yahweh" was complete (1 Chr 28:20).[27] This, in turn, strikes another ominous note for the narrative that proceeds from the after-clause. The Chronicler transitions from positive to threatening events and, while announcing the consummation of the cult in the monarchic period, creates uncertainty about the future role of the Davidic monarchy because the goal of Yahweh's benevolence and protection has been accomplished.

Finally, this after-clause also and perhaps most immediately invokes the parallel formula in the Hezekiah narrative in 2 Chr 32:1 and 32:9. There is an affinity developed and clearly intended between Josiah and Hezekiah in Chronicles. Both kings oversee or engage in similar activities, temple repairs, purges, reforms, and festivals, and both kings stand out among the post-Solomonic kings as most clearly conforming to the Davidic and Solomonic types. Indeed, only these two kings are compared directly with David (2 Chr 29:2; 34:2), and many typological connections are made that variously associate them with David or Solomon (and also Moses).[28] By invoking the Hezekiah narrative, in which Sennacherib invades Judah, the Chronicler invites

---

27. Although the promise is given through David to Solomon particularly, its ultimate fulfilment only occurs in the reign of Josiah, when the Chronicler asserts for the first time that "all the service of Yahweh was prepared" (2 Chr 35:16) and then transitions with the important passage under examination, "after all of this, when Josiah had prepared the temple" (2 Chr 35:20). Notably, 1 Chr 28 is the public proclamation of a private speech given in 1 Chr 22 and therefore lends weight to a programmatic reading of the promise, where Solomon embodies all David's heirs. For a fuller defense of this interpretation and exemplary treatment of the relationship between king and cult in Chronicles, see Riley, *King and Cultus*.

28. See S. J. De Vries, "Moses and David as Cult Founders in Chronicles," *JBL* 107 (1988) 619–39; S. Japhet, *I and II Chronicles: A Commentary* (OTL; Louisville: Westminster/John Knox, 1993) passim; Jonker, *Reflections*, 48–60; M. A. Throntveit, "The Relationship of Hezekiah to David and Solomon in the Books of Chronicles," in *The Chronicler as Theologian: Essays in Honor of Ralph W. Klein* (ed. M. P. Graham et al.; JSOTSup 371; London: T. & T. Clark, 2003) 105–21.

readers to compare these stories and also introduces, into the ominous tone, the hope that Josiah, as Hezekiah before him, will respond faithfully and receive some measure of deliverance from whatever is to come.

From the multilayered opening of the after-clause, the Chronicler proceeds to set the scene. The story unfolds that Necho, the king of Egypt, went up to fight at Carchemish on the Euphrates, and Josiah went out to oppose him (35:20). While the setup seems at a cursory glance quite simple, it is actually somewhat unusual. It is Josiah who initiates this conflict with a foreign monarch. In contrast to the war report in Hezekiah's reign, the foreign monarch is not attacking Judah. Necho confirms this through his messengers: "What have I to do with you, king of Judah? I am not going up against you today, but against a kingdom at war with me; and God commands my hastening. Cease opposing God, who is with me, so that he will not destroy you" (35:21). Necho's message to Josiah, however, not only confirms that Josiah is belligerent; it is also ad hoc prophetic speech that warns Josiah of his destruction, by authority rooted in divine revelation. The contrast with Sennacherib's proud posturing and blasphemy is striking (32:9–19); even so, it is not altogether unusual in the world of Chronicles that a foreign monarch should employ the language of the Israelite cult. In fact, as Ben Zvi argues, the Chronicler exhibits a clear tendency to "Israelize" the speeches of most foreign monarchs—most notably the king of Tyre, the queen of Sheba, and Cyrus—and so, in some sense, he appropriates Necho as well.[29]

In the case of the king of Tyre and the queen of Sheba, the "Israelization" of their speeches serves to give added weight to their subjective views concerning Solomon and also to emphasize Solomon's preeminence. The relationship implied in these speeches clearly elevates Solomon and subordinates the foreign monarch, who not only recognizes and pays tribute to Solomon but, in some sense, is blended into Israel. In the case of Necho and Cyrus, however, the "Israelization" serves a different purpose. These monarchs, quite remarkably, invoke the deity to authenticate and legitimate their actions and consequently their right to authority over Judah. As such, Necho's claim that God is with him is incredible and, at least to an extent, undermines Josiah's authority as ruler over Judah. This claim actualizes that which the nar-

---

29. E. Ben Zvi, "When the Foreign Monarch Speaks," in *The Chronicler as Author: Studies in Text and Texture* (ed. M. P. Graham and S. L. McKenzie; JSOTSup 263; Sheffield: Sheffield Academic Press, 1999) 209–28.

rative world has already hinted at through the absence of Yahweh's blessings and the absence of any statement that God was with Josiah.[30] In addition, the provocative implications of the introduction, set up by the after-clause, now openly confront Josiah (and readers) in Necho's message; because Josiah has prepared the temple, Yahweh's promise to remain with the Davidic king is fulfilled, and Yahweh can justly transfer authority over Judah to another house.

Necho's message, therefore, heralds a radical political realignment that occurs only two other times in the text: at Saul's death (1 Chr 10) and at the division of the kingdom (2 Chr 10). In these cases, the Chronicler depicts schisms between past and present political realities and attributes these schisms to God's judgment. In the division of the kingdom, God brings about the separation of the northern tribes and denies Rehoboam the right to reconstitute a unified Israel (2 Chr 10:15; 11:1–4).[31] At Saul's death, God transfers the kingdom from Saul's House to David's House. This transfer of the kingdom is especially relevant to the present text and gives particular poignancy and irony to Necho's claim. According to the Chronicler, Saul dies and the kingdom transfers to David because Saul fails to fulfill Yahweh's command or seek his advice (2 Chr 10:13–14). Now, Josiah, who fulfills Yahweh's command to prepare the temple and who seeks his advice through the prophet Huldah, faces a similar fate: death and the transferal of the kingdom to a foreign monarch. Of course, Necho's foreignness (and thus the apparent incredulity of the message) invites the reader, at

---

30. This is admittedly somewhat contentious in that Josiah's reforms, the temple repairs, the finding of the book, Huldah's prophecy, the covenant-renewal ceremony, and the Passover can and even should be regarded as signs of blessing apart from any explicit statement of divine approval; contra Halpern, "Sacred History," 35–56; Mitchell, "Ironic Death"; J. W. Wright, "Beyond Transcendence and Immanence: The Characterization of the Presence and Activity of God in the Book of Chronicles" in *The Chronicler as Theologian: Essays in Honor of Ralph W. Klein* (ed. M. P. Graham et al.; JSOTSup 371; London: T. & T. Clark, 2003). Nevertheless, the absence of an explicit statement of blessing and approval so common in the reports of David and Solomon and the post-Solomonic kings up to Hezekiah must have some significance, and it seems to me that this is best understood in terms of the transferal of the kingdom from the Davidic monarchy to foreign kings.

31. However, observe the important nuances highlighted by G. Knoppers, "Rehoboam in Chronicles: Villain or Victim?" *JBL* 109 (1990) 423–40; idem, " 'Battling against Yahweh': Israel's War against Judah in 2 Chr 13:2–20," *RB* 100 (1993) 511–32; and also, M. Boda, pp. 249–272 in the present volume; as well as the slightly different interpretation offered by E. Ben Zvi, "The Secession of the Northern Kingdom in Chronicles: Accepted 'Facts' and New Meanings," in *The Chronicler as Theologian: Essays in Honor of Ralph W. Klein* (ed. M. P. Graham, S. L. McKenzie, and G. N. Knoppers; JSOTSup 371; London: T. & T. Clark, 2003) 61–88.

least temporarily, to regard the message as untrustworthy—perhaps this god that Necho invokes is not Israel's god—and consequently this maintains the suspense of the narrative. Notably, however, the Chronicler gives no explicit indication that this foreignness motivates Josiah's subsequent decision to reject Necho's warning.

Rather, at this point in the narrative, the Chronicler takes an even more peculiar and unexpected turn; the Chronicler reports in 35:22 that Josiah 'disguised himself' (התחפש). The Chronicler apparently employs the disguise topos to further the ironic comparison between Saul and Josiah and introduce parallels between Ahab and Josiah.[32] The Chronicler notes in 1 Chr 10:13, among the grievances against Saul that justify the transferal of the kingdom to David, that Saul consulted a medium. In turn, this note refers to the story in 1 Sam 28:4–25 in which Saul 'disguises himself' (יתחפש) in order to consult a medium by stealth about a battle with the Philistines. In relation to Ahab, the disguise topos occurs twice. It is present in 1 Kgs 20:35–43, in which a prophet 'disguises himself' (יתחפש) in order to conceal his identity from Ahab, the king of northern Israel, and to elicit from Ahab a judgment that ironically serves to indict Ahab himself and consequently to justify a prophecy that Ahab will die in accordance with Yahweh's judgment. Most immediately, however, the disguise topos invokes 2 Chr 18, in which Micaiah, a prophet of Yahweh, prophesies that Ahab will not return from a battle against Ramoth-gilead (18:14–27). Ahab, nevertheless, 'disguises himself' (יתחפש) and goes into battle anyway (18:28–29). Notably, the parallel story in 1 Kgs 22 operates with 1 Kgs 20 to bring about Yahweh's judgment against Ahab with heightened irony.

In each relevant intertext, the story of disguise is told "at the expense of the king . . . [and] it is an unacceptable line of kingship which is condemned."[33] This stands in contrast to the topos as it is presented in other ancient Near Eastern texts. In those texts, the topos of disguise typically allows the king to escape their divinely ordained fate.[34] The

---

32. On these parallels and others, see also Mitchell, "Ironic Death," passim.

33. R. Coggins, "On Kings and Disguises," *JSOT* 50 (1991) 60. Coggins cites another possible intertext as being 1 Kgs 14, in which Jeroboam, the first king of (northern) Israel, has his wife 'change' (השתנית) herself to consult Ahijah the prophet about his son's illness. Yahweh, however, informs Ahijah of the ruse, who then prophesies the end of Jeroboam's Dynasty and the exile of northern Israel. While the verb is different, the topos is indeed the same and leads to a similar judgment against an unfaithful king.

34. For more on this topos in the ancient Near East, see J. Bottéro, "The Substitute King and His Fate," in *Mesopotamia: Writing, Reasoning, and the Gods* (Chicago: University of Chicago Press, 1992) 138–55; P. M. Goedegebuure, "KBo 17.17+: Remarks on an Old

biblical inversion of the topos ultimately serves to illustrate, at least in most of these cases, that attempts to avoid divinely ordained fate are ineffective because "nothing is hidden from God's sight."[35] With these intertexts in mind, the Chronicler's report that Josiah disguised himself relates the king's actions to the actions of Saul and Ahab as well as to the outcomes of these actions, sounding again an imminent political realignment. It also implicitly confirms that the Chronicler's Josiah understood Necho's message as a threat to his safety and thus a message of divine authority. Subsequently, the Chronicler, as the trustworthy narrator, explicitly authorizes Necho's message, in 35:22, by stating that Josiah did not listen (לא שמע) to Necho's words 'from the mouth of God' (מפי אלהים); thus, the Chronicler takes for granted that Josiah ought to have adhered to them as genuine divine pronouncements. As a result, there is no doubt that Necho's message comes with the authority of Israel's god and, coupled with the disguise topos, strongly foreshadows the final tragic outcome.

Notably, Josiah's refusal to heed Necho's warning echoes events in the Chronicler's account of the reign of Amaziah, when Amaziah goes to war against the Israelite king Joash (2 Chr 25:17–24). Like Josiah, Amaziah is belligerent and actively pursues the confrontation (2 Chr 25:17). Joash, like Necho, issues a warning that this will bring about disaster for the Judean king (2 Chr 25:18) and, like Josiah, Amaziah does not listen (לא שמע) to the warning (2 Chr 25:19). In slight contrast, however, the Chronicler does not attribute Joash's words to God but instead attributes Amaziah's obstinacy to God (מהאלהים היא). In any case, the result is disastrous for Judah: Joash defeats Amaziah in battle, takes the king and people captive, and plunders the temple (2 Chr 25:19–24). The shared motif of these two narratives—the refusal to heed warnings—always portends disaster in Chronicles.

Significantly, however, neither Josiah's disguise nor his refusal to heed Necho's warning is justification for the impending disaster. As Mitchell has astutely observed, these topoi are symptoms of an already

---

Hittite Royal Substitution Ritual," *Journal of Ancient Near Eastern Religions* 2 (2002) 61–73; R. Labat, "Le Sort des Substituts Royaux en Assyrie au Temps des Sargonides," *Revue d'assyriologie et d'archéologie orientale* 40 (1945–46) 123–42; S. Parpola, *Letters from Assyrian Scholars to the Kings Esarhaddon and Assurbanipal* (2 vols.; AOAT 5/1–2; Neukirchen-Vluyn: Neukirchener Verlag / Kevelaer: Butzon and Bercker, 1970–83; repr. Winona Lake, IN: Eisenbrauns, 2007) 2.xxii–xxxii. This topos is also found in classical texts: see, e.g., Arrian, *Anab.* 7.24.1–3; Herodotus, *Hist.* 7.15.

35. Coggins, "On Kings and Disguises," 61.

ordained outcome; they help to bring about the disaster but are not its fundamental justification.[36] In the case of Amaziah, the fundamental justification is explicit: "in order to hand [Judah] over, because they had sought the gods of Edom" (2 Chr 25:20b). In the case of Josiah, there is no comparable statement, so justification must be deduced from the account of Josiah's death and the narrative context as a whole.

In reporting Josiah's death in 35:23–24, the Chronicler again advances an ironic comparison with Saul and Ahab. Just as Saul (1 Chr 10:3; cf. v. 4) and Ahab (2 Chr 18:33) are shot by archers, archers wound Josiah (2 Chr 35:23). In addition, all three kings make final appeals to their retainers: Saul asks his retainer to kill him so he is not captured alive (2 Chr 35:4), while Ahab and Josiah ask their retainers to be removed from the battlefield because of their wounds ('because I am wounded' כי החליתי, in 2 Chr 18:33 // 35:23). This, however, is where the similarities end. The retainers of Saul and Ahab are unwilling or unable to comply with the requests, so Saul must take his own life (2 Chr 10:4), while Ahab's chariot remains trapped on the battlefield (2 Chr 18:34). By contrast, Josiah's retainer carries out the king's request (2 Chr 35:24). Consequently, unlike these unfaithful and impious kings, Josiah does not die on the battlefield, but he is returned to Jerusalem.

Once in Jerusalem, Josiah dies and is gathered to the graves of his fathers (35:24). This provides the ironic fulfillment of Huldah's prophecy. As Mitchell points out, the Chronicler puns Huldah's prophecy that Josiah would die 'in peace' (בשלום) by locating Josiah's death in "the foundation of peace," Jerusalem (ירושלם) and, in this way, showing the whole prophecy fulfilled.[37] In light of the disastrous and humiliating fates suffered by Saul, Ahab, and Amaziah, the prophecy actually remains, even in its horrible irony, a blessing. To die in Jerusalem, and not in captivity or on the battlefield, is something honorable in the world of Chronicles. Furthermore, as foretold, Josiah dies before the coming exile and destruction of Judah. This fateful end to the narrative suggests that Josiah's death is not a part of the paradigm of immediate reward and punishment; that is, Josiah is not punished for a refusal to listen to the words of Necho. Rather, the fundamental justification for his death is the inevitable *telos* of God's will, as revealed through the prophet Huldah. It is a necessary event in order to ensure

36. Mitchell, "Ironic Death," 424–25.
37. Mitchell (ibid., 423) also observes, "This use of irony is not unlike that used in fulfillment of prophecy in classical sources, for example, in Herodotus' story of Croesus' invasion of Persia and his loss of his empire (*Hist.* 1.53, 71, 91)."

the fulfillment of Huldah's prophecy and commence God's final judgment upon Jerusalem and the people, while sparing Josiah the experience of this judgment.

The Eulogy

The story of Josiah is completed with a burial notice (35:24), a eulogy to the slain king (35:25), and a summary that points readers to
sources with stories about Josiah that the Chronicler has left untold
(35:26–27). Although the burial notice and summary are conventions
carried over by the Chronicler from Kings and common to the reports
of most kings, they should not be overlooked. Often the Chronicler reveals much in the way that these conventions are particularized for
each king.[38]

The burial notice in 2 Chr 35:24 that concludes the account of Josiah's death secures his status among the good kings in Chronicles.
Solomon (2 Chr 9:31), Rehoboam (2 Chr 12:16), Abijah (2 Chr 13:23),
Asa (2 Chr 16:13–14), Jehoshaphat (2 Chr 21:1), Amaziah (2 Chr 25:28),
Uzziah (2 Chr 26:23), Jotham (2 Chr 27:9), and Hezekiah (2 Chr 32:33)
all receive a burial notice presented without significant discrimination
against them; these kings are honored in death to rest with their ancestors and assume a place in the City of David, explicitly or implicitly in
the graves of their fathers. Interestingly, only for Uzziah, Hezekiah,
and Josiah does the Chronicler explicitly aver that these kings were
buried in the graves of their fathers; and Uzziah only nominally so, in
order to ensure that the special provisions for him on account of his
leprosy are not read as a significant discrimination.[39] Josiah's burial

---

38. See esp. D. A. Glatt-Gilad, "Regnal Formulae as a Historiographic Device in the
Book of Chronicles," *RB* 108 (2001) 184–209.

39. The Chronicler does not mention that David was buried in the City of David and
obviously, as the progenitor of the dynasty, he is not said to have been laid with his ancestors (see 1 Chr 29:28). Of course, none of this counts negatively against David; rather,
it excludes him from the present list as a unique, yet equally venerable, case.

Uzziah's burial includes the note that he was buried with his ancestors, which is
qualified as "beside them in a field because of his skin-disease." The issue of impurity
raised in this case is not, however, meant to diminish the quality of Uzziah's burial, and
therefore the Chronicler insists that he was buried with his ancestors.

Several other kings are buried in the City of David, but the Chronicler explicitly
states that they were not buried in the graves of their fathers (2 Chr 21:20, 22:9, 24:25,
28:27, 33:20). The exception is important in that it shows: (a) that the normative case is
that kings are buried in the graves of their fathers, and thus for the kings of whom it is
not explicitly stated, it should be assumed (i.e., Solomon, Rehoboam, Abijah, Asa, Jehoshaphat, Amaziah, Jotham); and (b) that this discrimination in the burial notice is a
subtle judgment against the king.

notice is also quite distinctive in that it is followed by a eulogy; the only other kings to receive a eulogy are David (1 Chr 29:28) and Hezekiah (2 Chr 32:33), and these are much briefer than the eulogy accorded to Josiah.

In the Chronicler's eulogy, the grief paradigm in the Josiah narrative is fully realized, which as already noted replaces the usual joy paradigm for good kings. The torn clothes and tears of the king (2 Chr 34:19, 27) are now answered by the people's display of grief for their slain king. The word 'to mourn' (אבל) in 2 Chr 35:24 is used only one other time, in 1 Chr 7:22, and forms of 'to lament' (קין) and 'lamentations' (קינה), which appear in 2 Chr 34:25, are used only here in Chronicles; the latter is even used twice. Thus, the poignant irony of the Josiah narrative is that the only king who wept for his people is the only king for whom all Israel mourns; no other king is mourned in death. So immense is the grief that Jeremiah, the great prophet, laments for the king, and all the singers in Israel, male and female, speak of Josiah in their lamentations, to the Chronicler's day. It is, perhaps, irony upon irony that these lamentations should also become, in the Chronicler's words, 'a statute for Israel' (לחק על ישראל); in death, Josiah bequeaths to the cult another legacy: the ordinance of mourning, of lamentations, of grief. It is, of course, a bequest that could only have resulted from a tragic and untimely death. The lament of Jeremiah and the laments of all the singers of Israel are an enduring remembrance to the king of Torah and tears.

Like the burial notice and the eulogy, the summary of the sources of the untold stories of Josiah is also quite distinctive. It consists of two parallel statements:

ויתר דברי יאשיהו וחסדיו ככתוב בתורת יהוה

The remainder of Josiah's deeds and his *ḥesed* (pl.) are as written in the law of Yahweh. (2 Chr 35:26)

ודבריו הראשנים והאחרנים הנם כתובים על ספר מלכי ישראל ויהודה

His deeds, the first and the last, behold they are written upon the Book of the Kings of Israel and Judah. (2 Chr 35:27)

Although the last of these two statements is typically Chronistic, the first statement is unusual, rather enigmatic, and very suggestive.

In Chronicles, only Yahweh practices *ḥesed* toward Israel and its leaders (1 Chr 16:34, 41; 17:13; 2 Chr 1:8; 5:13; 6:14; 7:6; 20:21), as well as David toward Hanun (1 Chr 19:2) and toward Yahweh (2 Chr 6:42), Jehoiada toward Joash (2 Chr 24:22), Hezekiah toward Yahweh (2 Chr

32:32), and Josiah toward Yahweh. *Ḥesed* is the primary term in the Hebrew Bible to denote covenant loyalty and, as such, when not used of human-human relationships, overwhelmingly functions to characterize Yahweh's attitude and actions toward Israel or its leaders. It is, therefore, an extraordinary character trait to ascribe to humans in the context of covenant, as the Chronicler does for David, Hezekiah, and Josiah—so extraordinary, that it appears only once more in the Hebrew Bible (Nehemiah ascribes it to himself in Neh 13:14). It certainly links David, Hezekiah, and Josiah together as practicing common types of covenant loyalty in Chronicles and sets them apart from other kings.

More unusual than this (which at least has three parallels in the text) is the syntactic relationship of the phrase "the remainder of Josiah's deeds" to "his *ḥesed* is as written in the law of Yahweh" (2 Chr 35:26). The phrase "as written in the law of Yahweh" is used in the Hebrew Bible to indicate that "X" action was performed as "X" action is prescribed in the Torah, referenced by various essentially synonymous terms, where "X" is a statute or commandment, festival, or cultic practice authorized (or so claimed) in the Torah. Most scholars assume that the referent, or "X," of the phrase 'as written in the law of Yahweh' (ככתוב בתורת יהוה) is limited to 'his *ḥesed*' (חסדיו) and consequently that this phrase is appositional to the main clause that begins "the remainder of Josiah's deeds" and continues in the next verse with "and his deeds."[40] The Chronicler's syntactic construction is, however, ambiguous, and so it is unclear what the Chronicler intends to communicate. It also seems possible to read "the remainder of Josiah's deeds" and "his *ḥesed*" as a dual referent of the ככתוב ('as written') phrase, in which case not only Josiah's *ḥesed* but also the remainder of his deeds are as written in the Torah. This would be an extraordinary and certainly unique statement! Yet, even if the limited reading is preferable, the Chronicler creates a positive relationship between Josiah's *ḥesed* and the Torah that remains unmatched in the evaluation of any other king in Chronicles. Whatever else it may suggest, the Chronicler, at minimum, confirms the intimate connection between Josiah and the Torah established by the finding of the book and its application to his reforms.

---

40. See Japhet, *Chronicles*, 1058; W. Rudolph, *Chronikbücher* (Handbuch zum Alten Testament 21; Tübingen: Mohr, 1955) 333; and the extensive treatment of K. L. Spawn, *"As It Is Written" and Other Citation Formulae in the Old Testament: Their Use, Development, Syntax, and Significance* (ed. O. Kaiser; BZAW 311; Berlin: de Gruyter, 2002) 82–84, 113–16, 250.

The Power of the Text

Texts are unavoidably shaped by the communities in which and for whom they are written. Chronicles, therefore, reflects the political-cultural and religious reality of its community: the loss of independence, the experience of exile and restoration, and the emergence of Persian governance. The Chronicler also attempts to resolve problems of continuity and discontinuity with earlier texts, such as the Torah and Samuel–Kings, in the Josiah narrative. Historical impulses of the text, therefore, are not simply or even primarily an attempt by the Chronicler to show *wie es eigentlich gewesen*; rather, they constitute an ideological re-presentation of the community's historical traditions with the purpose of making them (intellectually and/or pragmatically) relevant to the community's present. A text such as this, then, aims to inscribe its ideological re-presentation on its audience in order to persuade them to a certain world view and to actions that reflect that world view.

The Audience

Naturally, the persuasive power and communicative intent of the text is dependent on the audience's access to the text and the readings and rereadings of the text for these audiences. Liverani, in a study of the "celebrative texts issued by the ancient kings," identifies three "spheres of audience and levels of mobilization" of these texts according to degrees of accessibility.[41] These spheres, relevant also to biblical texts such as Chronicles, are the "inner audience," the "wider audience," and the "outer audience."[42]

In the case of Chronicles, the inner audience consists of the Chronicler's community and literate scribes in other Yahwistic communities that received this text. This audience had direct access to the text, could read it and study it, and was presumably the most aware of the issues it is primarily meant to address. This inner audience is the only group with authority over the text; it can reject, rewrite, accept, and/ or disseminate it. Given this authority, any education of this audience

---

41. M. Liverani, "The Deeds of Ancient Mesopotamian Kings," in *Civilizations of the Ancient Near East* (ed. J. Sasson; 4 vols.; New York: Scribner, 1995) 4.2353.

42. See also Y. Levin, "Who Was the Chronicler's Audience? A Hint from His Genealogies," *JBL* 122 (2003) 229–45. I essentially agree with Levin's conclusions about the audience of Chronicles and have here used Liverani to systematize and categorize these conclusions in a way that I think is actually consistent with, though not explicitly articulated by Levin. Furthermore, my analysis of the audience(s) is ultimately more comprehensive, by virtue of the outer audience(s), than Levin's (if not as thoroughly defended).

through the text must be consistent with established norms or else be surreptitious, if the text is going to be accepted, studied, and disseminated.

The wider audience consists of the lay participants in the cult (mostly free adult males in Yehud and possibly in some centers outside Yehud, who acknowledge the religious authority of the inner audience). This audience receives the text filtered by the inner audience, who reads it to them and teaches them from it (either through homilies or other means). It is this audience that is the primary target of the text's ideologies.

The outer audience consists of those who do not participate, either by choice or by status, in the cult (women, slaves, foreigners, and so on). This outer audience receives the text, if at all, filtered by the wider audience, either as secondhand instruction or by simple cultural diffusion. While communication with this outer audience takes place, it is unlikely that this audience is in any significant way purposefully addressed in the text.

The Message(s)

The analysis in this essay "confirms the proposal that Jerusalem, the temple, the cult, and the absolute sovereignty of Yahweh are central elements of the Chronicler's ideology."[43] As seen, the structures and themes of the narrative, however they are construed or read, are all concerned to strengthen the centrality of these elements. These elements are not very controversial; more controversial is the way in which the Chronicler's representation of Josiah, in particular the account of his death, addresses problems of causality and the divine will, blessing and punishment, and leadership for the postexilic community.

Both the Josiah narrative and Chronicles as a whole repeatedly call attention to the law and the proper execution of the cult as the means to a proper relationship with Yahweh. This point is often made through the immediate reward-and-punishment paradigm, which inculcates the importance of fidelity and warns against infidelity.[44] In the Josiah narrative, however, readers encounter a significant obstacle to this paradigm for, whereas the Chronicler in 1 Chr 10 to 2 Chr 32 is largely consistent in showing that right action brings joy and blessings from Yahweh, the Josiah narrative not only fails to advance this ideal

---

43. I reached this same conclusion in "Breaking Down Unity: An Analysis of 1 Chronicles 21.1–22.1," *JSOT* 30 (2005) 221.

44. See again Dillard, "Reign of Asa," 207–18; idem, "Reward and Punishment," 164–72; Japhet, *Ideology,* 165–76; McKenzie, *1–2 Chronicles,* passim.

explicitly but appears to contradict it directly; Josiah's (nearly) ideal kingship and reforms appear to lead only to the specter of exile and the king's own death by Egyptian archers. Although it is possible that this inconsistency simply stems from redactional activity, a "convenient" solution of this sort negates one of the most ignored yet poignant and important themes of Chronicles, and the Josiah narrative in particular: the encouragement to faithfulness and *ḥesed* in the face of the inscrutability and/or judgment of Yahweh.[45]

Indeed, for a postexilic cultic community in the small province of Yehud, which is not nearly the size of even the Chronicler's Judah (let alone the Chronicler's Israel), the immediate reward of divine blessings for faithfulness that so many scholars have identified as the hallmark of Chronicles is a strange ideology to advance. Such a message would only serve to condemn the community as somehow inadequate, for it was too small, too beset by difficulties, too confined in its influence, too poor and powerless to claim that it was a faithful community in the tradition of David, Solomon, Hezekiah, and Josiah—all kings who, blessed by Yahweh, reigned over a glorious people in a promised land and established an authentic cult. Chronicles could not be the great *apologia* for the postexilic Jerusalem temple and its personnel that its content and many commentators suggest. Its message would simply ring hollow with those in the postexilic community and actually serve as a polemic against the postexilic Jerusalem temple and its personnel. Certainly, it must be admitted that this may be at least part of its message: the postexilic cult is failing because the traditions of David, Solomon, Hezekiah, and Josiah have not been effectively applied. However, the text is not so negative; it clearly is an *apologia* for the centrality of Jerusalem and the temple cult.

Consequently, it seems appropriate to conclude that the Josiah narrative is evidence of the Chronicler's much more complex system of cause and effect than immediate reward and punishment, a system more consistent with the situation of the postexilic community. Although it is true that the Chronicler often develops a correspondence between individual actions and rewards or punishments from Yahweh, there are many times in the text that this correspondence does not hold or, at least, the severity of the punishment appears inconsistent with the offense.[46] As Ben Zvi has observed, the Chronicler clearly presents the exile as unavoidable and unequivocally attributes the di-

---

45. On this theme, see especially Ben Zvi, "Sense of Proportion."
46. See ibid., 37–51.

vine judgment to "the transgenerational sin of Israel and its kings."[47] Interestingly, and perhaps surprisingly to some in view of the immediate reward and punishment paradigm, this is not entirely unexpected in Chronicles. Most notably, the multiplication of guilt or sin also brings about the invasion of Shishak (2 Chr 12:2),[48] which, as argued and like the exile, inaugurates a new political dynamic of service to foreign kings. Ben Zvi has noted that such moments of transgenerational guilt or, conversely, merit are typically associated with critical events.[49] To this extent, the Chronicler presents a world in which Yahweh's judgments are often inexplicable, at least from the perspective of the immediate reward-and-punishment paradigm.

In the Josiah narrative, the Chronicler presents the restoration of the temple and all its service as being under constant pall and threat. The blessings for this generation's faithfulness are deeply ironic and tragic; Josiah's promised reprieve is still death after battle, even if he dies in Jerusalem before the exile, the temple that is rebuilt is shortly destroyed, its completed service is ended, and the covenant that is renewed is soon broken. The solemnity of every accomplishment is highlighted by the absence of the joy and celebration that the Chronicler typically attributes to momentous occasions of this sort. Furthermore, the people receive in Josiah's death the cultic ordinance of lament, which is one genre in biblical literature that explicitly permits the people to challenge any injustice that befalls them. The lament would not be necessary in a world of the perfect correspondence of individual actions with rewards and punishments that some attribute to Chronicles; in such a world, there is nothing to lament because every event is the just consequence of a specific cause.

Because of the relationship of this theme to other parts of the book, it is unlikely that the Josiah narrative is a redactional anomaly; rather, it is an integral part, even climax, of the relevancy and affirmative message of Chronicles to the postexilic community. While the immediate reward-and-punishment paradigm provides encouragement that faithfulness is rewarded and evil punished, the Chronicler argues that inexplicable judgment and disaster from Yahweh can befall the faithful, and the proper response is continued faithfulness. This message, while seemingly negative in that it suggests a capricious and untrustworthy god, is actually positive because the cultic insider is

---

47. Idem, "Observations," 104; see also B. Halpern, "Why Manasseh Is Blamed for the Babylonian Exile: The Evolution of a Biblical Tradition," *VT* 48 (1998) 473–514.

48. Ibid., 477.

49. Ben Zvi, "Observations," 104, esp. n. 47; idem, "Sense of Proportion."

unlikely to accept that Yahweh is capricious and untrustworthy; therefore, he or she will assign the misfortune to some inscrutable good while perceiving from the text that misfortune of this sort is not necessarily an indictment or an indication of one's unfaithfulness. It also encourages faithfulness in the face of judgment because, through this faithfulness, a legacy is created for subsequent generations, just as Josiah provided a legacy for the Chronicler's own generation.

This, in turn, confirms the proposal that the kings of Judah in Chronicles are instrumentalized rather than idealized; they are—and this is admittedly a fine line—examples rather than models.[50] The king succeeds as a divinely ordained patron of the temple and its institutions.[51] He is invested with the power to build and order the temple and its service, interpret and apply the liturgical texts, call for and preside over national convocations, and maintain the defense of the city and its environs; he also bears the responsibility to enforce and maintain the covenant between Yahweh, king, and people. The faithful king's legacy and judgments are also binding on subsequent generations.

In one sense, this may seem an unassailable position of authority, yet it is important to qualify it. The king in Chronicles, as a patron of the temple and its institutions, is its servant. The king must adhere to the Torah; his authority to interpret and apply the liturgical texts is limited by the tradition itself and by prophetic words; and, he is accountable to Yahweh at all times and in all respects. No ruler in Chronicles other than Solomon, and possibly Abijah, perfectly succeeds in his mandate, and consequently there is no concerted attempt to idealize the kingship. In fact, the kingship is repeatedly presented as imperfect and the king repeatedly subject to the judgment of Yahweh revealed in the Torah. Thus, the Chronicler appears to advocate a political system that is only pragmatically monarchic and essentially theocratic.[52]

---

50. See again Jonker, *Reflections*, 33.

51. On this point, see esp. Riley, *King and Cultus*.

52. See J. E. Dyck, *The Theocratic Ideology of the Chronicler* (Biblical Interpretation Series 33; Leiden: Brill, 1998); cf. A. Labahn, "Antitheocratic Tendencies in Chronicles," in *Yahwism after the Exile: Perspectives on Israelite Religion in the Persian Era* (ed. R. Albertz and B. Becking; Assen: Van Gorcum, 2003) 115–35. Personally, I think the dichotomy between monarchic and theocratic is false for the ancient world; it is only useful here to distinguish between a view that emphasizes the necessity of or desire for an indiginuous, more-or-less independent state and monarchy, over against a view that many postexilic Judeans by and large accepted foreign rule, though admittedly they constructed it as peripheral and secondary to their supposed (and idealized) theocratic rule, which nevertheless was pragmatically realized through some form of hierocratic or gubernatorial leadership.

The Josiah narrative also explains the absence of a Davidic ruler in the Chronicler's own time and presents a world in which foreign kings can have rightful dominion over Judah/Yehud. Most of the kings who succeed Josiah are appointed by either Necho or Nebuchadnezzar, all are deposed and taken into exile by them, and all are severely judged by the Chronicler (2 Chr 36:1–21). The temple, the wall of Jerusalem, and the palaces they built are destroyed, and the land is made to lie desolate for 70 years to fulfill Jeremiah's prophecy in accordance with Yahweh's judgment against the people of Israel (2 Chr 34:24–25; 36:18–21). After this, Cyrus, roused by the spirit of God and made ruler of "the kingdoms of the lands" by God, invites the people to return and rebuild the temple (2 Chr 36:22–23); notably, it is not a Davidide who inaugurates this new era but the great king of Persia. The successive removal and exile of Josiah's successors, the final destruction of the city, as well as Necho's and Cyrus's claim to divine authority clearly undermines the authority, if not future legitimacy, of the Davidides as independent rulers in Judah:

> That the rule of Cyrus signals the termination of the Davidic dynasty can be seen by the application to him of two of the same emphases which were once operative in the dynastic promise to David: that the king reigns only under Yahweh and that the task of temple-building is linked with divinely established kingship. In receiving the commission to build the Temple, Cyrus inherits the chief symbol of the legitimacy of the Davidic dynasty according to the common ideological language of the ancient Near East, and according to the Chronistic narrative of the monarchy.[53]

The Chronicler likely accepts an ongoing right of the Davidides to some form of political leadership in the community—after all, the Chronicler preserves the Davidic genealogy into the postexilic age in 1 Chr 3:15–24—but the Chronicler is not clear about how this should be realized. The more salient reality of the Chronicler's presentation is the legitimation of foreign rule over Judah. In the final verses of the book, the Chronicler only expresses hope for a return from exile and a Second Temple. There is no expectation of or commission for a new Davidic kingdom.[54]

---

53. Riley, *King and Cultus*, 154.

54. By contrast, the Kings Historian ends on a more suggestive note with concern for the condition of the Davidides in exile (2 Kgs 25:27–30). The Chronicler's Davidic genealogy is the only certain evidence that the Chronicler has any abiding interest in the Davidic line into the exilic and postexilic periods, and there is no compelling reason to assume on this basis that the Chronicler necessarily supports the restoration of the monarchy. Personally, I think the assumption otherwise is strongly influenced by the

Through the "Israelization" of foreign kings, however, the Chronicler shapes, communicates, and reinforces for the community of the
text an ideological construction of foreign kings as dependent on Yahweh. Their authority comes from Yahweh and, ideologically, they are
not at the center of the community's life. So, for example, Josiah must
go out from Jerusalem to meet Necho, and Necho as well as the other
foreign kings in Chronicles are only successful when they speak in the
language of the Israelite religion.[55] The imperial throne, therefore, is
subordinate to the center that the Chronicler identifies as the presence,
knowledge, and law of Yahweh, as mediated through the temple and
its functionaries.

Conclusion

The sophisticated structure and the multiple themes and motifs of the
Josiah narrative point to a flexible interaction with the traditions that,
in turn, expands the potential readings and rereadings in a process
perhaps most akin to the homiletical traditions of contemporary Jewish and Christian communities.[56] This didactic and kerygmatic quality
of the text is the essence of its power and endurance. Through reading
and rereading the Josiah narrative in Chronicles, and reading it to
others, the community of the text advances and promotes its own ideals and values and receives encouragement in its present situation and
future goals. By reading and rereading the Josiah narrative in Chronicles ourselves, we are able to identify these aspects of the text and at

---

overstated interpretation that the Chronicler glorifies the Davidic monarchy, especially
vis-à-vis Samuel–Kings. The Chronicler's glorification of the Davidic monarchy almost
always relates directly, or at least indirectly, to the proper, divinely authorized establishment of the cult and its purity, legitimacy, and authority for the people of Israel. The ex-
altation of the Davidides in Chronicles serves that end rather than a political programme
for the restoration of the monarchy; however, compare Boda's essay in this volume.

55. In this respect, Sennacherib is the foremost example of the negative (2 Chr 32:1–
23). Regardless of Sennacherib's overwhelming power, his contempt for Yahweh ensures
that his attempt to conquer the center of Israel's community life—Jerusalem and the
temple—is thwarted.

56. On the relationship between rereading and homiletics, see P. J. Wilson and B. R.
Gaventa, "Preaching as the Re-reading of Scripture," *Int* 52 (1998) 392–404. For more on
the didactic and kerygmatic quality of Chronicles, see esp. L. C. Allen, "Kerygmatic Units
in 1 and 2 Chronicles," *JSOT* 41 (1988) 21–36; R. Mason, *Preaching the Tradition: Homily and
Hermeneutics after the Exile: Based on the "Addresses" in Chronicles, the "Speeches" in the Books
of Ezra and Nehemiah, and the Postexilic Prophetic Books* (Cambridge: Cambridge University
Press, 1990).

the same time identify some of the fears, anxieties, and insecurities of the community that the text attempts to overcome.

From the Josiah narrative, in particular, it is clear that the Chronicler and the primary community of the text are passionate Yahwists concerned with monotheistic worship centered in Jerusalem and its temple. They are interested in questions about leadership and temple organization and deeply concerned with the intersection of praxis and ideology in the cult and the life of the community. They are a community often rapt by their insecurity and dependence on foreign powers, as expressed through the subtext of exile and judgment. However, despite these insecurities, they remain committed to a theological tradition, which they understand in continuity with the past communities that wrote and disseminated the Torah and also, though perhaps less deferentially, Samuel–Kings and other books of the Hebrew Bible. This continuity provides the community with its self-identity, its sense of purpose in the world, its source of joy, and also, as evident from the Josiah narrative, its validation of lament. In a world of tragedy, perhaps the last of these is one of the most important legacies of the Josiah narrative.

Identity and Empire, Reality and Hope
in the Chronicler's Perspective

MARK J. BODA
McMaster Divinity College and McMaster University

Introduction

In his recent contribution to the Nadav Naʾaman Festschrift, Ehud Ben
Zvi provides wise guidance to all who dare to make claims for what I
am calling in this essay the "Chronicler's perspective":

> It cannot be emphasized enough that studies in Chronicles must clearly
> distinguish between the messages conveyed by a particular account, or
> portion thereof, and the messages conveyed by the book as a whole. The
> former are only strands in the dense tapestry of the latter. In other
> words, the messages of the whole evolved as the intended and primary
> rereaders (hereafter, "target readers") moved beyond the level of indi-
> vidual accounts (or sections thereof) and evaluated and reinterpreted
> their particular messages in a way that was strongly informed by the
> messages of other accounts. As a result, they developed a more inte-
> grated and integrating, sophisticated understanding of the theological
> positions shaped in and communicated by the book of Chronicles as a
> whole.[1]

To read Chronicles, then, is not only to study its various accounts in all
of their detail but also to recognize the intricate relationships between
these accounts and their place within the narrative shape of the entire
work.[2] Thus Ben Zvi continues: "The more one understands the literary and theological sophistication of the book of Chronicles, the more
one must pay careful attention to nuances, literary topoi, allusions,

---

1. E. Ben Zvi, "Observations on Josiah's Account in Chronicles and Implications for
Reconstructing the Worldview of the Chronicler," in *Essays on Ancient Israel in Its Near
Eastern Context: A Tribute to Nadav Naʾaman* (ed. Y. Amit et al.; Winona Lake, IN: Eisenbrauns, 2006) 90; see earlier idem, "A Gateway to the Chronicler's Teaching: The Account
of the Reign of Ahaz in 2 Chr 28,1–27," *SJOT* 7 (1993) 218–20, and his call to conduct
analysis of the Chronicler on "two levels."

2. The latter being what Ben Zvi calls elsewhere a passage's *Sitz im Buch* ("Gateway,"
218).

and references to other sections in the book that are present in each individual account."[3]

One might think that a similar sensitivity is to be found in the work of a scholar such as Jonathan Dyck who makes the humorous statement: "As I see it, the difference between your average punter and a literary or biblical critic is the fact that the critic reads books more than once."[4] By this, he means that the critic has read the ending of the book and thus is able to view the entire work through the lens of its conclusion. He suggests that a shortcut to a critical reading is to read the ending first.[5] Although there is certainly value in being sensitive to the final phase of the book of Chronicles (as articulated below), one should not assume that the ending is determinative for the entire work or that the ideology of the book is expressed most fully in the closing chapter. Yet there has been an increasing trend in work on Chronicles to focus exclusively on the final chapter as normative for the Chronicler's ideology. Probably most influential has been the work of Riley, who writes

---

3. Idem, "Observations," 90.

4. J. E. Dyck, *The Theocratic Ideology of the Chronicler* (Biblical Interpretation Series 33; Leiden: Brill, 1998) 77–78.

5. It is fascinating to me that Dyck's "shortcut" does not lead immediately to a rereading of Chronicles but instead becomes a point of departure into the book of Ezra–Nehemiah and the history of the Persian-period community. He takes the incomplete sentence at the end of Chronicles as an invitation by the Chronicler to "read Chronicles and Ezra–Nehemiah together; and not just the books of Ezra and Nehemiah but also the history of the post-exilic community to which it refers" (ibid., 83). In the present essay, I will argue that the final chapter of Chronicles demands first a rereading of Chronicles, sending the reader back to earlier points in the Chronicler's work, not to a separate work called Ezra–Nehemiah or to the history of the postexilic community. I am well aware that 1 Esdras does reveal a reading strategy in antiquity similar to Dyck's. There are, of course, two dominant views on the relationship between 1 Esdras, Chronicles, and MT Ezra–Nehemiah, the first being that 1 Esdras provides evidence for a corpus that predates the present form of MT Chronicles–Ezra–Nehemiah (as D. Böhler, *Die heilige Stadt in Esdras a und Esra–Nehemia: Zwei Konzeptionen der Wiederherstellung Israels* [OBO 158; Freiburg: Universitätsverlag / Göttingen: Vandenhoeck & Ruprecht, 1997]). The second view is that it is a later reformulation of the texts of MT Chronicles, MT Ezra–Nehemiah (as Z. Talshir maintains, *1 Esdras: From Origin to Translation* [SBLSCS 47; Atlanta: Society of Biblical Literature, 1999]; cf. R. G. Wooden, "1 Esdras," in *A New English Translation of the Septuagint and the Other Greek Translations Traditionally Included under That Title* [ed. A. Pietersma and B. G. Wright; Oxford: Oxford University Press, 2007] 392). I have adopted the latter view and so have concluded that the reading strategy found in 1 Esdras cannot be assumed for the original, implied readers of Chronicles but instead for a particular, ca. second century B.C.E., readership. It is instructive that the only extant version of 1 Esdras includes material only from 2 Chr 35–36, thus eliminating the bulk of the Chronicler's material, including the idyllic portrait of David and Solomon and the renewals of Hezekiah and Manasseh.

of 2 Chr 36: "As an ending to the work, the passage does not look to the shadowy indications of a Davidic restoration but to the firm promise of a restored Temple, thus identifying the Temple and its cultus as the permanent salvific contribution that the House of David has made to the nation."[6]

It is the intention of this paper to heed Ben Zvi's advice to evaluate the ways in which the book of Chronicles shapes the identity of its original readership in the Persian period. Close attention to the closing section of Chronicles suggests that the book seeks to shape identity within the enduring colonial realities of the Persian imperial environment. However, this identity shaping cannot be abstracted from the larger project of Chronicles, in which one finds many other instances where the book also clearly appeals to Persian-period conditions. It will be the contention of this paper that the book of Chronicles not only justifies present reality but also projects future hope. In this way, the many idealized portraits found prior to 2 Chr 36 also play a role in shaping the identity of the readers.[7]

The Death of Josiah, Exile, and Restoration

The final section of Chronicles, from the death of Josiah to the end of the book (2 Chr 35:20–36:23), transitions its original readers not only historically but also sociologically from the monarchial past to the colonial present. After tracing the reforms of Josiah in response to the discovery of the book of the law (chap. 34) and his celebration of the Passover (35:1–19), the Chronicler describes the demise of Josiah at the hand of

---

6. W. Riley, *King and Cultus in Chronicles: Worship and the Reinterpretation of History* (JSOTSup 160; Sheffield: Sheffield Academic Press, 1993) 143. Similarly K. Ristau, *Reading and Re-reading Josiah: A Critical Study of Josiah in Chronicles* (M.A. thesis, University of Alberta, 2004) 83; see also his contribution in this volume. Although I do not dispute the fact that "Chronicles reflects the politico-cultural and religious reality of the Chr's community" or what Ristau brilliantly describes as "the power of the text . . . to inscribe its ideological re-presentation on its audience in order to persuade them to a certain worldview and actions that reflect that worldview," I am not convinced that the Chronicler's aim should be subsumed into the "reality" described in the final chapter of the book.

7. Although Jonker adopts the view that the Davidic role has been assumed by the Persian rulers, his sensitivity to the larger narrative context ("Why then was the story of their own kings retold in this era?") leads him to suggest that Chronicles does express "constructive criticism *vis-à-vis* the Persian rulers"; L. C. Jonker, *Reflections of King Josiah in Chronicles: Late Stages of the Josiah Reception in II Chr. 34f* (Textpragmatische Studien zur Literatur- und Kulturgeschichte der Hebräischen Bibel 2; Gütersloh: Gütersloher Verlagshaus, 2003) 87.

Pharaoh Necho (35:20–27). While a military attack on a Judean king
following a phase of obedience is not odd in Chronicles (e.g., Hezekiah),
it is interesting that first in the direct speech of Necho (35:21) and subsequently through the narrator's voice (35:22) the Chronicler reveals
that Necho's actions and words are God's actions and words (35:21–22).
Significant connections between Josiah's death and the deaths of at least
Saul and Ahab, if not also Amaziah and Ahaziah, villainize Josiah and
reveal the loss of divine favor.[8] This signals a major juncture in the book
of Chronicles because, from this point on, not only will the Judean
monarchy be controlled by external imperial forces, but the Chronicler
will continue to identify various speeches and actions of subsequent
emperors with Yahweh. As Johnstone has so aptly written: "With the
death of Josiah the new phase of exile has now begun for Israel."[9]

This can be discerned in the subtle sequencing in the Chronicler's
description of the reigns of Jehoiakim and Jehoiachin in which the narrative evaluation "he did evil in the eyes of Yahweh (his God)" (36:5,
9) is followed immediately by a description of an invasion by Nebuchadnezzar (35:6, 10), suggesting a causal link between the two events.
This connection is heightened in the final example of Jehoiachin, in
which the narratival evaluation is expanded to include a reference not
only to doing evil in the eyes of Yahweh (35:12a) but also to failing to
humble himself before Jeremiah the prophet (35:12b) and rebelling
against King Nebuchadnezzar, "who had made him take an oath in
God's name" (35:13a). Not only does this place Nebuchadnezzar in a
group that includes Yahweh and Jeremiah, but the final phrase bolsters Nebuchadnezzar's role as vice-regent of Yahweh. Thus, as with
the two previous kings, when the wrath of Yahweh is aroused, Yahweh
brings up "the king of the Babylonians . . . Nebuchadnezzar" to exact
judgment upon Judah (35:17).

---

8. R. B. Dillard, *2 Chronicles* (WBC 15; Waco, TX: Word, 1987) 292; S. Japhet, *I and II
Chronicles: A Commentary* (OTL; Louisville: Westminster/John Knox, 1993) 1043; S. S. Tu-
ell, *First and Second Chronicles* (Interpretation; Louisville: John Knox, 2001) 241; Ristau,
"Josiah," 75–77; I. Kalimi, *The Reshaping of Ancient Israelite History in Chronicles* (Winona
Lake, IN: Eisenbrauns, 2005) 23; but especially the work of C. Mitchell, "The Ironic
Death of Josiah in 2 Chronicles," *CBQ* 68 (2006) 421–35. I am not convinced that Mitchell
has successfully undermined the validity of Josiah's Passover, something suggested by
the fact that her argument ends with a series of questions (p. 430).

9. W. Johnstone, *1 and 2 Chronicles* (JSOTSup 253–54; Sheffield: Sheffield Academic
Press, 1997) 2.260; more on the transition from Josiah to Jehoahaz in 2 Chr 35:25: "The
story of Israel now passes from monarchy to exile." Johnstone also argues that the
Chronicler's claim that the ending of the 70-year exile with the proclamation of Cyrus
(2 Chr 36) is also designed to identify the death of Josiah as the beginning of exile.

In 35:20–21, again Nebuchadnezzar is linked to Jeremiah as the Chronicler notes that his exile of "the remnant" is seen as a fulfillment of the prophetic word of Jeremiah. As with Necho, so also with Nebuchadnezzar, the Chronicler identifies an imperial figure as an agent of Yahweh. But even with this, the Chronicler is not finished. In his closing verses, he links Yahweh with the words and actions of yet another imperial figure, with Yahweh "moving the heart" of Cyrus "to make a proclamation" as fulfillment of the "word of Yahweh spoken by Jeremiah" (36:22–23).[10]

The Chronicler makes clear to his audience that its past loss of monarchial status at the hands of the Egyptians and Babylonians as well as its present colonial identity within the Persian Empire can be directly linked to Yahweh's will. The experiences in the demise of the state, the exile, and the restoration have all been superintended by a sovereign God who judges and saves and does so even through non-Israelite figures. The "promotion" of these imperial figures in the exile and restoration of Judah occurs at the expense of the Davidic House.[11] In the Chronicler's account, Judean kings serve at the whim of more powerful imperial forces—with Jehoahaz removed by Necho in favor of Jehoiakim, and Jehoiakim and Jehoiachin by Nebuchadnezzar in favor of Zedekiah.

But does this "promotion" mean future hope for the Davidic monarchy has been extinguished? The Chronicler's accounts of the last four kings of Judah accentuate parallels between the monarchs. None of the deaths of these kings is recorded by the Chronicler, even though the information was available for two of them in his source.[12] Three of the

---

10. H. G. M. Williamson, *1 and 2 Chronicles* (NCB; Grand Rapids, MI: Eerdmans, 1982) 419. Although Williamson considers 2 Chr 36:22–23 to be a post-Chronistic appendix "in order to point up the hopeful elements in the Chronicler's concluding words" as well as "directing the reader to the books where the continuation of the people's history may be found," the evidence I will introduce in my consideration of Hezekiah below suggests a close relationship between these verses and the account of Hezekiah; see I. Kalimi, *An Ancient Israelite Historian: Studies in the Chronicler, His Time, Place and Writing* (SSN 46; Assen: Van Gorcum, 2005) 151–53.

11. Ristau emphasizes this in his work, comparing this shift from Davidic to imperial kings with other key political realignments in Chronicles at Saul's death (1 Chr 10) and at the schism (2 Chr 10; "Josiah," 74–75).

12. My analysis here assumes that the Chronicler's Vorlage is essentially the text represented in MT Kings. In this I am obviously not following S. L. McKenzie (*The Chronicler's Use of the Deuteronomistic History* [HSM 33; Atlanta: Scholars Press, 1985]), who argued for the heavy reliance of MT Chronicles on MT Kings for 2 Chr 1–28 but argued for greater reliance on other sources for 2 Chr 29:1–35:19, and then after Josiah's death (2 Chr 35:20–36:23) for no reliance on MT Kings at all. See the critical reviews of McKenzie's work by

four experience exile in a foreign land—Jehoahaz to Egypt and Jehoiakim and Jehoiachin to Babylon—with Zedekiah's fate ignored. The
Chronicler notes that the two kings who were exiled to Babylon were
taken together with the treasures of the temple.

The conclusions that have been drawn from this evidence are controversial, to say the least. On the one hand, as Riley has argued, "by
denying the post-Josian kings such royal trappings as the statement of
their deaths and burials, and, to a lesser extent, the naming of the
Queen Mother, the Chronicler seems to undermine their full legitimate
status within the Davidic dynasty."[13] Furthermore, after introducing
Zedekiah's reign and rebellion in 36:11–13, the Chronicler shifts attention exclusively to the people as a whole for the description of the demise of the state, exile, and invitation to restoration.[14] For some, this
shift signals the end of royal hope, with the future lying exclusively
with the people, as the "remnant" (36:20) that works under the direction of God's new imperial vice-regent to rebuild the temple (36:22–23).

On the other hand, the absence of death notices may be an attempt
to highlight the enduring character of the royal line and to accentuate
the vast potential of a continuance of the royal line through the royal
figures in exile.[15] Furthermore, the link between Jehoiakim-Jehoiachin
and the temple treasures may be identifying subtly the line of Josiah-
Jehoiakim-Jehoiachin as the legitimate royal line for Judah,[16] while
also creating an inseparable link between the renewal of the temple

---

R. W. Klein, "Review of S. L. McKenzie: *The Chronicler's Use of the Deuteronomistic History*," *CBQ* 49 (1987) 478–79; and, especially, H. G. M. Williamson, "Review of S. L. Mc-
Kenzie: *The Chronicler's Use of the Deuteronomistic History*," *VT* 37 (1987) 107–14.

13. Riley, *King and Cultus*, 142–43.

14. The only reference to a Judean king after this point is the description of the plun-
der of "the treasurers of the king and his officials" in 36:18.

15. See Williamson, *1 and 2 Chronicles*, 412; C. T. Begg, "The Fate of Judah's Four Last
Kings in the Book of Chronicles," *Orientalia Lovaniensia Periodica* 18 (1987) 79–85.

16. Not developed in this paper is evidence from the Davidic genealogy of 1 Chr 3
that reveals the same historiographical structure evident at the end of Chronicles, that
is, a key break appears in the genealogy at Josiah, before which only a single Davidic heir
is identified, but after which multiple heirs are listed. I agree with Gary Knoppers that
the shape of the post-Josianic genealogy reveals enduring royal hope on the part of the
Chronicler (or post-Chronistic genealogist; *I Chronicles: A New Translation with Introduction and Commentary* [2 vols.; AB 12–12A; New York: Doubleday, 2004] 332–36; see idem,
"The Davidic Genealogy: Some Contextual Considerations from the Ancient Mediterranean World," *Transeu* 22 [2001] 35–50). Kelly notes that the genealogist shows interest in
the exilic Davidic Dynasty in the reference to "Jehoiachin, the captive" in 3:17, which is
"prospective and anticipates the king's fate in 2 Chr. 36:10" (B. E. Kelly, *Retribution and
Eschatology in Chronicles* [JSOTSup 211; Sheffield: Sheffield Academic Press, 1996] 164).

and the renewal of the royal house.[17] Interestingly, the Chronicler has transferred his source's description of a bronze-shackled royal journeying into exile from the figure of Zedekiah (2 Kgs 25:7) to Jehoiakim (2 Chr 36:6).[18] The shift then from king to people after Zedekiah may be further evidence of the Chronicler's focus on the Jehoiakim-Jehoiachin line. Bolstering this view is the Chronicler's presentation of Jehoiachin in which "the deportees were reduced to the person of the king, the booty was reduced to the precious vessels of the Temple and the siege and capitulation were reduced to the Babylonian king sending for Jehoiachin and removing both him and the vessels."[19]

While in the present paper I will offer a *via media* between these views, in the end, no matter how one resolves this debate, the closing chapter of Chronicles shapes the identity of the colonial audience. By concluding with the broken piece of Cyrus's proclamation (36:23), the narrative forms identity, first of all, by suggesting that imperial forces will control the political environment of the world, including Yehud; second, by demonstrating that these imperial forces will support the temple in Jerusalem;[20] and third, by linking the identity of the community with the people who have accepted or will accept the invitation to "go up" to Jerusalem in Judah.[21]

---

17. Williamson (*1 and 2 Chronicles*, 412) sees here a "deliberate parallel between the fate of the temple and that of the Davidic dynasty." Kalimi observes that, while the Deuteronomic History has the vessels cut up (2 Kgs 24:13), Chronicles has them taken intact (2 Chr 36:10) based on Jer 27:16–22; 28:3–6 (*Ancient Israelite Historian*, 118); see G. N. Knoppers, "Treasures Won and Lost: Royal (Mis)appropriations in Kings and Chronicles," in *The Chronicler as Author: Studies in Text and Texture* (ed. M. P. Graham and S. L. McKenzie; JSOTSup 263; Sheffield: Sheffield Academic Press, 1999) 206.

18. W. M. Schniedewind, "The Source Citations of Manasseh: King Manasseh in History and Homily," *VT* 41 (1991) 450–61.

19. Kalimi, *Ancient Israelite Historian*, 118.

20. Thus, Ehud Ben Zvi: "the texts discussed here are clearly consistent with the idea that the principal kings of the area are not necessarily evil, nor do they necessarily oppose the will of YHWH. . . . In particular, the concluding reference to Cyrus suggests not only that the rule of foreign kings over Jerusalem is not necessarily a bad thing, but, in fact, it seems to raise the possibility that YHWH's kingship over Jerusalem may be executed by Cyrus" ("When the Foreign Monarch Speaks," in *The Chronicler as Author: Studies in Text and Texture* [ed. M. P. Graham and S. L. McKenzie; JSOTSup 263; Sheffield: Sheffield Academic Press, 1999] 227–28).

21. 2 Chronicles 36:22–23 represents a proclamation that identifies the building of the temple with Cyrus, not the people. The golah is merely invited to "go up." This suggests that the implied reader is not to be associated with the community in the early Persian period, the phase in which the temple was rebuilt, but with the postconstruction community. The book appears to be encouraging "exilic" communities either to return to

Transition

But while this pro-empire identity is clearly offered to the reader at the conclusion to Chronicles, is this the only identity projected by the text onto its readers? Will imperial figures always be the conduits of Yahweh's rule and voice on earth? What are the limits to this colonial identity?

The final scenario offered in Chronicles is filled with potential ("let them go up") and suggests that, although imperial conditions provide a foundation for the present restoration experience of the community, this is just the beginning. It is easy for scholars who place the dominant rhetorical weight on the presentation of Judah in 2 Chr 36 to ignore rhetorical motifs that dominate the majority of the Chronicler's account. For these scholars, while certain ideals can be gleaned from the earlier accounts, these ideals are not to be related to larger-scale sociological shifts, especially a return to kingdom from colony. However, if the book's final phase is seen as shaping the imperial expectations of the colonial readers, then why would this not be true for the earlier portions of the book, which also present material relevant to a Persian-period readership and have implications for imperial expectation? That is, in the words of Ben Zvi, how does 2 Chr 36 function as but one strand within "the dense tapestry" of the book as a whole?

It has long been noted that the Chronicler shapes his story of the monarchy with a view to the present realities and needs of his Persian-period community. Dyck is typical when he claims: "It is clear that the Chronicler intended this story, like the history as a whole, to say something about the present day by saying something about the past. That is to say, the Chronicler's story of Israel has a paradigmatic, even atemporal, ahistorical quality which stands in tension with the narrative genre."[22] Duke highlights the way the David-Solomon phase of the Chronicler's history constructs a paradigm or model that not only is confirmed in the rest of Israelite history but also seeks "to induce the audience to take another step and to evaluate and classify the character and situation of their own generation" moving them to "self-

---

or at least to make a pilgrimage to the Jerusalem temple—what Kalimi calls "a practical 'Zionistic' encouragement of immigration from the existing Jewish communities in Diaspora to *Yehud Medinta*" (*Ancient Israelite Historian*, 156).

22. Dyck, *Theocratic Ideology*, 222. See also Schniedewind, who sees the Chronicler's narrative as typological ("Source Citations," 450–61).

analysis."[23] It is thus misguided to limit the paradigmatic function to only the context described in the post-Josianic materials.

It has long been observed that the idyllic period of David and Solomon provides the foundation for Second Temple administration and practice of worship. Furthermore, nearly every scholar working on the post-Solomonic phase of Chronicles has noted a multitude of connections between the accounts (especially about Rehoboam, Hezekiah, Manasseh, and Josiah) and the Chronicler's Persian-period audience. Thus it is necessary to take a closer look at the various models for interaction with empire that are provided in the post-Solomonic and pre-Josianic phase of the Chronicler's history, models that are designed to shape the identity of the original readers.

From Rehoboam to Manasseh

Rehoboam

Its literary position immediately after the completion of the David-Solomon idyllic phase lends the account of Rehoboam considerable rhetorical weight in Chronicles. In particular, this account provides insight into the Chronicler's view of foreign kings.

The Chronicler does not hide the reality of the schism that followed the death of Solomon.[24] However, excised from the account is any suggestion that his ideal Solomon was responsible for the division of the kingdom. Retained from his source is the characterization of Rehoboam as a foolish leader who rejected wise counsel, but this is carefully tempered in the Chronicler's unique Abijah speech in 2 Chr 13, which lays the blame squarely on the shoulders of Jeroboam and his worthless scoundrels, who took advantage of the young, indecisive, weak Rehoboam (13:6–7).[25] Although throughout the post-Solomonic

---

23. R. K. Duke, "A Rhetorical Approach to Appreciating the Books of Chronicles," in *The Chronicler as Author: Studies in Text and Texture* (ed. M. P. Graham and S. L. McKenzie; JSOTSup 263; Sheffield: Sheffield Academic Press, 1999) 121–22.

24. H. G. M. Williamson, *Israel in the Books of Chronicles* (Cambridge: Cambridge University Press, 1977) 110–11.

25. See G. N. Knoppers, "Rehoboam in Chronicles: Villain or Victim?" *JBL* 109 (1990) 423–40. Mark Throntveit argues that the Chronicler's presentation does show that the split was ordained by God (cf. 11:4) and that the north was justified in not following Rehoboam but that under Abijah they should have returned (*When Kings Speak: Royal Speech and Royal Prayer in Chronicles* [SBLDS 93; Atlanta: Scholars Press, 1987] 113–20). Although it is true that the Chronicler does retain the negative characterization of Rehoboam as young and foolish and does retain the statement that the split was God's doing, it appears that the early reforms of Rehoboam in 11:5–15 sufficiently renovated Rehoboam's character to justify a return by the north (so 11:16–17).

narrative the Chronicler consistently displays openness to northern Israelites, Abijah's speech makes clear that the northern kingdom as a political entity is illegitimate.[26]

The Chronicler's perspective on foreign kings further afield can be discerned as well in his account of Rehoboam. The Chronicler reveals that, after an initial phase of faithfulness, Rehoboam and his community ("all Israel") abandoned the law of Yahweh, an action that brought on the invasion of Shishak, king of Egypt. The prophetic message of Shemaiah identifies this foreign invasion and subjection as Yahweh's disciplinary action in order that "they may learn the difference between serving me and serving the kings of other lands" (12:8). This statement provides an interpretive window into the Chronicler's view of foreign subjection. Although foreign subjugation is used by Yahweh for disciplinary purposes, it is not an ideal condition but a means to an end. This statement thus functions as programmatic for the post-Solomonic account in Chronicles, providing a hermeneutic for interpreting interactions between Judah and foreign powers.[27]

Asa, Jehoshaphat, Jehoram, Ahaziah, and the North

The account of Rehoboam thus provides, first of all, perspective on Judah's relationship with the northern kingdom. In line with his negative attitude toward the northern kingdom as a political entity, the Chronicler excises all accounts of the northern kingdom from his post-Solomonic narrative except accounts directly related to Judah.

In his description of the faithful phases of the first three kings of the southern kingdom (Rehoboam, Abijah, and Asa), the Chronicler highlights how these royals either attracted faithful northern deserters to Judah (2 Chr 11:16–17; 15:8–19) or defeated the northern kingdom in battle (2 Chr 13). However, in his description of the final phase of Asa's reign, the Chronicler reveals that fear of the northern kingdom

---

26. As Williamson writes: "there are some indications that the Chronicler distinguished between the northern kingdom as a political institution and the population of the north as such" (*1 and 2 Chronicles*, 237; cf. idem, *Israel*, 139–40). Similarly, Sara Japhet: "the northern kingdom was established in sin, its existence constitutes a rebellion against YHWH, and its history is an unbroken chain of transgression leading up to destruction. Yet it is part of Israel, and without the members of the northern tribes, the people of Israel cannot be complete" (*The Ideology of the Book of Chronicles and Its Place in Biblical Thought* [Beiträge zur Erforschung des Alten Testaments und des antiken Judentum 9; Frankfurt am Main: Peter Lang, 1989] 324).

27. See Ristau, who sees in the plural "kingdoms" the notion that the Chronicler "presents the inauguration of a long-term political situation by which numerous foreign kings will rule the people" ("Josiah," 70–71).

tempted Asa to make a treaty with Aram (2 Chr 16), a treaty that is soundly attacked by the prophet Hanani (16:7–9), the abuse of whom led to Asa's foot disease. Asa's folly foreshadows the action of his son Jehoshaphat, whose alliance with the Omrides (Ahab, Ahaziah) was attacked by Hanani's son Jehu (19:2), and Eliezer, son of Dodavahu (20:37).[28] The danger of alliances of this sort is seen first in the corruption of Jehoshaphat's son Jehoram (21:6) and grandson Ahaziah (22:3, 5), and most dramatically in the near extinguishment of the Davidic Dynasty in the south by Athaliah, the Omride princess who embodies the inappropriate liaisons with the northern kingdom. It is clear that alliances with the local powers in the Levant are deemed unacceptable by the Chronicler. This is the first sign of the Chronicler's wary attitude toward cooperation with foreign entities, especially but not limited to those of the northern kingdom.[29] As Knoppers has noted: "the Chronicler advocates steering a course independent from Judah's neighbors and relying solely upon the deity."[30]

Ahaz, Hezekiah, Manasseh, and the Empire

As already noted above, the account of Rehoboam also provides insight into the role of foreign entities further afield, especially imperial powers. In this early period, Rehoboam's defeat at the hand of Shishak (Egypt) shows how forces external to the Levant can be used to discipline Judah (2 Chr 12), while Asa's defeat of Zera the Cushite reveals that foreign forces can be defeated with Yahweh's assistance (2 Chr 14; cf. 15:8–9). After Asa and before Ahaz, however, the focus of the

---

28. See Gary Knoppers on Jehoshaphat and the presentation of alliances in Chronicles ("Reform and Regression: The Chronicler's Presentation of Jehoshaphat," *Bib* 72 [1991] 500–524; idem, "'Yhwh Is Not with Israel': Alliances as a Topos in Chronicles," *CBQ* 58 [1996] 601–26). Also see Tuell, *First and Second Chronicles*, 210; contra R. H. Lowery, *The Reforming Kings: Cult and Society in First Temple Judah* (JSOTSup 120; Sheffield: JSOT Press, 1991) 101.

29. See also Ehud Ben Zvi, who concludes that the ideological implications of the Chronicler's presentation of the secession of the northern kingdom include the fact that "the Samarians are Israel" but that "their polity is separate from Yehud and should remain that way, because it is YHWH's will" ("The Secession of the Northern Kingdom in Chronicles: Accepted 'Facts' and New Meanings," in *The Chronicler as Theologian: Essays in Honour of Ralph W. Klein* [ed. M. P. Graham, S. L. McKenzie, and G. N. Knoppers; JSOTSup 371; London: T. & T. Clark, 2003] 85).

30. Knoppers, "Reform," 524; for a more detailed and nuanced study of Judahite identity in relation to foreigners, see Armin Siedlecki, "Foreigners, Warfare and Judahite Identity in Chronicles," in *The Chronicler as Author: Studies in Text and Texture* (ed. M. P. Graham and S. L. McKenzie; JSOTSup 263; Sheffield: Sheffield Academic Press, 1999) 229–66. He concludes: "Chr's view of the relationship between Judah and its neighbors is characterized by a constant mediation of tensions" (p. 265).

narrative is largely on smaller kingdoms within the Levant (Philistines, Edomites, Ammonites, Moabites, Meunites, Arabs, and Arameans).

That the account of Rehoboam prepares the way for later royal accounts that show interaction with powers outside the Levant has been highlighted by several scholars. First, Lowery notes considerable links between Rehoboam and Hezekiah, concluding that Rehoboam functions "to set the stage for Hezekiah's reform."[31] Japhet reveals that this function is not just related to the reforms but also to the battle that Hezekiah faced against imperial forces.[32] Her substantial evidence includes connections between the characterization of Rehoboam and Hezekiah, between Yahweh's treatment of both, between the two foreign invaders (Shishak, Sennacherib), and between the message of the two prophets who address the Judean kings (Shemaiah, Isaiah).[33] Second, Schniedewind highlights key links between Rehoboam and Manasseh, especially the fact that only these two kings repent in Chronicles (2 Chr 12:1–2), and both are presented using the vocabulary and imagery of survival from exile (see 12:7–8).[34] Rehoboam thus prepares the way for the key phase, when imperial forces press in on Judah in the wake of the fall of the northern kingdom. In light of this, the hermeneutic expressed in the Rehoboam account in 12:8 ("they may learn the difference between serving me and serving the kings of other lands") is especially applicable to the later phase, in which Hezekiah and Manasseh are highlighted as normative in the new imperial conditions.

Ahaz: Invitation to Empire

This imperial pressure appears at the end of Ahaz's reign, and with it the Chronicler signals a narrative shift in foreign interaction from smaller kingdoms to more distant and powerful empires. With the king experiencing significant defeat at the hands of Edomites and Philistines, Ahaz appeals to the kings of Assyria for help.

---

31. Lowery, *Reforming Kings*, 70. Lowery identifies this role in both Chronicles and the Deuteronomic History.

32. Japhet, *Chronicles*, 678–80.

33. Both Rehoboam and Hezekiah display arrogance followed by humility (2 Chr 12:1, 6–7; 32:24–25); for both, Yahweh's wrath is mitigated as treasures are taken but Jerusalem saved. The Chronicler has used the description of Sennacherib's invasion from 2 Kgs 18:13, 17 for his description of Shishak's invasion (2 Chr 12:4; "he [Shishak] captured the fortified cities of Judah and came as far as Jerusalem"; see 1 Kgs 14:25) and tempered it for Hezekiah (2 Chr 32:1). Both Shemaiah and Isaiah speak of repentance. Japhet concludes: "Thus the Chronicler has formulated the story of Shishak's campaign in analogy to Sennacherib's invasion in II Kings 18–19, even though his own version of the latter takes a much shorter form (cf. II Chron. 32.9–21)" (ibid., 679).

34. Schniedewind, "Source Citations," 453.

The Chronicler evaluates Ahaz's appeal to the kings of Assyria neg-atively, revealing in 28:20–21 that Tiglath-pileser offered him only trouble rather than help. As we have already seen, alliances with Ju-dah's closer neighbors in the Levant have been portrayed negatively to this point in the Chronicler's account and, not surprisingly, alliances with distant imperial powers are neither better nor effective.[35] Thus, as empire is first introduced in the final phase of the Chronicler's account, it is not affirmed. Not only is empire invited by a rebellious king, but its consequences are dire, resulting in the pillaging of the temple, pal-ace, and people.

The account of Ahaz plays a significant role in the book of Chron-icles, representing a transition between eras.[36] Ahaz's reign provided the greatest opportunity for the Davidic Dynasty since the schism un-der Rehoboam, because the demise of the northern kingdom during his reign removed "the final barrier to a reunited Israel."[37] However, in the words of Lowery, Ahaz and his reunited Israel "stand as the photo-graphic negative of the Chronicler's Davidic-Solomonic ideal,"[38] so that Ahaz "brings Judah to its darkest hour,"[39] which Japhet describes as a "uniformly black" script, "moving toward a climax of evil."[40] William-son sees in Ahaz a reversal of the conditions realized under Abijah near the outset of the Chronicler's depiction of the divided kingdom.[41] While under Abijah the Davidide is considered good and the northerners bad

---

35. See Knoppers, who discusses the various treaties; note especially the comparison of Asa and Ahaz ("Alliances," 601–26). Tuell makes an important link between Ahaz and Jehoshaphat, even though I disagree with his more positive reading of Jehoshaphat ("Je-hoshaphat saw the light, and was able to break free"; *First and Second Chronicles*, 210).

36. For this, see especially Ben Zvi, "Gateway," 218; Lowery, *Reforming Kings*, 128–29; and D. C. Raney, *History as Narrative in the Deuteronomistic History and Chronicles* (Studies in the Bible and Early Christianity 56; Lewiston, NY: Edwin Mellen, 2003) 144–48.

37. Lowery, *Reforming Kings*, 128–29.

38. Ibid., 129.

39. Ibid., 128–29. The role of Ahaz as marking the beginning of the end for Judah is also noted with regard to the Deuteronomistic History by N. Naʾaman, "The Deuterono-mist and Voluntary Servitude to Foreign Powers," *JSOT* (1995) 41 ("days of Ahaz mark the beginning of the period which ends with the destruction of Judah and the deporta-tion of its people"); H. Tadmor and M. Cogan, "Ahaz and Tiglath-Pileser in the Book of Kings: Historiographic Considerations," *Bib* 60 (1979) 505 ("The tenor of the story im-plies that the appeal of Ahaz to Tiglath-pileser marked the start of Judah's servitude to Assyria").

40. Japhet, *Chronicles*, 897. Ahaz is matched, in her estimation, only by Jehoram be-fore him and Zedekiah after him. Compare with Ben Zvi, who calls him "the worst king of Judah in Chronicles" ("Gateway," 229).

41. Williamson, *Israel*, 114–18; idem, *1 and 2 Chronicles*, 343–44. See especially the lexical links between 2 Chr 13:15–18 and 28:5–6.

as the south defeats the north, under Ahaz the Davidide is deemed bad
and the northerners good so that the north defeats the south. In this
context, what is demanded is a Davidide such as Abijah, not Ahaz.[42]

Whereas according to Smelik, in the Deuteronomic History the key
contrastive father-son pair in the divided kingdom is Manasseh and
Josiah,[43] in Chronicles this role is played by the father-son pair of Ahaz
and Hezekiah, with Ahaz taking the place of Manasseh as the nadir of
the southern history.[44] This nadir is described by Mosis and Dillard in
terms of exile, a typology that Ahaz shares with Saul.[45] DeVries echoes
this when he links Ahaz's chopping up of the temple vessels and lock-
ing of the temple doors as "a vivid type of the temple's desecration in
the coming exile."[46]

Key to the depths of Ahaz's rule is unquestionably his cultic offenses
and temple closure, but many have noted the consequences of his interaction with foreign powers. Tuell links the Chronicler's "unstinting
condemnation of Ahaz" to the fact "that he was the first king to suc-
cumb to a foreign power, and he did so willingly, without resistance."[47] In contrast to the David-Solomon ideal of receiving tribute

---

42. See also Kalimi, who notes contrasts between the kingdoms and Ahaz and Abijah (*Reshaping*, 334–35).

43. Christine Mitchell sees the father-son pairing as "one of the major structuring elements of Chronicles as a whole" (David/Solomon, Rehoboam/Abijah, Asa/Jehosha-phat, Jehoram/Ahaziah, Joash/Amaziah, Uzziah/Jotham, Ahaz/Hezekiah, Manasseh/Amon, Josiah/sons) but observes that the Ahaz-Hezekiah pairing is "a radical departure from the previous pairings," which had the son following or completing the father's work, while Ahaz and Hezekiah are "depicted as contrasts" (*The Ideal Ruler as Intertext in 1–2 Chronicles and the Cyropaedia* [Ph.D. diss., Carleton University, 2001] 299, 264). In this way the Ahaz-Hezekiah complex stands out in the narrative of Chronicles.

44. K. A. D. Smelik, "The Representation of King Ahaz in 2 Kings 16 and 2 Chronicles 28," in *Intertextuality in Ugarit and Israel* (ed. J. C. de Moor; Oudtestamentische Studiën 40; Leiden: Brill, 1998) 164, 181. Smelik writes: "We can point to the fact that Ahaz, under similar circumstances, did not convert. Moreover, his list of sins is even more elaborate than that of Manasseh. . . . Most transgressions attributed to Manasseh are also ascribed to Ahaz but Ahaz withal is reputed to have committed various other sins. He even closed the Temple. This means that in Chronicles the representation of Ahaz is more negative than that of Manasseh" (*Converting the Past: Studies in Ancient Israelite and Moabite Historiography* [Oudtestamentische Studiën 28; Leiden: Brill, 1992] 182–83).

45. R. Mosis, *Untersuchungen zur Theologie des chronistischen Geschichtswerkes* (Freiburger theologische Studien 92; Freiburg: Herder, 1973) 41–43, 186–88. See also Dillard: "[Hezekiah] showed the path to recovery from the difficulties and foreign domination under Ahaz" (*2 Chronicles*, 261).

46. S. J. De Vries, *1 and 2 Chronicles* (FOTL 11; Grand Rapids: Eerdmans, 1989) 366.

47. Tuell, *First and Second Chronicles*, 210. Note Mitchell, who contrasts Ahaz with "previous kings who had called for help from Yhwh (like Abijah)" ("Ideal Ruler," 266; cf. Ben Zvi, "Gateway," 227).

from the nations, Lowery notes that "Ahaz frantically stripped the temple and handed over Jerusalem's cultic and royal treasuries in a disastrous attempt to enlist Assyria's assistance (vv. 16–21)."[48]

In our work above, we have argued that the final phase of Josiah's reign represents a key turning point in the Chronicler's narrative, transitioning Judah from kingdom to exile, as Josiah's successors continue the trend of disobeying Yahweh. In similar fashion, the final phase of Ahaz's reign is depicted as an earlier turning point, one in which the Davidide invites an imperial power to help Judah but is followed by a successor who obeys Yahweh and repels the imperial forces. Both of these "strands" in Chronicles contribute to the "dense tapestry" of the book of Chronicles as a whole. It appears that the Chronicler had different models in mind for his audience's interaction with the empire, both of which contribute to the identity projected through the book.

Hezekiah: Opposition to Empire

As just noted, the Chronicler's account of Ahaz prepares the way for the appearance of Hezekiah. The reader is prepared for an Abijah-like figure who will be able to unite the kingdoms, but this will only be accomplished by a leader who embodies the David-Solomon ideals.[49] The Chronicler finds this sort of leader in the character of Hezekiah, who is universally hailed in scholarship on Chronicles as the "zenith for post-schism Judah."[50] The Chronicler not only devotes more space

---

48. Lowery, *Reforming Kings*, 130.

49. Throntveit notes the relationship between the speeches of Abijah and Hezekiah in the structure of the post-Solomonic history in the Chronicler. Throntveit argues that the Chronicler's history should be divided into three phases: United Kingdom, Divided Kingdom, Reunited Kingdom, with the latter beginning with Hezekiah (*When Kings Speak*, 113–20). So also Williamson (*Israel*, 131) argues for the unity of Israel under Hezekiah that "remains the situation until the end of the monarchy." These claims, however, appear to be too strong in light of the argument of G. N. Knoppers ("A Reunited Kingdom in Chronicles?" in *Proceedings, Eastern Great Lakes and Midwest Biblical Societies 9* [Cincinnati: Eastern Great Lakes & Midwest Biblical Societies, 1989] 74–88), who argues that the presentation of the subsequent reigns does not indicate an enduring situation of reunification. Knoppers does admit that "one of Hezekiah's achievements is clearly to effect some sort of reunification between Israel and Judah" but claims that this "is not unique" to Hezekiah, because it is accomplished by Asa and Jehoshaphat before him and Josiah after him (pp. 79–80). In my opinion, however, Hezekiah's accomplishments can be distinguished from those of Asa and Jehoshaphat, in that (1) Hezekiah is the first to accomplish this after the demise of the northern kingdom, and (2) the territory in view for Hezekiah is from Beer-sheba to Dan (30:5), as opposed to merely the hill country of Ephraim for his predecessors (15:8; 19:4).

50. Dillard, *2 Chronicles*, 228; see also Japhet, *Chronicles*, 936; Raney, *History as Narrative*, 159; Mitchell, "Ironic Death," 429. Baruch Halpern notes that much of the narrative tension in Chronicles disappears after Hezekiah's reign, so he thinks "the work was

to Hezekiah than any other post-Solomonic monarch,[51] but he also
takes pains to link Hezekiah with both David and Solomon (29:2–3, 27,
35; 30:26).[52] Halpern argues that Hezekiah forms an inclusion in the
Chronicler's account with the united monarchy,[53] while Williamson
shows that the strategy of the Chronicler is to return the reader to a
point just prior to Rehoboam's reign: "Thus in Hezekiah's recapitula-
tion of Solomon's achievements it is as though the Chronicler is taking
us back prior to the point of division where the one Israel is united
around a single temple under the authority of the Davidic king."[54]

Japhet's many connections between the accounts of Rehoboam and
Hezekiah, already noted above, bolster Williamson's claim, showing
how Hezekiah redeems Rehoboam's reign and provides the model
that should have followed Solomon. There is no question then that,
while Josiah represents the height of the post-schism phase of the Deuteronomic History, Hezekiah functions in this role in the Chronicler's
History.[55]

geared to climax and to culminate in the account of Hezekiah's reign." This is used by
Halpern as evidence of a source underlying Chronicles and does not appear to do justice
to the presentation of Manasseh. Nevertheless, he has highlighted the rhetorical role
played by Hezekiah in Chronicles ("Sacred History and Ideology: Chronicles' Thematic
Structure—Indications of an Earlier Source," in *The Creation of Sacred Literature: Composition and Redaction of the Biblical Text* [ed. R. E. Friedman; Berkeley: University of California Press, 1981] 52).

51. See G. N. Knoppers, "History and Historiography: The Royal Reforms," in *Israel's
Past in Present Research: Essays on Ancient Israelite Historiography* (ed. V. P. Long; Sources
for Biblical and Theological Study 7; Winona Lake, IN: Eisenbrauns, 1999) 557–78; cf.
Mosis, *Untersuchungen*, 189–92; Williamson, *Israel*, 119–25.

52. There is some debate over whether Hezekiah is linked to David or Solomon or
both; see the superb review of this by M. A. Throntveit, *When Kings Speak*, 121–25; idem,
"Hezekiah in the Books of Chronicles," in *Society of Biblical Literature 1988 Seminar Papers*
(ed. D. J. Lull; SBLSP; Atlanta: Scholars Press, 1988) 302–11; now idem, "The Relationship
of Hezekiah to David and Solomon in the Books of Chronicles," in *The Chronicler as Theologian: Essays in Honour of Ralph W. Klein* (ed. M. P. Graham, S. L. McKenzie, and G. N.
Knoppers; JSOTSup 371; London: T. & T. Clark, 2003) 105–21. Oddly, Japhet, although
admitting the connection to David and Solomon, eschews too much focus on Hezekiah
as "stereotypical 'type,'" emphasizing instead the "idiosyncratic" character of the figure
of Hezekiah (*Chronicles*, 998). But see Williamson, *Israel*, 120–25; Halpern, "Sacred History," 50–51. Mitchell shows links to the David-Solomon ideal not only in connection to
the glories of the ideal but also in the penitential response of David and Hezekiah; see
1 Chr 21 and 2 Chr 32:25–26 ("Ideal Ruler," 270–71).

53. Halpern, "Sacred History," 41, 50–51. See especially his link between 1 Chr 18:6,
13; and 2 Chr 32:22, and on the latter: "The verse appears to form an inclusion of Hezekiah with David, who also was saved wherever he went (1 Chr 18:6, 13)" (p. 41).

54. Williamson, *1 and 2 Chronicles*, 351.

55. A comparison of the Chronicler's evaluation of the festivals of Hezekiah and Josiah (compare 2 Chr 30:26 with 35:18) has suggested to some that Josiah is elevated above

It is important, however, to note, with Raney, that "Hezekiah not only mirrored the greatness of the past, but also served as an ideal model for what the Chr desired for his own post-exilic community."[56] In order to accomplish this, the Chronicler incorporates elements strikingly similar to the conclusion of the book. The transition from the "exile" of Ahaz to the "restoration" of Hezekiah is marked by the action of Hezekiah and the leaders of the city 'going up' (עלה) to the House of Yahweh (2 Chr 29:20), an action echoing the action of the community in exile, which is invited to 'go up' (עלה) to Cyrus's newly built House of Yahweh (2 Chr 36:23).[57]

In vocabulary identical to the words found in 2 Chr 36:23 (עבר [Hiphil] + קוֹל), where Cyrus sends forth his proclamation throughout his realm, in 30:5 Hezekiah and his Jerusalemite community send forth a proclamation beyond the narrow restrictions of Hezekiah's realm (Judah), extending an invitation to the community from Beer-sheba to Dan to come to Jerusalem to celebrate the Passover. Hezekiah's invited community has escaped the hand of the kings of Assyria (הַנִּשְׁאֶרֶת, 30:6), similar to the community that will escape (הַשְׁאֵרִית) the sword of the Babylonians (36:20). The invitation of Hezekiah is to 'return' (שׁוּב) to Yahweh, a return that will result in the 'return' (שׁוּב) of Yahweh to the remnant. This return is contrasted with the 'unfaithful' (מעל) behavior of the community's ancestors and involves submitting to Yahweh,[58] 'coming to/entering' (בוא) the sanctuary and 'serving' (עבד)

Hezekiah, at least in terms of cultic reforms. It is true that Hezekiah's Passover is compared by the Chronicler with the celebration during the time of Solomon, while Josiah's Passover is compared with the time of Samuel and that, furthermore, the Chronicler says of Josiah that "none of the kings of Israel had ever kept a Passover as Josiah did" (35:18). However, a look at his source in 2 Kgs 23:22 reveals that the Chronicler has excised the term "or of the kings of Judah," which may be his way of protecting the image of Hezekiah's Passover (see now Mitchell, "Ironic Death," 421–35). The reference to Samuel for Josiah's festival may indicate that, with Josiah's death and the beginning of exile, Judah has now moved into a phase similar to the premonarchial context of Samuel. The reference to David and Solomon for Hezekiah's festival (2 Chr 30:26) may indicate that Hezekiah represents the ideal of the monarchial age.

56. Raney, *History as Narrative*, 155.

57. Although the *Qal* of עלה is used often in Chronicles, most of the occurrences relate to engaging in battle. Those that are related to going up to a sacred place are related to only the figures of David (1 Chr 13:6 [Chr change]; 21:18, 19 [same]), Solomon (2 Chr 1:6 [Chr addition]; possibly 9:4 [same]), Hezekiah (29:20 [Chr addition]), Josiah (34:30 [same]), and the golah (36:23 [Chr addition]). [Chr change = the DtrH has different wording; same = both the ChrH and the DtrH are identical; Chr addition = part of a section not found in the DtrH].

58. For the phrase נתן + יד, see Lam 5:6; 1 Chr 29:24; Jer 50:15.

Yahweh. Although this return is not unrelated to repentance (submitting and serving), it is closely associated with the temple, just as is seen in 2 Chr 36:23.

The return to the temple of the people who are in the land will prompt not only the return of Yahweh's presence but also the return to the land of the people who are in exile (30:9), the same group that appears to be the target audience of the Chronicler in 36:23. As 2 Chr 36 intertwines the themes of captivity, escape, and attention to the temple, so does 2 Chr 30. But in chap. 30, one finds a Davidic figure rallying the people around the temple in the wake of the reemergence of a community after severe punishment by a Mesopotamian power, with a view to the return of still more from exile. These connections to the closing chapter of Chronicles suggest potential for a Davidic king to resume the role that had been taken over by Mesopotamian powers.

This connection to the Persian-period community is to be related not only to the cultic reforms found in chaps. 29–31 but also to Hezekiah's encounter with an imperial power in chap. 32. In this account, the Chronicler depicts the Davidic king as a figure who stood up and encouraged faith in Yahweh rather than fear of the king of Assyria and his vast army. This is stated succinctly by Dillard, who observes that Hezekiah "showed the path to recovery from the difficulties and foreign domination under Ahaz," a path that was intended as "lessons for the post-exilic community."[59] So also Raney highlights the parallel experience of Hezekiah's Judah and the Chronicler's Yehud, both of whom "had been denied access to the Temple and had been under the political dominance of a great Mesopotamian power."[60] Often emphasis has been placed on Hezekiah's role in renewing the temple cult without corresponding attention being given to his role in facing the imperial foe.

The key appears to be that Sennacherib speaks of Yahweh as a deity who cannot withstand his power (32:13–19), strikingly different from the imperial voices presented in chaps. 35–36, which suggest imperial forces that were in line with Yahweh's purposes. Chapter 32 provides a model in which a Davidic king could stand in opposition to empire, in particular, an empire that stands against Yahweh and his purposes.

It is clear that the Chronicler shapes the Hezekiah account to maximize connections to his Persian-period audience. In addition, the striking links between the account of Hezekiah and the final chapter of

---

59. Dillard, *2 Chronicles*, 261.
60. Raney, *History as Narrative*, 155.

Chronicles suggest that the Chronicler envisioned at least two scenarios for his audience's interaction with empire: the scenario at the end of the work, which relates most directly to the present reality of a Yehud under imperial domination; and the scenario in 2 Chr 29–32, in which a Davidic figure and Judean community faithfully support the temple cult and are emboldened to stand against an empire.

Manasseh: Empire as Discipline

Lying between the two scenarios of imperial domination and a faithful community standing against an empire, one finds yet another narrative account strongly shaped by the realities of the recent past of the Chronicler's audience. As many have noted throughout the history of scholarship, Manasseh is presented in the Deuteronomic History as the one whose sinful reign sealed the fate of the southern kingdom (2 Kgs 21:10–17; 23:26–27; 24:3–4).[61] Although the Chronicler does not ignore Manasseh's sin, his account provides additional material that promotes Manasseh as a model of the kind of response to discipline that can bring an end to exile and prompt renewed blessing (2 Chr 33).

2 Chronicles 33:11, with its depiction of Manasseh's exile to Babylon, subsequent humble prayer, and restoration to his kingdom, echoes the Chronicler's typology of exile and restoration so crucial to the Chronicler's Ahaz-Hezekiah and post-Josianic narrative complexes.[62] The striking difference, however, is that this time the exile and restoration occur within one reign, so that a royal figure in exile is restored to rule. A further difference is evident in the fact that in the post-Josianic complexes human repentance plays no role in the shift from exile to restoration. After a period of disobedience and discipline, it is merely the obedience of a later generation (golah) that is essential to restoration. In the Hezekiah account, repentance is essential in Hezekiah's letter to the people. The account of Manasseh, however, takes penitence to a new level, providing a model of penitence by a guilty exilic royal figure.[63] It is interesting that, while the reforms of Hezekiah are closely

---

61. However, one should not miss the deuteronomic presentation of Hezekiah's reign, at the end of which, Hezekiah's folly in showing his treasures to the Babylonian envoys prompts Isaiah's prophecy of exilic doom (2 Kgs 20:16–19).

62. See Mosis, *Untersuchungen*, 192–94; Williamson, *1 and 2 Chronicles*, 389; Dillard, *2 Chronicles*, 271; Schniedewind, "Source Citations," 450; Smelik, *Converting the Past*, 188; Raney, *History as Narrative*, 165.

63. Lowery emphasizes the penitential dimension of the Manasseh story ("Manasseh's story shows Israel the efficacy of repentance"; *Reforming Kings*, 185); so also Schniedewind, who calls Manasseh in Chronicles a "paradigm of a contrite sinner" ("Source Citations," 450).

linked to the people as a whole and while the call to return at the end
of Chronicles is addressed to a whole community in exile, the account
of Manasseh is focused on the exile of a single figure, a Davidide who
had clearly offended Yahweh. This is the first indication that Manasseh
is being presented, not merely as a model of penitence for the golah, but
also and possibly primarily as a model of royal exile and royal restoration.[64] It may be that the final three scenarios in Chronicles depict, in
reverse order, the restoration of the community (post-Josianic phase),
the restoration of the royal house (Manasseh), and the restoration of the
royal house and community together (Hezekiah).

But there is further evidence that the account of Manasseh is focused on the Davidic Dynasty. Just as the Chronicler's account of Hezekiah contains allusive links to the final phase of Judah's history, especially the restoration of the golah under Cyrus, so also the Chronicler's
account of Manasseh contains a fascinating link to the final phase of Judah's history. We have already noted the way in which the Chronicler
has shifted the deuteronomic description of the exile of a royal figure to
Babylon in bronze shackles from Zedekiah to Jehoiakim—a shift that
may signal the potential of the Jehoiakim-Jehoiachin line for the reemergence of the royal line.[65] What is interesting is how the Chronicler
uses this description to create a link between the exiles of Manasseh
(33:11) and Jehoiakim (36:6).[66] Important to notice is the common use of
not only the verb אסר with the preposition ב and נְחֻשְׁתַּיִם but also the
verb הלך and the destination of Babylon using the locative *he* (see figure
on p. 269). This evidence strengthens the view that the Chronicler is
using the Manasseh account to provide a paradigm for the Davidic
House. By forging a link between Jehoiakim and Manasseh, the Chronicler provides a model by which a Davidide may seek God's favor,

64. Contra most, who see this as a "symbol of post-exilic Israel": Lowery, *Reforming Kings*, 188; compare with Schniedewind, "Source Citations," 451, 453, 454; Dillard,
2 Chronicles, 271; Williamson, *1 and 2 Chronicles*, 389; Raney, *History as Narrative*, 165;
Philippe Abadie, "From the Impious Manasseh (2 Kings 21) to the Convert Manasseh
(2 Chronicles 33): Theological Rewriting by the Chronicler," in *The Chronicler as Theologian: Essays in Honour of Ralph W. Klein* (ed. M. P. Graham, S. L. McKenzie, and G. N.
Knoppers; JSOTSup 371; London: T. & T. Clark, 2003) 102.

65. Schniedewind (Source Citations," 451) and Johnstone (*1 and 2 Chronicles*, 2.267)
highlight the close resemblance between the description of Manasseh's exile in 2 Chr
33:11 and the description of Zedekiah in 2 Kgs 25:7.

66. Smelik, *Converting the Past*, 188; cf. Johnstone, *1 and 2 Chronicles*, 2.267. Probably
2 Kgs 25:7 has influenced both 2 Chr 33:11 and 36:6, but the intertextual link in Chronicles is designed to forge a relationship between Jehoiakim and Manasseh.

---

2 Chr 33:11 (Manasseh)

וַיָּבֵא יְהוָה עֲלֵיהֶם אֶת־שָׂרֵי הַצָּבָא אֲשֶׁר לְמֶלֶךְ אַשּׁוּר וַיִּלְכְּדוּ אֶת־מְנַשֶּׁה בַּחֹחִים

וַיַּאַסְרֻהוּ בַּנְחֻשְׁתַּיִם וַיּוֹלִיכֻהוּ בָּבֶלָה

2 Chr 36:6 (Jehoiakim)

עָלָיו עָלָה נְבוּכַדְנֶאצַּר מֶלֶךְ בָּבֶל וַיַּאַסְרֵהוּ בַּנְחֻשְׁתַּיִם לְהֹלִיכוֹ בָּבֶלָה

2 Kgs 25:7 (Zedekiah)

וְאֶת־בְּנֵי צִדְקִיָּהוּ שָׁחֲטוּ לְעֵינָיו וְאֶת־עֵינֵי צִדְקִיָּהוּ עִוֵּר וַיַּאַסְרֻהוּ בַנְחֻשְׁתַּיִם

וַיְבִאֵהוּ בָּבֶל

---

humble himself, pray, and "be brought . . . back to Jerusalem and to his kingdom" (33:13).[67]

The Chronicler links the penitent King Manasseh to his later, Persian-period readers through the exile-restoration motif and via the glorious-ideals motif. Manasseh's repentance suggests a connection with the earlier ideal royal penitent, David,[68] and Manasseh's restoration in Chronicles puts him in company with the great post-Solomonic monarchs of Asa, Hezekiah, and Josiah:[69]

Humbling himself before God	Hezekiah (32:26); Josiah (34:27)[70]
Removing the foreign gods/ the image	Asa (14:2, 4; 15:8, 16); Josiah (34:3, 4, 7, 33)
Removing the altars	Asa (14:2); Hezekiah (32:12); Josiah (34:4, 7)
Repairing the altar for the Lord	Asa (15:8)
Sacrificing to the Lord	Asa (15:11); Hezekiah (29:20–35)
Commanding Judah to worship the Lord	Asa (14:3); Josiah (34:33)

---

67. See also the evidence of links between Jehoiachin and Manasseh presented by Abadie, based on Ezek 19:9 and 2 Chr 36:10 ("Impious Manasseh," 102). Mitchell observes that Manasseh is "the only king who is depicted as starting out evil and ending up as a good ruler" ("Ideal Ruler," 272). In this way Manasseh stands out among the Davidides as providing a model for moving from the final depiction of the royal house in Chronicles to the Hezekiah-David-Solomon ideal.

68. Abadie, "Impious Manasseh," 96; cf. G. N. Knoppers, "Images of David in Early Judaism," *Bib* 76 (1995) 449–70. Manasseh's phase of infidelity is linked back to the depths of Saul's faithless consultation of mediums (2 Chr 33:6; compare 1 Chr 10:13; cf. Abadie, "Impious Manasseh," 97), thus accentuating the link to the penitent David.

69. For this list, see the chart in Smelik, *Converting the Past*, 184.

70. Compare with Rehoboam (2 Chr 12:6, 7, 12).

In contrast to his source, the Chronicler has renovated the character of
Manasseh and depicted him as a normative Davidic character through
association with the kings whose reigns displayed most thoroughly
the values of the David-Solomon ideal. Thus, as with Hezekiah, so
with Manasseh, the Chronicler's account connects the reign with the
royal ideals developed in the David-Solomon account, but also with
the communal realities of Persian-period readers. Manasseh provides
a model at least for the community as a whole, if not the royal house in
particular for the renewal of an independent Yehud.

Conclusion

What we discover in the final "imperial" phase of Chronicles is not just
one model for Judean identity in the shadow of empire but a series of
models. To use Ben Zvi's imagery, the Chronicler has interwoven several bright strands to create a dense tapestry bound together with the
thread of intertextuality.

In the closing chapter of the book, empire is treated positively because it fulfills the purposes of Yahweh, especially the reconstruction
of the temple. The people in exile are encouraged to follow the imperial
lead and join the colonial experience. Judean royal figures are over-
shadowed by imperial officials who have assumed the prerogatives
originally enjoyed by the Davidic line.[71] This closing model legitimizes
the present imperial reality of the Chronicler's readers, affirming the
constitution (golah), activities (temple rebuilding), and polity (colony)
of the Persian-period Yehudite community.

However, the Chronicler's vision of Judean identity should not be
reduced to this final picture, even in relation to polity. Ben Zvi's call to
"pay careful attention to nuances, literary topoi, allusions, and references to other sections in the book that are present in each individual
account" and to the overall shape of "the book as a whole" cautions us
from focusing too much on a single strand and ignoring the dense tapestry of the book.[72]

---

71. Kalimi has highlighted evidence in the Chronicler's presentation of Necho that
may temper or even neutralize this positive portrayal of at least this one imperial figure:
"The Chronicler made a considerable effort to reduce [Necho's] importance and to destroy his reputation by omitting his traditional exalted title, Pharaoh; by choosing other
ways to refer to him; by reducing the number of times he is mentioned in the text; and
by rendering him significant in a difficult situation; and so on" (*Reshaping*, 177).

72. Thus what Ben Zvi suggests for the image of the temple can be applied to the image of the empire and possibly the monarchy: "As the literati read and reread each literary unit in the book in a manner strongly informed by their knowledge of the other
units, a multilayered, multidimensional ideological image of the temple was shaped"

One should not ignore the key role played by the Rehoboam account, which is designed to shape the readers' understanding of imperial domination—that is, this is not the ideal but, rather, a temporary and purposeful measure. Wariness toward alliances with foreign political entities is first established in relation to foreign kingdoms in the Levant and then carried forward into relations with imperial figures in the account of Ahaz

Intertextual links in 2 Chr 36 usher the reader back to the earlier models of Manasseh and Hezekiah, who were the first to face the imperial threat after Ahaz's fateful alliance with Sennacherib. It is not surprising that the Chronicler alludes back to these accounts, because in the post-Solomon narrative they represent two of its rhetorical high points. The Chronicler's account of Hezekiah represents the narrative height of the post-Solomonic phase, and in this account the Chronicler showcases another model for interacting with empire, a model in which empire is not considered normative. Here the Davidic king is afforded a key role not only as a facilitator of worship at the temple but also as a catalyst for faith against blasphemous imperial hegemony.

Between the model of Hezekiah and the model of the post-Josianic phase stands a third model, Manasseh, a Davidic royal whose sinful behavior prompts a shift in the narrative portrayal of the empire. Now the same "kings of Assyria," invited foolishly by Ahaz into Judean affairs (28:16) but defeated by Yahweh in Hezekiah's time (32:4), are used by Yahweh to discipline the recalcitrant royal. In this case, the people are not mentioned; only the king goes into exile. Furthermore, because he sought Yahweh in humble prayer, Yahweh "brought him back to Jerusalem and to his kingdom. Then Manasseh knew that the LORD is God" (33:13).[73]

Therefore, although the Chronicler ends his account with the present reality of colony, one should not assume that this represents the Chronicler's ideal. Rather, his portrayal of Hezekiah places considerable rhetorical weight on this earlier phase of imperial interaction and suggests that there is still hope for independence.[74] It may be that

---

("Observations," 93 n. 15). One can discern Ben Zvi's openness to a multivalent approach to kingship in his excursus in "Gateway," 247–49.

73. Abadie notes the association between Hezekiah's exhortation to repentance (2 Chr 30:6–9) and Manasseh's example of repentance ("Impious Manasseh," 102–3). Interestingly, the Chronicler also makes a link between Manasseh's sinful phase and Ahaz, who sets up the reign of Hezekiah; see Kalimi, *Reshaping*, 333–34.

74. Relevant here is Williamson's response to the work of Mosis: "the Chronicler's glowing presentation of certain phases of Israel's past history could only have been intended to awaken fresh hopes and aspirations in the minds of his readers" (*Israel*, 135).

Manasseh displays the posture essential for kingdom renewal, and hope for renewal is placed in a figure emerging from the Jehoiakim-Jehoiachin line.[75]

In this way, readers who reach the end of Chronicles are invited to retrace the steps from the depths of exile through Manasseh to the heights of Hezekiah, the figure whose reign not only embodied the values of the ideal David and Solomon but also provided hope for the renewal of an independent kingdom united around the temple.[76]

---

75. This is bolstered by the shape of the Davidic genealogy in 1 Chr 3. See above, n. 16.

76. See further my *1–2 Chronicles* (Cornerstone Biblical Commentary 5a; Carol Stream, IL: Tyndale House, forthcoming).

Index of Authors

Index of Scripture

Deuterocanonical Literature